How to Answer "How'd You Do That?"

Revealing how you actually did a trick makes you look like an amateur. But you gotta say *something* when they ask how you did it. Here are a few snappy answers to get you started:

- ✔ "Quite well, don't you think?"
- ✔ "If I told you, I'd have to kill you."
- ✔ "I'm a genetic freak."
- ✔ "The question isn't *how* — it's *why.*"
- ✔ "What are you, from *60 Minutes*?"
- ✔ "Pure luck."
- ✔ "Can you keep a secret? Well, so can I."
- ✔ "Witchcraft. Didn't you see me wiggle my nose?"
- ✔ "Through years of tedious practice and self-denial."
- ✔ "What do I look like — the Masked Magician?"
- ✔ "Camera tricks."

What to Say When You Flub a Trick

Ideally, you never *would* flub a trick. If you've rehearsed in private until your acts of wizardry are smooth and comfortable, flubbing should be impossible. But when bad luck rears its ugly head, here are a few lines to have ready:

- ✔ "I forgot to compensate for the rotational effect of the Earth."
- ✔ "Hmm. It worked in the magic store!"
- ✔ "It's all part of the show, folks — the part that hasn't been rehearsed."
- ✔ "That's the first time that ever happened again."
- ✔ "It doesn't look as bad from my side."
- ✔ "The real magician will be here shortly."
- ✔ "I'm curious to see how I get out of this myself!"
- ✔ "Wow, it's so quiet in here, you could hear a career drop."

A Field Guide to the Audience

Most audiences enjoy the mystery, entertainment, and challenge of a magic show. But let's face it: At its core, magic is an assault on every law of nature we've ever learned — which makes some people's brains squirm. As you progress in your magical career, here are some of the rarer species of *spectatoris weirdus* to watch out for:

The Yellow-Bellied Grabber: This spectator can't resist grabbing your props. Before you perform, you'll find him circling you like a vulture, trying to peek into your stuff; after each trick, he's the first to snatch your props away in hopes of finding out how you did it. Turn him into your ally by choosing him to help with a trick that makes him look good.

The Ruby-Throated Guesser: Immediately after you've created some moment of impeccable, poetic magic, this species shouts out her theory as to how you did it. ("You switched it when we weren't looking!") That can rattle you if you're not used to it; have a clever line (or another trick) ready to go, just in case.

The Farfetched Guesser: This sub-class of spectator also likes to shout out guesses — but this variety comes up with incredibly *ridiculous* theories. They'll accuse you of writing down a prediction *in your pocket* during the tenth of a second when you were reaching for a pen, or of having magnets installed in your hands, or of having made a secret agreement with *everyone else in the audience* before the show started. Although most people recognize the absurdity of these guesses, the outbursts can still detract from the delicious final moment of a trick.

The Longbilled Believer: In this age of Psychic Hotlines, X-Files, and alien-abduction theories, an increasing number of audiences actually believe in magic. Do a mindreading trick for *this* kind, and you get almost no reaction at all — just a small, knowing smile and some nodding. It can be hard to impress one of these onlookers, since they've quietly believed *all along* that reality is a government conspiracy.

The Clueless Dodobird: Somebody who forgets his card, making your trick worthless — or, worse, doesn't follow instructions.

The Puff-Chested Boyfriend: In the presence of a girlfriend, a funny thing happens to this ordinarily easy-going species: He becomes surprisingly defensive, remarkably unreceptive to being entertained by the magic. He doesn't like her to see that he can be fooled.

The Fuzzy-Tummied Hatchling: Performing for children — or the childlike — can be one of the most rewarding experiences for a magician. A child doesn't yet have the ego of a Guesser or a Puff-Chested Boyfriend, and therefore isn't threatened by your magic. As a result, you can relax, focusing on what you're saying, on creating a feeling of mystery, on your delivery — and then bask in a young child's reaction of pure wonder and delight.

For Dummies: Bestselling Book Series for Beginners

Magic For Dummies®

Magic Words Worth Knowing

There isn't much jargon in *Magic For Dummies*. But the *field* of magic — videos, lectures, and other books — is filled with it. Here's a guide to some of the terms you'll hear most often.

burn — To watch a trick intensely, with an unblinking stare, immobile head, and general resistance to conventional misdirection. A spectator who's burning you clearly isn't there to be entertained.

clean — The blissful state when a magician's hands and props can be examined because they're not rigged in any way. Example: You're "clean" at the end of "The Ring off Rope" (see Chapter 5). The audience can inspect the props from now until doomsday without learning how you did the trick.

confederate — A secret assistant pretending to be an audience member. The confederate may, for example, subtly feed the magician information. Confederates should be used infrequently, and rarely as the primary "spectator" in an audience-participation trick (otherwise, their assistance will be too obvious).

false shuffle — To simulate shuffling the deck without actually altering the position of certain cards. Some false shuffles are designed to keep all 52 cards in their original locations. Other false shuffles, such as the one described at the beginning of Chapter 10, keep only some cards — such as the top or bottom one — in their original locations.

force — A standard magic procedure in which an audience member is offered what seems to be a fair and free choice (usually of cards) — but, in fact, the magician has predetermined the outcome. See Chapter 11 for several easy card forces.

French Drop — A sleight usually used to vanish a coin held at the fingertips. Magicians today rarely use the French Drop because of its unnatural appearance.

gimmick — A piece of equipment, unseen by the spectator, that helps the magician accomplish the effect. (You may also hear the adjective form, used to describe a prop that's been specially rigged: "You probably have a gimmicked pretzel.")

impromptu — Without advance preparation, using the materials at hand. Most of the tricks in this book can be done impromptu, since they involve ordinary, unprepared objects.

lap — To secretly drop something into your lap (when seated at a table) — or to retrieve an object already there. Never lap anything that has an open flame.

misdirection — Audience distraction. Misdirection is an essential magic skill — probably *the* most important one; by directing the audience's attention, you create opportunities to do tricky maneuvers where the audience *isn't* looking.

palm — A tricky move in which a card, coin, or other object is concealed in what's supposed to be your empty hand — for example, by pinching it between opposite sides of your cupped hand. There are many forms of palming: finger palms, thumb palms, back palms, and so on.

patter — What a magician says while performing.

play — To work as rehearsed (and to be enthusiastically accepted by the audience). Professionals often recommend tricks or presentations by saying, "This definitely plays."

riffle shuffle — The most common way to shuffle a deck of cards: The two halves of the deck are butted against each other, their ends interlaced by riffling, and finally mixed by pushing the two halves together.

routine — A series of tricks performed in a logical sequence, such as the two sugar-packet tricks described in Chapter 8.

sleight-of-hand — The secret manipulation of props (usually by the fingers) to generate a miraculous effect. When magicians speak, they drop the last two words: "He did a version of the trick involving sleights."

stacked deck — Also known as a "set-up" or "prearranged" deck. A deck whose cards the magician has pre-arranged, unbeknownst to the audience.

stage illusion — A trick that's big enough to be performed in a large auditorium. Examples of famous stage illusions: The Levitation; Sawing a Woman in Half; The Water Torture; Vanishing an Elephant.

sucker trick — A trick in which you let the spectators believe that they understand how a trick is done — only to have their "understanding" dashed.

vanish — (a verb, oddly enough): To make something disappear. "He vanished my wallet!"

For Dummies: Bestselling Book Series for Beginners

Praise for Magic For Dummies

"The primary message of magic is that we are all magicians, living in a magical world. However, most of us don't have a clue about how to access that magic. Until now. *Magic For Dummies* provides a wonderful introduction, not only to the "How it's done," but to the "How and why you can do it, too.""

— Tobias Beckwith, Producer and Manager

"This excellent introduction to magic is easy and fun to read. The information it contains is of as high a quality as many of the more difficult to obtain (and harder to understand) magical classics. Any one of the card tricks alone is worth the price of the entire book. I hope readers will appreciate and respect the value of these secrets."

— Daryl, the Magician's Magician

"When I first started magic, which was as far back as I can remember, I would have saved a lot of learning time if I'd had a copy of *Magic For Dummies*. It's got so much good advice and material, I'd heartily recommend it to anyone deciding to take up this fascinating business. But more importantly, it's very readable too."

— Billy McComb, Society of American Magicians
Hall of Fame, Vice President of The Magic Castle,
Hollywood, California, and Gold Star Member of
the London Magic Circle

"*Magic For Dummies* teaches more than the mere mechanisms of magic tricks. It imparts the psychological and dramatic essentials needed to share a pleasantly magical ambiance of temporary liberation from the tyranny of natural laws. If that isn't enough, it's also a hoot!"

— Looy Simonoff, Associate Professor of
Mathematics and Lecturer on Magic at the
University of Nevada, Las Vegas

"I wish this book were available years ago. All the impromptu magic you are about to learn represents an accumulation of some of the best effects in magic. Yes, this one book will make you the life of the party, and from here you may go on to a new career in magic."

— Tony Spina, President, Louis Tannen Magic
Company, World's Most Modern Studio, NYC

TM

BESTSELLING BOOK SERIES

References for the Rest of Us!®

Do you find that traditional reference books are overloaded with technical details and advice you'll never use? Do you postpone important life decisions because you just don't want to deal with them? Then our *For Dummies*® business and general reference book series is for you.

For Dummies business and general reference books are written for those frustrated and hard-working souls who know they aren't dumb, but find that the myriad of personal and business issues and the accompanying horror stories make them feel helpless. *For Dummies* books use a lighthearted approach, a down-to-earth style, and even cartoons and humorous icons to dispel fears and build confidence. Lighthearted but not lightweight, these books are perfect survival guides to solve your everyday personal and business problems.

Already, millions of satisfied readers agree. They have made For Dummies the #1 introductory level computer book series and a best-selling business book series. They have written asking for more. So, if you're looking for the best and easiest way to learn about business and other general reference topics, look to For Dummies to give you a helping hand.

Wiley Publishing, Inc.

5/09

MAGIC

FOR

DUMMIES®

MAGIC
FOR
DUMMIES®

by David Pogue

Wiley Publishing, Inc.

Magic For Dummies®

Published by
Wiley Publishing, Inc.
111 River St.
Hoboken, NJ 07030
www.wiley.com

Copyright © 1998 by Wiley Publishing, Inc., Indianapolis, Indiana

Published simultaneously in Canada

For general information on our other products and services or to obtain technical support, please contact our Customer Care Department within the U.S. at 800-762-2974, outside the U.S. at 317-572-3993, or fax 317-572-4002.

Wiley also publishes its books in a variety of electronic formats. Some content that appears in print may not be available in electronic books.

Library of Congress Control Number: 98-85846

ISBN: 0-7645-5101-9

Manufactured in the United States of America

15 14 13 12

1B/TQ/RS/QU/IN

About the Author

From age nine, **David Pogue** (page 17) was the magician at practically every birthday, street, and Halloween party in his native Cleveland, Ohio until the day he went to Yale. After graduating, he moved to New York City, where he conducted Broadway and Off-Broadway musicals for ten years. Along the way, he founded and taught the magic courses at New York's Learning Annex and the New School for Social Research.

In his other lives, David is the back-page columnist for *Macworld* magazine and the author or co-author of 15 books, including *Macs For Dummies, Opera For Dummies,* and *Classical Music For Dummies,* all published by Wiley Publishing, Inc. He teaches more than magic, too — his computer students include Mia Farrow, Carly Simon, Harry Connick Jr., Stephen Sondheim, and others.

David is a regular speaker at computer shows and user-group gatherings nationwide, and has been profiled in *USA Today,* in *The New York Times,* and on the CBS program *48 Hours.* He and his wife Jennifer Pogue, MD, live in Connecticut, where David is a first-time father, a frequent after-dinner trickster, and a member of the International Brotherhood of Magicians. His Web page is at *www.pogueman.com,* and his overstuffed e-mail box is *david@pogueman.com.*

About the Magic Consultant

Mark Levy (page 195) fell in love with magic when he was four years old, after the waiter at a local deli made the letter M appear on Mark's palm. Bitten by the magic bug, Mark haunted libraries, bookstores, and magic shops for the next 30 years, learning all he could about how to make letters appear on other people's palms.

Mark's trick inventions have been published in now-classic books and periodicals, such as Richard Kaufman's *CardMagic* and *CoinMagic, Apocalypse* magazine, and *Magic: The Independent Magazine for Magicians.* At his day job, Mark works in publishing, where he has currently sold over a quarter of a billion dollars worth of books, and was twice nominated for the *Publishers Weekly* Rep of the Year Award. Mark has written reviews for *The New York Times,* celebrity interviews (Leonardo DiCaprio!) for entertainment newspapers, and business articles for industry magazines.

He wishes to thank all his friends at Bookazine, and most importantly his dear family: Rhoda (his mom), Stella, Paul, Joyce, Gil, Joan, Irwin, and especially his father Sheldon and his Aunt Barbara, who would have been happy to see his name on this book. His e-mail address is *squanto2@aol.com.*

Acknowledgments

This book would have been only a hollow shell of its current self if it weren't for my longtime friend, magic and book expert Mark Levy. It was his brilliant idea to approach the Western hemisphere's leading professional magicians, inviting each to submit a favorite trick to include in this book.

Only one thing topped Mark's idea: his execution of that idea. He tracked down all the members of what we affectionately call our Advisory Pantheon, persuaded them to participate, and secured their submissions, biographies, and advice.

Along the way, Mark was a constant source of inspiration, ideas, and ingenuity, helping me to cull through hundreds of possible tricks for inclusion in this book. He was also a source of *chapters,* beautifully drafting the final four chapters in the Part of Tens, the glossary, and the short story in the Intermission.

My admiration and gratitude also flows to the pros who contributed their time and tricks to the book; you'll get to meet them in the following pages. Thanks, too, to the models who posed for the book's photographs. My original idea — that it'd be more fun for you, the reader, to see a different magician performing each trick than to stare at *me* for 408 pages — proves to have been right on, thanks to these friends' patience and good humor.

Thanks, too, to the friendly and expert Jon Racherbaumer, a pro with an encyclopedic knowledge of magic. He and Mark Levy were this book's technical reviewers, frequently reining me in from the brink of error.

As always, the team at Wiley was a joy to work with, including Senior Project Editor Mary Goodwin, Associate Project Editor Andrea Boucher, Acquisitions Editor Mark Butler — and Mimi Sells and Catherine Schmitz, who encouraged me to propose the book to begin with.

Finally, thanks to David Rogelberg; Steve "Shoes" Sanderson; photographic consultant Tim Geaney; and above all to the lovely Dr. Pogue and son, who stood by me (or crawled by me, as the case may be) throughout the writing process.

The Advisory Pantheon

A group of professional magicians contributed tricks, advice, and other material to this book. I call them the book's Advisory Pantheon. (*Pantheon* means "the officially recognized gods" or "a group of illustrious persons." In professional magic, these performers are both of the above.)

I'm presenting them to you here so that you can make a point of going to see them — they're tops in the biz — if you ever see that they're performing near you. Some of them have even provided contact information — just in case a little magic is what you or your special events require.

David Copperfield called **Michael Ammar** "the magician's magician." Michael has received six Academy of Magical Arts' "Oscars" — the most a magician is allowed to win. Michael has served as magic consultant to Copperfield, Doug Henning, Siegfried & Roy, and Michael Jackson. He's also kept busy lecturing, doing corporate magic, and producing a line of big-selling videos. E-mail: *ammarmagic@aol.com*

Mike Bent describes his act is an "homage to 'B' science-fiction and horror movies, comic books (not the stories — just those strange ads in the back), atomic visions of the future, brains, schlock movie gimmicks, and '50s hygiene films." His TV appearances include A&E's *Evening at the Improv* and *Caroline's Comedy Hour*, as well as Comedy Central's *Short Attention Span Theatre*. E-mail: *mikejb@aol.com*

Christopher Broughton brings class and humor to the stage in ways that stun his audience into applause. Using pop music to accompany his staged "playlets," Chris "bounces" a live dove off the stage floor and, in one truly astonishing moment, produces a *child* from his empty hands. The music industry's top stars — Puff Daddy, Busta Rhymes, and Gladys Knight, among them — have requested Chris to be their opening act. Phone: 702-876-8896

According to *Stagebill* magazine, **Eugene Burger** is "universally recognized as perhaps the finest close-up magician in the world." Using a few simple props, such as a candle and cards, Eugene creates miracles more astonishing than illusionists with a trailerload of apparatus. Twice Eugene has won the Academy of Magic Arts' Lecturer of the Year Award. He was prominently featured on PBS' *The Art of Magic,* A&E's *The Story of Magic,* and The Learning Channel's *Mysteries of Magic.* E-mail*: magicbeard@aol.com*

Lance Burton won the prestigious Grand Prix at the Fédération International Societé de Magic, with an act described by magic historian Mike Caveney as "the best twelve minutes in magic." That was in 1982. Since then, Lance's act has exploded into such brilliance that a major Las Vegas resort signed him up for an unprecedented *thirteen-year* run and honored him by building a theatre just for him — The Lance Burton Theatre. To magicians, Louisville, Kentucky is not known for bluegrass or horse racing. Instead, it's the birthplace of Lance Burton!

Not only is **Mike Caveney** considered "one of the funniest magicians in America" (says *The Hollywood Reporter*), but he's one of magic's premier historians (his latest subject: Carter the Great). Mike is a member of the Inner Magic Circle of London, has been nominated ten times as Stage Magician of the Year, and was twice named Lecturer of the Year by the members of the Magic Castle. He also runs his own publishing company, Mike Caveney's Magic Words. E-mail: *Caveney@aol.com*

At age 13, **John Cornelius** sorted magazines in the basement of a magic shop. Today, his mindblowing effects — one of which Doug Henning used as an opener for a TV special — earned John the International Brotherhood of Magicians' Creativity Award. John is the only American ever to win the Fédération International Societé de Magic world championship in two different categories — card and close-up magic.

Daryl has won The Magic Castle's Magician of the Year award six times — twice each as a close-up performer, parlor performer, and lecturer. Daryl sows the seeds of his magical wisdom in lectures, at workshops, and through the products made by his company. His video series, *Daryl's Encyclopedia of Card Sleights,* has become the best-selling series of its kind. Fax: (702) 435-7227. For a catalog of his tricks, write to P.O. Box 13821, Las Vegas, Nevada, 89112.

Doc Eason is carrying on a record-breaking 21-year run at Colorado's Tower Comedy/Magic Bar. There, Doc performs from behind the bar. Among his best known tricks: Doc not only finds the selected cards of 25 spectators, but he calls out each spectator's name as he goes ("Mary, this is your 9 of Clubs. Joel, here's your Jack of Diamonds . . ."). Phone: 970-927-3197. Web: *www.doceason.com*

Roberto Farini (or "Bob Farmer," as he is sometimes known) is unable to provide any biographical material about himself or "any other man of respect," owing to his "pledge of Omerta" (don't ask — we don't know what that is, either). All we can infer about him is that during his leisure time, Roberto enjoys thinking up tricks involving dismembered doll limbs, as you'll discover in Chapter 6.

Paul Harris's wild thinking and elegant invention has influenced a generation of magicians. Recently, Paul acted as magic consultant on David Blaine's controversial TV special; produced the Brett Daniels magic extravaganza in Mississippi; and was hired to make a scene in *Mission Impossible II* seem more impossible. Paul is developing his theory of astonishment, in which magic helps steer spectators towards a greater appreciation of life.

Bill Herz is one of America's premier corporate magicians. Corporations like MTV, Morgan Stanley, Time Life, and Coca-Cola hire him to custom-make magic tricks that get a company message across at meetings, banquets, and trade shows. Since 1987, his company, Magicorp, has sent magicians around the world to present their wonders at, and for, companies. You may have read about Bill in *Fortune, Forbes,* or *The Wall Street Journal.*

Jade has become one of magic's most elegant performers. Her act is homage to classical Asian magic, filled with parasols, flowers, and ceramic bowls overflowing with water. In one breathtaking illusion, Jade tears up bits of paper — then waves her fan and turns them into a dozen animated butterflies. Jade is an International Brotherhood of Magicians' "Gold Medal" award winner. Phone: Tobias Beckwith, Inc.: 702-697-7002

Kevin James has wowed spectators in some of the most demanding showrooms in the world, including at a command performance for Prince Albert of Monaco. As an inventor, he has designed illusions for David Copperfield, Doug Henning, and Mark Wilson; no wonder he was the guest editor for *Genii* magazine's special issue on magic creativity. His magic company is called Kevin James' Imagination Unlimited.

Aye Jaye, a comedian and a Clown Hall of Fame inductee, has been an entertainer since age four, when he appeared with his carnival-performer parents. Since then, Aye has performed at countless circuses, Radio City Music Hall, the Macy's Thanksgiving Parade, and the Rose Bowl. Aye is the author of the bestselling *Golden Rule of Schmoozing: The Authentic Art of Treating Others Well* (published by Sourcebooks Trade), and his new career is delivering "Schmoozing seminars" to corporations and business schools. Phone: 414-567-6673

Chad Long has been performing his casual, funny, engaging brand of magic since the age of thirteen — across the U.S., Canada, Europe, the Bahamas, and Japan. He performs regularly at trade shows, hospitality suites, sales meetings, banquets, and private parties. A multiple award winner, Chad has authored several magic books, and his tricks have been featured in magic publications and videos around the world. Phone: 904-274-2735. E-mail: *Shuffle1@mindspring.com*

Harry Lorayne has invented hundreds of tricks, which he's written about in his 25 magic books. On TV, you may have caught him performing a mind-blowing demonstration: remembering the first and last names of each of 500 people in the audience, each of whom was introduced to him only once. In short, Harry is the world's foremost memory training expert, having written 14 books on the subject, which have sold 8,000,000 copies worldwide.

Jay Marshall is the last of the living vaudevillians. For decades billed as "one of the better, cheaper acts," Jay and his hand puppet, Lefty, played (as Jay puts it) "the Hippodrome in Pottsville, Pennsylvania, the Palladium in London, and lots of places in between." Jay, along with his wife Francis, owns one of the world's most renowned magic shops: Magic, Inc. Phone: 773-334-2855

Jeff McBride is one of magic's superstars. In an act combining equal parts Kabuki theater, Shamanistic spirituality, and 22nd-century conjuring principles, Jeff coaxes water from the sky and levitates on beams of light. Jeff has won the Magic Castle's Magician of the Year award, as well as the rarely issued Star of Magic citation from The International Brotherhood of Magicians. Recently, Jeff has appeared on *Star Trek: Deep Space Nine* as Joran, a character written for him. Phone: Tobias Beckwith, Inc.: 702-697-7002

Tom Mullica is one of magic's funniest, most respected close-up performers. He delights the public in his Atlanta-based Tom Foolery Magic Bar Theatre and with his traveling show. Tom was featured in Penn & Teller's book, *How to Play in Traffic* (publihsed by Boulevard) and on *Late Show with David Letterman*. Currently, Tom is in Las Vegas, doing a daily tribute show to his comedic mentor and friend of 17 years, Red Skelton. E-mail: *poolery@aol.com*

Rich Marotta performs standard stage illusions, but with a hilarious difference. When "sawing a woman in half," for example, the star of the routine is a dummy — and its cloth innards tumble out as it's sawed in half. Assisted by his wife, Tamara Haas, Rich has brought laughter and mystery to the best known comedy clubs in the country (Caroline's and Dangerfield's), as well as to TV (*Comic Strip Live* and *The Showtime Comedy Club*). Phone: 212-532-5019. E-mail: *richmarotta@earthlink.net*

Mike Maxwell is a close-up performer, writer, editor, producer, director, and owner of the magic video and publishing house A-1 Multimedia. He published the complete works of Paul Harris as *The Art of Astonishment, Volumes I, II, & III*. Phone: A-1 Multimedia: 800-876-8437. E-mail: *gr8trix@aol.com*

Billy McComb received a medical degree from Queen's University in Belfast — and promptly went into magic. Since then, Billy has performed at Buckingham Palace and the London Palladium. He appeared in over 30 movies, plus his own magic TV series. Billy was the first non-American ever elected into the Society of American Magicians' Hall of Fame, and he received both the World Magic Summit's Living National Treasure Award and the Academy of Magical Arts' Lifetime Achievement Award. These days, corporations hire Billy to attend awards dinners disguised as "our British representative" — where he delivers a hilarious speech full of buzzwords and half-truths. The guests laugh until they fall into their cheesecake. Fax: (213) 850-5570

Jon Racherbaumer, this book's technical reviewer, came to the Big Easy in 1961 for the Madi Gras and is still recovering. He says, "New Orleans is in the land of dreamy dreams, where there is great food, music, and uninhibited celebrations of every kind. It is the greatest open-air asylum in the world. Every day is undeniably magical." Jon has written over 50 magic books, sired 7 children (Karen, Michael, Jona, Jonathan, Erika, Robynn, and Ry), survived voodo, Ann Rice mania, hurricanes, and the swampy heat. He can often be found at the Reality Check, an imaginary bar, with six characters in search of an unforgettable card trick!

As an illusionist, **Richard Robinson** has performed at venues from The Yale Art Gallery to Atlantic City's Trump Castle. Richard runs one of the most sophisticated magic sites on the Web — *www.allmagic.com*. In other careers, Richard wrote and produced live satellite radio broadcasts for Mick Jagger, Sting, Duran Duran, and Pat Benatar; wrote several books, including *Rock, Roll & Remember* with Dick Clark; produced records for Lou Reed, David Johansen, and The Flamin' Groovies; and directed some of the earliest rock videos for Blondie.

George Schindler was the national president of the Society of American Magicians before being elected into its Hall of Fame. While George specializes in performing his comedic miracles for corporate clients, he's also an expert at ventriloquism. You may have seen George in the Woody Allen movie *New York Stories,* in which he played Chandu the Great.

Jeff Sheridan is credited with restarting an entire art form in the U.S.: street magic. Before Jeff started performing his card, cigarette, and sponge-ball routines in Central Park during the 1960s, there were no American street magicians. Both the public and the magic fraternity paid attention — Jeff counted among his magic students teenagers Jeff McBride and David Copperfield. Recently, Jeff toured Germany in a show directed by movie impresario Werner Herzog. Phone: 212-969-0735

Looy Simonoff claims — get this — that he doesn't exist. If Looy did exist, however, he'd be a math professor at the University of Nevada, Las Vegas, teaching a celebrated course called Beginning Magic. The fictional Looy would be adored in magic circles, both for his wit and his wild effects. In one, for instance, he says, "I think I have a stone in my shoe" — and removes a rock the size of his *foot* from inside the shoe. Phone: 702-895-0361

Jim Sisti specializes in a demanding area: close-up restaurant magic. The restaurant's customers watch selected cards stick to the ceiling and magically appear under their own drinking glasses. Jim publishes a national newsletter for restaurant and bar magicians called *The Magic Menu.* Not all of his spectators have napkins in their laps — he also performs for corporations such as Norelco, Pfizer, and Hewlett-Packard. E-mail: *jsisti@ibm.net*

Tony Spina has been a regular on TV, including *The Tonight Show.* A winner of the Society of American Magicians' Magician of the Year award, he's served as consultant to David Copperfield, Doug Henning, and Woody Allen. But Tony may be best known as the owner of New York City's Louis Tannen Magic, arguably the most famous magic shop in the world. Phone: 212-929-4500. E-mail: *spinamagic@aol.com*

Jamy Ian Swiss has performed his riveting sleight-of-hand for audiences from Fortune 500 companies to Caesar's Palace to the Smithsonian. He has appeared on *48 Hours* (CBS), *Sonya Live* (CNN), *Nova* (PBS), and *The Art of Magic* (PBS); served as creative consultant on feature films and prominent magicians; and has lectured to magicians in 13 countries. He writes a column in *Genii* magazine; is a contributor to *Skeptic* magazine; and cowrote *The Art of Magic,* a companion book to the PBS documentary. Phone: (212) 581-7120. E-mail: *jamyianswiss@worldnet.att.net*

Dan Sylvester (also known as "Sylvester the Jester" and "The Human Cartoon") does things previously seen only on Saturday morning cartoons: His eyes bulge from their sockets; he threads a rope through his head and plays a tune; and he attaches a car battery to his ears, making voltage visibly shoot through his body. And that's just the opening! Dan has performed his outrageous miracles on many TV shows, including NBC's *The World's Wildest Magic* and Nickelodeon's *Make Me Laugh*. Phone: 562-867-4884

Johnny Thompson, along with his wife and co-star **Pam,** have won dozens of magic awards worldwide, some of which would require umlauts and tildes to cite. The Great Tomsoni & Co. (as they're known) are one of the earth's most hilarious, mystifying, and sought-after magic acts. While most performers spend a lifetime trying to be serviceable in either close-up or stage magic, Johnny can stun spectators five and 500 feet away equally adeptly. He has designed special effects for amusement parks and industrial shows, and he's also a virtuoso on the bass harmonica.

Torkova is never at a loss for pocket change. During his award-winning act, he produces hundreds of coins from thin air, to standing ovations. The *New York Post* calls Torkova's sleight-of-hand and misdirection abilities "unquestioningly among the best." While Torkova regularly performs for corporations and at international festivals, he also wows the likes of Dustin Hoffman and Don Johnson at private parties. Phone: 212-686-4050. E-mail: *torkova@earthlink.net*

Gregory Wilson performs and lectures worldwide — for Fortune 500 companies, comedy clubs, colleges, lavish yachts, and even backyard hot-tub get-togethers (where his polyneoprene tuxedo really comes in handy). He's a featured favorite at Hollywood's famous Magic Castle; the latest in his list of bestselling instructional videos is *Card Stunts: Cards that Disregard their Own Personal Safety for Your Entertainment Pleasure*. Best quote: "People often ask me if I can actually make a living doing magic. Of course, I don't mind if they ask that *before* the show." Fax: (949) 650-1135. E-mail: *theothergw@oco.net*

Meir Yedid was recently elected The Society of American Magicians' Magician of the Year — and is the only man ever to win that society's close-up championship twice. As a maker of magic tricks, Meir's braintrust of inventors includes Harry Anderson, John Bannon, Gene Maze, and Johnny Thompson. Meir also publishes a highly regarded online newsletter, MagicTimes. For a free copy, e-mail *meir@mymagic.com*. His Web site is at *www.mymagic.com*.

Finally, a super-special thanks to the other magicians who contributed time, expertise, and friendship: the hilarious and internationally famous Terry Seabrooke; the Amazing Jonathan, who really is amazing; Barry Lubin (also known as Grandma the Clown, a man who, at Ringling Brothers Clown College, majored in "Idiocy and Oops, with a minor in Stupidity"); Todd Robbins, America's most esteemed freakshow performer; C.W. Wolfe, voice-over artist extraordinaire; rubber-band genius Dan Harlan; creative genius Steve Fearson, who can levitate himself five different ways; Seth Ossinsky; skeptic Ray Hyman; Ron Bauer; Milt Kurt; Dick Zimmerman; grand illusionist David Seebach; Richard Kaufman; Zsajsha and Zeke Jaye; Erika Larsen and Jim Krenz of *Genii* magazine; Stan Allen of *Magic* magazine; super-agent and performer Peter Reveen; and Dave Goodsell of M.U.M. fame.

Photo Models

Winston Lindo
Matt Malloy
Carolyn Malloy
Bill Malloy
Kathleen Malloy
Jenny Henkind
Joe Ferraro
Mary Jo Hansen
Case Hansen
Tim Geaney
Adrienn Takacs
Trevor Clarke
Dorian Bailey
Agnes Sipos
Jennifer Pogue
David Pogue
Jane Lazgin
Bill Scatchard

Brock Emmetsberger
Gerry Fox
Steve Bowling
Jordan Brugg
Richard Ortiz
Mónika Csiszár
Carol Ferrier
Maria Elaba
Pat Pogue
Steve Sanderson
Ryan Hughes
Peter Hughes
Evon Malloy
Kerry Malloy, Jr.
Kerry Malloy, Sr.
Marissa Littlejohn
Ronald Thorpe
Chris Deur

Gerard M. Sweeney
Mary Jo Sweeney
Mark Levy
Stella Levy
Jan Deur
Susan Vogel
David Schmidt
Molly Malloy
Breanne Malloy
Eric Jankelovits
Bob Lincer
Andrea Csiszár
Alexander Paul
William Paul
Dan Jew
Virginia Fox

Publisher's Acknowledgments

We're proud of this book; please send us your comments through our Dummies online registration form located at www.dummies.com/register.

Some of the people who helped bring this book to market include the following:

Acquisitions, Editorial, and Media Development

Senior Project Editor: Mary Goodwin

Acquisitions Editor: Mark Butler

Acquisitions Manager: Kevin Thornton

Associate Project Editor: Andrea Boucher

Copy Editor: Stacy Riebsomer

Technical Editors: Mark Levy, Jon Racherbaumer

Photographer: David Pogue

Editorial Manager: Elaine Brush

Editorial Assistant: Paul Kuzmic

Editorial Coordinator: Maureen F. Kelly

Acquisitions Coordinator: Jon Malysiak

Administrative Assistant: Allison Solomon

Composition

Project Coordinator: Karen York

Layout and Graphics: Lou Boudreau, Linda M. Boyer, J. Tyler Connor, Maridee V. Ennis, Angela F. Hunckler, Todd Klemme, Jane E. Martin, Drew R. Moore, Heather N. Pearson, Anna Rohrer, Brent Savage, Janet Seib, Deirdre Smith, Rashell Smith, Michael A. Sullivan

Proofreaders: Kelli Botta, Michelle Croninger, Nancy L. Reinhardt, Rebecca Senninger, Janet M. Withers

Indexer: Sherry Massey

Publishing and Editorial for Consumer Dummies

Diane Graves Steele, Vice President and Publisher, Consumer Dummies

Joyce Pepple, Acquisitions Director, Consumer Dummies

Kristin A. Cocks, Product Development Director, Consumer Dummies

Michael Spring, Vice President and Publisher, Travel

Brice Gosnell, Associate Publisher, Travel

Suzanne Jannetta, Editorial Director, Travel

Publishing for Technology Dummies

Andy Cummings, Vice President and Publisher, Dummies Technology/General User

Composition Services

Gerry Fahey, Vice President of Production Services

Debbie Stailey, Director of Composition Services

Contents at a Glance

Introduction 1

Part I: Becoming Magical 7
Chapter 1: All Form, No Content 9
Chapter 2: The Instant Gratification Chapter 29

Part II: Wizardry Anywhere 43
Chapter 3: The Financial Wizard 45
Chapter 4: New Uses for Old Office Supplies 67
Chapter 5: What to Do with Other People's Clothing 85
Chapter 6: Take It Outside, Pal 99

Part III: The Restaurant Zone 121
Chapter 7: Cutlery Is Your Friend 123
Chapter 8: Playing with Your Food 143
Chapter 9: Matches Made in Heaven 163
Intermission 177

Part IV: Pick a Card . . . Trick 183
Chapter 10: I Could Have Dealt All Night 185
Chapter 11: The Build-Your-Own-Card-Trick Kit 223

Part V: Party Time 241
Chapter 12: Rope 243
Chapter 13: I Knew That! 255
Chapter 14: Group Hysteria 281

Part VI: The Part of Tens 303
Chapter 15: Ten Basics of Good Magic 305
Chapter 16: Ten Classic Moments in Magic History 311
Chapter 17: Ten Dead Magicians Worth Knowing 317
Chapter 18: Ten Things to Say When Things Go Wrong 323
Chapter 19: Ten Ways to Get More into Magic 325

Part VII: Appendixes 333
Appendix A: Magic Stores, Publishers, Societies, and Magazines 335
Appendix B: Magic Words: A Glossary 339
Appendix C: Trickography 345

Index 353

Cartoons at a Glance

By Rich Tennant

page 7

page 183

page 43

page 333

page 121

page 303

page 241

Cartoon Information:
Fax: 978-546-7747
E-Mail: richtennant@the5thwave.com
World Wide Web: www.the5thwave.com

Table of Contents

Introduction 1

   About This Book 1
      Where the tricks came from 2
      Of handedness 2
   How This Book Is Organized 3
      Part I: Becoming Magical 3
      Part II: Wizardry Anywhere 3
      Part III: The Restaurant Zone 3
      Part IV: Pick a Card . . . Trick 3
      Part V: Party Time 4
      Part VI: The Part of Tens 4
      Part VII: Appendixes 4
   Icons Used in This Book 4
   The Process of Learning a Trick 5
   Welcome to the Circle 6

Part I: Becoming Magical 7

Chapter 1: All Form, No Content 9

   The Anti-Gravity Pencil 10
   The Disappearing Anything 13
   The One-Legged Leg Vanish 15
   Fingertip Munch 18
   How to Get Rubbery 19
      The Stretchiest Thumb in the World 19
      The Stretchiest Finger in the World 21
      The Stretchiest Arm in the World 22
   Off the Wall 24
      It's a bird, it's a plane 24
      Social climbing 25
      The mugger nobody knows 26

Chapter 2: The Instant Gratification Chapter 29

   Two-Card "Sleight of Hand" 29
   The Tale of the Tightrope Walker 33
   The Pencil-and-Quarter Double Vanish 37

Part II: Wizardry Anywhere 43

Chapter 3: The Financial Wizard 45
Hard, Cold, Pencil-Breaking Cash 46
Sheep and Thieves 49
The Vanishing Quarter, Show-Off Edition 52
The Big Money Rises 54
The 7-Penny Reflex Test 57
Don't Show Me the Money 61
Heads or Tails: The Shadow Knows 64

Chapter 4: New Uses for Old Office Supplies 67
Pencil up the Nose 67
Cheapskate Houdini: The Triple Rubber Band Escape 70
    Stage I: The rubber band jumps 71
    Stage II: Locked in place 73
    Stage III: Dueling bands 75
The Antigravity Ring 76
Post-It-ive Identification 78
The Photocopied Card Trick 82

Chapter 5: What to Do with Other People's Clothing 85
Give Me a Ring Sometime — and a String 85
Walking through Ropes 88
Scarf Decapitation 92
Give That Purse a Hand 94

Chapter 6: Take It Outside, Pal 99
The Missing Spray-Paint Marble 99
The Ninja Key Catch 102
Straw through the Jaw 104
The Astonishing Straw-Wrapper Restoration 106
The Creepy Little Baby Hand 109
The $100 LifeSaver Trick 113
The Unforgettable "Cloudy" Toilet Paper 116

Part III: The Restaurant Zone 121

Chapter 7: Cutlery Is Your Friend 123
The Bendy Spoon, Part I 123
Bendy Spoon II: The Return 126
The Classic Salt Shaker Penetration 129
Forks a Lot 132
The Three-Mug Monte 134
Three-Object Monte, Freakout Edition 137

Chapter 8: Playing with Your Food 143

   A Sugar Substitute 143

   The Evaporating Sugar 146

   The Linking Pretzels 149

   Beans through the Orifices 152

   Bouncing the Roll 157

   The Floating Dinner Roll 158

Chapter 9: Matches Made in Heaven 163

   Making an Ash of Yourself 163

   Ashes through Someone Else's Palm 165

   The Three-Matchbox Shell Game 168

   Weighing the Matchbooks 171

   The Static-Electricity Test 173

Intermission 177

   A Day in the Life of a Semi-Pro 177

      Entertainment Weekly 179

      The Restaurant Summers 179

      The Offer 180

      The Show 181

      It's in the Cards 182

Part IV: Pick a Card . . . Trick *183*

Chapter 10: I Could Have Dealt All Night 185

   How to Shuffle without Really Accomplishing Anything 185

   You Do As I Do 187

   The Hands-Off, Mixed-Up, Pure Impossibility 190

   Aces by Touch 193

   Dealing to the Aces 195

   The Envelope, Please 198

   Soul Mates 200

   The "Pick a Number" Spelling Bee 203

   The Shuffling Lesson 207

   Sleight of Foot 211

   The Future Deck 215

   Dream a Card, Any Card 219

Chapter 11: The Build-Your-Own-Card-Trick Kit 223

   How This Chapter Works 223

   Forces 224

      The Cut Anywhere force 224

      The Under the Hanky force 226

      The Bottom-Deal force 227

      The Countdown force 228

Revelations 230
    The Geiger Counter 230
    The Jumping Out revelation 230
    Feeling by Muscle 232
    The "Name of the Card Is" revelation 234
    Slap It! 235
    The "Above and Beyond" revelation 236
    The Magic For Dummies Grand Finale 237

Part V: Party Time 241

Chapter 12: Rope 243

    The Classic Cut-Rope Restoration 243
    Ring off Rope 247
    Escape from the K-Mart Tie 251

Chapter 13: I Knew That! 255

    The Three-Card "Pick by Touch" Test 256
    The Triple-Prediction Spouse-Clincher 258
    The Math/Geography/Animal/Color Test 263
    Divide & Conquer 265
    The Book Test 268
    The Great Vegetable Prediction 273
    The Telephone Trick I: Call This Number 275
    The Telephone Trick II: Call the Phantom 279

Chapter 14: Group Hysteria 281

    The Torn and Restored Toilet Paper 282
    You Can't Do as I Do 285
    The Strength Test 288
    The Phantom Photo 291
    The Late-Night Party Murder Mystery 298

Part VI: The Part of Tens 303

Chapter 15: Ten Basics of Good Magic 305

    Don't Reveal the Secret — Ever 305
    Don't Repeat a Trick 306
    Know When to Start 306
    Know When to Stop 307
    Build Up Your Audience 307
    Suit the Tricks to the Crowd 307
    One Great Trick Is Worth Ten Not-Ready Ones .. 308

Keep at It 309
Act the Part 309
Make It Yours 310

Chapter 16: Ten Classic Moments in Magic History 311

Robert-Houdin Prevents War with a Trick 311
Herrmann Pulls a Coin from a Roll 312
Malini Produces a Block of Ice 312
Houdini Becomes Dangerous 313
Blackstone Saves His Audience 313
Richiardi Jr. Bisects His Daughter 314
The Great Tomsoni Capitalizes on His Mistakes 314
Doug Henning Comes to Broadway 315
Copperfield Changes the Scale of Magic 315
You See Your First Magic Trick 316

Chapter 17: Ten Dead Magicians Worth Knowing 317

John Henry Anderson (1814-1874) 317
Harry Kellar (1849-1922) 318
Servais Le Roy (1865-1953) 318
Howard Thurston (1869-1936) 319
Horace Goldin (1873-1939) 319
Joseph Dunninger (1892-1975) 320
Cardini (1899-1973) 320
Slydini (1901-1991) 321
Ed Marlo (1913-1992) 321
Dai Vernon (1894-1992) 322

Chapter 18: Ten Things to Say When Things Go Wrong 323

Chapter 19: Ten Ways to Get More into Magic 325

Watch Other Magicians 325
Read 326
Go to Magic Shops 327
Watch TV Magic Specials 327
Join a Magic Association 328
Read Magic Magazines 328
Surf the Web 329
    General magic 329
    Magic history 329
    Magic dealers 329
    Individual magicians 330
    Current events 330
Watch Magic Tapes 330
Take a Course 331
Perform 332

Part VII: Appendixes *333*

Appendix A: Magic Stores, Publishers, Societies, and Magazines 335
Magic Shops 335
Book and Video Sources 336
Organizations 337
Magic Magazines 337

Appendix B: Magic Words: A Glossary 339

Appendix C: Trickography 345
Chapter 1 345
Chapter 2 346
Chapter 3 346
Chapter 4 346
Chapter 5 347
Chapter 6 347
Chapter 7 348
Chapter 8 348
Chapter 9 349
Intermission 349
Chapter 10 349
Chapter 11 350
Chapter 12 351
Chapter 13 351
Chapter 14 351
Chapters 16 and 17 352
Chapter 18 352
Appendixes 352

Index *353*

Introduction

● ●

Maybe you've noticed: In this age of X-Files, Psychic Friends Hotlines, and a new UFO movie every month, magic is making an explosive comeback. David Copperfield, Lance Burton, David Blaine, and *The World's Greatest Magicians* specials appear on TV almost monthly. Maybe society needs a break from encroaching technology, or maybe we're just riding the upswing of the big spiritual pendulum — but there's no question that magic, as a hobby, a performance art, and a belief, is booming.

A magic trick creates a tiny, giddy, momentary bubble of disbelief. "That's *got* to be a trick," the audience says to itself — "... *almost* certainly." For a split second, you, the magician, have grabbed the spotlight in a way that nobody can resent. Magic is therefore the perfect skill for the business-person who needs an ice-breaker, the teenager who wants a self-esteem boost, the ham or klutz who needs a socially acceptable outlet, or the romantic who wants to impress dates. (I should know: I won my wife over with magic tricks!)

About This Book

Would you like to know how David Copperfield makes airplanes disappear? Would you like to saw beautiful women in half? Would you like to escape from a water tank on national TV?

If so, you've picked up the wrong book. Sorry about that.

In this entire book, there's not a single trick that requires a crew, not one trick bigger than an icebox, and not a single prop whose construction involves a table saw. Big TV stage magic is glorious to watch, but wait until you see people's faces when magic happens *in their hands*. Trust me on this: The joy isn't in knowing how other magicians work; it's in being the magician yourself.

I'll teach you how to perform *little* miracles. You can do them on the spur of the moment, using unprepared items you borrow on the spot: money, pencils, clothing, silverware. You'll be surprised at how just a couple of extraordinary stunts with ordinary things can add charm to your personality, impress friends, and land important job promotions.

And by the way: There's no real sleight of hand in this book. Not one of the tricks in this book require days of practicing "moves" over and over again. Out of the 841,302 magic tricks in the world of wizardry, I've found 100 that are astounding without being difficult. But you'll see that for yourself.

That's not to say, however, that doing magic doesn't require skill; I'm just saying that you don't have to have great manual dexterity. No, the talent required here is *showmanship*. Only a small percentage of doing a trick well is *trick*. Most of it, believe it or not, is presentation — timing, eye contact, style, and talking. Learn to put over a magic trick well, and you'll also find yourself improving at making speeches, telling jokes, and understanding politics.

Where the tricks came from

In most cases, the magician who makes up a new trick gets no money for it. The idea may catch on — at magic conventions, in conversation, in performance — and may get passed along from magician to magician, but the inventor doesn't get rich. As any lawyer will tell you, you can't copyright an idea.

As a result, magicians make it a point to honor the originator when they write about a trick. Professional magic books and videos are full of such crediting. The thoroughness of this may sometimes seem ridiculous — "This is a trick originally developed by Dai Vernon and adapted by Jay Marshall into a version Michael Ammar presented in his first video, with the ending twist added by Johnny Thompson" — but it's a sweet and noble tradition.

Although there's nothing *illegal* about publishing a bunch of tricks without acknowledging who thought them up, doing so is definitely not classy. That's why this book's technical reviewers and I have done everything we could to accurately credit the various inventors and refiners of each trick — you'll find the complete lineage of each trick in Appendix C, the Trickography.

As a result, all the tricks in this book were either dreamed up (or enhanced) by the 35 magicians who contributed material, or the tricks are so ancient and well-established that nobody can remember who invented them. (Or, as magician Aye Jaye would say, "Sure, I know who came up with that. It was Schlobotnik the Fool in 7 A.D.")

Of handedness

To keep everyone from going insane, I've written this book as though everyone's right-handed. If you're a lefty, simply scan the book into your word processor and do a global search, substituting "left hand" for "right hand" everywhere it occurs.

How This Book Is Organized

This book comes pre-sliced into five handy chunks.

Part I: Becoming Magical

The hardest part of getting into magic is just getting over what I call magician's stage fright. That's a lot like the traditional fear of failure in public, but compounded by the terror that somebody will figure out how you're doing the trick.

The first two chapters of the book, therefore, are risk-free. They're meant to ease you into the spotlight with tricks that are either pure humor (and very little mystery), as in Chapter 1, or so sure-fire (Chapter 2) that your confidence will skyrocket.

Part II: Wizardry Anywhere

The great thing about magic is that you can do it anywhere. This style of spontaneous, borrowed-prop magic is called *impromptu* magic, and it's the focus of these chapters. They cover tricks you can do with money, office supplies, other people's clothing, and stuff you encounter while out and about.

Part III: The Restaurant Zone

To a magician, a restaurant is like Prop Land. These chapters, which offer tricks you can do with tableware, food, and matches, are ideal for any magician who eats.

Between Parts III and IV, by the way, is a strange little written interlude I call the Intermission. A piece of fiction, actually, but a very telling one — that may inspire (or frighten) anyone considering a full-time career in magic.

Part IV: Pick a Card . . . Trick

These are some of the best — and most unusual — card tricks ever squeezed into a single chapter. A second chapter teaches you the basic components of a good card trick, in the hopes that you'll then be able to construct one of your own.

Part V: Party Time

Many of the tricks in this book take place on a stage no bigger than your palm. In these three chapters, however, you enter the world of *parlor magic* — tricks big enough to do standing up before a room full of people. Tricks with rope, mindreading, and rolls of toilet paper.

Part VI: The Part of Tens

Five top ten lists, for your winding-down pleasure. They'll give you insight into the traditions, history, rules, and humor of magic — and show you ways to get even more into magic.

Part VII: Appendixes

The book wraps up with three bursts of reference info. One is a glossary; one's a list of magic shops, publications, and organizations; and the Trickography credits the various magicians who have left their marks on the tricks in this book.

Icons Used in This Book

Cute little icons dress up the margins of this book. They're there to help you spot items like these:

This icon denotes something you have to do before performing. Because this book is so heavily slanted toward tricks that don't require much setting up, there aren't many of these icons.

The tricks in this book aren't difficult to do, but that doesn't mean they don't require practice. This icon clues you in to the parts that require the most rehearsal. Get this part smooth, and it's downhill from there.

Much of magic is acting, if not downright lying. You've got to pretend you're actually violating the laws of nature. Here are your moments to ham it up.

Misdirection, of course, is drawing the audience's attention to the wrong thing at the right time, so that you can get away with whatever sneaky deed is required. This icon indicates those delightful opportunities.

Most people love watching magic. Some, though, treat your performance as a challenge to be conquered, and you as a charlatan to be exposed. This icon tips you off to places where, if you're not careful, an audience member could ruin your trick.

 This icon points out subtle touches that enhance the illusion by playing upon human nature. You'll see.

 Yep, it's a tip: a sage morsel of good advice accumulated from battle-scarred experience.

The Process of Learning a Trick

So how do you learn a new trick? Read about it. Get the necessary props and try the trick in private. You'll usually know right away if the trick is going to be any good. For example, I recently tried out a trick that involves threading somebody's wedding ring over the four corners of a cloth restaurant napkin. Are you *kidding?* That's like trying to stuff a blanket through a straw. Next!

If the trick shows promise, though, most books advise you to try the trick in front of a mirror. (Now you know why magicians are so often in the bathroom.)

A mirror is great for letting you see what the audience sees, for making sure the secret isn't visible, for practicing moves. But it has one huge drawback: You have to watch the mirror as you do the trick! That's nearly impossible to do.

In the real world, you'll never be watching yourself; you'll just be doing the trick. Many tricks take advantage of *misdirection* — directing your audience's attention to the wrong place by looking there yourself. Well, guess what? It's impossible to practice misdirection in the mirror, because the minute you look away from the mirror, you can't see how you're doing!

Fortunately, you were foresighted enough to wait until the Camcorder Age to take up magic. The camcorder neatly solves the mirror problem: It lets you perform the trick exactly as you'd perform it for an audience, complete with misdirection, eye contact, and so on — *and* still analyze your own weak spots by watching the videotape playback.

Not everyone has, or can borrow or rent, a video camera. But doing so makes a huge difference to the speed of mastering magic. It's worth the effort.

Welcome to the Circle

Writing a book like *Magic For Dummies* is not without its risks.

Some professional magicians believe that magic is a private club, a closed circle to which newcomers are not welcome. One pro I know, who I'll call Floyd the Great, broke out in screaming red hives at the thought of a magic book for beginners. "Magic is for magicians," Floyd told me. "If you write this book, you'll be destroying the art!"

As the co-author of *Opera For Dummies,* I'm already familiar with art forms that some consider a private club. I know that there's an upper echelon of "experts" who, having clawed their way to the top over many years, feel threatened by the thought of throwing open the doors to anyone who's interested.

Ah, but I believe that these people have it absolutely backward. The art of magic will die if it *isn't* taught, if the excitement *isn't* passed on and amplified. After all, where the heck did Floyd get his start? You better believe that some book or some person taught *him.* I'm firmly of the belief that everyone should know at least a couple of magic tricks. The more people get interested in magic, the more they'll do it, invent it, watch it, buy it — and even become Floyd's fans and followers.

So prove them wrong. Make the art prosper by doing a few tricks really well. In doing so, you'll find your life enhanced in ways that have nothing to do with magic. You'll be more comfortable in front of crowds, more confident in everyday transactions, and more fun to be around. You may not believe in magic, but you'll be turned on to the magic of physics, of words, and of psychology. In other words, you may very well discover the magic of *magic.*

Part I
Becoming Magical

The 5th Wave   By Rich Tennant

In this part . . .

Ever had a nightmare where you're standing in front of a crowd to give a speech — but you can't remember what to say?

No wonder — fear of public embarrassment is coded into our genes. The self-working, confidence-building tricks in this part are designed to get you over the hump of stage fright. With these sure-fire miracles, you can gently adapt to being the center of attention.

Chapter 1

All Form, No Content

▶ How to get comfortable in the spotlight

▶ The importance of patter

▶ A few goofy, funny tricks to warm you up

*I*f you've read this book's Introduction (which I highly recommend), you already know that only a tiny percentage of a magic trick is *what* you do. The rest is *how* you do it: your sense of humor, timing, and talkiness. Hate to break it to you, but behind the scenes, some of the world's greatest magic tricks actually look pretty dumb. Out front, they look spectacular — but you may have to overcome a certain self-consciousness when doing them.

How can I possibly stress the importance of *personality* in magic? How can I cure you of worrying that you might get caught doing something silly? How can I hook you on the rush of entertaining people, even if you've never been a show-off before?

Hey, I've got it: I'll begin the book with tricks that are *nothing* but showmanship. These tricks aren't even tricks. They're optical illusions, hilarious visual jokes, laugh-out-loud quickies. These tricks aren't about fooling people; they're about *entertaining* people — which, after all, is the goal of magic. Because there's nothing for the audience to figure out, you won't suffer that kind of performance anxiety.

These tricks will, however, get you into the habit of performing. Try them out. Get a sense of how people react to you. Practice being onstage. See how it feels to talk as you go. (See the sidebar "The importance of patter" on the next page for more about talking and performing at the same time.) After you do a few of these, you'll be ready for the added excitement of astonishing *and* entertaining people; that's what the rest of the book is about.

The importance of patter

Patter is magicians' terminology for "what you say while you're doing the trick."

Not every magician talks while performing; some stage magicians, for example, hit Play on the CD player before doing their stuff. You, however, may find it a tad inconvenient to whip out a boombox as you sit down at the restaurant table or stand in line for movie tickets.

Except for the occasional mime, no magician performs in absolute silence; it's just too uncomfortable, and therefore less entertaining. Because the music thing isn't ideal for close-up, impromptu performances, you have to talk while you do your tricks.

Patter can take various forms. If you can't think of anything clever, just describe what you're doing. ("Now I'm going to insert this steak knife, which you've previously examined, into the melon . . ." and so on.) Sometimes you may be able to create a story line that goes with your trick. ("Centuries ago, there was a magical steak knife from India who fell in love with a forbidden cantaloupe . . .")

If you're a business person and you're going to perform a trick to begin a speech, it's usually easy to make up patter that ties in with your pitch. ("Now, most consultants are like steak knives plunging into a melon. They only tackle problems they already know they can solve . . .") The point is to say *something* as you go. Make it funny, make it serious and mysterious, make it New Age and life-affirming — just say something.

Because patter is a huge part of any good magic trick, I'm going to suggest patter for every trick in this book. If you use it, great. If you don't, replace it with your own homemade patter. Whatever you do, don't perform in silence.

The Anti-Gravity Pencil

You don't necessarily need a pencil for this trick. Advisory Pantheon member Richard Robinson, who recommended this illusion, uses a magic wand; but you could also call this trick The Anti-Gravity Pencil, Butter Knife, Letter Opener, Straw, Ruler, Magic Wand, or Other Long Skinny Doodad.

The effect: With great concentration and a furrowed brow, you clench a long pencil (or other long skinny doodad) in your fist. You hold it high above your head — and open your fingers one by one. But the pencil doesn't fall! It hangs there against your palm, defying gravity.

The secret: The only thing defying gravity is the index finger of your other hand. Like I said, this one isn't really designed to fool anyone older than about nine years old (although you may be surprised). But it sure *looks* good, and it's great practice for overcoming the "The-secret-is-so-stupid-I-can't-believe-I'm-doing-this" syndrome.

1. **Rub the pencil (or other doodad) up and down against your clothing, as though you're building up a static charge.**

   "Did you ever fool around with static electricity when you were a kid?" you might say. "We used to rub balloons against the carpet, and then they'd stick against the wall."

2. **Lay the pencil across your open left palm (photo A in Figure 1-1).**

   For added effect, you might pull it away from your skin a couple of times, as though you're testing the static charge.

3. **Close your hand into a fist. Grab your own wrist with the other hand, as shown in photo A. Turn your fist so the back faces the audience.** *As you do so,* **straighten your right index finger (which is out of sight) so that it pins the pencil against your palm (photos B and C).**

   You'll have to open a couple of your fist fingers briefly to let your index finger in.

   Yes, I know — you're worried that people will see this move. They won't. First, your turning wrist blocks your index finger's movement. Second, your audience isn't even tuned in yet — as far as they're concerned, you haven't even started the trick yet! If you act as though nothing important has happened yet, so will the audience.

   After you're in position, however, your attitude should change. *Now* you're into science. Now the hush falls over the crowd. Now get slow, deliberate, and highly mystical. Start *acting.*

   "The funny thing is — when the humidity is just right . . ." (It's okay to not finish your sentences here. You're much too busy concentrating.) "I've found that even heavier objects can sometimes — here, I'll just . . ."

4. **Raise your hands to the level of your head. Look at your hands. With a great display of difficulty, balance, and danger, open your fingers one by one (photo D).**

   Leave the thumb last; to the last moment, you want your audience to think, "Oh, big deal. The thumb is still holding the pencil." Then, when you finally do open your thumb (and the pencil doesn't fall), there's a moment of genuine shock or hilarity, depending on how seriously your audience is taking you.

   At this point, spread your open fingers wide. You might decide to move your hand slowly around, maybe even shaking it. You might even *roll* the pencil mysteriously up and down your palm (with your index finger), although doing so immediately gives away the secret. (Which is fine if you're doing this for comedic effect or for children.)

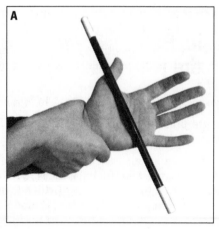

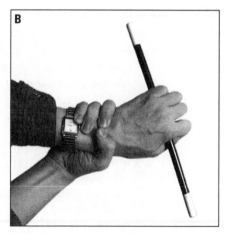

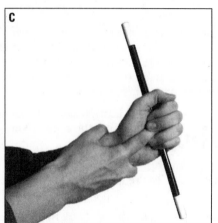

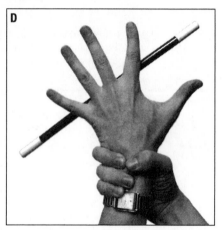

Figure 1-1:
At the outset, the setup looks innocent enough (A), here featuring a magic wand. After you've closed your left hand (B), your right hand (seen in C from behind) is missing a finger, although nobody will notice. And voilá . . . anti-gravity (D)!

5. **Finally, close up your fingers again and bring your hands down. Deliberately turn your left fist knuckles up — which perfectly conceals your right index finger sneaking back out of your palm and joining the other fingers on your wrist.**

    You've just reversed the move you made at the outset. There's nothing left for the audience to see but your left fingers opening, revealing an ordinary pencil that, by now, has lost its static charge.

If anyone actually looks mystified, you can now hand over the pencil: "You wanna try? It feels really neat!"

Otherwise, if everyone's smiling and thoroughly entertained, you might decide to (a) get back to work, (b) break your pencil with a dollar bill (see Chapter 3), or (c) push the pencil up your nose (see Chapter 4).

Truths of Magic, Part 1: Nobody questions the procedure

At one point in the Anti-Gravity Pencil trick that opens this chapter, you're supposed to grab your wrist with the other hand. In 1,000 performances, nobody will ever ask *why* it's necessary for you to grab your own wrist! Deep down, they'll assume you're trying to stabilize your fist, help lift it into the air, guard against germs, or whatever.

But the more important lesson here is useful in overcoming your shyness about doing magic: When it comes to how you do something, the advantage is definitely the magician's. For some reason, audiences simply don't question the *way* you do something; they just assume that the rules of the trick are a given.

Look: If a stage magician were *really* magic, he'd just stand there in the middle of Times Square with his assistant and slice her in half with a power saw. But he doesn't. He puts her in a box, on a table, on a stage, with the audience seated out front, blocking their view of his assistant before cutting her in half.

But not a single person complains about all that setup. To them, a woman still got bisected, and it's a darned-tootin' miracle.

The Disappearing Anything

You won't get far in your study of magic without hearing about *misdirection*. That's when you make the audience look at the wrong thing, so they completely miss the real action of the trick.

You probably assume that misdirection is very difficult, especially with an audience all around you. Actually, though, misdirection is amazingly easy, thanks to this handy piece of psychological trivia:

People look where you look.

If you're talking to me at a party and I look sharply at something over your shoulder, *you* turn and look, too. But if I'm looking you straight in the eye while I talk, you *must* look me in the eye. You can't help it. Meeting the speaker's gaze has been programmed in your DNA and reinforced every day of your life.

You probably assume, too, that you're new to misdirection. Actually, I doubt it. Misdirection goes on every day, all around you, in fields unrelated to magic. It happens in child-rearing. (**Thud.** "Waaaaaahhhh!" "Ooh, look, little Timmy! Here comes Mr. Teddy Bear! Lookie here!") It happens in politics. ("You had an affair while in office!" "Look out! There's a war in the Middle East!") It happens in relationships. ("You're late again." "Oh, yeah? Well, you forgot my birthday last week!")

Keeping your eyes on the prize

Beware one common misdirection pitfall of beginning magicians. Painfully aware that you're doing something tricky, and deeply worried that someone will catch you, you may try to cover your actions by staring at your *audience.* That is, if you're at dinner, you might unconsciously stare into the *eyes* of your date.

They, programmed (like all humans) to meet your gaze, will completely miss the trick. They'll also think something's wrong with you.

Instead, look above peoples' heads, as though you're going to chuck this poor croissant all the way to the rest rooms. And it's not *staring,* anyway; it's *aiming.*

You're about to see a trick that relies *purely* on misdirection. Mastering it will require a big mental gulp on your part — you won't believe you can get away with it — but it's super-easy and quite magical-looking. In short, I'll show you how to make *anything* disappear. Anything small, anyway.

The effect: You grab something small — a dinner roll, a $20 bill, a cork, a business card, an oyster, an egg timer — and toss it into the air, where it vanishes instantly.

The secret: It's all misdirection. You look where the thing is supposed to fly; everyone else will follow its trajectory. Trouble is, it won't be there. The trick is over before they start paying attention!

The fake-out toss is probably easiest to learn at a restaurant, where you're seated at a table. For this example, say you're working with a dinner roll.

1. **Hold the object in your right hand.**

   "Hey, have you read any of the new research about the aerodynamic properties of dinner rolls?" you might say. "Check this out!"

   Photo A in Figure 1-2 shows a dinner roll in pre-throw position.

2. **Drop your hand back and down, as though you're preparing to throw a Frisbee.**

   This all happens in one fluid motion, by the way.

3. **Simultaneously, turn your head out and to the right and *look* where the roll would go if you were really going to throw it.**

   Again, this is exactly what you'd do if you were going to toss a Frisbee.

4. **Drop the roll into your lap (the table hides it) and whip your hand in the direction you're looking.**

   Once again, your hand moves exactly as though you'd just tossed a Frisbee (photo B).

Figure 1-2: (A) shows the windup. You're looking where you're going to "throw the object." And then (B): It's all over.

Thanks to the power of your eyes and your violent hand motion, there's no way anyone can help jumping back and watching to see the roll's flight through the air. After about one second, they'll realize the roll is gone, and they'll immediately stare at your hands — which are, of course, empty.

The whole thing takes less than a second.

Don't be nervous, don't slow it down, and *don't look at the roll* once you've begun the windup. It's just a quick toss. If you can videotape yourself, you'll see how incredibly convincing this illusion is.

The One-Legged Leg Vanish

Here's another gag that won't fool anyone, but will have everyone thoroughly entertained.

The effect: You hold a coat or towel in front of your legs for a moment as you sing corny circus music. When you lift the coat, one of your legs has vanished — leaving only the shoe behind!

The secret: Pull your heel out of your shoe before you begin the trick. You then simply tuck your leg up behind the coat.

To prepare, grab a coat, towel, throw rug, or some other piece of opaque fabric big enough to cover your legs from the knees down. You'll have best results if you loosen your shoe before you take the stage.

1. **Stand with your feet together. Lower the coat so that only your shoe tips peek out.**

"All my life I wanted to do magic tricks," you might say. "But time after time, people would just say: 'Hey — try making *yourself* disappear!' and they'd burst out laughing."

2. **As you talk, pull your foot free of the shoe; your toe is touching the floor of the shoe for balance.**

Photo A in Figure 1-3 shows your starting position.

"The funny thing is, I took 'em seriously. I'm working my way up to making my entire body disappear into thin air. Wanna see what I can do so far?"

3. **Behind the coat, lift your free foot up, balancing on the remaining foot.**

Look down as you do this. (***Remember:*** The audience looks where you look.)

4. **Slowly lift the coat about two feet, enough for people to see that your leg is missing.**

It's actually a very funny sight — not what you'd call mystifying, but extremely weird (photo B). (Of course, it'd look at lot less weird if people could see you from *behind,* as shown in photo C.)

As you hold this position for a moment, you might fill the time by singing some corny show-biz tune, like the Johnny Carson theme: "DAAAH-dot-dot-daah, dahhhh . . ."

5. **Slowly lower the coat to your shoe tips again. Slip your free foot back into its shoe and whip the coat away to reveal your fully restored leg (photo D).**

Grace under Fire, Part 1

Kids, in particular, adore The One-Legged Leg Vanish. One six-year-old in my neighborhood nearly nailed me last summer, though. After a masterful performance of The One-Legged Leg Vanish, he yelled out, "Now make 'em *both* disappear!"

So I did what any self-respecting magician would do: I made something up. By sheer co-incidence, I was standing directly in front of the kid's back porch. A railing came down parallel to the staircase, and it ended with a post just about at the level of my hips.

I did the same trick — except I loosened *both* my shoes. Unbeknownst to the kids, I actually sat on the railing post, lifted up both my legs, and — sure enough — convinced the kids that I was now floating in the air!

Figure 1-3:
The preparation (A), the illusion (B), the secret (C), and the big finish (D).

Fingertip Munch

This trick is tacky, juvenile, and completely revolting. It's one of my favorites.

The effect: You've got a hangnail. As everyone watches in grotesque fascination, you begin nipping at your finger with your teeth. Deeper and deeper your finger goes into your mouth as you bite, until suddenly — *crrrrrunchhh!* — you accidentally chomp your own bone. The sound of splintering skeleton is loud enough to hear from the next table.

The secret: The sound of disintegrating bone is provided by a cough drop, peppermint, or other piece of hard candy you've previously socked away into your mouth. (Handy alternative: Slurp up an ice cube from your drink.)

The only tricky part to this whole affair is getting peoples' attention — and even that shouldn't be too tough. *"DARN!"* you can exclaim loudly. (That usually does it.)

1. **When everyone's staring at you, stare at your index fingernail, picking at it.**

   "I hate getting these hangnails. You ever get those?" Now start nipping at the edge of your finger with your teeth.

2. **Push your finger farther into your mouth and chew harder.**

   As the moment of truth approaches, ensure that your finger is actually *outside* of your teeth, between them and your cheek.

3. **After about four seconds, kick the hard candy into position between your back teeth with your tongue. Bite down hard.**

   Figure 1-4 shows the effect.

   What makes the trick (in addition to the horrific cracking, crunching sound) is that you *freeze* in horror, motionless, eyes wide, and let out just a tiny whimper of excruciating pain.

Figure 1-4: CRRRUNCH! The shattering of your bone has got to be heard to be believed.

After a moment of enjoying the crowd's aghast expressions, chomp two or three more times on the pieces of shattered candy, now pretending to enjoy the taste of fresh finger bone. Finally, pull out your finger, look it over, announce, "Got it!" and smile broadly.

How to Get Rubbery

You'll never get onto Letterman doing *these* tricks. You will, however, get people at the next table gawking and pointing. And you'll be able to entertain the kids on the airplane — you know, the ones in the seats in front of you who insist upon standing up and looking back at you all the way to London.

Here they are: three ways to stretch parts of your body in hilariously realistic ways. Learn to do these three stretchiness exercises with a straight face, and you'll be ready to perform *real* magic tricks without batting an eye.

The Stretchiest Thumb in the World

The effect: You grab your thumb and stretch it until it's nine inches long.

The secret: It's all in the twitching.

1. **Hold your left hand out. Give a couple twitches.**

   That is, flex all five fingertips twice, as though you're scratching an invisible dog's neck or slipping into a tight glove.

   That's an important move; you'll repeat this twitching every few seconds throughout the trick.

   "You wanna know why I'm such a great magician?" you can say. "It's because I'm double-jointed. Check it out."

2. **Grab your thumb with your right fist. Here's the twist: Stick your *right* thumb between the right index and middle fingers.**

   When you plop your right hand on top of your left thumb, the *right* thumb looks like your *left* thumb sticking out. (Photos A and B in Figure 1-5 should make this all clear.)

   After you're in position, twitch twice with all the "left hand" fingertips again. This time, however, your right thumb twitches with the left fingers, in perfect sync.

3. **Pretend to pull hard on your left thumb. Slowly pull upward with your right hand, so that it looks like you're stretching your left thumb.**

Make it look like you're really exerting yourself. Grunt. Actually, of course, your right fist is just sliding up the left thumb (photo C). Every half inch, pause and do two more fingertip twitches; those twitches go a long way toward making it look like your left thumb is still visible.

"See, I was born with this extra cartilage. It lets me stretch my fingers in unusual ways."

4. **As you pull, bend and even twist your "left thumb" in hideous directions.**

I like to turn mine, slowly, 180 degrees so that when I twitch, my thumb tip is pointing toward my shoulder, Exorcist-style. You can also try bending your "thumb" all the way backward so it touches your wrist. It looks really grisly.

If you keep stretching and twitching, eventually only the tip of your left thumb will still be concealed by the right fist.

Figure 1-5:
From your side the setup looks like (B); from the audience, though, it looks like (A). With plenty of grunts and grimaces, pull until your thumb is stretched (C). You can end the trick, if you like, by yanking your thumb all the way behind your back (D).

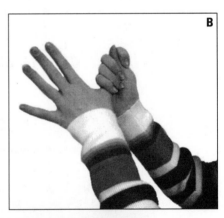

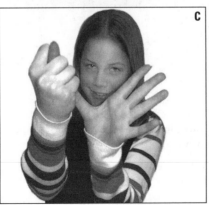

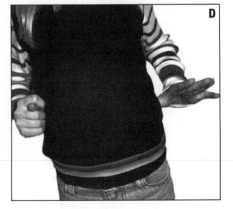

5. **End the trick by un-stretching, slowly compressing your thumb back to its normal length, and then taking your right hand away and showing your left hand back in its normal proportions.**

    Or you might make a sudden spasm, whipping your hands to either side of your abdomen, as shown in photo D. (Your real left thumb disappears behind your back.) Pause — and then twitch. It looks for all the world like you've just stretched your thumb all the way behind your back.

    Medic!

The Stretchiest Finger in the World

If you've just finished stretching your thumb, here's a great follow-up, especially if your audience is kids (or kids and adults).

The effect: You invite a kid to pull your index finger. Sure enough, it's stretchy, too — it doubles in length as the kid pulls!

The secret: It's all an optical illusion. Your index finger doesn't *really* stretch — I wouldn't publish any trick that could cut short any budding concert pianist careers.

1. **Put your right index finger between two fingers of your left hand, as shown in photo A in Figure 1-6.**

    Your right hand should be turned, so that your thumb is against your left palm, and your index fingernail points to the right.

    Hold both hands down low enough so that a kid can grab one of your fingers; in fact, your hands should be below the kid's chin level.

    "Hey, you — yeah, you with the hair. What's your name? Timmy? Okay, Timmy, wanna see how stretchy I am? Check this out. Grab hold of my finger. This one right here, the one I'm wiggling."

2. **Wiggle your right index finger. When Timmy grabs your fingertip, encourage him to pull.**

    "Okay, keep going . . . keep tugging — yeah, that's right — keep pulling . . . AIEEEE!"

3. **As he tugs, slowly let your right hand slide forward under your left. Don't open your left-hand fingers very wide.**

    As you can see in photo B, the effect looks exactly like your index finger just keeps growing until it's twice its original length. (What you're actually seeing is the top edge of your right hand. But it *looks* creepy as all get-out.)

Figure 1-6:
Two
pictures,
from the
spectator's
point of
view. The
right index
finger is
sideways
(A). Let your
assistant
pull it as far
as you
dare (B).

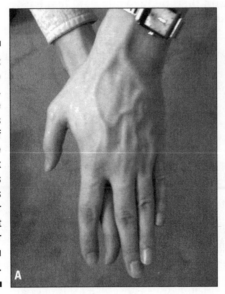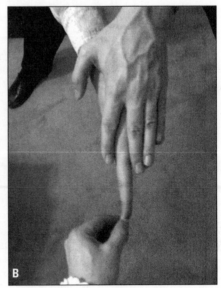

Figure 1-6: Two pictures, from the spectator's point of view. The right index finger is sideways (A). Let your assistant pull it as far as you dare (B).

4. **Finally, when Timmy has pulled far enough, pretend that your agony is the deciding factor in ending the experiment.**

   "Okay, that's enough! Quick! Push it back in! That's it, slowly — slowly . . ."

5. **Conclude by reversing the procedure, letting your right hand slide backward until your finger looks like it's the appropriate length.**

   Pull your hands apart. Vigorously snap your right hand in the air as though you're shaking off drips of water. "Wow, that actually felt pretty good," you can tell your young assistant. "Thanks for helping out!"

The Stretchiest Arm in the World

For this grand finale for the stretchy portion of your performance, you must be wearing some kind of suit jacket or blazer. Anything with elastic at the sleeves won't cut it.

The effect: You point out to your audience that your coat is a few sizes too big; your sleeves are positively hanging off your arm. No problem, though: With your other hand, you dislocate your shoulder, grab the newly freed arm, and stretch it until it's a full foot longer than it was before.

The secret: It actually has more to do with sliding than with stretching, but still, you won't believe how freakish this stunt looks.

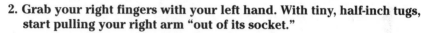

Before you begin, tug your right sleeve downward as far as possible. Scoot your shoulder backward in the coat to help with making your arm look very short. Hold your right arm out horizontally.

If you've set up everything right, only the tips of your fingers should be peeping out. Photo A in Figure 1-7 shows this starting position.

"People sometimes wonder where I get all the money to buy my magic tricks. Simple: I save on clothing! See, I don't care what size of clothes I get. If something's too big or too small, I just stretch my body to fit. Like this. Let me dislocate my shoulder here . . ."

1. **Use your left hand to karate chop your right shoulder (make a corresponding "Aaah —!" sound).**

   The idea is, of course, that you're trying to detach or dislocate your arm.

2. **Grab your right fingers with your left hand. With tiny, half-inch tugs, start pulling your right arm "out of its socket."**

   Let your right arm be tugged; help it along by shoving it farther and farther out of your sleeve. The optical illusion happens at your *sleeve edge*. People see the flesh sliding past that fixed vantage point — and get supremely grossed out.

   With each left-hand tug, your right arm moves, so your left hand's grasping point actually changes. Your first couple of tugs are on the fingertips; the next tugs are on the middle of the right hand; at the end, you're grasping your right *wrist* to continue pulling it out of your sleeve. At this point, push your shoulder forward, too, to help with the illusion of added length. It takes me about eight tugs to get to the absolute end of my limb, but then again, I'm Mr. Lanky.

   After you've stretched your arm to its max, hold for just a moment (photo B).

Figure 1-7:
Start with your arm as short as it goes (A). Start tugging. Stop when your arm is much too long (B).

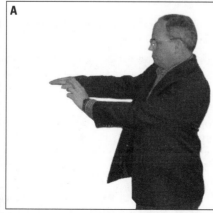

3. **Drop your arm, shaking both arms, as though you've just run the marathon.**

   "The things I do for fashion," you can mutter as you walk away.

Off the Wall

For the next series of witty stunts, you need an ordinary object found in homes, schools, and offices all over the world: a wall.

Actually, you need a wall that ends in an opening, such as a doorway. And you need an audience on the other side of that wall.

It's a bird, it's a plane . . .

The effect: They're all in there, having their cocktails and discussing metaphysics. You're late. You're embarrassed. You want to make an unforgettable appearance. So what do you do? *Fly* into the room, hovering three feet off the ground, floating halfway in, looking around, and floating casually out again.

The secret: No secret. Figure 1-8 explains it all.

1. **Stand just behind the doorway opening. Bend over as far as you can. Use one leg for balance (photo B).**

   You'll be amazed at how far over you can bend — and how much of your body you can show. Use the wall itself for balance, too, leaning into it.

2. **Move into position gradually, arms outstretched, head down, so it really looks like you're flying (photo A).**

   As you "hover," look into the room. If nobody's noticing your levitation, clear your throat loudly.

3. **When you've had enough, pull yourself backward out of the door frame again.**

Figure 1-8: (A): It's a bird! It's a plane! (B): Actually, it's someone standing on one leg!

Social climbing

The effect: This perfect follow-up to the previous stunt is a favorite of Advisory Pantheon member Looy Simonoff. This time, though, you enter the room by *climbing* in, as though you've just scaled the wall horizontally.

The secret: You're standing on one leg, just as you did when you were playing superhero.

Begin the effect standing a few feet behind the doorway opening. Stand on your left leg (if the wall is on your right). Bend over until your torso is horizontal. You're ready to make your appearance!

1. **Throw one hand "over" the wall . . . fidget until you've got a good grip and then throw the other hand over (photo A in Figure 1-9).**

   Only a couple of heads in the room will have turned at this point.

Figure 1-9: Who's coming over the wall (A)? Bit by bit, it's you (B). Thank goodness nobody knows how silly things look on *your* side of the wall.

2. **Strain. Pull yourself into view — just your head.**

   Ham it up; a little exertion-based grimacing helps quite a bit. At this point, somebody in the room has certainly heard your grunting and directed the group's attention to your efforts.

3. **Throw one elbow over, and then the other. Pause, look around the room, interrupt your panting long enough to say — "Oh . . . hi."**

   Photo B shows this happy moment.

   But uh-oh . . . this wall is slippery!

4. **Suddenly, pull back behind the wall with an "Augh!" sound, catching yourself only by your hands.**

   Feebly, strength fading, scrabble for a handhold with both hands. But in the end, it's no good; pull yourself back to your side of the wall as though falling, letting your last remaining hand whip out of view.

   (Crashing into the furniture a moment later, as you "hit the ground," is optional.)

The mugger nobody knows

The effect: Okay, you've had your fun. You've got the group laughing and admiring your chutzpah. Now it's time to get serious, to apologize for having interrupted conversations, to be yourself. As you stand in the doorway, smiling naturally, assuring the crowd that the worst is over, a hand reaches from behind the wall and grabs you by the neck, pulling you off balance and out of sight. No matter how many times you reappear, this backstage mugger won't let you go.

The secret: Once again, you're doing all the work yourself.

1. **Stand in the doorway, your right shoulder just behind the wall. Reach over to grab your own neck with your right hand.**

   This final effect doesn't work at all if people can see anything between your shoulder and your elbow. So stand close enough to the wall that nobody sees your upper arm (see Figure 1-10).

   Acting skills are essential here. Look shocked and worried.

2. **"Fight off" your assailant.**

   That is, after "he" drags you out of sight, reappear, mussed but okay — and now "he" has you by the face, or by the hair, or by the collar, again trying to drag you off your feet. With a little imagination — fueled by the riotous reactions of your audience — it's possible to carry on this way for 20 seconds or more.

And your reward? After you finally dismiss the mugger, you can pretend to be the victim of a very different kind of attack — a romantic one. The Hand reaches out from behind the wall, slowly, seductively, runs itself down your face and neck, and finally tugs playfully at your waist.

This time, you can pretend to be perfectly happy to leave the doorway.

Figure 1-10:
He's got
me!

Chapter 2
The Instant Gratification Chapter

· ·

In This Chapter

▶ The next step: foolproof but utterly mystifying tricks

▶ A blockbuster card trick

▶ A cut-and-restored string trick

▶ A double vanish — first a pencil, then a quarter

▶ The importance of misdirection

· ·

*T*he stunts in Chapter 1 loosen you up, hook you on the joy of being onstage, and help you overcome the sheer embarrassment of doing silly things in public. While they may even mystify some people, they'll mostly entertain.

This chapter offers you something even better: actual magic tricks. Tricks nobody will figure out. Tricks to get you started on the adrenaline rush of *amazing* people.

Better yet, the three tricks in this chapter are a rare breed: Although they're amazing, they're practically foolproof. Sure, they depend a great deal on your presentation; all tricks do. But if you rehearse these tricks a couple times beforehand and talk while you work, you'll find that these ridiculously easy tricks have a disproportionately powerful effect on your audience.

As you do these tricks, *act* as though you're actually doing something magical. Remember the old saying: "Sincerity is everything. If you can fake that, you've got it made."

Two-Card "Sleight of Hand"

There are no real sleight-of-hand tricks in this entire book. That doesn't mean, however, that you can't *pretend* to make frighteningly difficult moves with your fingers.

There's only one downside to performing this impossible-looking card trick: After it's over, nobody will play poker with you.

The effect: You let a spectator bury two cards deeply in the deck. After describing the hours of lonely magic practice you've been putting in, you announce that you're ready to try out a very difficult card manipulation for the very first time: You'll locate the two buried cards, pull them out of the deck, and slap them on top — with *one hand,* in *one second.* Needless to say, you succeed.

The secret: The two cards you bury in the deck aren't the same two cards that wind up on the top of the deck. But thanks to some clever psychological manipulation, nobody in a thousand years will notice.

1. **Borrow, or otherwise acquire, a deck of cards. Shuffle it a couple of times.**

   Start talking about how you've been trying to learn magic. You've spent hours learning sleight-of-hand maneuvers, standing in front of the bathroom mirror, practicing card manipulations until your fingertips bled.

   "I can't wait to show you what I can do — if I can do it," you might say. "But I need a couple of special cards."

2. **As you ramble, look through the deck for four cards and put them on top of the deck: the two black 9s and the two black 10s.**

   The order isn't important, as long as the top two cards don't have the same suit or number. *Good:* 9 of Clubs, 10 of Spades. *Bad:* Two 9s or two 10s. *Bad:* Two Spades or two Clubs. Photo A in Figure 2-1 shows a great lineup.

   You're about to pull *four* cards out of the deck, despite having just implied that you'll take out only two. So how come nobody complains? Because you're perfectly open with it; you're finding your special cards right in front of the crowd. Obviously, therefore, the fact that you're pulling out certain cards isn't going to be part of the mystery.

   Furthermore, you're not really "on" yet; you haven't taken center stage. Let other conversations continue; join in with the talk about sports and the weather; let people get the impression that the trick has not yet begun. Nothing is more boring than watching someone look for cards. Your audience will relax, zone out, stop watching. In fact, the risk isn't that they'll notice how many cards you set up — it's that they'll drive off to do some errands while they wait.

   On the other hand, there's nothing wrong with putting the four special cards on top of the deck beforehand *secretly,* if you get the opportunity. My point is that if you're in the middle of a series of magic tricks, and it would look fishy for you to run into the bathroom with the cards, it's perfectly okay to set up the deck right under their noses.

Figure 2-1:
Find the four cards and put them on top of the deck (A). Now begin the trick, showing the two cards fairly slowly, but always together (B). After your volunteer has pushed the two cards into the deck, do some kind of phony, sound-producing move (C). Triumphantly reveal them "back" on top of the deck (D).

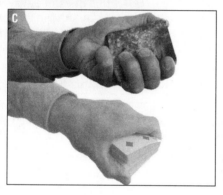

When your four cards are in position, you're ready. Turn to fully face the onlookers, straighten up, and square up the cards into a neat stack.

3. **Take the top two cards *together* and show them openly, as shown in photo B.**

"All right, I'm ready to show you my sleight-of-hand trick. We start with two cards: a black 9 and a black 10."

That's the key to the trick! In the entire performance, you *never name the exact cards.* You never *show* them separately, never *name* them separately. The hilarious part is that everyone will lean in, staring, checking up on your statement. Nobody will bother remembering *which* 9 and 10 you're showing.

PSYCH OUT

4. **Hand the two cards to one of the spectators, facedown. Ask her to stick the cards, separately, facedown, anywhere in the deck.**

   You can say something like, "I'd like you to stick these cards, *separately*, facedown, anywhere in the deck." Tell her to really bury them, pushing them all the way in, one by one.

   When that's done, go into slow motion. This is where you start acting.

5. **Hold the deck face-down on your palm as delicately as you would a glass that's full to the brim. Wrap your fingers around the deck, as shown in photo C.**

   "In magicians' circles, the move I've been working on is called the *Pinky Flesh Grab*. You probably can't see it from there, but those two cards aren't actually lost. I know exactly where they are. I've managed to bookmark each of their positions by pinching a tiny piece of my pinky skin at each location."

   Hold the deck high to "show" your audience. They can't see anything, of course, but they'll sure try.

   "Okay. Now, what I'm going to try to do — this doesn't always work, so no promises — what I'm going to try to do is pull those two cards back out of the deck and put them back on the top of the deck — with *one hand.* You won't believe how many hours I've put into this. Okay, watch."

   You've been moving slowly and cautiously to this point, like a coiled snake. Here comes the strike.

6. **Do *something* fast and audible. For example, quickly turn your hand palm-down and then back up again (photo C).**

   Obviously, this accomplishes exactly nothing, but it's so fast and so weird that your audience assumes you really *did* something.

   To help the illusion along, make a *sound* with the cards. While you're holding the deck tightly with your fingers, riffle the corner of the deck downward with your free thumb — *as* you do the palm-down/palm-up business. Your audience has just seen *and heard* you do something.

   Immediately after this fast action, slow down again.

7. **Push off the top two cards into your right hand — but before you show them, look at them yourself.**

   "Hey, it worked!" (Or just let your smile say this for you.)

8. *Now* **turn the cards around so the crowd can see them (photo D).**

   (That business about looking at them first yourself just underscores how difficult the trick was.) "And there they are, right back at the top of the deck!"

You may find this hard to believe, but only one person in 500 will notice that the cards are different — and even then, they probably can't be sure.

So why don't people notice that these are different cards? Let us count the ways:

- You use 9s and 10s, whose faces are covered with too many similar symbols to leave a visual impression. This trick *wouldn't* work if, for example, one card were an ace and the other a king.

- You never named the cards individually. You subtly asked your audience to confirm that you were holding a *black 9 and a black 10,* which you were. *That's* what they're looking for at the end of the trick.

- The audience assumes that the fast, confusing motion you made with your deck-holding hand had to have taken place for a reason.

- You acted so nervous about the trick's outcome, peeking at the top two cards before even showing them to make sure everything worked. Why would you have doubted the outcome if the cards were just sitting on top of the deck the whole time?

If you play up the sleight-of-hand angle, the illusion is irresistible. Afterward, slump back into your chair, depleted after the exertion, and shake out your hand muscles, smiling to congratulate yourself for a sleight well done.

And then, before the spectators have had too great a chance to think over what they've just seen, sit up straight and go into your next trick; see Chapter 10 for some ideas.

The Tale of the Tightrope Walker

Talk about idiot-proof! This miracle is so good, you'll cruise the streets of your town looking for more people to show it to.

The effect: Pattering on about a brokenhearted tightrope walker, you show two pieces of kite string. You ask a volunteer to hold one end of each string. You cover the remaining two ends with one hand — and they magically melt together, leaving a whole, unbroken piece of string. Your hands are completely empty, and your audience is completely floored.

The secret: Actually, you never *had* two piece of string. But people today tend to believe what they *see* — how foolish of them! — and by golly, they *see* two pieces.

Truths of Magic, Part 2: Give 'em something to believe in

In the Two-Card "Sleight of Hand" trick, the two cards your volunteer buries in the deck are already on top of the deck, where they've been sitting for the entire trick. Suppose, for a moment, that you *didn't* do that ridiculous business about twisting the deck and making a riffling sound. Suppose, instead, that just after the original cards were pushed into the deck, you simply said: "Okay, now look at the top of the deck."

Nobody would be impressed. They'd stare at you as though you'd completely lost your marbles. Everyone would *know* that the cards on top were different cards. Without some kind of intervening event, they'd know that the buried cards could not have moved to the top.

But if you pick up the deck and do some kind of maneuver, even if it's fast and blurry, you've planted reasonable doubt. You've given your audience something to work with — a clue. *Now* when the first two cards show up at the top of the deck, the onlookers can only assume that the fast, blurry movement had *something* to do with the outcome.

Let this serve as an introduction to one of the most important principles of wizardry: A trick is harder to figure out if you provide a semi-plausible possible explanation. Even when this explanation is clearly bogus, it's a mental distraction that throws secret-guessers off the scent.

For example, Chapter 13 offers some great mind-reading tricks. One of them ends by your naming a word somebody's thinking of. Now, let's be frank: Plenty of audience members are hard-core skeptics when it comes to ESP. They simply don't believe in it, never having seen proof that mind reading is possible.

If you were to simply blurt out the chosen word, everybody would know it's some kind of trick. But if you squint, muttering, taking your time — "I see a vowel — no, two vowels . . . I think a double letter — no, wait, I'm seeing *two* double letters . . . is the word — could it be — *beekeeping?* Is that it?" — if you do that, you've created enough mental distraction to create a reasonable doubt. You've got even the hard-core skeptics wondering, for just a moment, if you could have *actually* gotten an impression. "Hey, the magician only came up with one puny little word," they'll think. "It *could* happen."

The kind of string you use is all-important. Choose a *white cotton* string that's made up of twisted strands, as shown in Photo A in Figure 2-2. (Some people call it *butcher's twine.*) Brown twine won't work. Nor will rope, plastic string, or dental floss. If you don't have any white cotton string, visit a hardware store or drugstore and buy a ball.

Before you do the trick, cut off about three feet of string. At about the middle of the string, pull apart the strands of the string with your fingernails, as shown in the top part of photo A, forming inch-long loops on either side. If you can grab an equal number of strands on each side, better yet.

Now re-twist these newly created loops in the direction they seem to want to go. Twist and tug with your fingers until they look like string *ends* (as shown in the bottom of photo A). If you cover the joint with your fingertips (photo B), nobody can tell that you've actually got one long piece of string.

You're ready to begin.

1. **Hold up your "pair" of strings, hiding the joint between your finger and thumb.**

   "Did you guys read about the accident in the circus last month? Yeah — tragic business. They had this high-wire act from Russia. Guy named Komarynsky. Tightrope walking had been the specialty of the Komarynsky family for eight generations. And now the circus shows up here in *(name of your town here),* the poor guy's warmed up and ready to perform — and they find out that the tightrope actually broke during shipping."

   As you talk, casually display the strings. If you're nervous, keep the joint concealed by your fingertips. However, if you've plucked and positioned the strings enough, the rigged spot should actually be invisible enough that you *don't* need to hide it. As you handle the strings, you can:

   - Lay the middles of the strings across your open palm. (All four ends dangle down, together, just as they would if you really had two strings.)

   - Hold the strings, momentarily, by the *other* ends — the genuine pair of ends. (People assume the *far* ends are sticking together from static electricity.)

   - Hold *both* ends of the strings, pinching each "pair" of ends one inch from the ends.

   As long as you make these moves casually and naturally, they'll contribute, later, to the audience's memory of having seen two separate strings.

   "Well, the day I went to see this guy perform," you can go on now, "I took my little five-year-old *(niece/daughter/cousin/school friend)* to see the show, and she was crushed that she wouldn't be able to see the Great Komarynsky do his tightrope act. So I nobly stepped forward and offered my services as a magician!"

   At this point, you should again be holding the pair of strings by the joint.

Figure 2-2:
Pull apart
the middle
strands of
the string
and re-twist
until they
look like
ends (A). If
you hold the
joint, it
looks like
you've got
two pieces
of string (B).
Have a
volunteer
hold the
free ends
(C). Rub
magically
(D) — the
string heals
itself (E)!

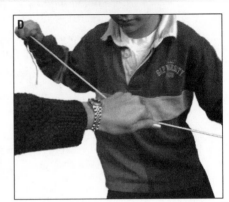

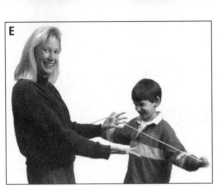

2. **With your free hand, take one of the genuine, dangling ends and put it into an audience member's hand. Take the other dangling end and put it in another spectator's hand.**

Or, if you're performing for one person, hand the second end to his *other* hand. You're still pinching the "two" remaining ends, as shown in photo C.

"I told the circus ringleader to fasten one end of the broken tightrope to each platform, like this. Hold that tight, okay?"

3. **Now *very* slowly and *very* deliberately, cover up the "two ends" you're holding with your free hand (photo D). Slowly and mystically rub your fist back and forth over the center of the rope.**

Inside your hand, you'll feel the phony ends dissolve as the loops straighten out; your rubbing actually serves to help the strands re-align into their original, string-like form. If your assistant isn't pulling the string tightly enough, *you* tighten the string by tugging the middle part toward you.

"And before the audience's eyes, I healed the two broken ends with one hand!"

4. ***Slowly* open your fist and hold it, palm open, just under the string, as the audience registers that you've actually done what you said.**

The effect, as shown in photo E, is mind-blowing; your audience can now examine you and that string until doomsday, and they'll never find anything that helps them solve the mystery.

You can't re-use the same spot on the same piece of string when you do the trick again, by the way; it will eventually fray enough to show the dirty work. Now you know why I suggested that you buy a whole *ball* of the stuff. (The other reason: I've got stock in the companies that make white cotton string.)

The Pencil-and-Quarter Double Vanish

Scattered through this book, you'll find a string of magical bonuses: magic tricks contributed by the Advisory Pantheon, which includes some of the most talented magicians in the world. By reading and trying these special effects, you'll get a great chance to see how each magician has cultivated a unique style. You'll also get to see how many different directions magic can take: Some tricks involve psychology, some require secret assistants, others take advantage of obscure scientific principles.

Truths of Magic, Part 3: Anticipate the dumb guesses

At the end of The Tale of the Tightrope Walker trick, I suggested that you finish the trick by holding your palm wide open and moving *very* slowly. Why?

Because of a pitfall of magic you'll encounter again and again: People make the *dumbest* guesses. "You switched the strings with another piece!" they'll shout. Or: "You had a pair of fake ends in your hand, and now it's in your pocket!" Or: "You have a trapdoor in your thumb!"

These may be patently ridiculous theories to you, but so what? If your spectators believe they're right, as far as they're concerned, they've figured out the trick.

Having performed most of the tricks in this book myself for years, I know the dumb theories most commonly shouted out. When possible, therefore, I'll steer you to performance techniques that serve as preemptive strikes against people's silliest guesses.

In the case of the tightrope trick, you'll torpedo your own masterful performance if you finish by (a) dropping your hand to your side, (b) stepping away, or (c) taking your hand away from the string but keeping it closed. Doing any of those things immediately draws attention to *you* and away from the string. If, instead, you leave your hand open, close to the string, palm visible, the final tableau is beautiful. Your audience is left with no leads whatsoever, and they're forced to stare at the white, whole string, wallowing in their inability to accept the impossible.

The following trick is a favorite of Tony Spina, who owns the world's largest magic store: the galactically famous Tannen's Magic Store in New York City (which you can read more about in Appendix A). (Nice guy to contribute a trick that doesn't involve buying *anything*, eh?)

You'll love doing this trick for two reasons. First, it's two tricks in one — a pencil vanishes, and then a quarter. Second, the trick works purely on *misdirection* (see Chapter 1) — misdirection so unbelievably powerful, not a person in the world can catch the sneaky parts. A fiery explosion behind you couldn't provide any greater distraction than the misdirection you use in this effect.

The effect: You show your audience a quarter — and announce that you're about to perform the Disappearing Quarter trick. You tap the coin with a pencil once, twice, three times — but the *pencil* disappears!

You apologize for the misfire. You show how you made the pencil disappear — you stuck it behind your ear! After exposing your own gag, you admit that you haven't actually delivered on your promise to make the *coin* disappear. So you tap it once, twice, three times again; sure enough, this time, the quarter is gone for good.

The secret: This is a *close-up* trick, designed to be performed right under your audience's noses. The misdirection makes it almost self-working.

1. **Show the quarter on your palm, which is at waist level. Point to the quarter with the tip of a long pencil, which you hold at the eraser end (photo A in Figure 2-3).**

   "Hey, wanna see a quarter disappear?" you can say. "No joke; I can make this quarter vanish right from my hand, while you're watching. Now, can you see the date on this quarter?"

   (That last question is optional. It's a gift I'm giving you if you're still nervous about relying on misdirection. The date of the quarter is irrelevant and never figures into the trick. But by *asking* if your audience can see it, you make them suspicious that this date will later become important. Result: Your "victim" is focusing even more on the quarter. Actually, though, this date business is training wheels; you don't need it once you're confident doing the trick.)

2. **Tap the quarter once per second, counting out loud as you go: "One. Two."**

   Throughout, look at the quarter. Do not look at the spectator. Do not look up.

   Before each tap, lift the pencil *all the way* up to the side of your head, as shown in photo B. Then bring the pencil all the way down to tap the quarter and say "One." Bring the pencil back again, to your ear, and back down to the quarter: "Two."

3. **The third time you lift the pencil, lodge it behind your ear. And then bring your empty hand down to the quarter and say, "Three." Open your pencil hand wide (photo C).**

   So powerful is the misdirection that most people won't even *notice* that the pencil's gone unless you say so! "Oh, man, look at that, I messed up! I made the *pencil* disappear!"

   Until you try this trick, you may not believe me that *nobody* will see you stick the pencil behind your ear. Everyone, *including you,* is looking downward at the coin in your hand. The pencil business is completely out of their field of vision, particularly if you turn the pencil side of your head slightly away.

   You'll get a great reaction from this first climax. People will look at your sleeves, on the ground, under your hand. Eventually, they'll spot the pencil behind your ear (unless you've got enough hair to conceal it) — but never mind; you're about to give away the secret anyway.

   "Okay, I admit it. That was just a joke. See, I just stuck it behind my ear! Check it out."

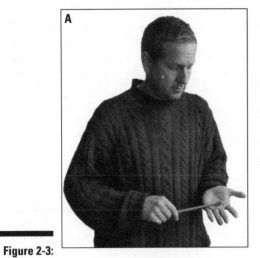

Figure 2-3:
Tap the quarter (seen in A and B from off to one side), bringing the pencil all the way to the side of your head each time. The pencil's gone (C). When you show where the pencil went (D), you've got a perfect chance to ditch the quarter in your pocket. That's how you're able to make it disappear (E).

4. **Turn your whole body sideways so that everyone can see the pencil — and *point to it*, too (photo D).**

   If there's one more powerful form of misdirection than looking at something, it's *pointing* to it. (If, because of your hairstyle, the pencil is completely hidden, pull it out instead of pointing to it.)

5. **Because the crowd is completely focused on the side of your head, you have two seconds of complete privacy to drop the *quarter*, hidden by your body from the audience, into your pocket.**

   Everyone is so busy staring at the pencil — and unaware that the trick is about to continue — that the coin could practically vanish in a *puff of smoke* and nobody would notice.

   Now turn to face your fans once again.

6. **Hold the quarter hand in front of you, just as you did before — but this time, it's closed into a fist. Point at it with the pencil again.**

   "But wait a sec: I promised you a disappearing quarter, and a disappearing quarter you shall have. Before your eyes, as promised. One . . . two . . . three!"

7. **Tap your closed fist three times with the pencil, exactly as you did the first time. On the third tap, open your fist wide, as shown in photo E.**

   The quarter is gone, and your reputation as a magician is well on its way.

Grace under Pressure, Part 2

The Pencil-and-Quarter Double Vanish is one of Advisory Pantheon member Tony Spina's favorite tricks. It's one of the first tricks he teaches his students, so powerful are its lessons in misdirection, focus, and timing.

But timing isn't always a magician's friend. Take the moment, for example, when Tony found himself at a nude beach, enjoying the sunshine — and a buddy handed him a pencil and a quarter. "Do that disappearing quarter trick for my friends!" said the buddy.

Now, let's face it: The power of misdirection drives most of that Double Vanish — but your

pants pocket handles the finale. On this beach, on this day, Tony *had* no pants pocket — that's a side effect of having no pants at all.

But Tony's a safe suntanner as well as a quick thinker. He did the trick perfectly — and fooled everyone on the beach.

He realized that the suntan lotion he'd applied was just sticky enough for the task. So instead of ditching the quarter in his pants pocket (at the moment when everyone was looking at the pencil behind his ear), he stuck it against his suntan-lotioned derriere!

Part II
Wizardry Anywhere

The 5th Wave   By Rich Tennant

FIDO MASTERS THE ART OF DISTRACTION

"...so he's showing me this pencil and quarter trick and I got my eye on the quarter and that's when he must have slipped off his leash and high-tailed it outta here."

In this part . . .

*I*mpromptu magic means tricks you can do it anywhere, on the spur of the moment, using only unprepared props you can borrow on the spot: money, office supplies, articles of clothing, and so on.

The next four chapters contain nothing but impromptu tricks, and there's nothing like 'em: they're miracles you can perform right under people's noses, up close, and without having to plan ahead.

Chapter 3
The Financial Wizard

- -

In This Chapter

▶ Breaking pencils with money

▶ Teleporting quarters, or making them vanish

▶ Making bills penetrate bills

▶ A "reflex test" that's fun for the whole family

▶ Making sure the money left on the table is yours

▶ Heads or tails? You always know

- -

*M*agicians adore money.

Now, by that I don't mean that we love money the way *everybody* loves money — acquiring it, investing it, and spending it (although magicians love all that, too). I mean we love to *play* with money, handle it, perform with it.

What's the big deal about money? Well, for one thing, it's everywhere. If you know a trick with coins or bills, you'll never, ever be caught without a prop. For another thing, money is above suspicion. Audiences are so familiar with money, and so confident in its government-issued officialness, that they can't imagine there's anything fishy about the bills or coins you're using. (Of course, that's not a safe assumption anymore, as any magician who's ever bought a double-headed quarter at the magic store can tell you.)

And finally, some money tricks are great because they put money at *risk*. Nothing's more exciting for a spectator who's just loaned you a $1 bill than getting a chance to take your $50 in exchange.

Hard, Cold, Pencil-Breaking Cash

You're about to learn the trick that got me started in magic at age seven. It's with a deeply welling sense of sacrifice that I reveal it now, for the first time, to the general public.

Okay, it's not quite such a big deal — in its original form, this trick appears in just about every magic book ever published. But the original version is also responsible for sending more novice magicians to the hospital than any other trick!

Do it my way, and you'll remain in one piece *and* blow your audience away.

The effect: You fold a dollar bill the long way, *really* sharply, muttering some pseudo-scientific mumbo jumbo about how the folded edge must be sharp. You persuade a volunteer to hold a pencil for you. With furrowed brow and a sharp snap, you succeed in cutting the pencil in half with the paper money!

The secret: Here's another trick that works by providing the audience with a bogus, but marginally plausible, explanation for what they're about to see. As long as they're busy trying to figure out if you're telling the truth, they'll completely miss the obvious solution.

1. **Borrow a dollar bill and a nice long pencil.**

   Or — because you're going to destroy the pencil during the course of this trick — provide one of your own.

   "Hey, can I borrow a dollar? Just for three minutes, that's all. See, I read this really cool article in *Scientific American* about the properties of cellulose, which is what they make paper out of. And paper money. I gotta show you this."

2. **Fold the dollar in half the long way.**

   Make a big deal about forming a sharp crease, even if it's a bedraggled bill. Drag your fingernail along the fold while the bill is pressed against the table. Look dissatisfied with your work, and then start flattening the bill against the table with the *pencil,* as shown in Figure 3-1, photo A. This is basically a non-speaking part; if you need to keep talking, just mutter something along the lines of: "Must . . . be . . . sharp . . ."

3. **After 30 seconds of this, slash the bill through the air a couple times.**

   You're gripping one end as though the bill is a Ninja saber, staring at it after each couple of whips as though you're looking for defects in your equipment.

4. Hand the pencil to your assistant and oversee the gripping process.

"Okay, I think this should work. Now, I need your help for this. I'd like you to hold the pencil like this." *Show* your friend by holding the pencil parallel to the floor between your two fists. As shown in photo B, the key to the grip is: *palms up!*

Encourage your assistant to hold the pencil at the very ends, making as much of the pencil visible to you as possible. "That's great," you might say (if necessary), "but move your fists even farther apart. This bill is *really* sharp, and I don't want anyone to get hurt. Hold it really firmly."

Swish your dollar/sword through the air a couple more times and then take position. Stand with your feet apart, as though you're about to do something incredibly difficult that requires a lot of balance. Hold the bill a couple of feet above the pencil (photo B). *Stare down at the pencil.* (Your audience will stare wherever you stare.)

Figure 3-1:
Make sure the folded bill is "nice and sharp" (A). Raise the bill high (B) and whip it down past the pencil (C) — and notice that the volunteer is holding the pencil *palms up.* The third time's the charm (D).

5. **Whip the bill, *hard*, down onto — and past — the pencil. Follow through, ending up as shown in photo C.**

   Of course, absolutely nothing will happen; a piece of paper can't *really* chop a piece of wood in half.

   Look perplexed at your misfire. Stare at the dollar. Apply even more pressure on the crease with your fingernails.

   "Huh! Man, the article said that it ought to work. The cellulose fibers in the paper are supposed to line up and give it a velocipital rigidity . . ."

6. **Take position again. Repeat the karate-chop thing with the bill — but this time, start with the bill even higher in the air and use even more force.**

   Once again, the bill strikes the pencil on its way down — and absolutely nothing happens.

   Your line: "*Darn* it!"

   Now your reputation is at stake. Get *really* determined. Third time's the charm. Start with the bill nearly above your head now.

7. **Once again, you're going to whip the bill past the pencil — but this time, smash it with your *fist*, not with the bill.**

   At this point, your arm is moving so fast, and you're swinging with such follow-through, that nobody will ever see what happened. Your hand is in table-pounding position, and the side of your fist — if possible, the curled-up-finger portion of your fist — breaks the pencil.

Truths of Magic, Part 4: Third time's the charm

In the Hard, Cold, Pencil-Breaking Cash trick, you try to break the pencil in half three times — but the first two times, you apparently fail. You've just met one of the most common and most successful dodges in all of magic: the "third-time's-the-charm" principle.

Why bother? Why not just smash the darned pencil the first time? Actually, the "third-time's-the-charm" principle has a number of powerful psychological effects. First, you *set a precedent,* teaching the audience what the routine is without actually saying anything. Second, you get them *slightly bored,* which is to say slightly less observant; by the third attempt, they've seen this all before, so they're not paying as much attention as they were the first time. On that third attempt, therefore, you can get away with changing one element of the ritual without being detected.

Third, the audience *thinks you're screwing up,* which adds some danger and fun to the proceedings. Now your trick has a miniature dramatic plotline: Will you overcome your failure and succeed in the end? Certain audience members, meanwhile, love seeing magicians botch tricks just because it makes them feel superior. The "third-time's-the-charm" routine gives them that rosy feeling for about a minute — and then you dash their hopes by proving that you really *are* superior, after all.

If you do this smashing with enough conviction (*real* conviction, not the acting you've been using thus far in the trick), you won't feel a thing. Both of you will be staring in amazement at the two shattered halves of the pencil in your assistant's hands (photo D).

Most magic books, by the way, tell you to stick your *finger* out and break the pencil with *it*. Are they *nuts?* About the only thing you'll break using *that* method is your index finger's proximal phalanx bone. No, use your fist if you ever want to play the piano again.

"Hey, wow, it works!" you can say. Hand the bill back to its rightful owner. "Careful with that! It's really sharp."

Sheep and Thieves

If you have trouble keeping patter going in your efforts at magic, you'll *love* this trick. Not only is it unbelievably easy to do and profoundly amazing, but its built-in story is foolproof and practically self-telling.

The effect: Prattling on about a couple of sheep thieves, you put five quarters on the table. Even though you pick up some of the quarters with each hand, at the end of your little tale of beefy shepherds and sleazy sheep resellers, all five quarters somehow wind up in the same hand!

The secret: This little miracle, a favorite of Advisory Pantheon member Johnny Thompson, has got to be among the most intellectually satisfying in the entire book. The principle behind the secret is simple: You've got an *odd number* of quarters. Therefore, you can't split the quarters equally between hands — a fact that will become increasingly important as the routine goes on.

You need *seven* quarters for this trick — five to represent sheep, and two to represent lowlife sheep-stealing scum.

1. **Hold one quarter in each hand, as shown in Figure 3-2, photo A. Put the other five quarters on the table.**

   Begin telling your little fable of livestock trouble in the Swiss Alps. "So there were these five prize-winning sheep, peacefully grazing in the prize-winning Swiss Alps," you can say. (This opening always grabs the attention of any sheep and Alps lovers in the crowd.)

   "Now, there were also these two sleazy *sheep thieves* who realized that these beautiful animals could be worth a fortune on the open sheep market. So the thieves hid in the two ancient barns that stood on either side of the meadow."

Figure 3-2:
Start with the five sheep on the table (A). When you pick up the quarters, start with your *right hand* (B). Nobody ever knows how many coins your hands really hold (C) — thus the surprise ending (D).

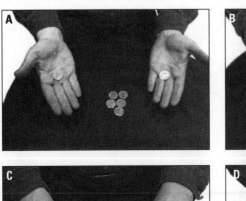

As you say all this, make your metaphor painfully clear — gesture at the five quarters on the table whenever you say "sheep," hold up your two quarter-holding palms whenever you say "thieves" or "barns," and so on. You don't want some bonehead to ruin the proceedings by saying, at the end of the trick — "So wait a sec. What do the quarters represent again?"

"Now, because these were prize-winning sheep, they were guarded by prize-winning *shepherds,* a couple of strapping former rugby players from the former Yugoslavia. But as soon as the shepherds left the meadow for the night, the two thieves dashed out of the barns. They grabbed the sheep and dragged them into the barns, splitting the flock between them."

2. **Pick up the five quarters, one at a time. Alternate hands. *Start with the right hand.***

"One! Two! Three! Four! Five!"

In case the *boldface* type didn't make it clear, you must pick up the five quarters individually, alternating hands as you go — right, left, right, left, right (photo B).

Now you're sitting there with closed fists and no quarters in sight (photo C). Resume the storytelling.

"The thing is, the two Yugoslavian shepherds, halfway home, noticed that they'd stopped hearing sheep noises. They ran back toward the meadow, but the thieves saw them coming. 'Quick! Put the sheep back right where they were!'"

3. **Put the five quarters back on the table, one at a time. Alternate hands. But *start with the left hand*.**

"One! Two! Three! Four! Five!"

If you've been keeping score at home, you realize that your left hand is now *empty*. But you, convincing Method actor that you are, don't let anyone know that. You keep both fists shut as you gesture and talk, just as though there's still one quarter in each.

There are now five quarters on the table; two in your right hand; and none in your left. But as far as the audience is concerned, you're right back where you started.

"By the time the shepherds arrived, everything was back to normal: Five prize-winning sheep contentedly munching. 'Huh!' said the shepherds in crisp Yugoslavian. 'Must have been our imagination. Definitely no sign of those sheep thieves we've been hearing about!' So they left again, heading home for the night.

"This was just what the thieves were waiting for. 'All right, the coast is clear,' they said. 'Let's grab the sheep again.' So once more, they snatched the sheep into the barns."

4. **Pick up the five quarters, one at a time. Alternate hands. *Start with the right hand*.**

"One! Two! Three! Four! Five!" (See photo B again.)

See what you're doing? Because you didn't start with the same hand when you put the coins *back*, you're quietly stockpiling quarters in your right hand, while depleting the left hand's supply. You wind up with five quarters in the right hand, and two in the left.

"But now, the shepherds were *sure* that they couldn't hear any baa-ing coming from the meadow. They went tearing back — saw that no sheep were in sight — and immediately got a funny feeling about those two barns. But when they threw open the barn doors, you know what they found inside? In the first barn, they found two thieves, fast asleep."

5. **Open your left hand to show the two quarters.**

"And in the other barn, they found all five prize-winning sheep, safe and sound."

6. **Open your right hand to show five quarters (photo D). Pour them onto the table for added effect.**

Why is this trick so adorable? Two reasons. First, it makes you *look* like you're a professional sleight-of-hand artist who spends six hours a day practicing — and yet it works automatically.

Second, it's got a story about sheep.

The Vanishing Quarter, Show-Off Edition

You wouldn't be much of a magician if you couldn't make a coin disappear — being able to do so is a requirement in the Magic Bylaws. (Or would be, if there *were* Magic Bylaws.)

Not only does this trick offer a vanish that comes as a total shock to the audience, but in the meantime, you've also entertained the crowd with your coin-catching skills.

The effect: You balance a quarter on your elbow — and then catch it in the air as you snap your hand downward. Big deal, right? But the second time you snap your hand down, the quarter is *really* gone. Your hands are completely empty, there's nothing in your pockets, and — as a handy bonus — you wind up with 25 cents.

The secret: This one you're going to have to practice. Not the *magic* part — only the catching-the-coin-in-midair thing.

In the privacy of your own home, balance a quarter on your elbow, as shown in Figure 3-3, photo A. (For the purposes of this discussion, let's say you're right-handed; put the quarter on your right elbow.) Now snap your hand forward; try to catch the quarter in midair, as shown in photo B. Rehearse this until you can catch it every time. Nothing does more damage to your budding reputation as *missing* the coin — or accidentally sending it flying into an onlooker's eye socket.

When you've got that talent down — and make no mistake, it's an excellent life skill anyway — venture forth into public.

1. **Borrow a quarter. Put the quarter on your elbow.**

   "Hey — can you do this?"

2. **Snap your hand forward, catching the quarter in midair. Show that you caught it.**

   Now, in fact, many people *can* do this. Many a seventh grader spends his study hall hours learning to catch coins from his elbow. (I actually learned to catch a *stack* of coins — at one point, a stack of pennies 21 high — from my elbow. But I'm weird that way.)

   So the answer to "Can you do this?" may be yes or no. It makes no difference.

   You're about to pretend that you're going to do the coin-catching thing a second time — but that's not what you've got planned at all.

3. **Turn the back of your right hand toward the audience and *pretend* to take the quarter with your left hand. Actually, just continue holding the coin in your right fist. Without stopping, assume The Position a second time. Pretend to put the quarter on your right elbow again.**

See the beauty of this arrangement? Your elbow is a flat plane that's at or above eye level, so nobody can see that there's no quarter there. Furthermore, you haven't *said* that this is going to be a magic trick. Nobody has any reason to suspect that you're going to make the coin disappear. They think you're just showing off with a coin catch you've been doing since seventh grade.

Here's the world's easiest move, known by advanced sleight-of-hand magicians as the "drop-it-down-your-shirt" move:

4. Drop the quarter down your shirt (photo C).

This action is completely invisible, partly because the audience is watching your *elbow,* and partly because people are getting sick of your stupid quarter-catching stunt. (Now you know why your parents always told you to tuck your shirt in, by the way. It's to prevent quarters from slipping through all the way to the floor.)

"Well, I bet you can't do *this!*" Really bellow that out. You've got to get the audience awake for your grand finale.

Figure 3-3:
This trick starts out as the old "I-can-balance-a-quarter-on-my-elbow-and-then-snatch-it-out-of-the-air-with-my-hand" gag (A and B). But the second time, it becomes the "I-can-also-make-a-quarter-vanish-into-thin-air" stunt (C).

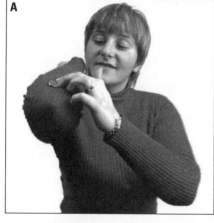

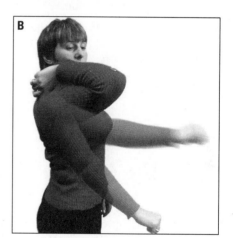

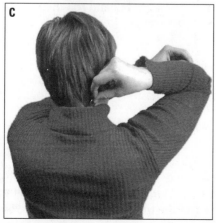

Truths of Magic, Part 5: The element of surprise

Most of the time, you should never repeat a trick. Such tricks as The Vanishing Quarter, Show-Off Edition work almost entirely on the element of surprise; throughout that trick, nobody even knows you're *doing* a trick! If you were to (a) repeat the trick or (b) announce what you're going to do before you do it, people would watch the coin like a hawk. If they're forewarned, they'll be more likely to catch you *not* handing the coin off to your right hand when you pretend to do so.

Many great illusions work on this principle: If the audience doesn't know what's coming, it doesn't know what to be looking for. Give them a second chance, and you ruin your own aura of magicalness.

5. **Snap your hand forward one last time as though you're catching the coin. Now, slowly, hold your right hand up and show that it's completely empty.**

   Show your left hand empty, too. Pull your pants pockets, if any, inside-out. Roll down your sleeves and shake them to show that nothing's there.

   Nobody is going to find that quarter (which is now resting comfortably at your waistline). They'll only turn up the quarter if they strip search you; your willingness to participate in *that* little exercise I leave up to you.

The Big Money Rises

Getting tired of coin tricks? Here's one with serious money — bills — that's half optical illusion, half brain teaser, and all magic.

The effect: You put a $1 bill on top of a $20 bill and roll them up together. Even though a volunteer pins them down, when you unroll them, the bills have changed places. Now the $20 bill is on top!

The secret: Of course, you can use any two bills for this trick, such as a $1 and a $5; one pro magician actually uses one American dollar and one *differently colored* bill from another country. For this example, I'll use a $1 and a $20. You can, of course, borrow these. The lender gets the curly bills back at the end of the trick, only heightening the mystery.

1. **Place the bills in a V that points toward you, as shown in Figure 3-4, photo A. The $1 bill is on top.**

   The long edge of the $1 bill isn't flush against the short edge of the $20, however; it's set into the $20 by about an inch, as shown in photo A.

"Funny thing about money," you might say. "In our society, the rich people always seem to have the upper hand. In government, in real estate, in taxes — wherever there's money, the big money always seems to come out on top. I'll show you what I mean. See how the small money — the $1 bill — is *on top* of the $20?"

Figure 3-4:
Start with the $1 inset by about an inch (A, shown from your angle; all other photos are from the spectator's viewpoint). Start rolling (B) until the $20 corner is about to disappear (C). Point to the $1 corner as your other hand conceals the $20 corner flipping over (D). Now ask to have the $20 pinned down (E). Unroll (F) the bills to see that the $20 has risen to the top!

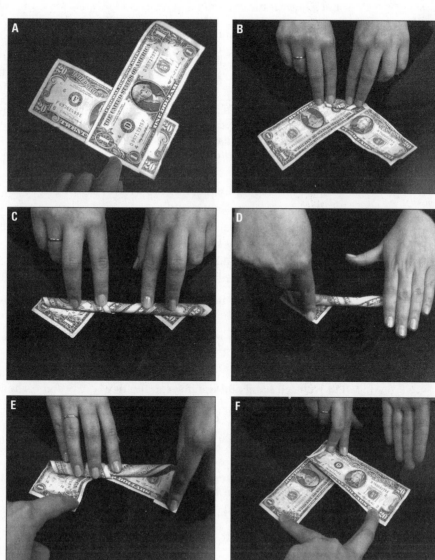

Your spectator will, of course, agree, probably accompanied by a big "So what?" expression.

2. **Peel up the overlapping corners of the bills (where they form a V), which is closest to you and start rolling the two bills away from you, as shown in photo B.**

   If it helps, by the way, you can roll the bills around a pencil or pen. That's one of those personal decisions of magical style that you, the budding wizard, will have to make yourself.

   Keep rolling until you're almost on top of the two far corners; as you can see from photo C, you come to the end of the $20 bill faster than the $1, thanks to the $1's inset starting position. Now there should be only the tiniest corner of the $20 peeping out from beneath the roll.

   "See, what happens in financial transactions is that big money and small money get mixed up in the chaos. For a split second, you can't see all of what's going on. What we really need is some regulation in these deals. Would you mind helping me out? Here, pin that down for me, would you?"

3. *Point* **to the exposed corner of the $1 bill, tapping it, as shown in photo D.**

   Apparently, you're just asking your spectator to pin it against the table with a finger.

   What you're *really* doing, however, is getting the spectator focused on the $1 bill while you're doing the funny business with the $20.

4. **Under cover of your left hand, roll the roll just a *hair* farther — far enough for the corner of the $20 to *slip out from under the roll.***

   Because of the bill's natural springiness, the corner flips forward to slap right down on the table again. Your left fingers block all of this action (as shown in photo D), which takes place in a blink.

5. **Lift your left hand and use it to tap the newly exposed corner of the $20.**

   "And you'd better pin this one down, too," you now say, indicating the $20 corner (photo E). "You've got to watch the big money closest of all. Okay, have you got both bills pinned down? Don't let 'em go anywhere. Don't let 'em move."

6. **Slowly begin *unrolling* the two bills, as your helper continues to pin the far corners against the table (photo F).**

   "See, the thing is, no matter how much we regulate, no matter how closely we watch, the big money always manages to come out on top. That's capitalism for you!"

   Sure enough, the $20 is now on top of the $1 (photo F). As far as your audience is concerned, you simply rolled the bills about halfway up and then unrolled them — and the bigger bill melted right through the smaller.

The 7-Penny Reflex Test

I'm giving you official permission to repeat this trick for the same audience, despite my dire warnings (in the Introduction) *never* to do so. A few tricks, like this one, are extremely small-scale miracles — no flames, no doves, and certainly no flaming doves — and only with repetition does it mount into a mind-blowing sensation.

I'm in love with this trick because it's pure psychology. In effect, your audience misdirects *itself,* as you'll see in a moment.

The effect: You challenge a friend to a reflex test. You count seven pennies into his hand — but no matter how many times you repeat the effort, you're able to grab the last penny out of his hand before he can close his fist to keep you out.

The secret: Actually, you never put the *sixth* penny into your helper's hand. But the real secret is the presentation — the way you (a) let a "dry run" lull your volunteer, (b) inflict your helper with performance anxiety, and (c) drop the seventh penny from a different hand to attract attention.

1. **Announce that you're about to try a reflex test. Display the seven pennies on your open left palm.**

   Take my advice: Arrange them in a group of three and a group of four — see Figure 3-5, photo A. (Why arrange them this way? So that your cynical audience can mentally *confirm* that you really have seven pennies. The last thing you need is some bozo claiming you never had seven to begin with. See "Truths of Magic, Part 3: Anticipate the dumb guesses" in Chapter 2.)

   "Hey, want to try a reflex test? I read this in *Seventeen* magazine. It's really fun. C'mon, wanna try? What are you, right-handed? Okay. Put your right hand out flat like this. Like a table."

   When your helper does so, as shown in photo B, continue with the explanation. The patter in this trick is *crucial.*

   "I've got seven pennies here. I'm going to count these seven pennies into your hand, one at a time. The *instant* the seventh penny arrives in your hand, I want you to slam your hand shut into a fist. As fast as you can. Pure reflex. Okay? Ready?"

2. **Begin transferring the pennies, one at a time, into your helper's hand, dropping one atop another. Simply pick up each one with your right hand and *place* it into his (photos B and C).**

   Do not *throw* the penny into his hand. Do not *push* it into his hand. Just set it there with a tiny clink. Count *out loud.* You should put one penny into his hand per second, or slightly slower.

Figure 3-5.
(A) Begin with seven pennies on your palm. (B) Count the seven pennies onto your volunteer's open palm. (C) From your point of view: You're just placing each coin, not tossing or pushing. (D) The seventh penny *drops* from your other hand!

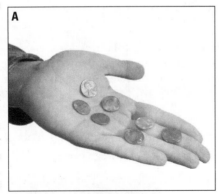

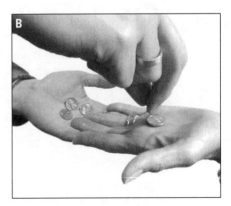

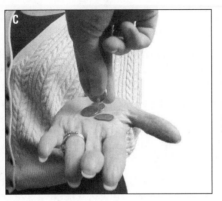

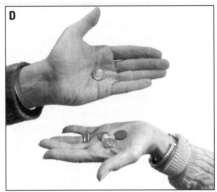

Photo C shows how to pick up each penny with your right hand: thumb in back, fingers in front. You can barely even see the penny.

"One. Two. Three. Four. Five. Six." Let your voice rise with anticipation on "five" and "six," although your rate of penny deposits should remain clock-like and steady.

3. **The seventh penny is different. Instead of picking it up with your right hand, *dump it* into his hand from your *left* open palm (photo D).**

If your assistant has any clue at all, he'll snap his hand shut into a fist as you've instructed him.

Stare at his closed fist, as though you're making mental calculations.

"Okay. Hey, you're pretty good. But now we're going to do something a little bit different. This is where it gets interesting. I'm going to need the pennies back, please."

4. Hold open your hand to receive the pennies.

When your helper gives them to you, arrange them once again in a group of four and a group of three on your palm.

Now you explain, *for the first time,* what the real point of all of this is.

"We're going to do the same thing again now. But this time, I'm going to grab the seventh penny *back* out of your hand — before you can close your hand into a fist! That's right: This is my reflexes against yours. Who's got the quickest nerve impulses? Here we go. Ready?"

5. Repeat the counting/penny-transferring business.

"One. Two. Three. Four. Five. Six!" Once again, set each penny into his hand. Once again, intensify your voice (but not your rate) as you approach seven.

But now comes the sneaky part.

6. Don't put penny number *six* into his hand. Instead, just clink it lightly against the pennies already there — and then drop your hand to your side as you turn your eyes to your left hand.

Your left hand should be rising, ready to *dump* the seventh penny, exactly as it did during the dry run (see photo D). And then it does the dump.

7. Dump the seventh penny into his hand from your *left hand*.

"Seven!" you say.

Do you understand now why you did that dry run? It wasn't to gauge your volunteer's speed. No, no — it was to *teach* him about how your left hand dumps the seventh penny. Now that you're doing the "reflex test" for real, all eyes have been trained to watch that left hand coming up to dump the penny!

Anyway, he'll slam his fist shut. Let one delicious moment of stillness pass. Then ask: "How many did you get?"

He'll open his hand now and find, of course, six pennies. This gives you plenty of time to hold up the penny *you've* still got.

"You're good, kid, but not good enough!"

Let your volunteer try the "reflex test" a couple more times. Why will he never catch the secret? Because the misdirection is *overwhelming.* Consider:

- ✔ You're *looking* at the left hand at the critical moment.
- ✔ The sixth penny clinks to confirm its arrival, just like all the others.

You Can't Catch the Money

Here's a *real* reflex test — not a bogus one, like the 7-Penny Reflex Test — that will provide hours of frustration for the whole family.

Hold a fairly uncrumpled bill by the end, as shown in the following photo. Ask an audience member to put her fingers at about the middle of the bill, as shown — close, but not touching, the paper. The patter is simple: "If you can catch it, you can have it."

Wait between two and five seconds and then drop the bill. That's it. Your volunteer *cannot* catch the bill, no matter how hard she watches — it's simply not possible. By the time her eye has signaled her brain to signal the hand to close, the bill has already fallen through her fingers.

What a fun way to kill a long ride on a crowded city subway!

✔ You've created incredible *verbal* misdirection by mentioning penny number seven over and over again. Check out the sample patter — by the time your volunteer is actually put to the test, you've referred to that seventh penny at least four times.

✔ The counting thing is so slow and lulling that everyone's practically asleep by the time penny number six comes along.

✔ Your subtle comment after the dry run — "Hey, you're pretty good" — makes your volunteer realize he's being *tested* in front of the crowd. He suddenly realizes that *you* aren't the one being judged as a performer here — *he* is! Suddenly he's worried about *penny number seven,* and his entire being will be focused on getting that penny before you do.

After two or three tries, quit while you're ahead — or find another spectator. If there *are* others in the crowd, somebody will certainly be pleading, "Let *me* try!" at this point. Indulge them. But always do the *complete* trick as described here, complete with the "dry run." That ritual is important in setting up the participant's expectations, assumptions, and performance-anxiety level.

Don't Show Me the Money

Eyes in the back of your head? Of course! If this trick doesn't convince your friends and family that you're a financial wizard, nothing will.

The effect: An audience member sits in front of four bills: three $1 bills and one $20. She randomly switches their positions while your back is turned. Yet somehow you know exactly where the $20 wound up.

The secret: This one works itself (thanks to world-famous memory expert Harry Lorayne, who contributed it). It'd have to work — you don't even participate in the trick! You do, however, have to do some mental work as you go, so pay attention.

1. **Arrange four bills on the table: three $1 bills and a $20. (See Figure 3-6.)**

   You can, of course, provide your own bills. But here's a much more fun way: *You* provide the $20 bill, but *borrow* the three $1 bills from a volunteer. Actually, if you have one, an even larger bill makes the trick that much more exciting.

   (You can also ask your *volunteer* to lay the bills out in any order she likes, although nobody's ever complained to me about not having a choice of bill order.)

   "Do you know what's wild?" you might tell the crowd. "I've done my own taxes for each of the last six years. And for six years in a row, I discovered on April 15 that I hadn't overpaid or underpaid the IRS by *a single dollar.* Every year, I find that I've got no refund due, and I don't owe any money, either — it somehow comes out exactly right every year. I guess I'm just really good at tracking money. Here — wanna see?"

Figure 3-6:
The starting
lineup for
Don't Show
Me the
Money.

"Tell you what we're gonna do," you tell the volunteer. "You contribute these three ones, and I'll contribute the twenty. If I make a mistake in my demonstration, you'll walk away with that twenty — not a bad return on your investment!"

"It's a simple game, really. I'm going to turn my back. I want you to mix up these bills. Whenever I say 'switch,' you swap the $20 bill with one that's next to it, like this."

2. **Demonstrate. Switch the positions of the $20 and one of the bills on either side by sliding them around on the table.**

   If the $20 is on the end, switch it with the bill next to it.

   "Easy, huh? Okay, I'm going to turn my back."

3. **Before you turn your back, remember the position of the $20 bill!**

   Imagine that the bills are at positions labeled 1, 2, 3, and 4 (counting from the left, as the spectator sees them). Remember where the $20 bill is as though your life depended on it.

4. **Turn your back and command your helper to make, in all, five switches.**

   "Okay, are you ready to start switching? Okay, here we go: *Switch!* And *switch* it again. Another *switch!* Oh, this is fun! Do it *again!* Okay, once more!"

In all, you should command your helper to make *five* switches. Don't make her aware that five is the magic number; make it seem as though you're making it up as you go. Keep track of how many times you've commanded switches, or the trick won't work; I usually count on my fingers.

Things get serious now. "All right. Now, I haven't seen what you've done. That $20 bill could be anywhere. But let me see here — I'm going to ask you to take away one of the bills and keep it."

Act as though you're concentrating. Hold your hand to your head; make a little humming sound; sway back and forth. If the overall effect could be confused for a migraine attack, you're doing it right.

5. **Tell your helper to take away the bill on the far left or far right.**

   Which one? Depends on whether the $20 bill's starting position was *odd* or *even*. If the $20 was in position 1 or 3 (odd numbers) when you turned your back, tell him to take away the *leftmost* bill (the odd-numbered end, position 1). If the $20 started out in position 2 or 4 (even numbers), tell him to take away the *rightmost* bill (the even-numbered end, position 4). Read this paragraph a couple of times; it's the only semi-tough part of the trick.

   "Now, I want you to take away — let me see — the one on the far (left/right)! And keep it. That one's yours."

   Don't ask me how it works. It just does. Although you can't see it, the spectator is now left with three bills — and the $20 is on *one end*. Unfortunately, you don't know which end. Fortunately, it doesn't matter.

6. **Command one last switch.**

   "Okay, let's keep going. Switch the $20 bill again."

   There's only one place your volunteer can move the $20 bill — and that's into the center! The rest is gravy:

   "All right. Now I want you to take away — and keep — um — the bill on the — *far left*. That should leave two bills left. If my sense of money is correct, one of them is the $20 bill. This is your last chance to make some big money: If I guess wrong, you walk out of here $19 richer. I want you to take away the bill — on the — *right!* And I'll keep whatever bill is left on the table!"

7. **Turn around and point triumphantly to the only bill left — your own $20 bill.**

   Pick it up and put it back into your wallet, purse, or pocket. (Or leave it out if you want to play the You Can't Catch the Money game described in the sidebar earlier in the chapter.)

   "That'll teach you not to play money games with a master of the 1040 form!"

Heads or Tails: The Shadow Knows

Ever since Advisory Pantheon member Gregory Wilson showed me this trick, I've been in love with it. Tricks that don't require anything more than a quarter are lovable all by themselves — but ones that could, in a pinch, help you win bar bets are even more attractive.

The effect: No matter how many times you flip a coin, you're always able to tell whether it's heads or tails up after you slap it onto the back of your hand. (And no, it's not a two-headed coin.)

The secret: You *feel* the quarter with your thumb in the split second between catching it and slapping it onto your hand.

1. **Flip a quarter (see Figure 3-7, photo A). Catch it on the way down — overhand — as shown in photo B.**

   Of course, this instruction presumes that you know *how* to flip a coin. I'll bet it's somewhere in one of those other *...For Dummies* books.

   If anybody's watching, you can ask: "Heads or tails?"

2. **As your coin hand completes its trip down and over to the back of your opposite hand, feel the quarter's face with your thumb (photo C).**

   You may not believe this until you rustle up a quarter and try it — but sure enough, the two sides of a quarter feel completely different. The heads side is smooth and soothing; the tails side has so much detail it feels like a Yellow Page done in Braille.

3. **Slap the quarter onto the back of your opposite hand, leaving it covered by the first hand as you call heads or tails (photos D and E).**

   Of course, you should call the *opposite* of what you felt with your thumb.

   When you make the call, look away from your hands. Get a misty look in your eyes and call it — heads or tails. (If your volunteer predicted heads or tails, add either, "You're right!" or, "No, I'm gonna say the opposite.")

4. **Lather, rinse, repeat.**

   Obviously, this trick is pretty stupid if you only do it once — *anyone* can call a coin once. Do it ten times in a row, though, calling the quarter every single time, and you've got yourself a doozy of a mystery — or bar bet.

   It's important, by the way, that you never really look at your hands after you've caught the coin. You don't want people guessing that you're somehow looking at the coin. You *do* want them guessing that, for the first time in their lives, they've actually met somebody with provable psychic powers.

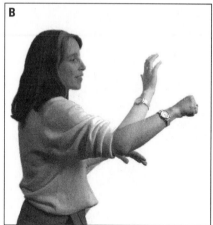

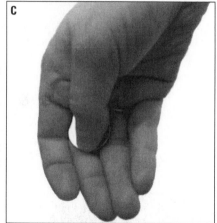

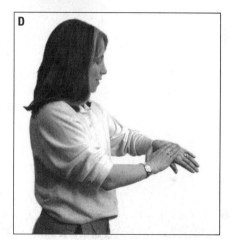

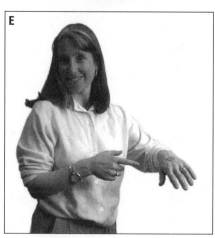

Figure 3-7:
Just flip the coin normally (A), but catch it claw-style (B). You have 1.2 seconds to *feel* the underside of the quarter (C) en route to slapping it on your hand (D). Correctly predict which side is up, and you're home free (E).

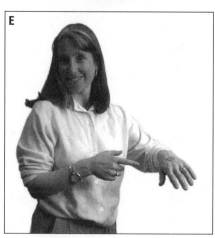

Chapter 4
New Uses for Old Office Supplies

• •

In This Chapter

▶ How to shove pencils up your nose

▶ Make rubber bands leap across fingers and help defy gravity

▶ Put Post-it notes to their best use yet

▶ Cards, the photocopier, and you

• •

*M*agicians view the world differently than other people. To a magician, the world is a gigantic playroom filled with potential props. Anything you can pick up — and many things you can't — is fair game for magic tricks.

Today's offices are *crawling* with small liftable objects (which may explain why companies have to buy new staplers, hole punches, and pencil sharpeners at the end of each year). This chapter takes you beyond the sheltered world of your own home and into the bustling, magically tantalizing corporate world.

Pencil up the Nose

Amazing isn't the right word for this trick. *Breathtaking* isn't the word, either.

Juvenile is more like it.

Still, nobody will forget the day you grabbed a sharpened pencil and shoved it all the way up your nose.

The effect: You grab a pencil and shove it all the way up your nose.

The secret: Not just any writing implement will do for this one. You need a longish pen or pencil. Above all, it must have a uniform size, shape, and color all the way down its shaft. Bulbous Mont Blanc pens are no good for this. Striped pencils don't work, either. You *can* use pencils with writing on them — but only if the *other side* is completely blank.

After you choose your weapon, you can start the trick:

1. **Point out your sinus problem.**

   For maximum effectiveness (that is, maximum grossness), tie your patter in to an attack of congestion. Let the "attack" interrupt something else you're saying at a moment when several onlookers are available.

   "So anyway, I was considering a 7.25 percent jumbo mortgage, but it was only adjustable after the first five-year term. So I thought I'd get something variable instead, and I — I —"

   Start squinching up your nose and sniffing loudly, both inward and outward.

   "Excuse me, I've got this — this congestion problem. It's acting up again. Let me just take care of it. Here, can I borrow this pencil?"

2. **Position the pencil.**

   Grab the pencil's eraser end with your right hand. Place the pencil tip just under your nostril, as shown in Figure 4-1, photo A. (If one side of the pencil has writing on it, the side with the writing on it should be away from the audience.) With your left hand, cover up your nostrils and the pencil tip, as shown in photo B.

   Your right hand position is spectacularly awkward, I admit, but nobody said magic was going to be painless. You're holding the eraser end of the pencil — but you're not grabbing it from the side, as a sane human being would do. Instead, you're holding it *from underneath,* so that your fingers and wrist are almost extensions of the pencil (see photo B). Your fingers are toward the crowd, your thumb is toward you.

3. **Slowly slide your hand up the pencil, allowing the shaft to slip behind your hand and wrist.**

   Do this with a great deal of grunting and grimacing; you're beyond words at this point.

   Of course, the pencil never actually moves. Your left hand protects your nostril from actual impalement, holding the pencil point exactly where it is. You're sliding your right fingertips up the shaft of the pencil, as shown in photos C and D; your hand and wrist conceal the pencil shaft (as shown in the transparent photo C). The whole sliding-up process should take about five seconds.

   Because the pencil is the same color all the way down the shaft, nobody can tell that it's not actually moving. (***Note:*** Do not *actually* insert the pencil into your skull.)

Figure 4-1: The tip goes near your nostril (A); hold it in place with your left hand (B). Keep the shaft hidden as you slide your right hand toward your nose (shown in C, transparently, and in D). After you've finished "clearing your sinuses," politely wipe off the pencil (E).

The optical illusion is unforgettable — *if* you hold your right hand and arm so that they completely block the pencil's shaft from view, and *if* you simulate sufficient discomfort. Try this in front of a mirror a couple times before you perform it. Think: What would your face look like if you *really* shoved eight inches of plywood into your cerebral cortex?

After the pencil has been "shoved" deeply enough — see photo D — you may wish to rest for a split second, or even wiggle the pencil slightly (you know — to loosen up your phlegm).

4. **Slowly extract the pencil.**

   Once again, you're really just sliding your right fingertips down the pencil shaft.

   When your right fingers hit the metal ridges of the eraser end, grab it and pull it free from your nose. Look skyward for a moment and inhale deeply, as though to demonstrate how freely you can now breathe.

5. **Be polite! Wipe off the pencil on your clothing (photo E) and graciously return it to the person who loaned it to you.**

Cheapskate Houdini: The Triple Rubber Band Escape

When you picked this book and saw the word *escape* in the index, you were probably hoping for something more along the lines of water tanks and handcuffs. But come on: I'll bet you don't even *have* a water tank. And bringing handcuffs to the office doesn't make people think you're cool — just weird. No, what you need is a trick you can actually *perform* on a day-to-day basis.

This trick starts out as a very old gag in which a rubber band jumps around on your hand. But with the additions of Stage II and Stage III, it turns into a much more impressive trio of feats.

The effect: You stick two fingers through a rubber band. Somehow, the band jumps to two *other* fingers.

Just to prove that there's no lightning-fast sleight-of-hand involved, you now add a second rubber band. You use it to tie off all of your fingertips — and yet the first rubber band *still* manages to leap around from finger to finger.

Finally, just as the mob is about to accuse you of witchcraft, you top yourself. You add a *third* rubber band, placing it around the opposite pair of fingers. Now, even with *both* rubber bands locked in place by the one across your fingertips, they manage to exchange places with a single snap.

The secret: What's great about this trick is that there's nothing sneaky going on with those rubber bands. But although your audience will quietly return to their homes and try all night to duplicate your feat, they'll wind up unsuccessful, defeated, and blistered.

Stage 1: The rubber band jumps

For the first miracle, you need only a single rubber band. Size counts; the super-spindly ones are less effective than slightly wider ones, for example. Colored bands are great. A rubber band about two inches long, unstretched, is ideal.

1. **Put a rubber band around your left index and middle fingers, as shown in Figure 4-2, photo A.**

   "You know, Houdini's famous for escaping from jail cells, locked water tanks, and things like that," you might say. "But as a boy, he started much smaller. In fact, legend has it that he first got the escapism bug from a simple *rubber band,* which he would sort of imprison on his fingers, like this. My *first two fingers.*"

   Calling attention to *which* fingers the band is on is always a good idea. Whenever you can accommodate the easily confused in your crowd, do so.

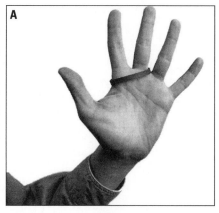
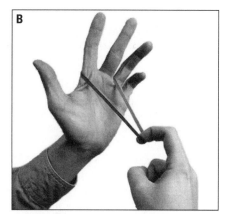
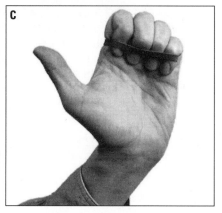
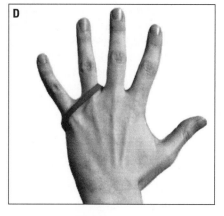

Figure 4-2: (Photos A, B, and C are from *your* view.) Start with an ordinary rubber band (A). Use your other hand to create an opening (B) into which you slip your fingertips (C). When you open your hand, the band leaps to the adjacent pair of fingers (D).

2. **With your right index finger, pull the palm-side strand of band toward you about four inches.**

   As you can see from photo B, you've just created a triangular opening in the band.

3. **Fold all four left fingertips into the open loop (photo C), taking care not to let the backside loop slip off. Let go of the rubber band with your right hand.**

   The band should snap against your fingertips. "What Houdini discovered," you can continue, "is that certain rubber bands have minds of their own. Even if you imprison one of these special rubber bands on two fingers . . ."

4. **Open your left fingers, taking care not to let the *palm-side* band slip below your fingertips as they open.**

   The band jumps, all by itself, to your *other* two fingers (photo D). Don't ask me how it works — just be grateful that it does.

   ". . . it can escape to the other two fingers whenever it feels like it."

When you're first trying this trick, it's perfectly okay to perform Steps 2, 3, and 4 as three separate steps, as slowly as you need to, even in public. The trick works perfectly well as a puzzle.

But after you've practiced enough to do Steps 2, 3, and 4 *smoothly and continuously,* in one motion, the trick really starts to look great as an optical illusion. Eventually, you should get to the point where the audience sees the rubber band *snap* (when you release it with your other hand) onto the other two fingers.

As you try to speed up the steps, however, don't fall into the common beginner pitfall of trying to *throw* the rubber band away from you, or manually flip it forward, in Step 3. Your right hand should pull *toward* you and then let go, never moving forward.

After you've nailed making the rubber band jump from your index/middle fingers to your ring/pinky fingers, make it jump *back again!* There's nothing to it: Simply repeat Steps 2, 3, and 4. See the beauty of it? Now you can make the rubber band leap from side to side on your hand, each time with the satisfying sonic *thwack* of rubber against skin, until your entire audience has packed up their things and gone home.

Stage II: Locked in place

But wait — there's more!

"Houdini quickly discovered, however," you can continue, "that people suspected him of using sleight-of-hand to make his rubber band jump. They accused him of doing *this* — really, really fast."

1. **With your right hand, pull the rubber band completely up off your fingers. Then place it manually on your other two fingers.**

   This looks unbelievably dorky, but that's the whole point.

   Put the rubber band back on your first two fingers.

   "So Houdini decided he'd prove them wrong. He took a *second* rubber band, like this, and he *sealed off* all four fingers. This way, there was no way he could remove the first rubber band by hand."

2. **Loop a second rubber band around each of your fingertips, fully twisting the band between each finger, as shown in Figure 4-3, photo A.**

   If you can find a rubber band that's a different color from the first, the effect is much stronger.

   "The crowds were much bigger now, there in Houdini's backyard in the suburbs. Big drunken men placed bets that Houdini couldn't make the rubber band jump if his hand was locked off like this. And yet somehow, the magic still happened."

3. **Make the rubber band jump to your fingers, just as you did in Steps 2 through 4 of Stage I.**

   You read that right. The fingertip rubber band does *absolutely nothing!* The trick works exactly the same, whether there's a fingertip-sealing rubber band or not. The jump looks better this way, but you don't have to do anything different to make the first band leap from one side of your hand to another!

   Make the first rubber band jump back and forth a couple of times, exactly as you did before the "sealing off" band was in place.

Stage III: Dueling bands

Just when you sense that your audience has had enough of this, grab a *third* rubber band. Now, I encouraged you to find a contrasting-color band to use in Stage II of this trick — but this *third* rubber band *must* be a different color than the first. (I guess it's okay if the fingertip-sealing-off band matches one of the two around the base of your fingers, although the trick is better if *no* two of the three bands are the same color.)

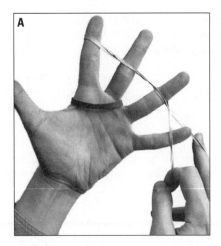

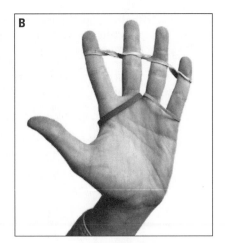

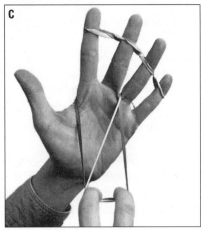

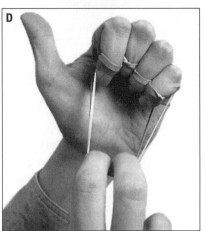

Figure 4-3: All of these photos are from *your* perspective. (A) shows how you "seal off" your four fingers. (B) is the setup for the dueling bands. Pull out a loop that includes *both* bands (C), put your fingers into that loop (D), and let go (E). When you open your fingers (F), the bands switch places.

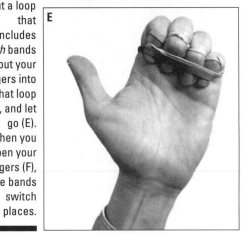

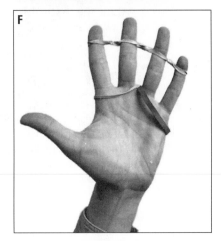

1. **Take off the fingertip band for a moment. Place the third rubber band around your ring and pinky fingers; the original band should be around your index and middle fingers.**

   Figure 4-3, photo B, should make this setup clear (although you won't add the fingertip band until the next step).

   "Now, by the time Houdini was six years old, the neighborhood was getting pretty tired of his little rubber-band stunt. So on his seventh birthday, he attempted the greatest challenge of his career so far: The Double-Rubber-Band Sealed-In Finger Switch."

2. **Replace the fingertip-sealing rubber band, as shown in photo B.**

   "The challenge, of course, is to make the two rubber bands down here —" (and here you point to the two bands looped around two fingers apiece) — "switch places before your eyes."

3. **Hook your right first two fingers inside the palm side of *both* bands.**

   You'll have to make *two* tiny dips with the tips of your right fingers, hooking first one band and then the other, but otherwise this is much the same move as Step 2 of Stage I. (See photo C).

4. **Pull the bands toward you, making a triangular loop. Fold your fingertips once more, this time inside of *both* rubber bands, as shown in photo D.**

   If you're observant, you've probably noticed that you're doing nothing more than repeating Steps 2 and 3 from Stage 1 with *two bands at once.*

5. **Let go with your right hand. As (or after) the rubber bands snap against your folded fingers (photo E), straighten them up (photo F).**

   The two rubber bands jump, exchanging places. (Now do you see why they have to be different colors? You'd have a hard time convincing the audience that anything happened *at all* if the two were identical.)

   "And — *voilà!* — despite the impossible odds, the rubber bands really did exchange places!"

   There's nothing to stop you from repeating Steps 3 through 5 a couple of times, making the two differently colored bands trade places a few more times.

   Then take all the bands off. One at a time, shoot them far over the heads of the audience, as described in the sidebar "How to shoot a rubber band" coming right up.

How to shoot a rubber band

Shooting a rubber band from your hand is not, technically, a magic trick. You will not find David Copperfield on national TV snapping a rubber band into his Las Vegas audience.

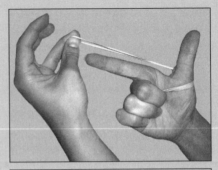

Still, doing so comes into the same category as many magic tricks: "Doing something cool that other people can't do."

Form your right hand into a gun shape, as shown in the first photo. Pinch one end of the rubber band against your palm with your middle finger. Pull the other end tight toward you, behind and around your thumb, and away from you — stretch the far end all the way to your index fingertip. Let the tension hold the far end of the band against your index finger, as shown in the second figure.

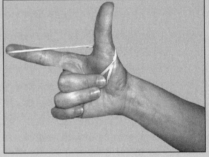

Now aim carefully (skies and ceiling make wonderful, lawsuit-free targets); when you're ready to fire, just release your middle finger. The band shoots surprisingly far, straight, and true.

The Antigravity Ring

Wow, is this trick freaky-looking. Not only that, but it's got some extremely realistic pseudo-scientific mumbo jumbo to go with it.

The effect: You thread somebody's finger ring onto a rubber band that you're holding taut. As you prattle on about the earth's rotational axis, you show how, when you cock the rubber band at a particular angle, the ring slides along the rubber band *uphill.*

The secret: There *is* science behind this one, but it's got nothing to do with the earth's axis. It has more to do with rubber bands' innate desire not to remain stretched out.

1. **Break a rubber band.**

   "Do you guys ever read *Scientific American?* Man, I could read that magazine for days," you could say. "Last month they had this great feature on nucleotide isotopes. *Awesome.* And that story in November, where they subjected quark ions to sub-G forces? I couldn't sleep for nights!

"But the neatest thing is in the current issue. All about gravity and geothermal physics and stuff like that. They even had a little experiment you could try. Want to see?"

2. **Borrow somebody's ring.**

"Can I borrow your ring? Thanks . . . ooh, it's a nice one, too. I'll do my best not to dent it any more than necessary."

3. **Thread the ring onto the rubber band. Now stretch your hands apart — but keep *much* more of the band in your left hand than in your right.**

That is, grab the rubber band at about the halfway point with your left hand — and near the right end with your right. You should have a loose piece of rubber band hidden inside your left hand.

Stretch your hands until they're about a foot apart, as shown in Figure 4-4, photo A. Start with the ring hanging closer to your *right* hand.

Figure 4-4:
There's a lot of band hidden in your left hand (A). The anti-gravity ring(B)!.

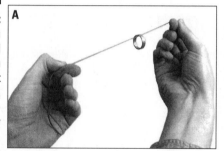 

"Now, you're probably already familiar with the force of gravity. You know, gravity? The attraction of all matter toward all matter? Force equals mass times acceleration? Look. *This* is gravity."

4. **Raise your right hand higher than the left, so that the ring begins to slide down the sloping rubber toward your left hand.**

Let the ring get to within a couple of inches of your left hand.

"But this *Scientific American* article pointed out that there are lots of less famous forces. For example, the earth isn't perfectly upright as it spins in space; it's actually tilted on its axis by 23 and a half degrees. This is one of those weird scientific phenomena, like how water drains counterclockwise when you're below the equator . . ."

5. **Turn your body this way and that, as though trying to find the magic geophysical "sweet spot."**

"In this case, if you stand in *just* the right position, you can actually *cancel out* gravity. You have to match the earth's angle of 23 and a half degrees. Let's see . . ."

6. **Gradually relax the tension of your left fingers, so that the rubber band begins to slide out through your fingertips.**

   The relaxation of tension is completely invisible. The only outward sign that the rubber band is actually sliding out of your hand is that the ring now starts *moving uphill* toward your right hand, as shown in photo B.

   ". . . and the ring is actually pulled *uphill,* away from the force of gravity!"

After the ring reaches your right hand, or you're out of excess band, or people are applauding and throwing money, stop. Let go with your right hand, hand the ring back to its owner, and hand the rubber band out for inspection.

Post-It-ive Identification

Mike Bent, a Boston magician on this book's Advisory Pantheon, used to sell this trick for real money. Lucky for you, he's donating this jaw-dropper in the interests of making you a better — and certainly more unusual — performer.

This is also the only trick I can think of that uses Post-it notes.

The effect: You ask somebody in the crowd to choose a card. You grab a pad of Post-it sticky notes and a magic marker. You write down your guess about what the card could be — but get it wrong. You try another stab at guessing the card — wrong again. Finally, in desperation, you tug the first page of the pad of Post-it notes. To the utter astonishment of everyone in the office (or office-supply store), this pad of Post-it notes falls into a long trail of *linked,* accordion-style sheets. The name of the chosen card is written plainly on the ladder of sticky notes, one letter per sheet.

The secret: Most of the tricks in this book require you to do nothing beforehand except practice a few times. This one involves a trip to the mall — the most worthwhile trip you'll make all month.

To obtain your special prop, head to Staples, Office Depot, or a similar office-supply store. Buy a pad of Post-it *Pop-Up Note Dispenser* refills. On this kind of pad, the notes are sticky at alternate edges, forming a fanfold effect. (A regular pad of Post-it notes, all gummed on the same edge, won't work.)

Because of the zigzag nature of the way your Post-it pages are connected, you're going to need some way designate one edge as the "top" of the pad — the edge that, if this were a *normal* pad, would be the spine. To make this decision, position the pad so that the free edge of the top sheet is facing *away* from you. You're now officially looking at the pad "upright." Make a tiny pencil mark across the "spine" of the pad, which at this moment is the edge farthest from you, right across the edges of the pages (see Figure 4-5, photo A). From now on, we'll call that that *top* of the pad.

Figure 4-5: Make a tiny pencil mark at the "top" of the pad (A), so you'll know how to hold it when it comes time to perform. Write "C-E-O-F-C-L-U-B-S" on every other page, starting with the third sheet (B). Complete your volunteer's cut (C). At the climax of the trick, the pad spells out the chosen card (D).

Grab your black magic marker. Beginning on the third sheet, write on *every other page* the letters that spell out "C-E-O-F-C-L-U-B-S." That's not a typo — leave off the A at the beginning of *Ace of Clubs.* The result is shown in photo B: A fanfold card revelation that's missing only the first letter.

On top of this stack, press on two blank, *regular* Post-it notes, both gummed at the "top" edge. You're ready to begin. Grab a deck of cards, put the Ace of Clubs on the top of the deck, and go forth in search of an audience.

1. **Fake-shuffle the deck as you talk.**

   By fake-shuffle, I mean shuffle the deck in such a way that you *leave* the Ace of Clubs on top of the deck. (When you're riffling the two halves of the deck into each other, let the *Ace* half finish last, that's all.) See "How to Shuffle without Really Accomplishing Anything" in Chapter 10 for details.

   "Hey, I just learned a really cool new mind-reading trick," you can say as you shuffle. "Will you help me see if it's any good?"

2. **Set the deck down. Ask your volunteer to cut the deck into halves.**

   "Okay, I'd like you to cut the deck into two piles. Just pick off about half the deck and set it down."

3. **Pick up what was the *bottom* half of the deck and place it crosswise on top of the *other* half, as shown in photo C.**

   Now comes the critical moment: You need to say *one more thing* to your volunteer. You need your volunteer to forget exactly what's gone on with that cutting business.

   "Very nice — you made a very nice cut. Hey, that's good — you made the cut, get it?"

   (Bad jokes and good magic go together like Regis and Kathy Lee.)

4. **Pick up the top half of the deck and tap the bottom half with it. Tell your volunteer to memorize the card you're tapping.**

   In other words, you want your assistant to peek at the top card of what's now the bottom pile.

   "Okay, great. Now take a peek at the card you cut to. Memorize it as though your life depends on it."

   If you think about it, that top card (of the bottom pile) *isn't* the card that was cut to; it's actually the card that was originally on *top* of the deck. But that fact is hopelessly forgotten by now.

   When the peeking is over, throw your half of the cards back onto the deck.

   "Here, take this half. Shuffle the deck so I've got no hope of finding your card again."

Although you may not realize it, you've just pulled off a very sophisticated magic maneuver: In magicians' lingo, you've *forced* a card. You've made your unsuspecting victim "freely choose" a card that, in fact, *you* selected beforehand. (You'll find many more clever forces in Chapter 11. You're free to substitute any of those forces for this one; I'm suggesting this particular "cut to any card" force because it's not only foolproof, it's pitifully easy.)

5. Pick up the Post-it pad and your black magic marker.

(If you're *really* good, you'll find that you can casually riffle the pad of Post-it notes to show that they're blank — by riffling the "top" edge, the one you marked with the pencil mark. Lo and behold, they all look empty when riffled that way! Don't make a big deal out of it — it's not as though anyone suspects a pad of Post-it notes already has writing on it. And don't forget to turn the pad around again before you start writing on it!)

"Okay. Now you've got a card in mind, and I've got nothing but a magic marker. Hey, that's good — *magic* marker, get it?"

When the hilarity subsides, continue. "Here's the deal: I'm going to try to guess what card you picked. Um — but because this is a brand-new trick I've never really done before, I get three guesses, okay?"

Unless you've chosen a real jerk as your helper, you'll get the okay.

6. Concentrate deeply. Write a big fat *3* on the top page of the pad.

"All right — all right. I'm seeing an odd number. I'm seeing — a — a *three.*"

Show what you've written on the pad. "Am I right?"

No, you're not. Let your panic begin to show. "But it *was* an odd number, wasn't it?"

The answer, of course, is yes. "Yeah, I thought so. But *that* wasn't a guess! That was just a statement of fact. I've still got two guesses left."

7. Rip off the top page and crumple it up. Concentrate deeply. Write a big fat *7* on the next page.

"I got it! I got it! You picked a seven! . . . Didn't you?"

Once again, you're wrong. (Spectators *love* this stuff.) Now you're deeply concerned. "All right, all right . . . one more try."

8. Rip off the 7 page and toss it. Concentrate deeply. Write the letter *A* on the top page of the pad.

"It was an *ace,* wasn't it?" Turn the pad around so that the "top" edge is toward you, so that your volunteer can read the A upright.

"Unfortunately, I haven't yet said the ace of *what.* And I'm out of guesses! At this point, I guess the only way out of this mess is to use — well, real magic!"

9. **Pick up the top sheet, the A sheet, by the "top" edge. Pull gently upward, revealing the full word ACE OF CLUBS spelled out down the chain of sticky notes (photo D).**

"Sooner or later, I knew I'd get it!"

The Photocopied Card Trick

Ever seen a room full of office workers faint simultaneously? Let me tell you, it's a sight not to be missed.

Yet that's exactly what you'll get as a reaction to this card revelation, a stunning contribution of Advisory Pantheon member Michael Ammar. Talk about funny, offbeat, and *impossible* . . .

The effect: A volunteer chooses a card. You never look at it, never touch it. You bring out a photocopied page that shows a million face-up cards and a single face-down card — you mention that you were fooling around on the Xerox machine earlier in the day. You prove your omniscience by asking the spectator to inspect the face-up cards in the printout. Her card isn't among them! You're amazing!

"Hah, hah," she smirks, pointing out that *lots* of cards probably aren't visible in the mixed-up photocopy. Determined, you then flip over the page — and there, on the *back* of the original printout, are the *backs* of all the cards — and the only face-up card is the chosen one!

The secret: You've *forced* the chosen card. In other words, the card is the same every time you do the trick — unless, of course, you've spent a *lot* of time at the copying machine.

1. **Before you perform, prepare your photocopy.**

To do so, put the 4 of Clubs face-up on the glass of a copying machine. Spread the rest of the deck, facedown, all around, until there's no glass left showing. Make a photocopy of this arrangement. (Anybody passing by the photocopier may look at you funny, but that's a small price to pay.)

You've just recorded Side A; as you can see from Figure 4-6, photo A, the result is a picture of a *face-up* deck with a single face-down card in the middle.

Return to the copying machine. Repeat the procedure, but this time turn all the cards over. Start with a face-*down* 4 of Clubs in the middle — and surround and cover it with the rest of the cards, faceup. Photocopy this arrangement onto the *back of the first* one, so the result is a two-sided sheet of paper. (This "back side" is shown in photo B.)

Have this printout handy. Grab a deck of cards, put the 4 of Clubs on the top, and venture forth to find a victim.

2. Force the 4 of Clubs on a spectator.

If "huh?" is your reaction to this instruction, then you clearly haven't yet visited Chapter 11, where the full majesty of *card forces* is introduced. As you may have read in "Post-It-ive Identification," earlier in this chapter, to *force* a card means to offer your volunteer what seems to be a free choice — but is actually no choice at all. Chapter 11 offers a wide variety of such forces; when you have a moment, peruse that chapter to see if there's a force you like better than the one described here.

The force I'll provide here is incredibly easy. Begin by shuffling the cards in such a way that the top card stays on top — that is, release that side of the deck *last* as you riffle the two halves of the deck together. (See the beginning of Chapter 10 for details on this *false shuffle.*)

"Name a number between 1 and 15," you now ask your spectator. Suppose the answer is nine. "What I'd like you to do is to deal off nine cards, like this: one, two, three, four, five, six, seven, eight, nine." As you do this, demonstrate — deal the cards off the deck onto the table, making a pile of nine cards. If you really stop to think about it, you'll realize that you've just reversed the order of the first nine cards.

"When you get to number nine, I want you to look at the card and memorize it. Okay? Easy enough? Here you go."

Pick up the little pile of cards on the table, put them *back on top of the deck,* and hand the deck to the volunteer. When she reaches the ninth card, remind her to memorize it without showing it to you. Then ask her to bury it in the deck and shuffle.

"All right, put the cards somewhere where I can't touch 'em," you now continue, reaching for your photocopy. "All right, it's safe now: loud and clear, what was the card you chose?"

When she names the card, bring out your photocopy. Make *sure* you handle it in a way that nobody suspect's it's double-sided. Place it on the table or desk, side A upward (see Figure 4-6, photo A).

Figure 4-6:
The prepared photocopy is two-sided. Shown here is side A (A) and side B (B).

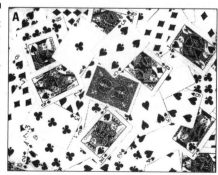
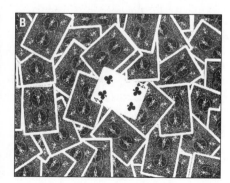

3. **Show the volunteer how you've "correctly" predicted the card.**

"The 4 of Clubs, you said? Awesome. Look at this — earlier today, I was goofing around with the Xerox machine. The incredible thing is, I *knew* that you would choose the 4 of Clubs. If you inspect this printout, you'll see that one card is face-down. All the others are face-up — but the 4 of Clubs is *not among them!*"

Let a moment of inspection go by, and then add, for those who haven't had quite enough caffeine, "You see? So the face-down card really was the 4 of Clubs!"

You're sure to get one of those looks that seems to say, "Er, your *other* tricks are really a lot better than this one."

You may even get a comment along the lines of, "That's the stupidest trick I've ever seen. There are *lots* of cards that aren't visible in this mess."

In which case, you have yet to show your, well, trump card.

"No, I'm serious. That card really *was* the 4 of Clubs. Look, I'll show you."

4. **Turn over the sheet of paper to reveal the face-up 4 of Clubs.**

I hope your office floor is carpeted. Fainting from a standing position can be hard on an audience.

Truths of Magic, Part 6: The card you chose

The world is filled with card forces like those described in Chapter 11. Some involve fancy sleight-of-hand; others are much easier. All, however, leave the spectator with virtually no free choice of cards.

If the spectator ever stops to think about what happened, though, you're doomed. "Why wasn't I allowed to just *think* of a card?" he might say.

That's why, for decades, magicians have used a subtle lie in their patter: They refer to "the card you chose." In the case of the card-counting force described in "The Photocopied Card Trick," of course, that line is patently ridiculous. The volunteer didn't really *choose* that card; that card just came up at a certain position in the deck.

But using such a reference is a psychological manipulation that helps the audience forget the *mechanics* of how the card was chosen — and re-paints what actually happened as having been a free selection.

Chapter 5

What to Do with Other People's Clothing

In This Chapter

▶ Pulling borrowed rings through borrowed strings

▶ Pulling ropes through borrowed torsos

▶ Pulling scarves through borrowed necks

▶ Pulling goofy stuff from a borrowed purse

*F*rom the point of view of your victims — er, that is, audience members — the things you do with your *own* props are fairly impressive. But when you do magic with their *own* personal possessions, magic becomes truly astounding.

In this chapter, you'll find out how to do stunts involving your spectators' most personal possessions — the ones they're wearing.

Give Me a Ring Sometime — and a String

The funny thing about this classic effect is that it's not really magic. I mean, it's not as though you actually do anything sneaky — there's no *secret* to it. Yet the resulting expression on the onlookers' faces will prove that *they're* convinced you just did something paranormal.

Or abnormal, anyway.

The effect: You borrow somebody's ring. While it's securely threaded onto a loop of string held up by a volunteer's fingers, you manage to make a few deft twists and pull the ring right off the string.

The secret: All you have to do is move three loops of string, but they have to be the *right* three loops or you'll wind up looking like a seventh-grader playing Cat's Cradle.

Advisory Pantheon member Eugene Burger, who recommended this trick, suggests a brilliant solution to the how-to-learn-it problem: Put tiny pieces of tape in the correct places on the string loop, as shown in Figure 5-1, photo A. Label these points X, Y, and Z, as shown in the figure. (Don't forget to remove the tape before you perform the trick in public. You don't want your adoring fans thinking you need training wheels.)

Oh, and one other how-to-learn-it tip: Practice by looping the string onto your own toes (instead of somebody's thumbs). That way you can mess up a few times without wrecking the trick prematurely for your own relative, best friend, or significant other.

1. **Tie a two-foot piece of string into a loop. Borrow somebody's finger ring.**

   "For this trick I'm going to need to borrow an article of clothing. The more expensive and personal, the better. Something with deep senti-mental value. How about a nose ring? Anybody? Anybody? All right then, a tongue stud? No? I don't suppose anyone has a navel ring either? Well, all right, how about your wedding ring, sir? May I borrow that for just a few minutes? I promise you'll get it back. In some form."

2. **Thread the ring onto the loop of string. Loop the string over somebody's upright thumbs, as shown in photo B.**

   The ring should be roughly centered between the thumbs.

   "Now what I want to achieve here is a sort of goal-post configuration. Ma'am, if you'd be so kind as to give me a Siskel-and-Ebert two-thumbs-up sign, like this, just as though you're really enjoying the trick so far."

   "That's perfect. I'm going to thread the ring onto the string, like this, and then use your thumbs as the hitching posts, like this. I think you'll agree that unless there's some sort of deep disturbance in the laws of physics today, there's no way I can get the ring off the string — without taking the string off or breaking something in a permanent way."

   Unless your volunteer has no familiarity with the laws of nature, she'll undoubtedly agree.

   "But as a magician, of course, my job is to violate the laws of physics whenever possible. I'm going to get this ring off without damaging anything — and without taking the string off of your thumbs. I'm allowed to put string *onto* your thumbs, though, like this."

3. **Grab point X on the far strand with your left index finger. Pull it toward you, *over* the near strand.**

   Your left-hand, point-X finger remains in this position until the final step (just as you see in photo B).

4. **Almost simultaneously, grab loop Y (on the near strand) with your *right* index finger. Pull it over and to the left of your left hand. Loop it over the thumb on your left, from front to back.**

   Photo C should make this maneuver relatively clear. (Throughout these maneuvers, you can ignore the ring; let it go about its business.)

   As you do this looping-over-the-thumb business — which should all take place in a matter of two seconds — say, "One!"

5. **With your right hand, pull point Z (on the near strand) to the left, just as you did with point Y. This time, loop it over the spectator's thumb on your left from *back to front*, as shown in photo D.**

Figure 5-1:
For easier practicing, tape labels onto your practice loop (A). Begin by hooking the back loop at point X and the front loop at point Y (B). Bring loop Y over the thumb on your left (C). Do the same with loop Z on the near strand (D). Finally, grab the ring (E) and pull it free (F).

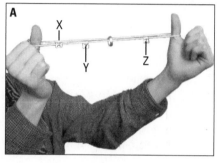
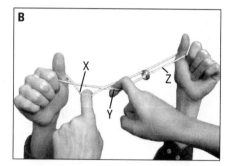
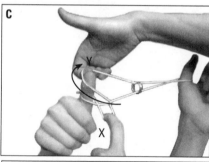
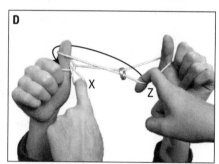
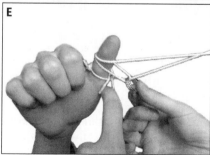
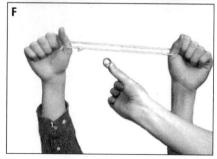

Again, you should do all of this within a matter of seconds. And say, "Two!"

Actually, the trick is over. The only thing holding the ring onto the string is your left hand, which still maintains its hold on the original loop (photo E).

6. Remove your left hand. Wiggle the ring with your right hand as you pull it down and away from the strings.

The ring comes completely free, to thunderous applause — see photo F.

But where's the theatrics in that? If you're interested in making the effect a little more magical, remove the ring this way instead:

Cover the ring with your right hand. Release point X with your left. Slide your ring-covering right fist back and forth along the string a couple of times, as though you're a magician. Finally, let the ring drop into your waiting left hand. At the same time say, "Three! And there's the ring, free at last."

The volunteer is right where she began — with a loop of string over her thumbs. You should now pick up the ring from your left hand, show it around, and accept the flowers flung at you.

"I'm happy to reveal how I did this one, by the way," you can lie. "See, there's a hole in the ring! It's true! Yep, there's a hole. Right here where your finger goes."

And you can poke your index finger through the ring a couple of times to make your appalling joke even more obvious.

Walking through Ropes

Most of my favorite magic is done without preparation — with ordinary objects that haven't been secretly prepared — and on the spur of the moment. Every now and then, though, a trick comes along that, despite requiring a little bit of preparation, is so amazing, it's irresistible.

This trick is one such blockbuster. It's just freaky enough that you might want to have a local therapist's business cards ready to hand out afterward.

The effect: You pull two pieces of rope through a volunteer's body *and* his clothing.

The secret: The rope we're talking about is clothesline. White, "braided cotton" (as the package often says) clothesline from a hardware store. This is the rope magic tricks are made of, as you'll discover in Chapter 12 — it's a staple of magicians' tool kits because it's soft, pliable, and looks great onstage.

You need two eight-foot pieces of clothesline. Before you go onstage, you've got a bit of homework to do. Lay the pieces of clothesline next to each other on a table, ends even — and tie a loop of white thread tightly around the exact center. If it's heavy-duty thread, two loops may suffice; if it's standard thinness, wrap the string a few times before tying the knot. The result should resemble Figure 5-2, photo A — in fact, the thread is so hard to see that it's barely visible, even in the photo.

After the ropes are prepared in this way, spend a few minutes handling them in private. You'll discover that the tiny white thread in the center isn't visible from a few feet away. You can even hold the ropes by the ends (as

Figure 5-2:
Handle the ropes mostly by the center, concealing the white thread (A). When the time comes, switch your grip so that one rope's ends protrude from each end of your hand (B). Help your volunteer put on his jacket, threading the ropes behind his back (C). Finally, cross one rope from each side (D), hand the far end to another volunteer (E), and pull sharply (F)!

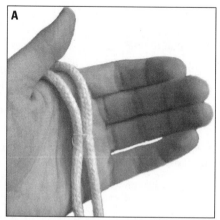
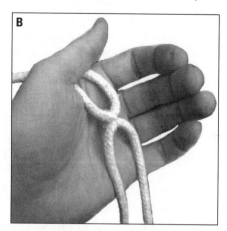

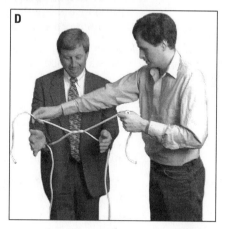

long as the ropes are dangling, parallel and side-by-side), clutch them by the middle (thus concealing the thread), stroke them while you talk, and so on.

1. Invite two volunteers to help you. One must be wearing a jacket.

Any kind of jacket will do — blazer, winter parka, windbreaker, suit coat, raincoat — anything. At this point, you should be holding the rope by its thread-tied center, letting the ends trail out of opposite ends of your hand; if you were to open your hand, you'd see something like Figure 5-2, photo A.

"Welcome to the stage. What are your names?" (Volunteer-relations etiquette is a hallmark of classy magicians.)

"I hope you don't mind my calling you up here, but I couldn't help but notice your jacket. As I'm sure you realized when you bought it, jackets like these have some special properties. Have you been aware of your jacket giving you special powers? I mean, other than keeping you warm and attracting admiring stares from passersby?"

As you talk, don't be afraid to casually toy with your ropes. Run one loosely closed fist down them, for example.

"Actually, I can prove to you just how remarkable this coat is. But first, I need you to take it off. All off. I mean take the *jacket* all off."

2. As your helper removes his jacket, you're holding the rope centers with your left hand. Slide your fingers among the strands of rope so that you double them back, as shown in photo B.

Let gravity help you reposition your grip — let the weight of the long rope ends assist in getting the rope ends reconfigured. Now two ends of the *same rope* protrude from each side of your left hand. The thread holds the centers together. (Of course, you've practiced beforehand enough to know how much pressure and fiddling might actually break the little thread and ruin the trick before it's even started.)

"Excellent. Wow, this is a *great* specimen of coat, too. You could easily get $50,000 for this on the magicians' open market.

"Now, if you don't mind, I'd like you to hold one pair of ends in each hand — and then put your jacket back on again. Here, I'll help you."

3. Standing behind your volunteer, put one pair of rope ends into his right hand, and the other end into his left hand.

Of course, if you really stop to think about it, you've just put both ends of the *same* rope into his right hand, and both ends of the *other* rope into his left.

But you don't have to worry about his pulling apart the threads that hold the ropes together. After all, the ropes are eight feet long, and he's holding the *ends.* The only way he could put tension on the middles of the ropes would be if he's half human, half pterodactyl.

"Your magic coat, sir," you might say in your best British-accented butler's voice. Hold the coat open for him.

4. Help your volunteer put his jacket back on as he carries the ends of the ropes down his sleeves (photo C).

The threaded center of the ropes is now behind your volunteer's back, inside the coat.

"Okay, so now you're right back where you started, except that you've got a pair of ropes threaded through your sleeves and behind your back. Just think of 'em as the world's most obvious loose threads.

"All right, you can let go of the ropes now. They're not going anywhere."

5. Take *one rope* from each sleeve and tie them in a single overhand knot, like the first step in tying your shoes (see photo D).

The idea here is to return one end of each rope to the opposite side, as you see in photo D. Don't tie a *double knot,* or you'll have some big explaining to do later.

"In fact, just to make sure *you're* not going anywhere either, I want to just tie you into place with a knot, like this. You can never be too careful with magic-trick volunteers, you know."

6. Ask your second volunteer to hold one pair of rope ends. You hold the other pair.

"If you wouldn't mind just hanging on to these ends of the ropes, I'd appreciate it. And I'll just hang on to the other ends."

Take a step back, so that the final pose resembles photo E.

"Now, I said that your jacket has some unusual powers, and I meant it. In your cultural education, you may remember some famous clothing through history: Superman's leotard made him bulletproof, Spider Man's outfit had web-spraying machinery, and Batman's outfit had an entire hardware store built into the belt. But *your* coat — your coat can make you walk through solid objects. I'm completely serious.

"In fact, I'll prove it to you. At the moment, you've got two ropes behind your back and through your sleeves. At the count of three, I want you to take a step backward. I want you to will yourself — and your jacket — to *dissolve* through the ropes. Right through your body, right through the jacket, setting you completely free. I know it seems impossible, but you've got to *believe* in your clothing."

7. Give final instructions to your second volunteer — and then do the deed.

"I'm going to count to three. And on three, you and I are each going to give the ropes a tug as our friend here dissolves. Pull forcefully, too — we don't want these ropes getting caught on his liver or something, halfway through his body. Ready? One — two — *three!*"

On three, give your ends of the ropes a sharp pull (just as your second volunteer does). That tug breaks the white thread behind the jacket owner's *back*. In a split second, *both ropes* are suddenly in front of the jacket owner, who's now entirely clear of the ropes (photo F). Everybody — audience and both volunteers — will be equally befuddled. By now, the tiny piece of white thread has brushed off somewhere or fallen to the floor undetected. Everything — ropes and jacket — can be examined.

"This is a great thing! Think of the possibilities — on your way out of here, you can just walk straight out through the walls!"

This is a *great* trick. Don't discount it just because of the need for secret preparation; get some clothesline and try it!

Scarf Decapitation

Here's a terrific decapitation effect that you can adapt to almost any circumstance — anything that's long and soft, you can pull through your neck. A winter scarf works great, but you can also use a tie, a piece of rope or string, a woman's scarf (if it's long enough), dental floss, or whatever.

In the figures that illustrate this trick (check out Figure 5-3), I've indicated — with great big labels X and Y — the two places you'll be handling this scarf. Fortunately, after you've learned the basic maneuver, you'll be able to go in public and perform the trick without big black letters floating around your head.

The effect: You wrap a scarf around your neck — and then pull it completely through your throat.

The secret: Actually, the scarf is never really around your neck, thanks to the clever way you wrap it to begin with. Sorry about the length of these instructions — it's a lot of words for a 10-second trick — but without your coming over to my living room, this is the best way I can show you. Follow the photos, spend 15 minutes in front of the bathroom mirror, and you've got yourself a portable miracle.

Figure 5-3: Grab opposite ends of the scarf (A) and don't let go! Pull X to the left, forming a loop that gets caught against your neck by the other end, which you wrap left across your body, up, behind your neck, and back down the right side (B and C). The hard part is over — grab the ends (D) and pull on through (E).

1. **Drape the scarf around your neck. The right end should hang lower than the left.**

   "When I was a kid, I always hated it when my mom got me all bundled up for cold weather. I mean, come on. Snow pants? Rubbers? Those little elastic clips that hold the mittens onto the end of your sleeves? It's a wonder I had any self-esteem at all."

2. **Grab the right piece of scarf (marked X) with your left hand at about armpit height, as shown in Figure 5-3, photo A. At the same time, reach across to grab the left-hand scarf with your *right* hand (marked Y).**

   Notice that the left hand is higher than the right. Notice that your hands are crossing your chest to grab the *opposite* ends of the scarf. Notice that all of this happens simultaneously, taking less than a second.

3. **Pull piece X to the left, straight across the front of your neck. Simultaneously, bring piece Y straight up, left, back, and around the back of your neck.**

   Photo B should make this procedure clear. Basically, you're just pulling a loop of X to the side while the real action — your right hand's awkward trip forward, up, and around over/behind your head — takes place.

   As your right hand pulls piece Y back around to the front of your body (now on the right side of your head), pull loop X (which your left hand has been holding all this time) around behind your neck so that nobody really sees it. In photo C, the loop is on its way back as the right hand comes down and forward. Let go with both hands.

   "But even then, I was a magical little kid. If mom ever put something on me that I didn't like . . . "

4. **Grab both ends of the scarf, as shown in photo D. When you've got everybody's attention, yank the scarf forward through your neck (photo E).**

   " . . . I'd just pull it off, right through my body!"

   Serving suggestion: A loud grunt, jerking your head backward, and an overall depiction of effort all enhance the illusion.

Give That Purse a Hand

Advisory Pantheon member Meir Yedid is not what you'd call a straight-laced fellow. His magic is anything but restrained and proper. In fact — how does one put this? — well, let's just say that one of his magic books lists about ten fun activities he can do with a fake rubber hand (such as leaving it sticking out of his car trunk as he drives around town). This trick is one of them.

I realize that asking you to locate a fake, hollow, rubber hand is a small violation of my promise at the beginning of this book that you'll need only everyday objects found around the house. I'm guessing you don't have a fake rubber hand lying around the house, unless you're Meir Yedid.

Still, your friendly neighborhood novelty shop probably sells them. If all else fails, you can order fake rubber hands, item #39/935, from the Oriental Trading Company, 800-228-2269 (at this writing, anyway). Unfortunately, you can't buy just one — you get one dozen fake rubber hands per package (for $18).

But look at the bright side: you'll have presents ready for eleven of your friends' birthdays.

The effect: You borrow a purse or book bag, mentioning that much may be learned about a person by examining what's in her bag. You reach in and begin pulling out the most alarming and bizarre items — a marshmallow, rubber cockroach, a fake mustache, a doll's hand, and so on. Just when everybody thinks you couldn't possibly pull out anything odder, you reach into the bag and pull out a life-size fake rubber hand!

The secret: All of the bizarre stuff starts out *inside* the hollow fake rubber hand. In the process of reaching inside, you deliver the entire hand-full into the purse.

By the way: A prepared container full of items you intend to magically produce out of nowhere is called a *load* in magic-ese. And that's what I'll call it in the following steps.

Before you begin the trick, load up your rubber hand. Figure 5-4, photo A, shows a typical amount of junk ready to load.

You'll have to do a bit of hunting in order to find stuff that's (a) small enough to fit into the hand, (b) big enough to be seen, and (c) bizarre enough that people will know right away they didn't *really* come from your volunteer's purse. (I'm sure there are parts of the country where a rubber cockroach, fake mustache, and marshmallow are perfectly normal items to pull out of the average person's purse. Gauge your scavenger hunt accordingly.)

The Oriental Trading Company's fake rubber hands aren't the biggest in the world, but you'll greatly aid your own cause by snipping off the fake red blood that lines the wrist. Not only is blood inappropriate for this trick, but snipping off a bit of the wrist gives you a wider opening into which you can stuff stuff.

Now stick the loaded hand's thumb into your rear right pants pocket (photo B). If you don't have pants, wear something with a belt or a waistline and stick the hand's thumb into *it*. The point is that you should be able to face your audience without them knowing that there's a stuffed fake rubber hand sticking out behind you.

You're ready to go.

1. To begin the performance, borrow a purse.

There's probably some equivalent item you could borrow if your audience has no purse-bearing members — a winter hat, say, or a belt pack — but you'll have to use your own imagination here.

"May I borrow somebody's purse or bookbag? I promise you'll get it back in one piece. However, I warn you that I will want to look inside."

Figure 5-4:
Stuff your fake rubber hand with the weirdest little objects you can find (A), and then hook it on your back pants pocket (B). When you've borrowed a purse, shove the loaded hand inside (C). Pull out the bizarre items one at a time (D).

For best results, look for a smallish purse. You don't want some huge handbag that actually *could* contain a huge assortment of items, including some weird ones. Yet the purse should be big enough for you to shove your hand (and your fake hand) into it without obstruction.

"Thank you very much. What's your name? Amy? See, Amy, I believe that you are what you carry. I think that we can learn a lot about a person by the items she carries with her at all times. I'd like to test my theory with your purse."

2. **Open the purse and stare inside. Turn so that your left side faces the audience; as you do this, grab the rubber hand's wrist with your right hand.**

"I can't believe this — look at all this stuff you've got in here!"

3. **Shove your right hand — carrying the rubber hand along with it — deep into the purse.**

Why won't anyone see the fake hand going in? Easy:

- Because nobody's expecting one.

- Because you're looking at the purse, so everybody else is, too.

- Because your motion is fairly fast.

- Because the fake hand looks, more or less, like it's *your* hand.

Yes, you can see the fake hand going into the purse photo C, but that's because it's a photo that's frozen in time.

4. **Leave the fake hand in the purse. Pull the first bizarre object out of the wrist — and out of the purse (photo D).**

"The first object that can tell us about your personality is this — this — pacifier? Amy, do you have an infant at the house? No? Then I'm afraid I'm going to have to ask you about this pacifier. Do have a license for this thing?"

5. **Continue pulling objects out of the rubber hand inside the purse, making witty and hilarious comments about each.**

- "A mustache!? Is this what you use when you don't want to be recognized?"

- "Aha — bikini bottoms. May I remind you that it's February? Now that's optimism."

- "A Malibu Barbie Cheese Grater. I don't even want to *think* about what *this* says about your personality . . ."

  And so on. Put each item on your table (if any) before proceeding to the next.

6. Finally, pull the rubber hand itself out of the purse.

"Now, there's one more thing in the purse I think we'd better talk about. All right, I can see why you'd carry around some of those other things — sort of. But I mean, can you explain — *this?*"

To conclude, graciously thank your purse-donator and return the purse to her. As you continue to stare at the phony appendage, your final line of patter is a no-brainer:

"How about a hand for Amy?"

Chapter 6

Take It Outside, Pal

In This Chapter

▶ Wreaking havoc at the hardware store

▶ Making an impression at your front door

▶ Creating a new facial orifice at McDonald's

▶ Causing a scene with a straw wrapper or doll hand

▶ Tricks you can perform anywhere

The beauty of impromptu magic is that it's the ultimate *portable* hobby. You can suddenly start showing off in the kitchen, the subway, or in the movie theater — a statement you can't make about such hobbies as, say, skeet shooting or the four-man bobsled.

This chapter offers tricks designed *just* for performances when you're out and about: at a barbecue, in the hardware store, at a fast-food restaurant, and so on.

And the next time you see a bobsledder, smile with sympathy.

The Missing Spray-Paint Marble

Spray-paint marble. Now, *there's* a phrase you don't use every day.

But the little rattling marble inside a can of spray paint is every bit a part of modern-day culture as, say, hearing-aid batteries or spray cheese — nobody talks about them much, but the world would be a greatly diminished place without them.

And therein lies the beauty of this trick, an invention of Advisory Pantheon member Chad Long. Not only do you get to do something truly amazing in a truly unexpected place (the hardware store, art-supply store, or Home Depot), but for just a few delicious moments, you also get to pretend to be a nut case.

The effect: In a hardware store, paint store, or Home Depot-type store, you call a clerk over. You complain that a can of spray paint is defective: It doesn't contain the little rattling marble that's supposed to mix the paint when you shake the can. You demonstrate the problem by shaking the can. Sure enough, there's no rattle — total silence.

But that's okay — you explain that you don't like going into paint stores unprepared. You pull a marble or ball bearing out of your pocket and slam it through the metal walls of the can. Instantly, the marble's rattling loudly around inside the can, as it should have been all along.

The secret: A magnet pressed against the side of the can prevents the actual ball bearing from rattling.

Now, not just any old fridge magnet does the trick for this trick. You need something fairly high-powered, such as one of those black, inch-wide, two-inch-long, science-kit magnets you may have had as a kid. (If you can't find one in your local magnet store, try American Science and Surplus, 847–982–0874.)

It's also worth noting that not all spray-paint cans cooperate with this trick. (Krylon brand, for one, does.) Sometimes the walls of the can are steel, which tends to intercept the magnet's force and prevent the steel ball inside from noticing the magnet.

Once you're in the store, therefore, you have three orders of business. First, experiment with different brands of paint until you find a can whose marble can be silenced by the magnet. Second, put the actual marble or ball bearing — the one you've brought from home — into your left pocket. Third, hide the magnet in your right hand, pressed against the side of the spray-paint can (near the bottom), as shown in Figure 6-1, photo A, so that the little steel marble inside doesn't rattle when you shake the can.

Experiment until you know how hard you can shake the can without dislodging the actual rattler; in my experience, you can shake it pretty darned hard.

Thus prepared, find a clerk.

1. **When you have a clerk's attention, shake the can to show that there's no marble inside (photo B).**

    "Excuse me," you can say. "This is exactly the right color paint for my project, but this can is defective. There's no rattler inside to mix up the paint."

    This, by the way, is the most delicious moment of the trick. You get two delightful experiences: playing the role of the psycho customer from hell and witnessing the poor clerk's reaction to what's certainly the most bizarre complaint of the year.

    "Actually, maybe I can fix this myself. I think I may even have a spare marble on me."

2. **Pull your right hand (and the magnet) away from the can. Pretend to fish in your right pocket for your extra marble.**

"I was almost sure I had one . . ."

3. **Pull your right hand out of the pocket, leaving the magnet behind. Transfer the can to your right hand, as your *left* hand goes into your *left* pocket — to pull out the marble.**

This fishing action is shown in photo C. Display the marble triumphantly.

"Ah! See, I knew I had one! Look, if you don't mind, I think I'll just use my own marble."

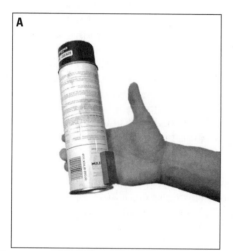

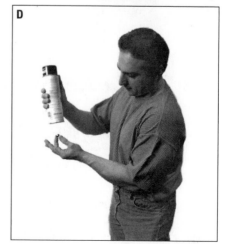

Figure 6-1:
The secret, of course, is the hidden magnet (A). Complain to the clerk (B). Fish for a marble (C). Finally, slam it through the metal walls of the can (D).

4. Slam the marble in your left hand onto the bottom of the can (photo D). At the same instant, begin shaking the can so that the newly released, *real* marble begins rattling loudly.

The illusion is spectacular. One moment you've got a non-rattling can and a marble outside it, the next the can's rattling happily.

So what about the external marble, which still rests in your left hand? No big deal. Anyone within eyeshot is, guaranteed, staring at the much more interesting sound, sight, and motion of the spray-paint can. Move your right hand forward with the can, offering the can to the clerk for inspection.

That's the perfect cover for dropping your left hand to your side, fingers curled to hold the marble — or even slipping your hand into your left pocket in a charming, self-conscious sort of way.

Chad's bonus tip: This trick works beautifully in reverse, too. As a variation, consider calling over the store clerk to complain that there's a *hole* in the can. Start shaking the can (so that it rattles) with both hands — your left contains your own personal marble, your right hides the magnet, held slightly away from the side of the can. At the key moment, release the marble so that it drops to the floor; go chasing it as it rolls down the aisle. The more disturbed you act, the better.

At this point, let the magnet stick to the side of the can to deactivate the can's internal marble. You can show the clerk how the can is now silent — and if you think it appropriate, you can even put the external marble "back into" the can by following Steps 1, 2, and 3.

No matter how you perform this trick, you can be sure that your hardware-store visit will quickly become legendary, talked about over dinner tables and loading docks for years to come.

The Ninja Key Catch

The Ninja Key Catch isn't something you do in your standard block-party magic show. Rather, it's a two-second stunt you do when you're opening the car door — or your house door — for friends or a date. Either way, with this trick, you cement your reputation as the James Bond of the neighborhood.

The effect: As you approach your car or house door in readiness to unlock it, you toss your key ring into the air. When you snatch it out of the air, the onlookers are stunned to see that you've managed to grab *exactly* the correct key — and in precisely the right position to instantly insert it into the lock.

The secret: Before tossing your keys, *remove* the key in question from the key ring — it's held in your hand the whole time.

PREP WORK

1. **Get your loose key in position — hidden in your right hand (if you're right-handed).**

   Figure 6-2, photo A, shows this starting position.

   "Shall we go in?" (This trick isn't what you'd call patter-heavy.) "Watch this!"

2. **Toss your key ring into the air (photo B).**

   It really doesn't matter which hand does the tossing.

TIP

3. **As the key ring is falling, push the loose key forward with your thumb, as shown in photo C. Catch the key ring with your bottom three fingers (photo D).**

   The effect looks snazzier (and is less susceptible to detection) if you *shoot* your hand out to catch the key ring.

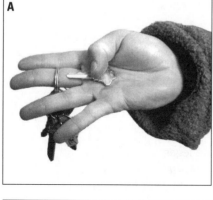

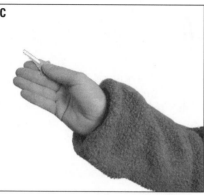

Figure 6-2: Prepare by getting the loose key lined up in your hand (A). Toss the keys (B); use that fifth of a second to push the hidden key into position (C); and catch the falling keys in your lower fingers (D).

4. Smoothly insert the protruding key into the lock, open your car or house, and smile modestly.

Chad Long, who came up with this one, goes even farther: Loose in his pocket, he carries around a *duplicate* of his house key. That way, he doesn't have to remove it from his key ring (and put it back on afterward) every time he wants to do the Ninja Key Catch. After he's inside the house, he just tosses the key ring onto the counter. If his friends get suspicious and begin to check out the keys on it, they'll discover nothing fishy; the house key is securely bound to the ring.

Like many of the greats in magic, this trick isn't difficult enough to qualify as sleight-of-hand — but it does take practice. Work on the catching part until you can do it smoothly and convincingly. (Throwing your key ring inexplicably into the air and having it clatter to the ground makes you look not so much like James Bond as Barney the Dinosaur.)

Straw through the Jaw

In Bali, Indonesia, when darkness falls and village fires are lit, local magicians perform what they call the Trance Dance — basically a chanting, dancing routine of magic tricks whose common thread is self-mutilation. The dancer performs the Jumping on Broken Glass Trick, the Light-Bulb Eating Trick, the Sticking a Wire through His Own Cheek Trick, and other stunts not found in the average beginners' magic kit.

If you're reading this book, you're probably a long way from Bali. And yet the ability to seemingly damage your own flesh in grisly ways is still a great way to enhance your popularity. Here's Advisory Pantheon member Kevin James' kinder, gentler self-mutilation effect. Its locale requirements are much easier to come by, too — instead of a village bonfire, all you need is a local McDonald's.

The effect: You stick a plastic drinking straw up through the bottom of your chin — all way into your mouth.

The secret: Before you perform the trick, cut off a couple inches of a second straw. Keep this two-inch piece in your mouth between your gums and your cheek. Even with this setup, you'll find that you can talk, smile, and even drink. (Note: For maximum popularity enhancement, do not swallow the straw.)

Go ahead, ask it. If you're at a fast-food restaurant, where on earth do you find a pair of scissors with which to cut off a straw piece? Kevin James cuts off the straw piece with his teeth. If you can't live with your dentist's disapproval, however, you may prefer to carry with you a small pair of scissors or a pocketknife. If you're in a pricier restaurant, maybe you can find a steak knife to do the job.

You're a magician. Find a way.

1. **Place the end of a full-length straw against the underside of your jaw, as shown in Figure 6-3, photo A.**

   As you can see, your right hand holds the bottom end of the straw. Your left hand pretends to position the top end against your skin, although its actual purpose is to conceal the fact that the plastic isn't actually traveling into your flesh. (If you enjoyed the Pencil up the Nose trick in Chapter 4, all of this is probably sounding distinctly familiar — it's essentially the same trick.)

   Say, "Hey, check it out!" (When it comes to self-mutilation tricks, patter is definitely secondary to shock value.)

   Going into a trance is optional.

2. **With great expressions of acute pain and effort, slide your right hand up the straw, as though pushing upward, about four inches.**

   The straw doesn't actually move, of course; your fingers just slide upward, hiding the straw's lower extremity, just as you hide the pencil in Chapter 4's Pencil up the Nose trick.

3. **Meanwhile, inside your mouth, use your tongue to line up the small straw piece vertically.**

   This is the hardest part of the trick — the one you should rehearse endlessly in front of a bathroom mirror. The idea is to make the straw piece line up *perfectly* with the straw that's beneath your jaw. For best results, use your tongue to press the straw piece against your lower teeth, pinning it there.

   When you can get the straw piece to stand proud and tall by pinning it with your tongue alone, with its top end unsupported, you're ready for action; go forth and stupefy. But if you can't get the straw piece to remain perfectly vertical, consider propping it up with your upper teeth (or the gums just *behind* your upper teeth).

4. **Open your mouth to reveal that the straw has penetrated all the way into your mouth, as shown in photo B.**

   While gagging and wincing, turn your head to give everyone present a brief look at your disgusting accomplishment.

   Finally, you're ready to back out of it.

Figure 6-3: Starting position for sliding the straw into your jaw (A). Actually, the straw is just sliding behind your hand. (B) shows the final illusion.

5. **Close your mouth. Maneuver the straw piece back between your gum and your cheek while sliding your right hand back down the straw, simulating pulling the straw out of your flesh. When you reach the bottom, pull the straw "out" and smile pleasantly.**

You might wipe the underside of your chin with the back of your hand as a finishing touch; it's not polite to bleed in public.

As for the piece that's still in your mouth — well, that's this trick's weak point. The best solution is to leave it there until you can conveniently ditch it (by, for example, coughing violently into a napkin).

And if somebody asks to *see* inside your mouth, stare back in disbelief, mutter, "You're dis*gust*ing!" and launch into the following trick.

The Astonishing Straw-Wrapper Restoration

All right, you're actually supposed to use this trick to turn a pencil into a pen, or some other boring transformation of one skinny object into another. But Advisory Pantheon member Mike Caveney uses straws and their wrappers. And because the annals of magical literature are so woefully devoid of tricks involving straw wrappers, it was a natural for this chapter.

Alas, today's fast-food establishments tend to serve their plastic straws *without* wrappers, relying instead upon straw dispensers as the sole defense against the transmission of gruesome germs. But if you spend a long enough time with a touch-tone phone and the Yellow Pages open to "Restaurants," you'll surely be able to find at least one dining establishment in your area where wrapped straws are offered to the clientele.

Gather your friends and propose a visit to that quality eatery.

The effect: You place a straw side-by-side with its empty wrapper on a napkin. You roll up the napkin, incant a few magic words, unroll the napkin, and lo! — the straw has somehow managed to get *back into* its wrapper.

The secret: You've got a second straw, still in its wrapper, hidden beneath the napkin. The sneaky napkin-rolling method swaps the naked straw for the fully clothed one.

Prepare this second straw before you actually start doing any magic. There's nothing to it, really: Just rip about an inch of wrapper off of one end. (This detail isn't strictly necessary. But the fact that one end is gone from the wrapper will later help to throw your audience off the scent. "Well, *maybe* the straw somehow got slid back into its wrapper from one end . . .")

When you're ready to do the trick, throw your napkin onto the table with the wrapped secret straw underneath. (Getting it under the napkin isn't very difficult because — if you've got any manners at all — the napkin itself has been in your lap thus far in the meal, safely out of sight.)

The napkin should lie in a diamond shape, as shown in Figure 6-4, photo A, where you can also see that the secret straw lies horizontally under the napkin.

It's at this point, by the way, that you start learning more than you ever wanted to know about today's exciting napkin-manufacturing industry. You discover, for example, that the cheapest paper napkins are see-through, and therefore no good for this trick — but that the nicer, larger, multi-ply paper napkins work well. You learn that most cloth napkins are great for hiding straws — but a few look suspiciously lumpy.

Now it's show time.

1. **Place a naked straw and its wrapper side by side on the napkin, as shown in photo A.**

   Note that the under-side straw is closer to you than the topside straw. Also note that *both* straws are closer to you than the napkin's horizontal, corner-to-corner midline.

"You know what's always struck me as funny?" you might begin. "That we humans are modest. We don't like to be naked in public. Most people get weirded-out when even our *pets* see us naked. But really, this discomfort is a natural instinct. And it's not confined to people, either. Pets get shy. So do plants, interestingly enough. Even inanimate objects sometimes. Like this straw, lying here shivering and cold without its clothing."

("Its clothing," of course, refers to the paper wrapper. Help along the less sophisticated audience members by pointing to the wrapper as you say this.)

Figure 6-4:
Begin with the secret straw, shown here by a ghostly image, underneath the napkin (A, which shows things from your side; all other photos taken from the spectator's side). Grab both together and begin wrapping away from you (B). When the corner flips (C), pull the corners apart (D) to reveal the fully dressed straw (E).

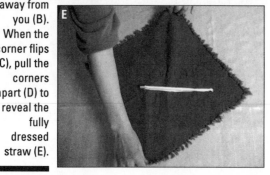

2. **Through the cloth, grab *both* straws and begin rolling the napkin's center away from you, as shown in photo B.**

   "If we relieve the nude straw's anxiety by giving it some privacy, like this . . ."

3. **Keep rolling until the bottom corner of the napkin flips *under* the roll, and the top corner flips *over,* as shown in photo C.**

   ". . . its natural tendency is, well . . ."

4. **Grasp the two corners that just flipped — and tug them apart, as shown in photo D, to reveal the fully-clothed straw in all its glory (photo E).**

   ". . . to get dressed!"

   This trick does not, alas, end "clean." Everything at this moment is *not* inspect-able; the original straw and wrapper are now underneath the napkin.

   That's what *misdirection* is for.

5. **With your right hand, pick up the visible, wrapped straw and hold it at eye level, showing everyone. With your left hand, "wipe" the napkin (and everything under it) back into your lap.**

   If you perform Steps 4 and 5 smoothly and naturally, nobody will question your actions. You're showing the newly wrapped straw, handing it around. Chances are good that the missing tip of the wrapper will further occupy the skeptics. All of this provides further cover for your ditching the napkin — and the evidence along with it.

The Creepy Little Baby Hand

This trick, a contribution of Advisory Pantheon member Bob Farmer, is a matter of personal taste. More than any other trick in this book, it requires a certain willingness to creep out those around you. But in the right hands, it's a shocker that will have everyone looking at you with renewed alarm.

The effect: You clasp your empty palms. From nowhere, a doll's arm reaches out from between your hands, gropes around your palm, slinks back into your hands — and then vanishes abruptly.

The secret: You're wearing the doll's arm on your pinky. Because the doll's arm is flesh colored and skinny — just like your pinky — it's nearly impossible to see, especially head-on. That handy little fact makes the end-of-trick vanish almost self-working.

Grace under Fire, Part 3

Boston, 1995: It was the Society of American Magicians' national Stage Competition. Torkova, one of this book's advisers, entered the contest — it was his very first competition.

He had perfected his own special version of The Miser's Dream, a classic trick in which the magician reaches out with his bare hand and plucks a coin out of the air. He drops it into a bucket and then reaches out again — another coin. The coins begin appearing faster and faster, and with much clinking, the bucket slowly fills up with money.

Torkova was performing without patter, accompanied only by his tape of Scott Joplin's familiar ragtime tune, "The Entertainer"; part of the charm of his act was that he caught coins in time to the beat of the music.

Imagine his horror, then, when the theater's sound system croaked in the middle of his routine. The music stopped — and so, for a moment, did the magic. Torkova didn't know what to do; for a split second, he thought he was dead in the water.

But the tune to "The Entertainer" is familiar enough; to help the show go on, a couple of Torkova's magician friends in the audience began *singing* the melody. Torkova, inspired, smiled, faced the audience, and conducted them, encouraging them all to join in the song. Soon enough, the supportive audience was gleefully singing his music — and Torkova went right back into his routine.

A few moments later, the sound system sputtered to life again. Incredibly, the tape had continued running in the meantime; when the speakers came back on, the music resumed at almost exactly the right spot in Torkova's performance. Without missing a beat, he concluded the performance on the final chord — with the appearance of a huge wad of dollar bills at his fingertips.

The crowd, inspired by his good spirits and grace under fire, went crazy, giving him a standing ovation. A couple of older magicians in the back of the theater had tears in their eyes.

And, oh yes — Torkova won the competition.

Now, the most difficult part of this trick takes place before you try it — *finding* a doll's arm. Because the Yellow Pages listings are on the limited side when it comes to "Doll Limbs — Retail," you'll probably wind up having to buy an entire doll. Garage sales, "doll hospital" shops, and neighbors with grown-up children are good sources of *used* dolls (and arms); toy stores offer new ones, although you'll pay top dollar (and wind up wasting 90 percent of your purchase). You're looking for a doll whose arm size is such that it could fit neatly onto your pinky.

After you've got the doll home, pull its arm off. You need the shoulder end to be open so that you can stick your pinky into it; this may entail cutting off a part of the shoulder end with a pair of scissors.

Wedge your right pinky into the little arm's shoulder-end opening, and you're ready to begin.

1. **Casually and briefly show both hands empty.**

   You have *not* announced, "Ladies and gentlemen: The Baby Arm From Nowhere Trick!" In other words, don't make a big deal of showing your hands empty; nobody is expecting anything yet. According to the Bill of Magicians' Rights, hands are assumed to be empty until proved otherwise.

   So a momentary display like the ones shown in Figure 6-5, photos A and B, will do nicely. That is, start with your hands palm-down (photo A), where the little arm is bent under your right hand, and then flip them palms-up, hiding the arm beneath the left hand (photo B).

   "Let me show you something," you can say.

2. **Turn your left hand over to clasp your palm-up right hand (photo C). Under cover of this hand-turning, fold up your right pinky, placing the doll's arm between your two hands.**

   Photo D shows the baby arm in birth position — what your audience would see if your left hand weren't there.

   "From the empty darkness of my hands, may I present . . . *LIFE!*"

3. **Slide your pinky toward your wrist, so that the doll's hand and arm come into view (photo E). Move it so that it appears to be grasping, clutching, desperate to escape your hands.**

   You're pumping your pinky, making small circles with the doll arm, doing everything in your power to simulate a horrifying tiny creature clawing its way out of your hands. (Some magicians even put a dime on the base of their right thumb — whereupon the little hand reaches out, grabs the coin, and drags it back into its little hand-womb.)

   Practice this part before you perform it in public. Of course, you should practice *any* trick — but practicing *this* one is fun. You'll find, to the dismay of your friends, family, and employer, that you can spend hours by yourself in the broom closet doing nothing but playing with your little doll's arm.

   When you've finished manipulating your little baby arm — about ten seconds is plenty — you're ready to make the whole thing disappear.

   "And just as quickly, may I present . . . *DEATH!*"

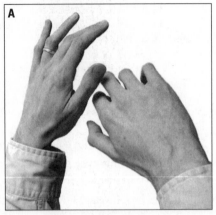

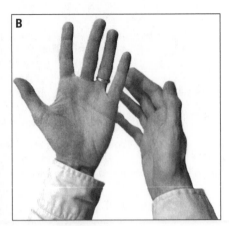

Figure 6-5:
Show your hands empty (A), even though the doll's arm is actually on one pinky (in photo B, a piece of the baby arm is slightly exposed for clarity). Fold up your hands (C); if you were to take your left hand away, you'd see the arm in ready-to-emerge position (D). Finally, let the arm emerge (E). End by clapping your hands (F, as seen from the audience's viewpoint).

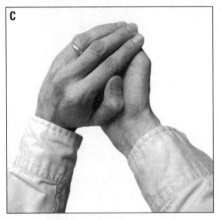

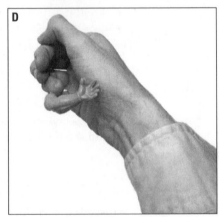

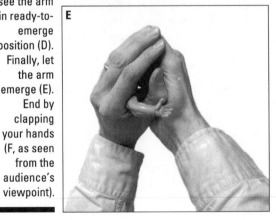

4. Clap your hands.

If you do so with your fingers splayed apart and pointing directly into the eyes of your audience (photo F), the doll's arm on your pinky won't be noticed. At this point, everyone's eyes are peeled for an *object,* some little piece of flesh-colored plastic to come flying onto the floor. Thanks to the laws of optical perspective, your pinky's unusual length (and the fact that your pinky has tiny *fingers* on the end) isn't noticeable.

To finish up, drop your hands to your sides, curling your right pinky into the palm so that the doll's arm is once again hidden. Alternatively, you could shove your hands (or just your pinkies) into your pockets in an "aw-shucks" posture for a moment, thus ditching the tiny arm.

The creepiness and oddness of this trick must be seen to be believed. I can think of no better way to make the guy next to you on the subway excuse himself and move to another seat.

The $100 LifeSaver Trick

Some of the world's best tricks are stunts that take place without the audience even knowing about it. This kind of trick goes on constantly — in politics, law, relationships — but only magicians are up-front about it.

This hilarious gem, a favorite of Advisory Pantheon member Bill Herz, is a perfect example. Nobody will ever know that you've even *done* a trick — but they'll never forget you or the day they saw you pull a $100 bill out of a roll of LifeSavers.

The effect: At a store or restaurant, you ask the clerk for a roll of LifeSavers. But for some bizarro reason, you're fanatically fussy over *which* roll you're given. You explain that the LifeSavers manufacturer is running a contest, hiding $100 bills inside random rolls of LifeSavers, and you think you can identify the special rolls.

When you're finally satisfied with the roll you've chosen, you pay for the candy — and then, right there in the store, you open the package to find a $100 bill tightly rolled inside!

The secret: You've got a duplicate roll, pre-stuffed with the bill inside.

1. **Before going out, carefully open a roll of LifeSavers. Roll up a $100 bill so tightly that it'll fit into the holes, as shown in Figure 6-6, photo A.**

   This isn't a trivial bit of surgery, by the way. LifeSavers are wrapped twice (not counting the printed outer label): once by waxed paper, and again by silver foil. (It's amazing how much trivia you pick up as a magician.)

Your task is to open the foil and waxed paper in such a way that it can be *put back* without looking horribly obvious. Fortunately, you won't have to make the damage *completely* undetectable — a roll of LifeSavers has two ends. Perform your operation on the end that's *opposite* the tiny dental-floss pull-string; later, in the store, you can conceal the doctored end in your hand as you open the pull-string end.

But the roll of LifeSavers itself isn't your only difficult task. You must also roll a $100 bill tightly enough that it can be shoved down the tunnel formed by the LifeSaver holes. (And you must *get* a $100 bill, which may be your most difficult task of all.)

Rolling a bill into that tight a tube isn't easy, but it can be done. Get used to it: patience and repetition are the trademarks of good magic preparation.

Before Step 2, one more point: this trick is best performed when you're *with* people. The cash register of a restaurant is a great place to do the trick — just after you've dined with your friends, for example. The candy counter at a movie theater is also great, because you're sur-rounded by other patrons as well. You *can* do this trick alone — at a convenience store, for example — but then the only person who'll be impressed is the cashier (and anyone else in line).

Put the doctored roll of candy in your right pocket (pants, coat, what-ever). Put a dollar in the left pocket.

2. **Approach the counter. Ask for a roll of LifeSavers (the flavor that matches your prepared roll, of course). But be very fussy (photo B).**

Reject the first couple of rolls. Direct the clerk to a *particular* roll. "Could I have a roll of LifeSavers, please? This kind here? No, I'm sorry, I really need to you get me *that one*. Right there — no, to the right. Yeah, that one."

3. **When you're handed the roll, jam both hands immediately into your pockets, as though looking for money (photo C). In your right pocket, swap rolls of LifeSavers. Pay for the candy.**

Your hands come out of your pockets, then, with your prepared LifeSavers in your right hand and the dollar in your left.

As you wait for the change, turn the roll over in your hand, inspecting it. Here comes the key patter:

"Okay, I own this now, right? I've definitely paid? These are definitely my LifeSavers?"

The more people that hear you ranting, the better.

"See, Nabisco — that's the company that makes LifeSavers — is putting a hundred-dollar bill inside random packs of LifeSavers. But I know how to tell which packages have the money. At least I think so. I found this out on the Internet."

4. Rip open the untouched end of the LifeSavers. Pull out the money. Unroll it. Go crazy (photo D).

The LifeSavers may adhere to the $100 money tube, looking like dinky little — well, life preservers around its waist. But who cares? You're rich now.

"Look! I won! I can't believe it! I won! Yes! I can't believe it — I've never won anything in my life!"

Unroll the money and show it all around (unless you're in *that* kind of neighborhood), stuff it into your pocket, and shake hands with the cashier.

Magician Bill Herz reports that he's done this stunt dozens of times — and that it blows onlookers' minds. In many cases, if you wait around, you'll get to witness a stampede of other customers buying and tearing up the cashier's remaining stock of LifeSavers, hoping to be equally lucky.

Figure 6-6:
Pre-stuff a roll of LifeSavers with a $100 bill (A). Make a big deal over *which* roll of LifeSavers you're getting (B). As you "hunt" for your money, shove your hands into both pockets (C) and swap the rolls — so that you can get lucky (D).

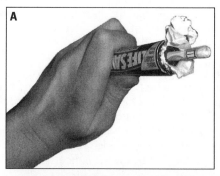

Dan Sylvester's Bubblous Glasses

Not all of magic is *magic*. Much of it is pure entertainment, even when it's not mystifying.

Advisory Pantheon member Dan Sylvester is a case in point. He buys a cheap pair of glasses (from a garage sale, for example) and pops the lenses out. He then dips the empty frames into a bowl of bubble-blowing solution — you know, the stuff kids run around with on summer days. (You may have to experiment with various brands and concentrations before you find one that clings satisfactorily across your empty glasses frames.)

Then out he goes into public, his glasses duly prepared with films of bubble solution. At an appropriate lull in the conversation, he removes his glasses, clears his throat, and gently blows — as the lenses bulge out, spherize, and finally float away across the room!

The Unforgettable "Cloudy" Toilet Paper

If you've ever seen Advisory Pantheon member Jeff McBride perform, you know that his graceful style is high in visual impact. Consider yourself lucky, then, that he's contributed one of the most unusual and beautiful tricks your friends will ever see at a picnic.

The effect: After showing your hands empty, you pull off several yards from a roll of toilet paper. As you question why toilet-paper packaging always stresses the cloud-like nature of each brand, you and your audience watch in amazement as fountains of water begin shooting up several feet into the air — out of the middle of your wad of toilet paper. The streams of water seem to go on forever, rising and falling at your command; finally, you toss the absolutely ordinary blob of tissue into the audience.

The secret: The fountain of water is produced by a Glaxon T-7 Irrigator, a compact electrical pump first developed for use in greenhouses. Transparent flexible hoses conduct the water from a concealed tank into two tiny spigots at your fingertips. You can order the T-7 for $495 from Glaxon, P.O. Box 4175, San Francisco, CA, 94107.

Just kidding.

Actually, this trick costs next to nothing: the fountain comes from an ordinary toy balloon. Some clever handling ideas and even cleverer laws of physics keep it dry and hidden until you want the shower to begin.

Before the magic show, track down an ordinary toy balloon, of the type you might see at a birthday party. Size matters; you want a balloon that's big enough to hold about a quarter of a cup of water without even starting to stretch.

Hold the balloon's neck up to a faucet. Your instinct will probably be to put a *lot* of water in. Don't; in fact, you shouldn't even put enough water into it to make it start stretching. A little bit of water will go a very long way, as you'll find out shortly.

Tie the balloon's neck in a knot. At this point, it's just a limp, blubbery bladder that would be considered a dud in any self-respecting water-balloon fight. Here's where it gets weird: Find a pin. Start poking holes into the round end of the balloon (opposite the tied neck), as shown in Figure 6-7, photo A. If you've underfilled the balloon correctly, you'll find it surprisingly difficult to poke these holes, since there's so much slack in the rubber.

But if you push far enough, the pin will go through. You might find it handy to make *two* holes at a time, pushing the pin all the way through both sides of the balloon each time. The number of holes to poke is up to you, but eight or ten will produce a delightful fountain.

Impressively enough, the balloon doesn't leak. Because you've put so little water in, you can pocket it, handle it, toss it, all without leaking. In fact, only if you squeeze the thing fairly assertively does the fountain appear, as you can find out for yourself in the comfort of your own shower.

Slip the balloon into the core of a roll of toilet paper, as shown in photo B. (If the balloon is too big to slide in, you've overfilled it.) Set the roll down on whatever table you'll be using when you perform — sideways, not standing up — somewhere where it won't roll. If you can roll up your sleeves, or wear something with no sleeves at all, all the better.

Now you're ready to — well, roll.

1. **Pick up the toilet-paper roll with your left hand, holding it horizontally.**

   "I'll tell you one job I'm glad I don't have: marketing toilet paper," you might begin. "I mean, there's so many things you can't say on TV . . . you can't even really talk about what your product is *for.*"

2. **Insert two left-hand fingers horizontally into the roll to serve as a toilet-roll holder (photo C).**

   You may want to "steady the roll" by pressing your right palm against the right-side core opening, so that your left fingers don't accidentally push the balloon out.

3. **Start unwrapping tissue from the roll, wrapping it around your right hand as you go (photo D).**

   "In fact, it seems like there's only one thing toilet-paper ads do say: how *cloudlike* their brand is. Have you noticed that? The packaging all has pictures of clouds. Toilet paper is supposed to be as soft as a cloud, as white as a cloud, as light as a cloud . . . "

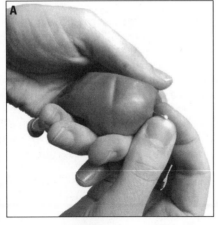

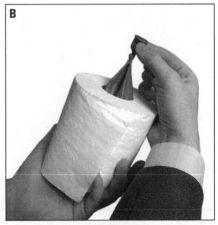

Figure 6-7: Puncture the slightly filled water balloon with a pin (A) and then sock it away (B). When you perform the trick, let your left hand serve as a TP holder (C) and then unwrap some around your right hand (D).

4. **Detach the unwound wad of toilet paper from the roll.**

    "But the other day, I saw this new brand on sale. At the magic store, of all places. I didn't know why they were selling bathroom supplies at the magic store, but the price was good, so I bought a roll. You won't believe what this new stuff is called: Cloudy."

5. **As you say this, tip the roll (with your left hand) upright into your right hand, so that the balloon falls out of the roll and into your waiting palm (Figure 6-8, photo A).**

    The balloon is completely concealed by the huge blob of toilet paper. Your excuse for transferring the roll in this way is to hold it up, as though on a pedestal (photo B), as you say: "Cloudy."

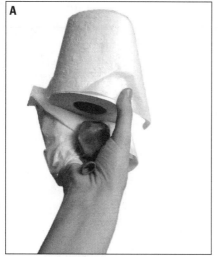

Figure 6-8:
Dump the balloon into your waiting right hand (A, shown from your side) as you present: "Cloudy!" (B). Position the tissue and the balloon (C, from your side), and then let the shower begin (D).

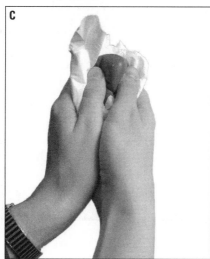

"I didn't really know just how far they were willing to go with this cloud theme, though, until I got home . . ."

6. **Set the roll down with your left hand. Use both hands to adjust the tissue wad so that it conceals the balloon without blocking its pinhole jets (photo C).**

In other words, fluff the paper in such a way that it provides an open-air channel for the water volcano that's about to erupt. In the process, you may want to extract your right fingers from their tunnel in the middle of the wad, re-gripping the wad from the outside.

". . . and that's when my Cloudy toilet paper started — to — *rain.*"

7. Squeeze the balloon so that the water sprays out of the pinholes.

The effect is dazzling. You can vary the height of the spray by squeezing with more or less pressure. Because the streams of water are so silvery and fine, you're not actually using up water very quickly. The fountain can continue for a minute or more, although you probably shouldn't test the limits of your audiences' novelty-wear-off factor.

If you planned ahead in Step 6, and adjusted the balloon so that your right hand alone controls the squeezing, you can use your free hand at this point to gesture gracefully at the fountain, controlling its height via magical hand movements (photo D).

At this point, you're batting a thousand; you've got sparkling streams of water shooting from your hands and an audience with no clue where it's coming from. If you're performing at a picnic somewhere and you don't have a table, you can end the trick by wadding up the toilet paper in your hand and tossing it into a garbage can.

If you do have a table, however — one that the spectators can't see behind — here's a more convincing way to end the trick.

8. With your left hand, pick up the roll of toilet paper from your table.

If there's a tail of tissue that's slightly unrolled from the roll, all the better. This roll is about to go sailing through the air, and a streamer of unwound tissue will only make its flight more dramatic.

"Can't you just see the ads for this new toilet paper? Cloudy: It's *lighter than air!*"

9. As you say that, throw the roll out into your audience. As it's flying through the air, let the balloon fall from your right hand behind the table.

Don't drop the toilet-paper wad; just let the balloon fall to the ground. The onlookers (including you) are watching to see who catches the roll of toilet paper you threw. It's the perfect misdirection opportunity to ditch the empty balloon.

Optional tag line: "That's the last time I'll buy toiletries at the magic shop!"

10. Immediately after tossing the roll, toss the now-empty toilet-paper wad into the crowd, too.

When the audience tells their friends about the trick later, they won't remember that you tossed out the roll and *then* the wad, as a one-two punch. They'll say, "And then this fountain of water came out of the bunch of toilet paper. But when the magician threw the toilet paper into the audience, it was perfectly normal. It was barely even wet!"

Part III
The Restaurant Zone

In this part . . .

*E*nough traipsing around your office, picnics, and hardware stores. Now you're ready for the bigtime, the limelight, center stage, the close-up magician's native habitat: the Restaurant Zone. This is the enchanted land where all the world's a prop, built-in audiences sitting at fixed distances are everywhere, and the lighting is just right.

Take a seat, survey your available weapons — salt shakers, silverware, napkins, wine glasses, companions waiting for the entrée to arrive — and proceed to establish your innate amazingness.

Chapter 7
Cutlery Is Your Friend

. . . .

In This Chapter
▶ Stunts with spoons and saltshakers
▶ Fun with forks
▶ Magic with mugs

. . . .

*J*ust sitting down at a restaurant table is a giddy experience for a magician. All around are small, loose objects, ripe with potential. Especially tantalizing: silverware. Not only is silverware shiny, eye-catching, and familiar to the audience, but it's also guaranteed to be waiting at any restaurant you visit.

Unless you're eating at an Ethiopian restaurant, of course. Then you eat with your hands. But you should have thought of that before you took up magic.

This chapter is a guide to the wonders that you can perform at the dinner table — at home or at the restaurant — with knives, forks, spoons, glasses, plates, and other inedible paraphernalia.

The Bendy Spoon, Part 1

In my junior-high cafeteria, there were three ways to enhance your status using only a spoon: (a) hang it from your nose, (b) fling Jell-O cubes with it, or (c) "bend" it by pressing the bowl flat against the table, meanwhile pretending that your hands still held the handle.

Trouble is, all the kids already knew that last trick. Furthermore, because you couldn't *see* the spoon's handle sticking out of the top, the effect wasn't very convincing. This updated version of the Bendy Spoon trick offers a clever spin on the old junior-high-cafeteria illusion.

The effect: With appalled spectators all around you, you pick up a spoon and bend it nearly double against the tabletop. Then, just as the hysterical waiter comes running over to intervene, you open your hands — to reveal a perfectly straight, untouched spoon. Ah, the power of mass hypnosis!

The secret: Before you do the trick, fish a nickel out of your pocket. You'd be surprised at just how much the smooth, shiny edge of a nickel looks like the top of a spoon handle.

1. **Get the nickel into push-up position.**

   That is, pinch the nickel with your thumb against the inside of your index-finger knuckle, as shown in Figure 7-1, photo A. Don't let anyone see the nickel yet; pull it down below knuckle level with your thumb. Now you're ready to start.

2. **To begin your performance, pick up a spoon with your other hand.**

   "Hey, you guys," you might say. "I love the food at this place, but can you believe how cheap the silverware is!? I mean, look at this!"

3. **Assume the position.**

   Grab the spoon with both hands, right hand (containing the nickel) on top. In the process, push the nickel *slightly* upward, so that the shiny rim pokes over your index finger, as shown in photo B.

   The bowl of the spoon is digging vertically into the tabletop, the left hand's pinky is the *only* finger wrapped around the handle, and the right hand holds the nickel at the point where the handle's end might plausibly be.

   Your hands should overlap. Otherwise, if you were to put one hand atop the other, your spoon would look like it's 10 inches long (photo C.)

   "I mean, what do they make this stuff out of — aluminum foil!? Look at this!"

4. **Lean forward, grunt, and start "bending" the spoon.**

   I'm serious about the grunting and leaning — it *makes* this trick. You want to create the impression that this particular silverware is more substantial than, say, aluminum foil.

   As you "press," here's the key move: Let the spoon handle come toward you, slipping out the back of your hands. Your hands, meanwhile, angle forward *away* from you. The bowl of the spoon slowly flattens out to the table, as shown in photo D.

   Because your hands remain upright, the effect is that you're bending the spoon into an L or even a C shape. Your left pinky is the spoon's pivot point (photo E), but otherwise you're barely touching the spoon.

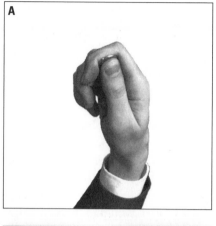

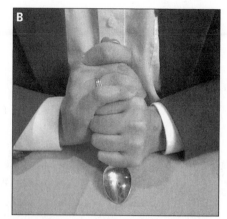

Figure 7-1:
The secret nickel (A). No one must know! The top hand should overlap the bottom hand (B). Don't stack your hands, or the handle will look unnaturally long (C). Bend the spoon slowly (D). If your left-hand fingers were to open, (E) is what your spectators would see from the side. Finally, ditch the nickel and the spoon (F).

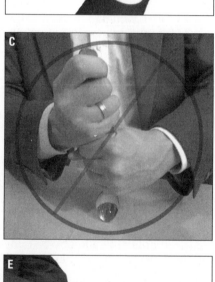

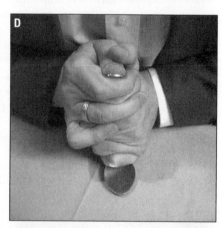

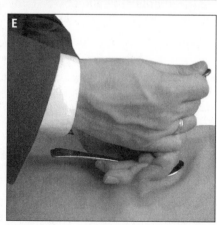

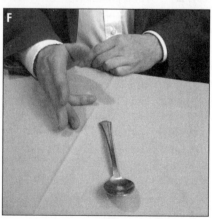

Let the spoon appear to slowly collapse until your nickel is nearly parallel to the table, as shown back in photo D. Freeze this way for a second; it's okay to lift the whole assembly up off the table, if you want.

"The only problem with this kind of demonstration," you then say, "is that it gets me in trouble with the waiters. It's times like this that it's good to be a magician, so I can show you that it was all an optical illusion anyway!"

5. **Toss the spoon in front of you onto the table.**

Trust me: Every eye in the joint will be locked on the shiny, moving spoon. You have a full five seconds of absolute privacy to drop the nickel into your lap behind the table edge without detection (photo F).

Now, of course, you've got a befuddled and amused crowd and a normal spoon sitting on the table in front of you. Wouldn't it be great if you could, say, now pick up the spoon and do a follow-up grand finale?

You can. Read on to "Bendy Spoon II: The Return."

Bendy Spoon II: The Return

How'd you like to perform a low-rent version of the trick that made Israeli magician Uri Geller famous? The guy made international TV — and a lot of money — by bending silverware with the force of his brain. Now you, too, can bend silverware — all the way into oblivion. This trick makes a perfect follow-up to the Bendy Spoon, Part I.

The effect: You start weakening the middle of a spoon by bending the halves back and forth. As the spoon softens, you point out that the molecules are warming up, loosening, spreading farther and farther apart — until the spoon vanishes entirely, right out of your hands.

The secret: As I've said, a typical restaurant couldn't be a better setup for magic tricks if it had trapdoors and a box office. In this case, your lap serves as a handy dumping ground for the spoon — long before anyone suspects that the trick has even started. All you need to pull this off is a teaspoon of acting ability, a tablespoon of chutzpah, and a plain old teaspoon.

1. **Position the spoon so that it's lying in front of you, as shown in Figure 7-2, photo A.**

In other words, the spoon is a foot from the table's edge and parallel to it.

"I was watching some seventies reruns last night, you know? *The Dukes of Hazzard,* the *Brady Bunch,* and *The Six Million Dollar Man.* Now *that* was art!" you might say.

"But I also saw an old Johnny Carson show where his guest was Uri Geller. Remember him? The guy who could bend metal with his mind? He'd hold a spoon out in front of him, and then it would just wilt like a dandelion. Well, I've been working on the same trick."

Figure 7-2: Getting the spoon ready (A). Picking it up (B). What really happens to it (C). Bending the halves (D). And breaking them apart (E). Not shown: your triumphant grin as you show your hands empty at the end.

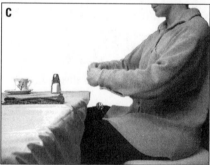

2. **Cover the spoon with both hands. In the act of "picking it up," slide it toward you, right off the table edge and into your lap.**

All of this happens in *one smooth motion,* as shown in photo B. (Smooth? Of course it's smooth, since you've spent time on it before performing in public. You've practiced picking up the spoon for *real* to see what it might look like.)

The instant your fingers clear the table and the spoon drops out of sight into your lap (photo C), close your side-by-side fists around the emptiness where the spoon was. (Make an effort not to go "Ow!" when the spoon strikes your thighs.)

Your hands never stop; they lift up about eight inches above the tabletop. Keep looking at your hands. Pretend that they still contain the spoon. Act. *Act!*

3. **Start bending the "spoon," back and forth, weakening it.**

Make it bend the way it really would: At first, it's stiff, so you can't bend it very far or very fast. And, as in the Bendy Spoon, Part I, your face and hands should exhibit the strain of the effort. As the center of the spoon handle "heats up," you can bend the ends farther and faster (photo D), always keeping your hands together.

"My spoon-bending trick isn't quite as impressive as Uri Geller's, 'cause I have to do the bending manually," you should say. "I use pure muscle instead of brain waves. But it's really fun to do, and it kinda feels good, and it's a great way to get some attention when you need a waiter."

By now your bending is fast and furious. Slow down now.

"Eventually, the middle of the spoon handle gets so soft you can just — kind of — pull it apart."

4. **Twist the halves of the "spoon" handle, as shown in photo E. By snapping your thumbnails against each other, "click" the spoon halves apart.**

In other words, you break the "spoon" by pulling your hands apart — and the sound effect is provided by your thumbnails clicking against each other. (The thumbnails are in ready-to-click position in photo E.)

At this point, you're sitting there with two empty fists.

"But even though Uri Geller's trick is more mysterious, mine has a better ending. See, I've got the spoon so loosened up that the molecules have completely disintegrated."

5. **Rub your fingers against your palms, as though wiping off something sticky — and then slowly open your hands to show them empty.**

Once the shock has registered, look longingly at your ice cream, turn to whoever's sitting next to you, and ask: "Hey — can I borrow your spoon?"

The Classic Saltshaker Penetration

Let's be frank: There's not a magician alive who doesn't know this trick. It's been in every magic book since the first caveman sawed a woolly mammoth in half. Do this trick at a magic convention, and you'll be laughed out of the joint.

On the other hand, this trick only *became* so popular because it's so darned good. Even if magicians yawn with boredom, *non*magicians generally respond to this effect by becoming regular churchgoers or falling unconscious.

The effect: You claim to be able to make a quarter melt through the tabletop. After repeated attempts, however, you change your mind and make an entire *salt shaker* dissolve through the table — and the shaker lands on the restaurant floor with a resounding clunk.

The secret: If there's a better lesson in magic than this particular miracle, I don't know what it is. The trick's secret relies on the Big Two of magical principles — surprise and misdirection — and the misdirection is not only pathetically easy to create, but overwhelmingly effective.

1. **Borrow a quarter. Place it on the table eight inches in front of you.**

   Wait until a moment when the table is relatively cleared of dining debris — maybe before ordering or between the meal and dessert. Clear your throat with authority.

   "Hey, want to see me make a quarter dissolve through the table?" you might say. "It's incredibly difficult to do, and I'm not sure I can pull it off, but it's really great when it works. Anyone got a quarter I can borrow?"

   It doesn't really matter what kind of coin it is. Put it in front of you, where your dinner plate would normally go. Clear away any glasses or other dinner detritus so that your dining companions have a clear view.

2. **Cover a saltshaker with a napkin.**

   Just take your napkin (paper works better), fold it in half or quarters (whichever is just large enough to cover the shaker), and drape it over the saltshaker. (The folding-up helps make the napkin opaque, and also helps it retain its shape.)

   Mash the napkin around the shaker with your fist, so that the napkin, if gently removed, would retain the shape of the saltshaker. Grip the bottom of the shaker, pinning the napkin around it, as shown in Figure 7-3, photo A.

Figure 7-3:
The napkin takes on the shape of things to come (A). When you move it aside, the saltshaker makes a hasty exit (B). Following your second "failure," move the shaker to the *side* (C). Finally, smash the "shaker" through the table (D).

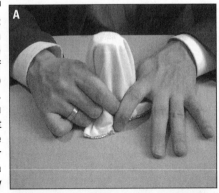

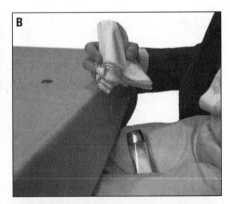

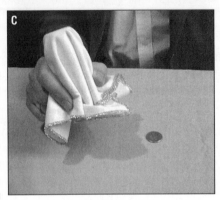

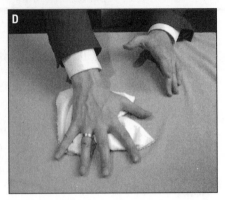

If you feel the urge, you can narrate as you go ("The best magic happens in the dark!") — but really, you don't need to comment at all on what you're doing. Instead, it's better to babble on about how difficult it is to make a metal coin dissolve through two inches of solid Formica.

3. **With great nervousness, put the covered shaker over the coin.**

   Fidget a bit, as though you're preparing to do something sneaky with your hands.

   "All right then, I think we're ready. Here we go. The Coin through the Table — a modern miracle in one act. One . . . two . . . *three!*"

4. **Lift the saltshaker all the way to the edge of the table — and *stare at the coin*. Release just enough pressure on the napkin so that the saltshaker drops into your lap.**

   Read this step again — it's the entire trick. The whole world waits to know whether or not you made the coin disappear. Everybody's staring at the coin. Including you.

All of this presents a window of misdirection wide enough to drive a sport-utility vehicle through. Your hand rests on the edge of the table, as shown in photo B — and lets the saltshaker quietly fall onto your thighs. (P.S. Don't crush the empty napkin shell by accident.)

You'll find that this misdirection works much better if:

- You consciously squeeze your legs together, so that the shaker doesn't slip through to the floor with an embarrassing shattering sound.

- You stare at the coin and utter an expression of dismay that the trick didn't work, such as "Darn!" or "Jeez!" or "Whoa mama!"

- You actually point to the coin with your other hand and *say* something. "I don't get it! It worked when the guy in the magic shop did it!" (If there's any misdirection more powerful than looking at something, it's *pointing* to it.)

5. **Slide the coin a few inches farther from your body. Cover it up again with the empty, saltshaker-shaped napkin.**

   You're going to try again. "Okay, I get another chance; I *told* you this is hard. Ladies and gentlemen: The Coin through the Table, take two. Stand back! One . . . two . . . *three!*"

6. **This time, move the napkin-holding hand to the *side* to expose the still-not-disappeared coin (photo C).**

   Get it? Instead of pulling your hand off the coin *toward* you, as you did in Step 4, this time you move your hand to the side. Why? So that, by the end of the trick, your audience will have forgotten that the salt-shaker was *ever* near the edge of the table. (This is also why you keep nudging the coin farther toward the middle of the table with each attempt — so that the audience will gradually forget that the coin started out close to the table's edge.)

   Now, as far as the crowd is concerned, you've really blown it — twice. Your utterances of frustration should be somewhat more emphatic this time.

   "Jeez, I just don't understand it! I swear, it's not supposed to be this tough. You know, maybe the coin has to be tails-up" (or "heads-up"). "Maybe that's it."

7. **Flip the coin over and set it down again — this time even farther toward the center of the table. Put the napkin/shell over the coin for the third time.**

   "All right. Third time's the charm. The Coin through the Table, take three. This is it! One . . . two . . . *three!*"

8. **Lift your free hand high above the table. Bring it down suddenly onto the napkin shell, smashing it flat against the table. At that precise instant, open your thighs so that the actual saltshaker clatters to the floor.**

   As far as the audience is concerned, you just slammed the salt shaker completely through the tabletop. One instant it was there, the next it was gone (photo D). Talk about mind-blowing!

   Don't worry about breaking the shaker. Ninety-eight percent of the world's salt shakers are constructed to withstand drops from table height.

   The other two percent should be destroyed anyway.

   Now, if the restaurant floor is carpeted, you won't get the satisfaction of hearing the shaker land. It doesn't matter — some wiseacre will *always* peek underneath to see if the shaker really went through. And there it always is, lying on the ground directly underneath its original, top-of-table position!

9. **Pull the edges of the napkin until it's completely flat against the table.**

   Smile sheepishly. "At the last moment, I changed my mind," you might say. "I figured at this rate, it'd probably be easier for me to make the *saltshaker* dissolve through the table instead of the coin!"

10. **Peel up the napkin by one corner, revealing the complete absence of anything saltshaker-like.**

    Why make such a big deal about pressing the napkin flat and then peeling it up? Trust me on this: If you don't, some dullard will inevitably spoil the perfection of the moment by asking to see what's in the crumpled-up napkin!

    Sure, you *could* show him the napkin at this point if he were to ask — there's nothing to find — but why mar the majesty of the moment? Much better to pre-empt any lingering suspicions by flattening and peeling the napkin yourself.

    All that's left at the table now is a quarter and your friends' admiring faces. What better moment to pick up the quarter and make *it* disappear, too? See Chapter 3 for some choice possibilities.

Forks a Lot

In the realms of magic, there's not a lot you can do with forks. The literature is filled with stunts involving spoons and knives, but the great sages have been strangely silent on the subject of their tined siblings.

There's actually no secret at all to this trick — science does all the work for you — but your audience will be left nonplussed nonetheless. Which is, after all, the whole point.

The effect: You balance two forks on the edge of a coin, and the coin on the edge of a glass, as shown in Figure 7-4, photo B. The whole thing looks utterly impossible, a clear violation of the law of gravity — and yet there the whole affair sits, gently teetering, until the onlookers fall to their knees and hail you as a god.

The secret: Okay, the secret is that the long handles of your forks move the forks' center of gravity until it's directly over the edge of the glass. But forget all that mumbo jumbo; as far as you're concerned, it's just plain magic.

1. **Slip a quarter between the top two tines of two opposing forks, as shown in Figure 7-4, photo A.**

   Actually, the bigger the coin, the more astounding the trick. If you can find a silver dollar or half dollar, all the better. But a quarter works fine, too. The important thing is to use *identical* forks, preferably the slightly smaller salad forks, and slip the coin between their *top* two tines. The forks don't intertwine or anything; one's simply in front of the other.

   You'll find all of this setup a bit awkward. The first time you try the trick, the coin will probably slip out of the forks a few times, and your forks may fall away. Keep with it. Be patient. The road to magical nirvana is strewn with danger, Grasshoppa.

2. **Bring the forks/coin apparatus over to a glass. Place the near end of the quarter on the rim of the glass. Slide the forks to the far edge of the coin. Fiddle with the positioning until the forks are stable, and then gingerly take your hands away.**

Figure 7-4:
The forks go on the far edge of the coin's rim (A). Once balanced on the glass (B), the forks sure look weird.

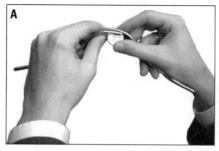

As I said, there's no secret move in this one; the only tough part is having the patience to find the "sweet spot" where the coin, forks, and glass all balance. (The glass doesn't have to be full, but it must be heavy enough not to fall over, which makes you look not so much gifted as klutzy.)

Once you've got the hang of hanging the forks, you can actually start them rocking forward and back as you take away your hands. The whole thing teeters, looking even more creepy and impossible.

In fact, this whole effect is so surreal (photo B) that I don't think you even need patter. The setup takes only ten seconds, and after that, the sweet silence of disbelief is the only sound you need.

The Three-Mug Monte

If you had fun with Don't Show Me the Money, described in Chapter 3, you may enjoy this dinner table follow-up. This trick, a favorite of Advisory Pantheon member Jim Sisti, is named for the *Three-Card Monte,* a card trick performed to this day on the streets of New York, in which unsuspecting tourists are tricked into betting $20 a pop that they can follow the movement of a red queen as it's rapidly slid around the table among two black cards. (**Hint:** The tourist never wins.)

Truths of Magic, Part 7: Don't pre-announce the trick unless you're lying

As you get more into magic, you'll discover that professional magicians almost never tell the audience what's about to happen before it happens. After all, surprise is one of the magician's weapons; if the audience knows what to watch for, the job of mystification is that much harder.

There are only two cases when telling the audience what to expect is okay. First, if you've got a trick that's unbelievably foolproof — if nobody will figure out how you did the trick even when they know what's coming — then pre-announcing the outcome only heightens the apparent impossibility of what you're going to do. (The Tale of the Tightrope Walker in Chapter 2 is one such trick.)

The other time it's okay to announce what you're about to do is when you're *lying.* In such cases, your announcement serves as psychological misdirection. You get the audience all pumped up about watching for the *wrong thing,* leaving you a terrific opportunity to do something else entirely.

In The Classic Saltshaker Penetration is a classic example. You announce that you're going to make the *coin* vanish. You barely even mention the saltshaker. Nobody will hold it against you that you baldly lied to everybody — they're in too much shock.

In this version, however, _you_ play the part of the hapless sap. Your spectator gets to do the sliding around. And yet this time, you always win.

The effect: A spectator hides a Pepperidge Farm Seasoned Salad Crouton under one of three identical overturned coffee cups. While your back is turned, the volunteer slides the cups around, mixing them up as much as desired. But when you turn around again, you instantly identify the cup that's covering the hidden object.

The secret: One of the coffee cups (or mugs, or even paper cups) has a tiny marking. It could be a chip on the handle; it could be a discoloration on the bottom edge; it could be a tiny pencil mark or gravy stain that _you_ make before you start the trick. As long as one of the cups is secretly identifiable, the trick works itself!

1. **Place the three cups upside-down on the table.**

   "Ever hear of an old swindle called the Three-Card Monte? They do it on the streets of major cities. They slide three cards around, a red queen and two black cards. They get a passing tourist to bet $20 that he can follow the movements of the red queen as the card guy slides them around. Of course, the tourists always lose their money."

2. **Introduce the object to be hidden underneath.**

   I say "object" because this trick doesn't have to be done with a Pepperidge Farm Seasoned Salad Crouton. You could just as well hide a crumpled dollar bill, wine cork, or glass eye.

   "But in this little version, I'm going to let _you_ be the smooth operator, and _I'm_ going to be the sucker. I'm going to turn my back. You're going to hide this crouton underneath one of the cups. And then I'll let you switch the cups around. But even so, I'm going to be able to tell you where the hidden thing is — just by trusting my _vibes._ Wanna try?"

   Not one person in 100 will decline such a delightful opportunity to make a fool of the show-off.

3. **Explain the rules.**

   "Okay. Let's call these cup positions One, Two, and Three." Indicate the three cups' positions as they sit there, left to right, as shown in photo Figure 7-5, photo A. "When I turn my back, hide the crouton underneath one of the cups, and then I'll tell you what to do."

4. **Memorize the position of the marked cup (position 1, 2, or 3), and then turn your back.**

   "All right, have you hidden the crouton under one of the cups? Great! Now I'd like you to swap the positions of the _other two cups,_ the ones that don't have the crouton. Tell me when you're done."

Figure 7-5:
See the black smudge (exaggerated for clarity) on the middle cup (A)? In (B), the marked cup isn't where it should be.

Whatever other part of this trick you may forget, don't forget this key step — instructing your helper to swap the two *non-crouton* cups! That move makes the trick work.

5. **Let the swapping begin!**

   Continue instructing your helper. "Actually, you don't need me to tell you how to mix up the cups. You can swap any cups you want, two at a time, as many times as you want. All I ask is that each time you swap, you tell me which two you're switching. Call it out. Say, 'One and three! Two and one!' And so on. Okay? Go for it!"

6. **As your volunteer calls out pairs of cup names, silently track the position of the *marked* cup.**

   In Step 4, you memorized that the secretly marked cup was in position 1, 2, or 3. Whenever your volunteer announces a swap, mentally update the position of the marked cup. Stick out one, two, or three fingers (in your pocket or under your armpit) to keep track.

   For example, suppose the marked cup started out as the middle cup (position 2). You start out by sticking out two fingers. The volunteer calls out, "One and two!" (Your cup is now in position 1, so keep only one finger extended.) The volunteer says, "Two and three!" (Your cup is unaffected. It's still in position 1.) The volunteer yells, "One and three!" (You update your cup to position 3, so you stick out two additional fingers.) And so on.

   Let your volunteer keep swapping cups until everybody's getting itchy to go home and watch TV.

   "Okay, are you finished swapping? May I turn around now?"

7. **Turn around. Stare at the three cups briefly, and then look away. Hold your hands over them, as though feeling their vibes. Turn over the two cups that *don't* hide the crouton — one by one.**

"I sense that the secret crouton is . . . is . . . *not* under this cup. And it's *definitely* not under this one."

8. **Finally, grab the correct cup and flip it over, revealing the crouton.**

"*Here!* Aha! I did it! Where's my twenty bucks?"

Oh, yeah — I guess it'd help if I told you *how* to know where the crouton is.

When you face the cups, compare the position of the marked cup with the position it *should* be in (according to your finger-tracking). The rules are simple:

- ✔ If the cup is where it's supposed to be, you've found your crouton. It's under the marked cup. (So if your fingers indicate that the marked cup is in position 2, and it *is* in position 2, the crouton is there.)

- ✔ If the marked cup should be in position 2 but it's *actually* in position 1, then the crouton is under the *other* cup (cup 3). That is, if you expect to see the marked cup in one position, but it's in another position, forget the cups in both of those positions. The crouton is under the remaining cup.

- ✔ Another example: You turn around. Your fingers claim that the marked cup should be in position 3 — but you see that it's actually in position 2. The crouton is under cup 1 (photo B).

What's so baffling about this trick is that in most cases, even your *volunteer* has lost track of where that crouton is! The fact that you turn around and confidently reveal its location is therefore doubly mystifying.

You have my permission to repeat this trick — using a different volunteer, if possible — at the same sitting. After that, though, move on to something less reminiscent of sleazy hucksters on the streets of New York.

Three-Object Monte, Freakout Edition

The previous trick is a *great* trick, but it's still a trick. The intellectuals in the audience will never figure out how you did it, but they may be left with the vague impression that it had something to do with calling out the names of the cups.

And they're right. If you were *really* magic, you'd be able to find the crouton by ESP alone.

Truths of Magic, Part 8: The confederate army

Using a confederate — also known as a stooge, a plant, a secret assistant — is controversial in magic circles. Purists consider them a violation of the ground rules: magic, they believe, should rely on *your* talents, not some secret helper's. They believe that using a plant is somehow cheating, somehow diminishes the challenge of the art.

Other magicians occasionally use confederates, realizing that some tricks (such as "Three-Object Monte, Freakout Edition") are so good, the use of a confederate is forgivable.

Only you can decide where you stand with confederates; two of the tricks in this book (one in this chapter, one in Chapter 14) require one.

If you do decide to use a silent assistant, here's a tip: get married. A spouse makes the perfect plant, since (a) over your years of going out together, you get very good at your silent signals; (b) you don't ruin the trick by having to explain it to many different new confederates, and (c) you can giggle about it afterward.

That's what makes the Freakout Edition of the same trick, a creation of Advisory Pantheon member Greg Wilson, so powerful. In this one, you seem to operate on feeling. There's no cup-swapping at all. No number-calling, no finger-tabulating. Just a freakish ability to *know*.

In this version, the crouton isn't necessary. Nor, for that matter, are the cups. You can use three of *anything;* Greg Wilson uses cardboard bar coasters or cocktail napkins, mainly because he can write on the underside of one beforehand in case he wants to pull off the Risky Optional Miracle Ending, described in a moment.

The effect: A volunteer touches one of three coasters while your back is turned. You return and correctly identify which one was touched. You repeat the experiment several times — and your guess is always right.

The final (optional) mind-blower: the spectator simply *thinks* of a coaster. If all goes well, you still guess which one — and you prove that you knew ahead of time. You turn over the chosen coaster to reveal a message, in your handwriting: "I *knew* it!"

The secret: This trick requires a *confederate* — a friend who's in on the trick, but nobody else knows it. Your confederate uses a subtle, silent code to signal which cup was selected.

1. **Arrange three coasters on the table.**

   "Hey, will you guys help me with a little experiment?" you might begin. "I was reading about alpha waves in this month's *Omni* magazine. You know, brain waves. Scientists usually can't measure alpha waves without attaching electrodes to your skull, but apparently there's actually some leakage into the air. Look, let's try something. I'm going to close my eyes. While I'm not looking, I want you to rotate one of the coasters. Turn it all the way around till it's facing the same way again. OK? Here we go. Let me know when you're done."

2. **When you open your eyes again, sneak a glance at your confederate's hands.**

Here's the key to the trick: your confederate's eyes were fully open while the coaster was being turned. She knows exactly which one was chosen.

With her hands on the table, she puts her right hand over her left (if the right coaster was chosen) — or her left over her right (if the left coaster was chosen). If the middle coaster is the one, your confederate's hands don't touch at all — they can be anywhere she wants. The photos in Figure 7-6 make this clear.

Don't stare, don't be nervous, don't take long; just get a glimpse of her hand positions, and you know. If possible, get the picture peripherally — don't look directly in her direction at all.

3. **Think for a moment, and then make your "guess."**

"I'm gonna say it's — *that* one. Was that it?" Thump one of the coasters with your fist.

It was, of course.

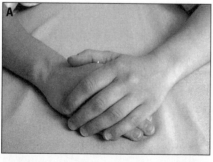
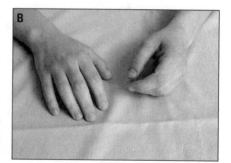
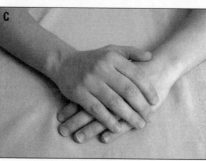

Figure 7-6:
These are the hands of your confederate. The upper hand tells you which object was chosen: the leftmost object (A), the middle object (B), or the rightmost (C).

4. Repeat the "test" several more times.

There are only three objects; just doing the trick *once* successfully could have been chance. The trick gets better as you repeat it.

With each repetition, increase the apparent difficulty. For example:

Second time: "I know, you probably think I was peeking. All right, look — I'll turn my back this time. Do it again." As promised, you turn your back. Yet when you turn around again, you're still able to "guess" which object was handled.

Third time: "OK, listen — let's make it harder this time. Don't turn the coaster this time — just *touch* it, all right? Let me see if I can still pick up any trace of alpha waves, just enough to steer me to the one you touched."

Fourth time: "Listen, let's do it again — but this time, don't make any sound when you touch it. Don't thump or anything. Just lay a couple of fingers on it, silently. Here we go."

Fifth time: "You know what? I think I'm getting the hang of this. One more time. This time, don't even touch it. Just sort of hold your hand over it for a couple of seconds."

After five or six times, you've clearly established your superior alpha-wave-detection skills. Thank your volunteer for helping, assure him that you haven't yet worked your brain-reading skills up to picking up credit-card numbers, and call it a great trick.

Once you're comfortable doing the trick, if you're a gutsy kind of person, you might want to consider the Risky Optional Miracle Ending. It works only once out of three tries. But anyone who sees you succeed (that 33 percent of the time) won't sleep for weeks.

5. *Risky Optional Miracle Ending:* Let your volunteer *think* of one of the coasters.

"One last thing. I really think I'm getting good at this alpha-wave thing. Let's do one final experiment. This time, I'm going to turn my back, and I want you to just *think* of one of the coasters. Focus on that one coaster (with your brain, not with your eyes)."

Your confederate can't help you now — she doesn't know which coaster was chosen, either. This one's up to chance. You've got one-in-three odds of guessing correctly.

Turn around and study the coasters. Make your "guess."

Actually, of course, you choose the coaster with the message on the bottom. Remember? Thinking ahead to the possibility of doing the Risky Optional Miracle Ending, you wrote "I *knew* it!" on the underside of one of the napkins or coasters.

You're going to be wrong two-thirds of the time. If you're wrong, don't sweat it. Shrug and say: "What do I look like, a mindreader!?" Failing on this final attempt doesn't dilute your accomplishment of having been right five or six times in a row; it's still a killer trick.

If you're *right,* however, your audience may form a cult to worship you on the spot.

Especially when you add: "In fact, it wasn't brain waves this time. It was the other skill I've been working on — foreseeing the future. See?"

Turn over the coaster to reveal the "I *knew* it!" message, and sit back to enjoy the pandemonium. Within a nanosecond, one of the onlookers will lean forward and grab at the other two coasters, turning them over to see what's written under them.

The answer, of course, is nothing. The bottoms of the other two objects are as blank as your audience members' minds when they try to guess how you pulled off this killer trick.

Chapter 8

Playing with Your Food

. . . .

In This Chapter

▶ Fun with condiments

▶ The Linking Pretzel trick

▶ How to put beans through your orifices

▶ Bouncing — and levitating — your dinner rolls

. . . .

*A*h, food! The handiness of it! The ordinariness! The abundance! The ability to have your prop and eat it, too!

From the dawn of humanity, eating has meant getting together — it's a social occasion. Consider: Where else, as a magician, do you get a built-in audience with time to kill, a table concealing your lap, and props everywhere? It's got Magic Op written all over it.

It's important to get *any* trick down pat before you perform it in public. But practicing your mealtime magic is especially important. Mess up one of *these* tricks, and you've got nowhere to hide. You must sit there, wallowing in your shame and making small talk, until the check arrives and you can make your ignominious escape.

A Sugar Substitute

This has gotta be one of the best tricks in the book, right here. Advisory Pantheon member Gregory Wilson notes that this trick is astounding, unexpected, easy to do, and — best of all — "clean" at the finish. (*Clean* means that all damning evidence — anything the audience could find that would ruin the trick — is long gone. All that's left are ordinary, ungimmicked materials that don't give any hints about the trick's secret.)

The effect: You drop a wadded-up sugar packet into your fist. But when it comes out the bottom of your fist, it's turned into *Equal* (or another sugar substitute), equally wadded up. Your hands are empty, and there's no trace of a second sugar packet.

The secret: You really do have two packets — one of real sugar and one of Equal. But the series of steps makes the switch appallingly easy, and the trick is un-figure-outable. (You can use the same series of steps, by the way, to convert almost anything into anything: sugar into money, a white Kleenex scrap into a blue one, coal into diamond, and so on.)

1. **Before you begin, crumple up an Equal packet and wedge it into your left fingers, as shown in Figure 8-1, photo A.**

   You're entitled to frown at this first instruction. "What, just crumple it up in full view of everyone at the table?"

   No, of course not. Do the preparation early in the meal, when somebody is telling some drawn-out story about how they bought Intel at 13 and 7/8. Fiddle absently with the little bowl of sugar packets that inhabits nearly every restaurant table on earth. Make off with an Equal packet without making a big deal of it, without saying anything, without even looking at it. Nobody knows you're going to do a trick — for all they know, you're taking a packet because you think your food could use a non-nutritive sweetener.

   If you're nervous about all of this, fine — go to the restroom and, en route, snag an Equal packet from some *other* table. But in the heat of normal dinnertime conversation, people truly aren't interested in you and your sugar bowl.

   After you've got the packet, wad it up as small as you can. Wedge it between the base of your ring finger and pinky, as shown in photo A. Even with the wad of packet thusly wedged — or *palmed,* as pro magicians would say — your left hand should be able to maneuver pretty well. For example, it should be able to assist the crumpling of a real-sugar packet, as you do in the next step.

2. **Grab a real-sugar packet and wad it up.**

   "Hey, have you guys heard about the latest studies on cane sugar? They've been doing some wild chemical tests on it. They found out that if you compress sugar granules into a very small space, like this . . ."

3. **Holding the Equal-equipped hand like a tube, drop the real sugar packet through your hand and onto the table (photo B).**

   Stare at the sugar-packet wad on the table as though the trick didn't work.

   "Huh. Wait a sec."

4. **Pick up the sugar wad by dragging it along the table surface, *all the way to the edge* (photo C), and then drop it back through your left hand.**

Pretend you're trying your little science experiment again.

"So when they analyzed the sugar molecules under heavy compression, they found that —"

But once again, the trick doesn't work. The sugar packet is lying right where it was the first time (photo B).

Figure 8-1:
Prepare by wadding up an Equal packet and wedging it between two fingers (A). Drop a real sugar packet through your hollow fist (B) — and pick it up again by dragging it toward you (C). That way, when the sugar drops into your lap the third time around (C again), you're ready to reveal the Equal packet instead (D).

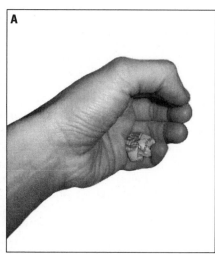

A

B

C

D

5. **Pick up the sugar wad, once again dragging it all the way to the table's edge. This time, however, let it drop into your lap. Without stopping, bring your empty right fingertips, still in wad-holding position, above your left hand. Pretend to drop the packet through your left hand a third time — but this time, let the pre-wadded Equal packet drop out of your left hand.**

"Ah! There we go. See, if you compress sugar enough, it turns into some *equivalent* substance! Get it? Equivalent? Equal?"

6. **As the gales of laughter surround your pun, unfold the Equal packet and clearly show it to your audience (photo D).**

Note how smart the model is in photo D. By splaying her fingers, she's making it painfully clear that both hands are completely empty. The fact that you're clean at the end of this trick is, of course, one of its greatest features. (She's also showing a packet of Sweet 'n' Low instead of Equal, but hey — magicians have to work with whatever's on the table.)

If the Sugar Substitute trick gets a good reception from your dining companions, consider plowing right ahead into another killer trick — the Evaporating Sugar, described below. Do that, and you've got yourself a *routine* — two or more tricks that fit well into a logical sequence — and you're a much better magician than someone who can only do one trick in a row.

The Evaporating Sugar

This trick is even better than the Sugar Substitute bit, if such a thing is possible. This one is based on a trick by Brad Stine, as performed by Gregory Wilson, who's clearly got a thing about condiments.

If you've been flipping through the book looking for an easy, mind-blowing, extremely unusual trick to try, you've found it.

The effect: You open a sugar packet and pour all the sugar into your fist. But when you open your hand, it's empty. Just a teaspoon of sugar makes the magic go down.

The secret: There's no sugar in the packet to begin with. But nobody needs to know that.

Like the Sugar Substitute stunt, this one requires a little advance work. Early in the meal, snag a packet of sugar. (See "A Sugar Substitute" for some advice on how to snag a sugar packet. If you feel self-conscious about doing the prep work in full view of the onlookers, excuse yourself to the bathroom and do the dirty work there. But I'll confess: I usually just do the preparation in my lap, underneath the table.)

In the privacy of the restroom or your own lap, shake all the sugar down to one end of the packet. Using a knife, key, or fork tine, rip a slit across *one side* of the sugar packet at the bunched-up end, about $1/4$ inch from end of the packet. (By bunching up the sugar at one end, you've created a cushion that prevents your cutting implement from going all the way through both sides of the packet.) Don't worry if the slit is ragged-looking; that's a *good* thing. Figure 8-2, photo A, shows this process under way.

After you make the slit, dump out all of sugar except a few grains (photo B). If you're in the bathroom, the sink or garbage can makes a nice final resting place for the sugar. If you're operating in your lap, pour the sugar into your napkin. (Then bunch up the napkin and sit on it, or something, so you won't accidentally shake out the napkin at the end of the meal, which would tack something of an anticlimax onto your magic miracle.)

Finally, slip the prepared packet back into the sugar bowl. Let your innate sense of misdirection and timing be your guide here. You might wait until somebody's showing off her engagement ring, there's a crash in the kitchen, or the entrees are being set down. Or you might absentmindedly grab *several* packets, toy with them, and put them back into the sugar bowl with your packet now among them.

In any case, the hard part is over.

1. **Begin the trick by taking your special packet out of the sugar bowl.**

   If you've just performed "A Sugar Substitute," your line of patter can practically write itself.

   "No, seriously, though, the FDA *has* been doing studies on sugar. They've figured out that it's got a boiling point and an evaporation point, just like water does. Look, I'll show you."

2. **Rip off the top edge of the packet, right along the lines of your previous tear.**

   As shown in photo C, you've just destroyed the evidence of tampering forever. Toss the little quarter-inch-tall strip onto the table or your plate.

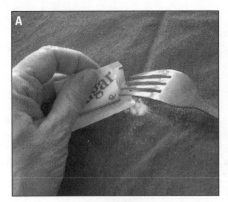

Figure 8-2:
Before you begin, make a slit (A). Ditch the sugar (B). After opening the packet (C), "pour" by holding the packet close to your fist opening (D), and even shaking it up and down (E). The vanishment (F) won't soon be forgotten.

Before doing the phony pouring in the next step, take a moment to make the sides of the paper packet bow outward, so that the packet doesn't look totally flat. From the audience's point of view, you're just puffing out the opening to make pouring easier.

3. **Make a fist. Use the other hand to "pour" all the sugar into it.**

As you can see in photo D, this pouring action entails putting the mouth of the packet right down into your fist. "Pour" by tilting the packet until it's completely upside down.

If you can manage to spill that tiny bit of leftover sugar onto your hand or the table, all the better. You've just proven beyond a shadow of a doubt, psychologically speaking, that everything is normal.

4. **Enhance the illusion by "shaking out the last few grains."**

That is, change your grip on the packet — now you're holding it by its bottom edge and shaking it up and down, tamping it into and out of your fist (photo E). *Bonus fakeout factor:* The rubbing of the paper against your fist makes a little rushing sound that could very well be the sound of sugar pouring out.

5. **Toss the empty packet onto the table. Hold your fist high, still clenched as though it contains a teaspoon of sugar.**

"Now here's the chemical-reaction part. If I let my own natural body heat work on that sugar for just a moment, the sugar starts getting liquidy inside my hand — and then it actually starts to *evaporate.* Ooooh, I can feel it! There it goes!"

6. **Open your fist (photo F).**

The expressions on your dining companions' faces tell you what magic is all about.

By the way: Don't be worried if a few grains of sugar wind up on your fist hand. Actually, that's *good.* A few stray grains convince the audience that there *was* really sugar in that packet — and leave them even more baffled by the ones that got away.

The Linking Pretzels

Magic's full of linking things. Linking rings. Linking paper clips. Linking, Nebraska. (Magic's also full of bad puns.)

But how will you ever make a name for yourself linking things that people have linked before? Link your *pretzels,* however, and you'll be able to say: "Hey look, I linked two pretzels!"

And how many people can say that?

Well, Advisory Pantheon member Chris Broughton can; he's the contributor of this charming snack-food trick.

The effect: You hold up two mini-pretzels. You toss one pretzel into the air — and snap a second pretzel against it. When the flour settles, you've managed to *link* them in midair.

The secret: Two pretzels are pre-linked but hidden in your hand. The rest, as they say, is acting.

Before the trick begins, in the privacy of your own laboratory, break off one loop of a pretzel. Link a second pretzel onto it; use your saliva as glue to press the broken-off loop back to its parent pretzel. (Rubbing the broken-off piece's two ends against your tongue for five seconds should provide enough sticking power.)

Figure 8-3, photos A and B, make all this clear. After wetting the broken ends, hold the broken pretzel piece in place for about ten long seconds. You'll be amazed at how invisible the broken spots are after the pieces are reconnected.

As the figures also make clear, you'll have best results using *mini*-pretzels for this trick — the kind served on airplanes, for example. Standard-sized Thin or Ultra Thin pretzels have less surface area to support a reattached limb by spit alone. Those larger pretzels are also harder to conceal in your hand.

All right — you're ready to go onstage!

1. **Display a loose pretzel in your left hand. Display *one* of the linked ones in your right (the other linked pretzel is hidden).**

   Photo C shows this starting arrangement from your viewpoint. Grip the visible pretzel by one loop so that, if you were to open your lower fingers, the linked pretzel would drop down into view (photo D).

   Here's your patter: "Hey, look what I can do!"

   (Sometimes there's just no point in hiding the real reason for doing a trick — which is to establish that you're the coolest person in the room.)

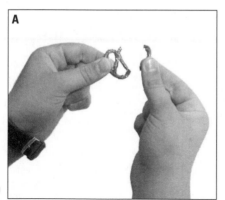

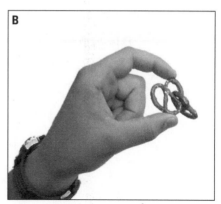

Figure 8-3: Before you begin the trick, break off a loop (A), link it to another pretzel, and press it back together (B). Start by showing what seems to be one pretzel in each hand (C is taken from *your* side). Toss a pretzel from the other hand (E) — and catch it as you release the linked pretzel (F).

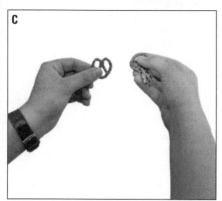

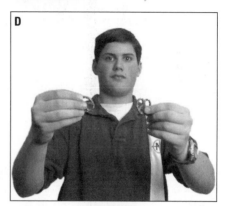

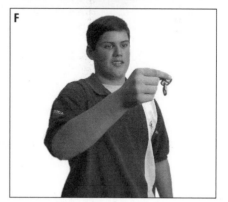

Alternative pretzel magic for the klutzy

If, despite a good 20 minutes in your bedroom, you can't seem to master the pretzel-catching thing you need to pull off in The Linking Pretzels, you don't have to abandon the promising field of snack-food magic altogether. For example, you can still get great mileage out of the spit-as-pretzel-glue concept.

Instead of throwing a pretzel and "catching" it in midair, try this: Start with the linked pretzels in your right hand (as shown in Figure 8-3, photo C, although your left hand in this case

would be empty). With the open bag of pretzels in front of you, slash your right hand into the bag, as though trying to hook something. Try this twice without success. The third time, release the linked pretzel hidden in your hand.

When you pull your hand out of the bag, you've created the illusion that you linked your handheld pretzel with one of the *loose* ones in the bag — without actually requiring any hand-eye coordination whatsoever.

2. **Toss the left-hand pretzel into the air (photo E). Catch it in the fingers of the right hand — and simultaneously release the linked pretzel (photo F).**

    The pretzel you threw winds up caught in the lower fingers of your right hand, but all eyes are on the two linked pretzels now dangling in full view, to the shock and astonishment of all.

This is not, by the way, one of those tricks you can run through in the pantry a couple of times before going out into the living room with it. The Move — catching a falling pretzel at the very moment you're unclenching your fingers to release a hidden linked one — is something you'll have to rehearse until it's smooth. But look at the bright side: Pretzel-catching is a skill that stays with you your entire life and requires much less of a commitment than, say, learning French.

    All right. You've caught the mini-pretzel and successfully released the linked one. Now how do you ditch the hidden one?

    How 'bout this low-tech method: Pop the whole clump of pretzels into your mouth — and eat the evidence.

Beans through the Orifices

The next trick has phenomenal potential for two different kinds of magicians: (a) those who like to create a true aura of the paranormal, and (b) those who like to gross out as many people as possible. Either way, Beans through the Orifices — a specialty of Advisory Pantheon magician Tom Mullica — is unforgettable.

The effect: You insert four beans into various skull orifices — your tear ducts, nose, and ears, for example. After considerable contorting, blinking, and snorting, you manage to suck all four beans through your interconnected sinus cavities and spit them out your *mouth.* Yummy!

The secret: Fear not — you will not actually be asked to propel foreign objects through your cranial cavities. Instead, before inserting a bean into an orifice, you moisten the bean with your mouth — a perfect opportunity to sneak one bean at a time into your mouth *in advance.*

1. **Talk about Indian mysticism and your war days.**

   "You know, when I was stationed in Bombay during the Korean War" — this line of patter is especially entertaining if you're under 25 — "I met an ancient Indian doctor who told me something fascinating about the human body. He told me that all of the various cavities in your head are interconnected! Isn't that wild?"

2. **Show your four beans.**

   "This old Indian guy showed me how to prove it. He took four little lentil beans, like this."

   Hold out your left hand so that you clearly display the four beans. Lentils, frozen peas, or little kidney beans are about right. In a pinch, you can also use match heads, Tic Tacs, or spitballs. (Beans tie in best with the Indian body-magic patter, however; Tic Tacs in 1950 in India were remarkably scarce.)

   "This works best with a little lubrication. You take one bean at a time, like this —"

3. **With your right hand, reach into your left hand to take a bean — fingers toward the audience, thumb toward you. But take *two* beans. Put them directly into your mouth.**

   If you cup your left hand, nobody will see how many beans remain. Keep your left hand in bean-pinching position (shown in Figure 8-4, photo B, although we haven't reached that step yet) all the way to your lips so that nobody can tell you've stolen an extra bean.

4. **Swish saliva around in your mouth. Take *one* bean out of your mouth with your right hand and put it onto the top rim of your left fist.**

   If you can *spit* one bean out without accidentally showing the second one (as shown in photo A), great. Either way, you should now wind up with one bean in your mouth — tuck it between your gums and cheek, if you like — and one on the top of your left fist (photo B).

Figure 8-4:
Moisten "one" bean and spit it out (A). Then pretend to take it from your left fist (B), but actually knock it back inside (C). Insert the nonexistent bean into your eye socket (D). Repeat with subsequent beans, sticking them into your ear canal, other eye, or nose (E). Finally, the beans reemerge from a central location (F).

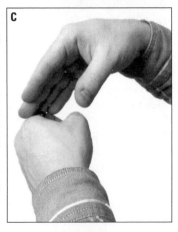

Why are you putting the bean on your fist? Because you need it there for the upcoming bean vanish. But to make this bean rest stop seem necessary for the trick, take this moment to blink your right eye excessively two or three times, as though warming up.

"Okay, now. We put the first, pre-moistened bean into the tear duct. Like this."

5. **Pretend to pick up the bean from the left fist. Actually, though, just brush it into the hole formed by your left fingers (photo C).**

Clever little vanish, huh? Your fingers brush the top of your left fist as though picking up the bean. But in the process, your right fingertips scoot that little wet bean right back into the fist.

Kindly remember to close up your left pinky, however, so that the bean doesn't fall all the way through your fist and land on your sneaker.

6. **Without stopping, move your empty right fingertips up to the corner of your right eye (photo D). Pretend to insert it into the tear duct.**

By "pretend," I don't just mean move your fingertips there. Ever get a speck of dust in your eye? It's *annoying.* Now imagine a speck of dust the size of a Tic Tac, and you'll appreciate the acting challenge ahead of you. This should *not* look pleasant. Don't draw out the moment — three seconds of blinking and squinting is plenty — but don't deprive your audience of the impact, either.

"All right," you say when it's over. "Three beans left." And, indeed, if you show your left palm openly now, there are truly three left. (One's still in your mouth.)

"And now let me prepare the second bean."

7. **Repeat Steps 3, 4, and 5.**

That is, pretend to put one bean in your mouth to lubricate it — but actually take *two* beans. Swish the beans around in your mouth and spit out, or take out, only one. There are now *two* beans in your mouth, but nobody knows that.

Put the newly moistened bean on your left fist, take a deep breath (to justify this moment), and "pick it up" again (brushing the bean into your left fist in the process).

8. **Put "Bean #2" into your ear canal. Pretend to ram it way down inside with your right pinky.**

If the ear-canal business is a bit much, you could always just stick Bean #2 into your *other* tear duct. The important thing is to simulate profound discomfort.

When this stage is over, you can show that, indeed, only two beans remain on your left palm. "All right: Bean Three. Let me moisten it up a little . . ."

9. **Repeat Steps 3, 4, and 5. Then put "Bean #3" up your nostril with a sharp, snorting inhaling sound (photo E).**

Act it up! Nothing gooses a quiet crowd like seeing you vacuum a bean up your nose.

"All right. One bean left. And this one goes straight into the mouth." (What you think — but do not say — is, "To join the three I've already got in there!")

10. **Put the final bean directly into your mouth. Begin a gruesome sequence of contortions, snorts, eye blinks, and facial tics as you "work" the beans through your sinus cavities and back into your mouth.**

"With enough suction," you can splutter between spasms, "you can actually maneuver the beans — back — into — the mouth through the — sinus — cavities . . ."

11. **Hold out your palm in front of your mouth. One by one, spit out the four beans (photo F).**

There they finally sit, glistening with spit, phlegm, tear fluid, and ear wax. Hold out your hand to an onlooker.

"Wanna heat these up?"

Bouncing the Roll

Surely you've been there: You're dragged out to dinner with your spouse's ex. Or you're roped into attending the most boring corporate luncheon in creation. Or you're out to cash in on the "free five-star dinner for two" you won in exchange for sitting through a sales pitch for a timeshare resort — and the five-star restaurant turns out to be a greasy spoon where only the cockroaches eat right.

The challenge: How do you express your contempt for such meals without being a brat? Try this little gag.

The effect: You pluck a dinner roll out of the basket and bounce it off the floor. It's so old and rubbery that it rebounds high into the air.

The secret: You actually throw the thing back up into the air (below table level), with a little help in the sound-effects department from your foot.

1. **Pick up a dinner roll. Express your unhappiness with its freshness.**

"Yikes," you might say after gnawing it. "I'd say these rolls are a few days past their peak of flavor perfection. *Look* at this!"

2. **Pretend to slam the roll downward to the floor (see Figure 8-5, photo A).**

   Your hand should start above table level and finish below the table. Let a tenth of a second elapse, and then:

3. **Stomp your foot to represent the roll hitting the floor. A fraction of a second later, (below table level) toss the roll high into the air.**

   This tossing business (photo B) is a wrist movement only; your arm and shoulder shouldn't move. From the audience's side, it looks like photo C.

   Practice the timing and the tossing. It won't look very impressive to *you,* but from the audience's side, the effect is hilarious — it looks like you just bounced the roll off the floor.

4. **Catch the roll on its way back down and put it back into the basket.**

   And next time, do your homework before going out to eat at a joint like this!

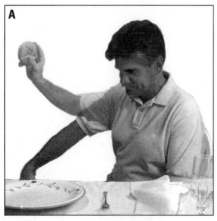

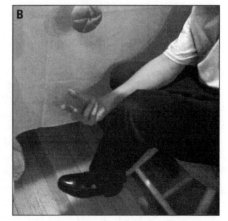

Figure 8-5: From the audience's point of view, you throw a roll down toward the floor (A) — and it bounces back up again (C). Actually, though, your foot provides the sound effect, while your hand provides the return propulsion (B).

The Floating Dinner Roll

The experiments with sugar packets at the beginning of this chapter point out the beauty of *routing* — performing nicely related tricks in succession. If Bouncing the Roll gets a good reaction but the dinner is *still* boring everyone silly, you could follow up with this somewhat more mystical dinner-roll illusion.

Now, in the life of magic you'll lead after reading this book, you'll almost certainly hear some magician, magic book, or magic magazine refer to The Zombie, which is a famous illusion. The Zombie is a display of unbelievable beauty when performed well — a shiny chrome sphere rises from its stand, lifting the big silk scarf that covers it. The ball seems to float around with a mind of its own, peeping over the top of the scarf, scooting down around the edges, and occasionally darting into the center of the scarf so violently that the magician is tugged along.

As stunning as The Zombie is, you, the novice magician, probably won't find many occasions where it looks natural to whip out a chrome sphere. So here's a trick, recommended by Advisory Pantheon member George Schindler, that creates the same kind of effect — and can be almost poetic if you perform it well.

The effect: You cover a dinner roll with a napkin. Slowly, magically, it seems to rise up, floating into the air underneath the napkin, apparently under its own control. Finally it lands again. You take the napkin away, and there's the roll — just an average dinner roll.

The secret: Behind the napkin, you stab the roll with the fork. You're actually controlling the roll from the corner of the napkin (thanks to your hand on the fork). But knowing how it works is only 5 percent of this one. The remaining 95 percent is in the showmanship.

1. **Put a roll on your plate. Cover it with your napkin. Grasp your fork's handle through the corner of your napkin.**

   (Hint: Paper napkins don't work for this. Cloth only.)

   If you've draped your napkin artfully, it can cover up the fork, too. Note to right-handers: Although the fork probably started out on the left side of your plate, you've got a whole meal in which to place it to the right side, where it'll be in good position for this illusion.

2. **Under the pretense of adjusting the napkin, steady the roll just long enough to stab it with the fork.**

   All of this goes on beneath the napkin. But if you were to lift the napkin, you'd see the shenanigans shown in Figure 8-6, photo A (which is shot from your point of view).

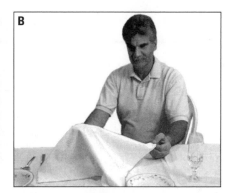

Figure 8-6:
If you looked under your napkin, you'd see the roll that you stabbed with your fork (A). As you concentrate on the roll (B), it starts to rise (C). The roll takes on a mind of its own, lunging from side to side (D) and resting on your napkin (E). Finally, you break the roll in half to show it was all magic (F).

During your practice sessions, experiment with *where* to stick the fork. If the tines pierce the crust somewhat below center, you may get more leverage when it comes time for the levitation.

You *could* make up some patter about how the chef has added too much yeast to the rolls, and they've been rising too much. You could also use this trick as a follow-up to Bouncing the Roll, described earlier in this chapter, saying something about how, apparently, *all* the rolls are airborne tonight.

But you may find that something more serious sets a better mood for this freaky display. "Every now and then, when the conditions are just right," you might begin, "and the company is good, and the meal is perfection, everything feels a little bit lighter than air. Even the humble dinner roll just seems to become enchanted."

3. **Grasp both near corners of the napkin — thumbs on top, fingers beneath. Pinch the fork handle (beneath the cloth) between your right thumb and forefinger. Slowly, steadily, turn your hands under, rotating the fork to a steeper angle, pushing the roll upward against the middle of the cloth.**

Photo B shows the early stages. Stare intently at the roll. Try to make it seem disconnected from you. You're just holding the cloth, remember — you've got nothing to do with the levitation.

Very slowly, majestically, let the roll and cloth "lead" your hands up off the table (photo C).

4. **As the enchantment builds, let the roll start pulling the cloth upward, outward, backward, left, and right.**

Photo D shows one of these lunges.

Once you get good at creating the mood and the motion, you may even want to try this advanced maneuver (not suitable for all roll shapes): Let the napkin hang straight down, flat, from between your hands. To do that, you'll have to angle the fork away from the cloth so that the roll is suspended in space in front of your chest, hidden by the napkin.

That's a great-looking move in itself — as though the roll has just vanished — but the best is yet to come. Slowly, carefully, without making your finger movements apparent, guide the fork back up to the top edge of the napkin, so that the roll peeps out from behind the cloth (photo E). Let the napkin sag slightly, so that the roll appears to be resting on the top edge.

After a moment of this, let the roll fall out of sight again — only to erupt into the center of the cloth, beginning another lunge again (as shown in photo D).

5. **After you've made your point, let the roll slowly sink to the plate or table again. With your left hand, reach under to hold the roll steady — and then whip the napkin — with the fork — away. Ditch the fork in your lap.**

As a final touch, break open the roll (photo F), as though to show that there's nothing inside it. What you're actually doing, of course, is destroying the evidence that the crust was ever pierced.

The Floating Dinner Roll is one of those tricks that cries out for a camcorder to help you practice. You can't look into a mirror to see how well you're performing, because your eyes, riveted to the roll, are an essential part of the picture.

Grace under Fire, Part 4

Advisory Pantheon member Chad Long won't soon forget performing at a Halloween party a couple of years ago. The costumes were great, the crowd was rowdy, and Chad was about to do a sensational card trick.

The audience member who volunteered to help him for one card trick was dressed as a pirate, complete with eye patch and machete (a razor-sharp sword, usually used to hack through sugar cane). Unfortunately, this particular pirate had drunk quite a bit too much rum.

Chad shuffled a deck of cards, and then set it down on the table. "Now, if you wouldn't mind cutting the deck for me."

That's all the invitation the staggering pirate needed. He grabbed his machete, whirled it over his head, and brought it down with all his might on Chad's deck, chopping halfway through the deck — and missing Chad's thumb by a fraction of an inch.

Shaken but not stirred, Chad pulled himself together.

"Okay then," he said. "Why don't we try a nice coin trick?"

Chapter 9

Matches Made in Heaven

· ·

In This Chapter

▶ Making ashes dissolve through your hand

▶ Making ashes dissolve through someone else's hand

▶ Fun with matchbooks and matchboxes

▶ Making matches — and amazed spectators — leap into the air

· ·

Matches are classic magic props: cheap, accessible, and easy to hide. They also make the tricks you're doing more satisfying thanks to the infintesimal simulation of danger. Speaking of which, the tricks in this chapter generally don't come even close to igniting anything valuable, like the house or human flesh. Still, they *are* matches. Use discretion when your audience includes children, vandals, or pyromaniacs.

Making an Ash of Yourself

Nothing livens a dull get-together like experiments that involve chemicals dissolving through human limbs. This trick, the ultimate close-up effect, falls squarely into that category. It's suitable for bar bets, catching the eye of attractive strangers, and auditioning for *The X-Files*.

The effect: You make a diagonal mark on your palm, using a sooty, burned-out match as your magic marker. When you make a similar slash — going the opposite direction — on the other side of your hand, it mysteriously melts away and reappears on your palm, forming a perfect X with the original slash. Not to be performed for the easily freaked out.

The secret: The act of closing your hand transfers soot from the opposite halves of the original slash, neatly forming an X.

1. **Break off the head of a burned match against an ashtray or plate.**

   Studies have shown that the burned *neck* of a match does better as a "magic marker" than the head itself; therefore, a match that's had the chance to burn down just below the head works best.

   "Have you ever studied ancient Incan mythology?" you might begin. (Feel free to substitute your own obscure culture.)

2. **With the burned-out match, draw a diagonal slash that crosses over the life line of your left palm (see Figure 9-1, photo A).**

   The slash should be dark. If you're not getting much soot from your match, try a different angle, a different match, or a different trick.

THE HARD PART

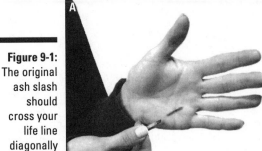

Figure 9-1: The original ash slash should cross your life line diagonally (A). When you close your fist tightly to make the second mark (B), and then "rub it through" your hand (C), you wind up making a carbon copy of the original slash on your palm (D).

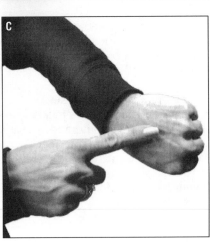

"The ancient tribal chiefs believed that a single mark on the hand made of finely burned bamboo ash could serve as an indicator for a person's future happiness."

3. **Close your left hand into a tight fist. Turn it palm down. Using the same match, make a similar slash on the back of your left fist (photo B).**

Technically, you should make this slash at 90 degrees to the original one. But what with all the fist-making and knuckle-turning, who's keeping track?

"The test goes like this. The Incan priest would make an identical mark on the back of your hand going the opposite direction . . ."

4. **Throw the match away. With your right index finger, rub the back of your left hand until the slash disappears (photo C).**

Don't ask me why match-soot marks disappear when rubbed. Just be grateful for this chemical anomaly.

"According to the legend, only one outcome of this test can foretell a life of happiness, fulfillment, and wealth. And that's if rubbing the mark makes it melt through your skin, through your muscle, through your bone, all the way through to . . ."

5. **Open your left palm to reveal the X, as shown in photo D.**

"*. . . the other side!*"

Now, you'll only have an X on your palm if (a) you made the original slash diagonally across the fold in your palm flesh, (b) the original slash was nice and dark, and (c) it was at the correct angle. The trick works by transferring each half of the original slash mark to the flesh on the opposite side of your palm fold. So if you just make a random marking, when you reopen your hand, you'll find nothing but a random marking.

And according to ancient Incan legend, *that* means the trick's a flop.

Ashes through Someone Else's Palm

This trick, suggested by Advisory Pantheon member Jade, makes a great follow-up to Making an Ash of Yourself (see the previous trick). The concept of ashes dissolving through a hand is the same as in the Making an Ash of Yourself trick — but this time, you make them dissolve through someone *else's* hand.

The reaction you get to this trick, however, is ten times greater than the slash-on-the-palm trick. Nobody will buy that baloney about ancient Incan rituals — but *this* trick will keep them awake nights.

The effect: You put some ashes on the back of a volunteer's hand. When she rubs it, the ashes disappear and show up on the inside of her palm.

The secret: You place some ash on her palm before the trick even begins.

You won't be able to get away with using burnt-match soot in this trick. Instead, you need genuine, Grade A, government certified ashes. In these modern times, the usual source of ashes — cigarettes — is increasingly scarce in restaurants and workplaces.

But the resourceful magician isn't daunted. If you really want ashes, burn a napkin corner on your bread plate. Or substitute another material altogether, such as pepper or sugar grains (although ashes are less noticeable during the trick and more visible at the climax).

In any case, the dirty work takes place before the trick even starts. Get a dab of the ashes on the tip of your right middle finger before anyone suspects you're about to do a trick. (If you're using pepper or an alternative condiment, you may have to lick your middle finger first.) Thus prepared, you're ready to begin.

1. **Ask a volunteer to hold out her hands flat. Demonstrate.**

   "Hey, let me show you something." (Or, if you've just finished the Making an Ash of Yourself trick, start out by announcing that ashes tend to dissolve through *anyone's* flesh, as you are about to demonstrate.) "Hold out your hands like this."

2. **Take her hands, your thumbs on top, and pull them several inches toward you, as though correcting her positioning (Figure 9-2, photo A).**

   "Right about here — good," you can say.

   The real purpose of this action, of course, is to transfer some of the ashes to her palm without her being aware of it. Don't wipe, don't press, don't even think too hard that you're getting stuff onto her palm; if you touch her hand for that instant, the transfer takes care of itself.

   Congratulations — the hard part is over.

3. **Dip your right middle finger (the ashy one) into the ashes on the plate or ashtray.**

   Notice how cleverly you just destroyed the evidence that you had ashes on your fingertip. Now there's *supposed* to be ash on your fingertip. (By the way, you can now invite your volunteer to take away her non-ashed hand. Its services will no longer be required.)

   "Now, if you don't mind, I'm going to put some ashes on the back of your hand," you can say. "And just to make sure there's no funny business, close your hand into a fist, okay?"

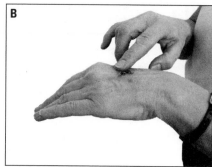

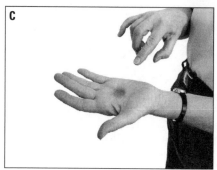

Figure 9-2:
The transfer takes place when you're adjusting your volunteer's hand positions (A). She rubs the ashes into one fist (B) — only to find that the ashes have penetrated (C)!

4. **Transfer some of the ash onto the back of her hand (photo B). Instruct her to rub them into invisibility.**

   "Now, I'm going to back off here. I want you to do this entire trick yourself, because this is where it really starts to get freaky. What I'd like you to do is rub those ashes with your other hand. Keep rubbing until they evaporate and disappear."

5. **Instruct your volunteer to open her hand and look at it (photo C).**

   "The ashes may have looked like they were evaporating, but actually they were dissolving directly through your hand!"

   And indeed, if all went well, those ashes you transferred to her palm in Step 2 are plainly visible — a black smudge that serves as a testament to your powers over time, space, and the universe.

The Three-Matchbox Shell Game

The *shell game* is an ancient favorite of scam artists all over the world. The smooth operator hides a pea underneath one of three nutshells on a table. She then slides the shells around a few times; when she stops, she gets a sucker to bet $20 that he knows where the pea is now. Naturally, the sucker always guesses wrong, and the smooth operator pockets the $20.

In this delightful variation, a favorite of Advisory Pantheon member Christopher Broughton, you don't have to rustle up those hard-to-come-by nutshells. Ordinary match boxes do the trick — and wow, what a trick.

The effect: You put a nickel into one of three matchboxes on the table. After switching the boxes around a few times, you challenge your onlookers to guess which box contains the coin. They're always wrong, no matter how carefully they try to keep track.

(Please note: This betting game is for entertainment purposes only. In other words, spend the money you win on movies and other entertainment.)

The secret: The matchboxes are empty the whole time. But thanks to a rattling matchbox strapped to one wrist, you can make *any* of them seem to contain the nickel just by shaking it.

This trick is *fairly* impromptu. That is, it requires some setup, but you can do the pre-trick surgery on the spot wherever you're going to be performing. Excuse yourself to the bathroom (for example), secretly armed with two matchboxes and (if you're at a restaurant) a dinner knife.

Cut a slit at the back end of one matchbox's drawer. The slit must be big enough to let the nickel slip out quietly, as shown in Figure 9-3, photo A.

While you're still in the bathroom, put a nickel into a second matchbox. With a rubber band, fasten this matchbox tightly to your left wrist, underneath your sleeve. (Your watchband, if you have one, might also work to hold the matchbox in place at your wrist.) If you're not wearing long, slightly loose sleeves, run home and change.

Photo A, left hand, shows this setup. Get the idea? Whenever you shake an empty matchbox with your left hand, you and your audience will hear the rattling of the coin in your wrist-strapped matchbox. The illusion is irresistible.

Whenever you shake an empty matchbox with your *right* hand, on the other hand, you and your audience will hear nothing. The matchbox is empty.

1. **When you're ready to perform, place a duplicate nickel into the slitted matchbox. Place it on the table. Close the drawer.**

   Because there really is a nickel in the box at this point, you can use your right hand to rattle the box.

   "Ever hear of the shell game?" you can begin. "It's a classic con. The huckster puts a pea under one of three walnut shells on the table, switches the shells around, and then bets the crowd that they can't find the pea. Nowadays, the only place you find peas and walnuts under one roof is at the grocery store, so I'll substitute a nickel and three matchboxes."

2. **Pick up the coin-holding matchbox with your right hand. Hold it vertically in the air — so that the slot is pointing directly down into your hand — and shake it to rattle the coin.**

   "Okay, I'm giving you notice," you can say as you shake the box. "The coin is starting in this box right here."

3. **Let the nickel slip out of the slit and into your waiting hand. Set the empty box back on the table.**

   Obviously, your audience doesn't know you've just let the coin out of the box. As shown in photo B, the entire "steal" is concealed inside your fist.

   "Okay now — follow the money!"

4. **Mix up the matchboxes on the table (photo C).**

   At the outset of your little swindle adventure, don't move the boxes around very much. Just exchange them four or five times, and do it slowly.

   "All right. Who knows where the nickel is?" Let your audience guess.

5. **Prove the audience either right or wrong by shaking the guessed matchbox with your left or right hand (photo D).**

   Now the fun begins! Suppose the audience guesses the middle match-box. Pick it up with your right hand (which, by the way, keeps the hidden nickel — clenched in the middle, ring, and pinky fingers — for the entire duration of the trick). Shake the box. To the audience members, who are sure that they've guessed the correct box, the resulting silence is deafening.

   "Ooh, close, but no cigar box," you might say as you shake the silent, empty box. "You've got to pay closer attention! It's actually over here, in *this* box!" And now you pick up one of the other boxes with your *left* hand; when you shake the matchbox, the sound of your hidden wrist box seems to confirm that the coin is present.

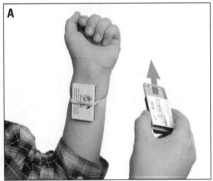

Figure 9-3:
Your preparation in the restroom: a matchbox rubber-banded to your wrist, and another with a slit in it (A). As you pick up the matchbox, steal the coin (B). Then the game is on (C); the real coin is clenched in your right hand throughout. You show that the spectator's guesses are wrong by shaking a different box with your rattling left hand (D). Finally, "dump out" the coin from any one of the match-boxes (E).

Occasionally, though, tease the audience by "letting" them be right. Do so by picking up the guessed matchbox with the *left* hand and shaking *it.* Once again, the sound of the nickel in your wrist-strapped box immediately identifies the matchbox you picked up as the one containing the coin.

In other words, you play God here. You let the audience guesses be either right or wrong depending on which hand you use to pick up the guessed box.

If you're betting your audience a penny per guess, therefore, you might let them be right during "practice rounds" where no money is actually at stake. But after they've put a penny on the line, then, of course, you can consistently prove them wrong.

All of this hilarity can continue for as long as you deem appropriate. I can't give you a precise routine; it's different every time you perform. You have to gauge when it's time to quit according to your audience's reaction — keep going while they're thrilled and baffled; stop when they're bored or pulling Mace dispensers from their wallets.

6. **When it comes time to end the trick, pick up any matchbox. Turn it upside down. Push the drawer out into your right hand — and let the hidden nickel drop onto the table (photo E).**

The coin looks as though it's dropping from the matchbox, not from your hand.

At this point, you're not exactly clean; your matchboxes can't be inspected, or the audience will discover the slit in one of them. Therefore, the best way to finish the trick might be to scoop up all three boxes, shove them into your bag or your pocket, and issue a final warning to the crowd. "Next time, never play betting games with a known magician!"

Weighing the Matchbooks

This little puzzler, a favorite of Advisory Pantheon member Jim Sisti, is helped along by a bogus pseudo-scientific explanation that could just *possibly* explain what's happening. In the meantime, you've performed an impressive stunt that could apparently go wrong and make you look foolish.

Audiences love that stuff.

The effect: While your back is turned, an audience member tears one match from one of seven matchbooks on the table. Just by weighing each matchbook in turn, you're able to identify which matchbook has thus been lightened.

The secret: Fortunately for those of us who aren't actually supernatural, the method for this trick has nothing to do with the weight of the matchbooks. Instead, you've prepared the matchbooks by jamming their covers shut. When you return from hiding your eyes, you simply check to see which cover is now closed loosely.

Incidentally, not every matchbook on earth is jammable. The trick works best with seven *different* matchbooks; if that's what you plan to use, test each before beginning the trick to make sure its cover will stay jammed. On the other hand, if you're at a restaurant and all you can come up with is seven *identical* matchbooks, the trick's still good — just make sure the particular matchbook type you're using is jammable.

1. **Lay the matchbooks in a row on the table. Under cover of pretending to pre-weigh each book, jam its cover shut, hard.**

   Almost simultaneously, check to see if each matchbook cover is satisfactorily jammed (by imperceptibly tugging with your thumb). Figure 9-4, photo A, shows this testing in progress.

   "I've been spending my weekends in sensory-deprivation tanks down at the Y," you could begin. "I'm trying to heighten my sensitivity to the five senses. Look, I'll show you how far I've come."

2. **Explain the rules.**

   "I'm going to turn my back. While I'm not looking, I'd like you to open one matchbook, tear out one match, close the cover, and put the matchbook exactly back where it was. There must be no visible sign to tip me off as to which matchbook you selected. Don't put it back upside-down or get coffee stains on it or cough nervously when I approach it. Okay, ready? Here I go. Let the sensory deprivation begin."

   The tearing-out-a-match business is, of course, pure verbal misdirecton. It has absolutely nothing to do with the trick.

3. **Turn your back until the volunteer indicates that the deed is done. Turn to face the matchbooks. Pick up one or two at a time, as shown in photo B, as though you're weighing them.**

   What you're really doing is subtly tugging at each matchbook cover with your thumb to see if it's still tightly jammed. When you find the matchbook cover that isn't, you've got your man (or in this case, your match).

   "Now, what I'm going to do here is to heft each matchbook," you can say while you work. (It's fun to stare thoughtfully into space as you compare matchbooks. Because your actual tip-off doesn't involve looking at the matchbooks, avoiding them with your gaze only adds to your credibility as a super-sensitive weigher.)

   "I'm going to try to identify which matchbook is now one match lighter."

Figure 9-4:
In pre-weighing (A), you're actually jamming each cover shut. When the big moment comes (B), you can easily identify which book has been opened.

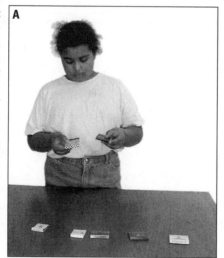
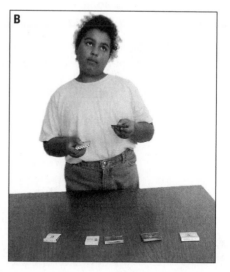

4. **After "weighing" all of the matchbooks, return triumphantly to the one with the loose cover. Hold it up accusingly and ask if it's the one.**

"I'm going to say it's — this one! Am I right?"

And of course, you are. You're always right — you're the magician.

The Static-Electricity Test

Advisory Pantheon member and sleight-of-hand guru Dan Harlan had plenty of tricks to suggest for inclusion in this book. Most, alas, are so technically difficult, they'd probably require surgery to have extra joints installed in your fingers.

This one, however, is a priceless classic. You can do it with wooden matches, as Dan does, or you can do it with toothpicks, as I do. You can do it using your own hand as a platform, or you can use the edge of a table. You can perform it for other people, or you can do it for your own amusement for hours on end.

The effect: You balance a toothpick or wooden match off the edge of your hand. You take a second one and rub it on your sleeve to build up a static charge. Explaining that negative ions repel, you touch the tip of the "charged-up" stick against the tip of the first one — which leaps four feet up into the air with an audible static pop.

Yet for some reason, nobody else seems to be able to repeat your little science-fair project. You shrug it off; must be your magnetic personality!

The secret: Static electricity has nothing to do with it. You simply flick the end of the "charged-up" match or toothpick with your middle fingernail — in a small, undetectable way. The other match's trajectory into space, however, is anything *but* small and undetectable.

1. **Lay a toothpick or wooden match at the edge of your left hand or the table.**

   In these photos, I use toothpicks. They're slightly easier to work with.

   "Did I ever tell you about my seventh-grade science-fair project?" you can ask the onlookers as you balance Toothpick 1 on the edge of your hand (or the table, or even someone else's hand). Only an inch or so needs to hang off the edge.

   "It was pretty cool," you continue. "I proved that certain kinds of wood, like the Adirondack Pine used in toothpicks" (or "wooden matches") "can conduct a charge just as well as iron does. All I have to do is build up an electrostatic charge here . . ."

2. **Rub Toothpick 2 vigorously against your sleeve.**

   Instead of rubbing it up and down, rub it repeatedly in one direction, lifting it away from your sleeve between strokes. You'll see why in Step 5.

3. **Bring the far end of the "charged-up" toothpick close to the end of Toothpick 1 (see Figure 9-5, photo A). Assume launching position.**

   By "launching position," I mean the hand grip shown in photos B (what your audience sees) and C (what the wall would see if it could crouch down really low and peer into the shadow of your hand).

   The grip is everything. After rubbing Toothpick 2 on your sleve, pinch it hard between your thumb and index finger, about $1/2$ inch from the end (photo C). You should find it relatively natural to press your right middle fingernail (if it's long enough) or fingertip (if you have stubby nails) against the near end of the toothpick.

   Check your positioning: Thumb on top, index finger underneath, middle finger underneath, too, pressing upward on the end of the wood. In order for your charged-up toothpick to be perfectly horizontal, you'll probably have to cock your wrist down at a slightly unnatural angle.

   "Once you've built up enough negative ions, you touch it against another toothpick that hasn't been charged, and watch out —"

Figure 9-5:
Balance on toothpick off the edge of your hand (A). Bring the "charged up" toothpick's tip just underneath (B). Let your middle finger do the snapping (C) — pop goes the tabled toothpick on its own little space mission (D).

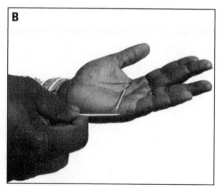
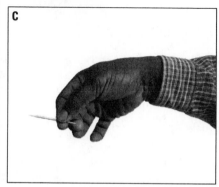

4. **Position the tip of your "charged-up" toothpick so that it's just underneath the tip of the other one (photo B). Snap your middle nail (or fingertip) upward against the end of the toothpick.**

   Photo C shows the snap just before it happens. The movement feels a lot like you're snapping your fingers — except you're snapping your middle finger against a piece of wood instead of your thumb.

   Two wonderful things happen if you've done this right: first, the far end of the pinched toothpick makes a tiny but powerful snap upward. The other pick goes flipping high up into the air. Second, if you've managed to do the snapping thing with your middle finger *nail,* there's an audible click. Of course, it's your nail popping past the end of the toothpick, but it *sounds* like a static charge going off.

   As the other toothpick goes flying, finish your sentence: "— negatives repel!"

5. Offer the onlookers a chance to try.

Of course, there won't be any electricity when they try. They'll rub until their sleeves are almost worn through, and then they'll touch the tips of the toothpicks — and absolutely nothing will happen.

Frown and look confused. "Jeez, that's odd. Maybe it's because you're rubbing back and forth," you can say. "I think you're canceling out the charge. Try rubbing all in one direction, as I did."

They try that; still nothing happens.

Ever helpful, you can now theorize that the sleeve fabric is causing the problem. "I don't know. Maybe it's the material of your shirt. Here, try mine."

Offer your sleeve for toothpick-rubbing. Naturally, this gesture will only attract attention from more people.

Eventually, after enough frustration, some obsessive spectator usually begins to suspect foul play. This is where the trick becomes its most glorious: He'll correctly assume that you're flicking the toothpick — but wrongly assume that you're doing it with your *wrist*. He'll bend down and try to flip the table-edge toothpick into the air by jerking his whole hand upward.

Funny thing about toothpicks (or wooden matches), though: some bizarre law of reverse physics applies to them. The harder you jerk your hand upward, the less the table-edge toothpick jumps! Your skeptical friend will succeed only in knocking Toothpick 1 pathetically onto the floor.

The mystery, confusion, and entertainment factor continue to grow as you go. This, my friend, is magic.

Intermission

*T*he vast majority of the world's magicians are amateurs.

Now, in magic, the word amateur is nothing to be ashamed of. *Amateur* doesn't imply anything about your ability, as the word might when applied to, say, a brain surgeon. It says only that magic isn't your primary source of income. There are some *incredibly* talented amateur magicians.

The next largest group of magicians is *semi-pro*. These people have day jobs. They do magic on the side — for parties, for conventions, for other paying customers as they come along — but magic is a secondary career.

Finally, a very small percentage are professional magicians. You might imagine that professional magic is the most glamorous, exciting career on earth — and, to be sure, it is very rewarding. But it's also a brutally competitive job, with an unsteady paycheck that won't make you rich unless your name is David Copperfield, Penn & Teller, Lance Burton, or Siegfried & Roy. It's hard work, too; you must constantly keep abreast of new effects, work them into your act, and somehow get your gear and your assistants to the right place at the right time.

At the moment, I'm guessing you fall into the amateur class. But suppose you become hooked on magic. Suppose you get offered money to perform somewhere — and you get the tingle of imminent Semi-Pro-hood. What then?

To help you visualize what lies down the road, I'd like to tell you about a certain semi-pro magician I know. I'll call him Alex (although his real name is Harold Bernstein, 273 Parklane Dr., Minnewonka, WI, 39924; phone (514) 388-3827, fax (514) 231-4776; e-mail *hbernstein@bookworks.com*).

A Day in the Life of a Semi-Pro

Alex's obsession with magic began when he was six, when his mom bought him a paperback book called *Spooky Tricks* at a first-grade book fair. From that book, Alex learned how to make a coin cry and how to make it look like he was sticking pins into his thumb through a handkerchief.

Alex's classmates adored these tricks. They'd ask Alex to repeat them again and again — which he did. Eventually, through, his classmates saw the piece of sponge that made the coin cry and the piece of carrot that Alex stuck the pins into under the handkerchief.

Without these prized secrets, Alex felt less special. He vowed to learn new tricks that were so deceptive, none of his friends would spot their secret workings. He hit the library. All the magic books were in section 793.8 in the Dewey Decimal system — his first time on the grown-up side of the library.

These musty old books intimidated him at first, with their two-inch-long words and ancient-looking photographs of hands performing complicated card and coin manipulations. He did, however, continue to practice, impressing his family with his enthusiasm. Alex's father was so pleased with his son's newfound interest that he promised to buy him a few small tricks at the local magic shop.

The shop was the size of Alex's room — and it was stuffed into the corner of an amusement arcade. If there were magicians shouting "Presto" and "Abracadabra," you couldn't hear them over the electronic gun fire and sound of "Game Over" music.

The shop's display case looked like a thief had rifled through it, leaving feather flowers, metal tubes, black vinyl wallets, and colored ropes flopped about. An elderly man with weary, uncombed hair, leaned over the glass counter. "Interested in magic, young man?"

The elderly man reached into the display case and pulled out an orange-and-black silk handkerchief. "There's a spirit around here," he said to Alex, "a friendly spirit, like Casper the Ghost." He dropped the handkerchief onto the counter, and searched the upper parts of the arcade with his eyes. "The spirit around here is named Myron, and here he is!" With that, the man grabbed at the air and slid "Myron" under the handkerchief.

"I've got him trapped," said the man, as he held the edges of the cloth against the countertop. The center of the handkerchief suddenly bulged, rising four inches in the air. "Now Myron," said the man to the spasming handkerchief, "this youngster just wants to visit. Don't be a pain in the behind." Myron sank back down to the counter and squirmed again within the cloth. "Okay, Myron, we're glad you came by, even for a little bit," said the man. And with that, he pulled the handkerchief off the counter, following Myron's invisible path back up into the arcade rafters with his eyes. Alex, too, turned to look.

"Is that hard to do?" asked Alex's dad.

"Not if he practices."

After Alex practiced enough to do the trick with the confidence it deserved, he performed Myron for his friends (never making the mistake of performing it for the same people twice). Of course, after people saw how good the Myron trick was, they wanted him to do others. Alex added to his repertoire with tricks he bought from the magic shop, as well as tricks from the books.

Entertainment Weekly

In time, Alex became a proficient technical magician. By the time he hit his middle teens, Alex could duplicate many of the sophisticated maneuvers he saw the adult hands do in the library books he'd read years earlier.

Strangely, though, his party audiences seemed more pleased with Alex's simple store-bought tricks — like Myron — than the advanced finger-flicking tricks he liked to wow people with. At one children's party, the kids turned their back on him while he was doing coin rolls across his knuckles — but laughed themselves silly when he did a simple trick where a hand puppet found a selected card.

Alex made the connection: People wanted _entertainment._ They longed for a story, for funny remarks, for tricks that blended neatly into other tricks. If Alex's technical tricks could be adapted to these rules, they could stay in his show. If not, they had to leave.

As he grew into a full-fledged girl-crazy late teen, he decided to bring his magic out of people's homes and into a more public arena. At the magic shop and during get-togethers of the local magic association, he heard magicians talk about getting hired to perform in a restaurant as a real proving ground.

"Look, Alex," said Joel, an experienced restaurant performer, "you've got a lot going against you in restaurants. For one thing, the owner might not want you disturbing the diners. For another, the restaurant might have so much traffic already that they don't need you. And for another, the waiters and waitresses might not like you because they think you're horning in on their tip money. But there are ways to handle all those situations."

The Restaurant Summers

Alex decided to give it a try. After an interview, he got hired at Our Gang Too, a gourmet-burger place at the edge of the city.

Alex's starting salary was $25 an hour, which was fine with him (although he knew experienced performers in fancier restaurants who were getting $80 an hour). He was expected to work two nights a week, six hours each night, and generally contribute to the merriment of the dining experience; this, too, was fine with Alex. His schedule left him free to do homework, practice magic, and give performances at birthday and block parties. The parties weren't regular gigs, but they netted him $125 for an hour's work. That was fine to start with, although once again, Alex knew pros who were making much more (at somewhat classier parties) — over $1,000 a show.

Alex worked at Our Gang Too for the last two summers before college. But the restaurant work was an education in itself. For one thing, he learned quickly that angles are important in a surrounded restaurant. While hiding a coin in his palm, for instance, an eight-year old-girl at the table behind him yelled out, "There it is," stopping the trick in its tracks. Only Alex's quick wit saved the day; he pretended that he had *meant* to "flash" the coin, turned the whole thing into a bit of comedy, and proceeded with a different trick.

He learned plenty about psychology and human nature, too. Alex discovered that many men don't like to be fooled in front of their dates. Men would deliberately lie about the names of the cards they selected, grab at props, and make fun of Alex's sports coat during a performance. He learned to stay away from couples who looked like they were dating — unless they called him over to the table.

Alex didn't do much performing in college — at least, not for money. But after graduation, he thought he'd take a shot at being a professional magician. He moved in with his roommates, put an ad in the paper, and waited for the phone to ring.

It didn't ring often. After a few frustrating months, one of his buddies told him about a marketing job at a local marketing company. Alex figured he knew a little bit about human nature, if not about marketing; he took the job.

And that's how Alex became a semi-pro magician.

The Offer

Alex liked his work; in fact, he stuck with the job for five years, working his way up, working parties on weekends as a magician. But he never stopped nursing the possibility of going pro.

Opportunity knocked in a funny way. Charlie Youngblood, one of Alex's former roommates, worked for a local financial-software company called Moneysoft. The company was trying to come up with a clever presentation for PalmWorld, an upcoming computer trade show.

"Alex, listen," said Charlie on the phone. "Last year, MacroSolutions had a magician at their Comdex booth. It was a great draw. Would you wanna come and do some tricks at our booth next month? We could do a whole theme of it; you know, 'Moneysoft — making magic for money managers.' What do you think?"

Alex had never done trade-show magic. He wasn't sure what to expect at a trade show, having never attended one. He didn't even know who to ask for guidance; trade shows mean big money, and most magicians guard their ideas about them for fear of losing the gigs.

Still, Alex knew that this trade-show job could be his entrance into one of the most important and lucrative performing arenas. If he did well and made a name for himself, he could be well on his way to becoming a full-time pro. *But magic is magic,* he thought. *If I do Coins Across in front of someone who's about to eat a steak and baked potato or someone walking around a convention center, it's still Coins Across.*

After auditioning for Moneysoft's events manager and arranging time off from his day job, Alex made a mental list of his most attention-grabbing effects, eliminated the ones that were too small to be seen around a crowded booth, and thought about ways of reworking each to integrate Moneysoft's message.

The Show

The day of the convention, Alex was cautious but confident. He began his morning with a trip to a nail salon. He didn't bother telling his buddies at work that he was getting a manicure — they might not quite understand. But like most magicians, Alex figured that 50 people at a time were going to be staring at his hands; his nails may as well look as neat and clean as possible.

Alex also wore a $500 suit for the day's performance — an investment he could afford because Moneysoft was paying him $1,100 for eight hours work. (Charlie Youngblood's boss had given Alex a "letter of agreement" guaranteeing him the money. It also specified a $550 "kill fee," which Alex would get if, for some reason, Moneysoft backed out of the arrangement.)

The performance space — Moneysoft's $50,000 booth — was carpeted and well-lit, and it offered ample area to set up.

Charlie dropped by to remind Alex that the convention doors were about to open. Soon business professionals would be striding past the booth, grabbing brochures and free Moneysoft mouse pads. Most of them would intend to blow right past the booth. It was Alex's job to stop them with witty patter and a well-timed miracle.

As the customers began milling around the convention floor, Alex opened a large felt bag. He pulled out his set of ten-inch, chrome-plated metal rings. "These are The Chinese Linking Rings," he began. "I like to think of them as representing your own business. You've got sales, you've got product, and you've got accounting. . . ." Although his memorized patter was flowing, the tie-clip microphone threw Alex off. He was used to a much more intimate performance style.

Alex jangled the rings together, counting them from one hand to the other in hopes of attracting a curious crowd. Men and women in business suits more expensive than Alex's smiled at him, and then continued on; even though a crowd was gathering, the steady stream of people walking away was distracting.

On the other hand, a beautiful brunette sales rep from the booth across the aisle was clearly enjoying the magic.

"The mystery of the linking rings!" began Alex, shouting now. A Moneysoft salesman put a finger to his mouth, indicating to Alex that he should lower his voice.

After the linking rings, Alex launched into his Cut and Restored Mouse Cord trick (which, until the night before, had been his Cut and Restored Rope trick). "Without proper financial tracking," he began, "all you get is a disconnect." He pulled out his pair of shiny scissors and prepared to cut the cord.

Now there's a guy who looks interested, Alex thought, noticing a convention member concentrating hard.

"Excuse me," shouted the guy. "Will your software run on the new Pentium III?"

"I'm sorry," said Alex, his momentum lost. "I'm the company magician. I don't know the product. If you wait right here, though, I'll try to find a salesman."

It's in the Cards

By the end of the day, Alex was beat. He'd stood for eight straight hours, conducting 30 consecutive mini-performances. Charlie Youngblood was thrilled. He wanted foot traffic, and he got foot traffic.

But the trade-show thing wasn't the perfect gig that Alex had pictured. He was constantly aware that the showgoers weren't there for magic; they were there for software. The performance situation stressed him: He could hear his own amplified voice, but he couldn't hear his audience's little murmurs and reactions, which made Alex feel detached. The angles were terrible — there were eyes on him from all sides; there wasn't much in the way of a stage, which confined Alex to a three-foot area all day; and the size of the booth ruled out some of Alex's best stuff — his close-up card and coin moves.

As he packed up his stuff and began thinking about the second day of the show, however, Alex noticed something: The little holder he'd set out with his business cards was nearly empty. Along with the software brochures and the free mouse pads, it looked like at least 30 people had walked away with his name and number. And one of them, he distinctly remembered, had been the beautiful brunette sales rep.

He smiled to himself as he carried his magic case out toward the car. *Maybe it wasn't so bad after all,* he thought. *Maybe this is just the beginning.*

And, of course, he was right.

Part IV
Pick a Card . . . Trick

The 5th Wave — By Rich Tennant

A1 "Sniffy" Bedwick was one of the truly great Sleight of Nose artists.

Pick a card. Any card.

RICHTENNANT

In this part . . .

Card magic is a field unto itself; some magicians perform *nothing* but card tricks. Because there are several trillion card tricks to choose from, you'll find some real blockbusters in the next two chapters. The first chapter in this part offers a selection of utterly baffling, unusual, and highly entertaining card miracles; the second teaches you the components of a card trick, so that you can make up your own variations.

Chapter 10

I Could Have Dealt All Night

In This Chapter

▶ Finding the chosen card in four impossible ways

▶ Predicting the future in two incredible ways

▶ Finding the aces in three astonishing ways

▶ A playing-card love story

*U*nfortunately, magic has a few occupational hazards. One of them is having some nerd run up to you at a party in the middle of your brilliant performance to say, "Hey, I know a trick, too!" Out comes a deck of cards. For the next 45 minutes, you stand there, toes falling asleep, as Cardo the Magnificent does some interminable card trick that involves dealing off the entire deck into piles. One card at a time. Three times through the deck. "And *now* which pile is your card in?"

Hello, Dr. Kervorkian?

The quantity of boring card tricks is a crashing shame, because *good* card magic can transport an audience to another realm. In the hands of an expert — or even a beginner doing *decent* tricks — card magic can take your breath away.

After culling through hundreds of thousands of candidates, allow me to present a few *superb* card tricks. Tricks people will talk about. Unusual tricks that go miles beyond "pick a card." And tricks that do not, under any circumstances, require you to deal off the entire deck a card at a time.

How to Shuffle without Really Accomplishing Anything

You probably know the usual way to shuffle cards — cut the deck in half, place the halves end to end, riffle the edges together, and finally, push the halves together (see Figure 10-1, photo A). Magicians don't call this "the usual way," though — they call this a *riffle shuffle*. Not only does using actual terminology sound more impressive, but "riffle shuffle" is actually kind of fun to say, too.

Over the last decade, while you were out enjoying movies, vacations, and human companionship, some magicians were sitting at home, spending their waking hours practicing card manipulations. These pros are so good that they can do a phony riffle shuffle that leaves all the cards in exactly the order they started in.

I have no intention of teaching you anything that takes ten years to master. However, you may want to consider spending ten *minutes* to learn a phony riffle shuffle that leaves *one* card undisturbed — either the top or bottom one. This fake shuffle is extremely useful in the other tricks in this chapter.

1. **Split the deck into two halves. Place them end to end, as though you're about to do a normal shuffle. Keep track of which half was originally the top half.**

   Suppose, for the sake of this discussion, that you're trying to keep the *top card* the top card.

2. **Start riffling the ends by releasing cards with your thumbs. Let the final few cards fall from the top half of the deck.**

   Pretty painless, eh? By timing the riffling so that you control which cards fall last from your thumbs, you can keep the top card on top even if you repeat the riffle shuffle several times. Photo B shows this action.

So what if the object is to keep the *bottom* card in its place? No problem. In Step 2, simply begin with the cards falling first from what was originally the bottom half of the deck (photo A).

Do all of this smoothly and casually, and you create the psychological impression in your onlookers' minds that the entire deck was truly mixed.

Figure 10-1:
A fake riffle shuffle involves controlling which cards fall first (A) and which fall last (B).

You Do As I Do

You Do As I Do (u∗du∗az∗i∗du), *n.* — Any trick in which a magician and a volunteer follow exactly the same steps — whether with cards, rope, or any other props — and in which the outcome of the magician's manipulations are either (a) surprisingly different from the spectator's or (b) identical despite overwhelming odds.

Here's one such You Do As I Do trick. Rustle up two decks of cards and an unsuspecting victim. Few magic tricks have such a huge impact with so little technical expertise on your part as this one.

The effect: You and a volunteer each shuffle a deck ridiculously thoroughly. You each memorize a card out of the middle of the deck. After cutting the decks, you and your volunteer locate your cards in each other's decks. Against all odds, it turns out that you and your volunteer both chose *the same card.*

The secret: The shuffling and cutting is all legit, and the choice of cards from the middle of the deck is real, too. But because you know the name of the card on the bottom of your volunteer's deck, you're able to hunt down *her* chosen card.

1. **Put two decks on the table. Give the preliminary instructions.**

   "Most card tricks use only one deck of cards. But that's way too easy. I'm going to use two decks — one for you, and one for me. Go ahead — take your choice."

   When your volunteer has picked up a deck, you can continue. "Now, this trick is called You Do As I Do, and it's called that for a very good reason: You and I are going to do everything in stereo. We're going to take every step exactly the same, all the way through the trick. We'll start by shuffling the heck out of our chosen decks. You start. I'll shuffle exactly the same number of times as you."

2. **Pick up whichever deck was left for you; shuffle it as your helper shuffles hers.**

   "Done? All right. Now, let's exchange decks. I want you to be comfortable that *you* mixed up the deck *I'm* going to be using."

3. **As you hand over your deck, memorize the bottom card.**

   Although this moment is the key to the entire miracle, it's not actually very difficult, as shown in Figure 10-2, photo A (that's you on the left). Just hand your deck to your volunteer in such a way that the bottom card is visible — and whatever you do, don't forget the name of the card.

Why won't your volunteer get suspicious? Because (a) she doesn't know what's coming, and (b) she's busy trying to hold up her own end of the trick.

All right — you've swapped decks. And in your head, you're chanting the name of the card you glimpsed. "4 of Hearts . . . 4 of Hearts . . . 4 of Hearts."

4. **Instruct your partner to remove any card from the middle of the deck, memorize it, and place it on top of the deck — and then to cut the cards. You do the same.**

"Now here's where it gets interesting," you can say. "We're going to turn our backs. We're each going to take one card from the middle of the deck and memorize it. Ready? Okay — assume the position."

You should each turn away. As you've promised, you, too, are going to pull a card out and look at it (photo B). But whereas your volunteer is going to remember her card, you *ignore* yours! (You may even want to close your eyes as you "look" at it, so that you won't be confused.) Just keep chanting: "4 of Hearts . . . 4 of Hearts."

"Have you memorized a card and put it back on top now? Wow, what a coincidence — me too! Now let's turn to face each other again. Well, hello there!"

Figure 10-2:
As you hand over the deck, memorize the bottom card. You each draw a card (B) — but ignore yours. Swap decks; her card will be just to the right of yours (C). The revelation is astounding (D).

A

B

C

Yours Hers

D

Set your cards down. "Now let's both cut our cards. You know, like this." Demonstrate — pick up half of your cards, set them down, and put the former bottom half on top.

When *you* do this, nothing important happens relative to the trick. But when your volunteer cuts her own cards, she's unwittingly placing the bottom card (the one you know!) right on top of the top card (which is the one she memorized). In magic terminology, the 4 of Hearts is your *key card.* You don't know what her card is yet, but now it's right next to a card you *do* know.

Actually, if it seems more convincing, you and your helper can cut the deck *multiple* times. As the "Truths of Magic, Part 15: Cutting cards doesn't accomplish much" sidebar explains, cutting the deck more than once doesn't separate your key card from her chosen card.

All right — your key card and hers are now snuggled up together in her deck. Somehow you've got to get that deck *back!*

5. **Switch decks again. Instruct your volunteer to find her card in the deck you just handed her.**

   "Great. Now you take my deck. I'll take your deck. I want you to find your card in *my* deck, and I'm going to locate my card in *your* deck. And when you find it, slap it facedown onto the table. And I'll do the same."

6. **Find your key card the deck she just handed you — and pull out the card to the *right* of it. Put it onto the table, facedown.**

   Take the deck she handed you in Step 5. Scan it from left to right, as shown in photo C. You're looking for your key card, the 4 of Hearts. Thanks to the cutting in Step 4, her card is *just to the right* of your key card. Pull her card out and slip it facedown onto the table.

   Make every effort to find "your" card before she finds hers. The trick is much more amazing that way — if you put your card onto the table first, you've just ruled out the possibility that you somehow *saw* the identity of her card as she was setting it down.

   "All right — I've found my card. Just set yours right down here next to it." When your helper has done so, it's time for the big wrap-up speech.

   "Now remember, this trick is called You Do As I Do. We were supposed to do everything exactly the same: We shuffled the decks the same, pulled out a card the same, cut the decks the same, and so on. But if we've really done everything identically, we should have even chosen the *same card.* I know that's nearly impossible, but let's have faith. Turn over both of those cards together and let's see how we did."

7. **Let your volunteer turn both cards up together.**

   Very few images are as powerful as the sight of two cards, chosen at random by two people from two different decks, turning up identically on the table (photo D).

Truths of Magic, Part 9: Cutting cards doesn't accomplish much

In the trick You Do As I Do, you may be alarmed at the instruction to cut the cards. You've gone to all this trouble to memorize the bottom card — won't cutting the deck mess everything up?

Not at all. If you really stop to think about it (which, fortunately, few spectators do), cutting a deck of cards actually accomplishes very little. Yes, it rearranges the cards somewhat — but no card is separated from the cards on either side of it! If two cards are together now, they'll still be together after the cut. Unlike a shuffle, a cut lets any individual card *mean* it when it says to the card next to it, "We'll always be together."

"Ah," I can almost hear you saying, "but what if you cut exactly between two cards? Then they're separated!"

"Good point," you can almost hear me answering. "But that just puts one on top of the deck, and the other on the bottom. If you cut the cards a second time, they're brought right back together!"

In other words, if you examine the deck (as in Step 6 of You Do as I Do) and discover that your memorized card is at the bottom of the deck, you know that that freak occurrence — a cut exactly between the important pair of cards — has come to pass. But so what? You know that your volunteer's card is, as always, "to the right" of it — in this case, on the *top* of the deck.

The Hands-Off, Mixed-Up, Pure Impossibility

This one's my kind of trick: Strikingly unusual. Almost entirely spectator-operated. And so baffling, even I don't know how it works.

But boy, does it work. All you have to do is remember the instructions to give to your soon-to-be-stupefied volunteer.

The effect: While you're not even looking, your volunteer shuffles a deck, memorizes a card, turns a chunk of cards face-up, and then shuffles and cuts the deck some more. The result is a mishmash — some cards faceup, some facedown. And yet, with your Psych-O-Vision abilities, you're able to locate the chosen card just by touch.

The secret: You tell me!

1. **Ask a volunteer to shuffle the deck and then divide it into three roughly equal piles.**

   "You know what I hate about most card tricks?" you might begin. "It's all that meddling by the magician. The *magician* shuffles. The *magician* holds the cards. Well, big mystery — obviously, the magician is doing something that you're not aware of.

   "I mean, if there really were such a thing as magic, then I ought to be able to have you do all the card handling. I shouldn't have to handle the deck at all. So let's do that. Go ahead. Take the deck. Shuffle it to within an inch of its life."

   When the spectator is finished, give the next instruction: "Great. Now just split up the deck into three piles, all about the same size."

2. **Turn your back. Instruct your helper to memorize the top card of one pile — and then to flip the pile upside-down in between the two other piles.**

   "I'm turning my back now. It's nothing personal — I just don't want to be accused of any funny business. Pick up any one of those piles. Shuffle it some more. Then peel up the top card, just enough to peek at it and memorize it."

   When that's done, go on: "Terrific. Now this is going to seem a bit peculiar, but I'd like you to turn your pile over, so it's faceup. Set it on top of one of the other piles that way — faceup. Got it? All right, now put the remaining pile on top, so that you've sandwiched your pile in the middle of the other two."

   If you were to turn back around, you'd see the card sandwich shown in Figure 10-3, photo A.

3. **Tell the volunteer to shuffle the deck once and then to cut it.**

   "You're doing great. Now square up the deck and shuffle it, just as though it were a normal facedown deck."

   At this point, it's safe for you to turn around again as you continue directing the action. "Looks good. As a matter of fact, give it a cut for good measure."

4. **Take the deck from the volunteer and show him how mixed-up the cards are.**

   This is the juiciest moment of the trick. Turn the deck faceup and fan them so that you both can see the cards' faces.

   "Look at this — oh, my! You've made a complete mess of things! Now how am I *ever* going to find your card in that!?"

   And sure enough, the deck seems to be a mess. Faceup and facedown cards seem to be randomly mixed all through the deck.

Figure 10-3: Your spectator makes a three-pile sandwich (A). Look for a stretch of faceup cards (B). Reveal the card with the Geiger Counter thing (C).

5. Look for a long unbroken patch of faceup cards.

Despite the crazy, mixed-up appearance of the deck, it always contains one long stretch of faceup cards — usually near the bottom of the faceup cards (which is to say the *left* as you fan the cards from left to right). This stretch of faceup cards usually "wraps around" to the front of the deck, as shown in photo B. There may be *more* than one stretch of face-uppers, but you're looking for the longest one.

At this point, the chosen card is the *first facedown card* to the *left* of this run of faceup cards (as shown by the tip of the long arrow in photo B). Even though you can't see its face, you now know exactly which card was chosen.

Now, you could fill a chapter with dramatic ways to reveal a card after you've identified it. In fact, I've done just that — Chapter 11 contains a million different ways. In other words, you're welcome to substitute a different ending for this trick.

If you're not in the mood to skip ahead to Chapter 11, though, try this dramatic revelation:

6. **Spread the cards across the table or floor in a ribbon. Hold the cards flat with your left forearm.**

   "Are you familiar with a Geiger counter?" you should now ask. "One of those radiation detectors that makes little clicks? Well, I've got a Geiger counter for cards. I can tell which card you're thinking of just from the *sound*. Watch this."

7. **Pick up one card and drag its corner across the cards on the floor so that it makes a clicking sound as it goes. Home in on the facedown chosen card.**

   You'll get the best clicking sound if you bend the card slightly, as shown in photo C. First stroke across the entire ribbon of cards. Then stroke again across a smaller swath — continue stroking and homing in on the chosen card. Stare thoughtfully into space (not at the cards) as you do this, pretending to focus only on the sound of the clicks.

8. **Finally, push the facedown card forward, out of the ribbon. Ask the volunteer to name the chosen card for the first time — and then turn it over to show that you were right.**

   If you've done this right, this should *completely* wig out anyone within eyeshot. Let's face it — you couldn't even *see* the chosen card's face! You pushed it out of the ribbon while it was still facedown. There's no *way* you could do this, especially when you never even handled the cards.

   If this trick were any more miraculous, you'd be getting calls from the Sainthood Committee of the Vatican.

Aces by Touch

Lance Burton may be one of the top magicians alive. He may have his own Las Vegas show in his own Las Vegas *theatre*. But he's young enough to remember a few killer tricks that don't require backstage machinery, acrylic trunks, and beautiful assistants.

Here's one such trick. Not only is it impressive to watch and difficult to figure out, but it involves the four aces — and for some reason, the appearance of the four aces in card tricks always seem to scream "master magician!"

All you need is a deck of cards, a coat with an inside breast pocket, a shirt with a breast pocket, and an audience. Beautiful assistant optional.

The effect: You put the shuffled deck into your jacket pocket. Through touch alone, you manage to locate — and pull out — the four aces, one by one.

The secret: Before going onstage, you've put the four aces into your *shirt's* breast pocket.

By the way: While you're in the broom closet stuffing your shirt's breast pocket with aces, you may as well put the Ace of Spades closest to your body, so that you can pull it out last. For some reason, audiences associate the Ace of Spades with power, fertility, and a healthy complexion.

1. **After you have the four aces socked away, offer the deck for shuffling.**

   "Hey, anyone want to know how magicians do some of the best card tricks? Here, I'll show you. I'll expose one of the greatest unspoken secrets in magic. But I need your help. I need you to shuffle the deck until it's just a shadow of its former self."

2. **After the shuffling, hold open your coat. Ask the volunteer to confirm the emptiness of your inside jacket pocket (Figure 10-4, photo A) and then to put the deck into that pocket (photo B).**

   "Nicely done. Now I want you examine my inside coat pocket here. Make sure there's no trapdoors, mirrors, or hydraulic machinery in there. Looks okay? All right then, I'd like you to put the entire deck into the pocket. I'm not even going to handle the deck. What I'm about to show you is 99 percent magician-free."

   After the deck is inside your coat pocket, let go of the jacket.

   "Here's the great secret of magic that very few people realize: With enough training, a magician gets to the point where he can recognize individual cards by *touch*. You know, the magician puts a card back into the deck, but somehow manages to find it again? Well, now you know how it's done — the magician is simply feeling the ink on the card, looking for the particular texture of the one you chose."

3. **Reach inside your coat and pretend to feel around (photo C).**

   "I'm not *that* good yet," you might say as you fish around, "but I've learned to locate 4 of the 52 cards. Here, watch. This one feels like . . . yes, I think I've found one . . . "

4. **Pull the first card from your *shirt* pocket and show it to all comers.**

   ". . . yes, this definitely feels like it's — an ace!"

   Of course, because your coat hides your hand, nobody knows that you're actually pulling the card from your *shirt* pocket.

   "Now let's see if I can find one of the others . . ."

5. **One at a time, with a terrific simulation of concentration and fiddling, pull out the remaining aces.**

   Pull out the Ace of Spades last, just for audience appeal (photo D).

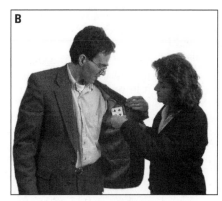

Figure 10-4:
After your pocket is inspected for emptiness (A), the deck is put into your coat (B). Pretend to feel around for the touch of the cards you're looking for (C). Pull them out one at a time (D).

By the way, if all of this seems too pat, too easy, too perfect, you can always magnify the apparent difficulty of the trick by pulling out a *wrong* card. That is, during one attempt, actually *do* pull a card out of your inside jacket pocket. Show it, apologize for your mistake — "Oh no! — Wait a sec!" — and put it back into your jacket pocket before successfully pulling out an ace.

Only "mess up" once, though. You don't want people to think you're losing your touch.

Dealing to the Aces

Here's a perfect follow-up to Aces by Touch (see the preceding section). You're sitting there with a deck in your pocket and four aces on the table. Wouldn't it be nice if you could take advantage of this delicious position? After all, ace tricks hold a special appeal.

And the only thing better than an ace trick is one performed entirely by an audience member — like this one.

The effect: You hand the deck to a volunteer, who deals out four piles at random. You ask him to turn over the top card of each deck — and it's the four aces!

The secret: The aces start out on top. By dealing down *twice,* the volunteer unwittingly reverses the cards' order — and puts the four aces right back on top.

1. **Scoop up the four aces, put them on top of the deck, and give a couple of false shuffles as you talk.**

   By *false shuffles,* I mean the scam described at the beginning of this chapter in the section "How to Shuffle without Really Accomplishing Anything." In this case, just let the top chunk of cards fall *last* as you riffle the two halves of the deck together. You want the aces to stay right where they are — on top.

   This isn't as fishy as it seems, by the way — nobody knows yet that you're about to perform an ace trick. For all they know, you're just "resetting" the deck in preparation for some other trick.

   And what, you may ask, are you supposed to do if you *didn't* just perform the Aces by Touch trick? Are you forced to abandon this follow-up effect just because you didn't wear a sport coat today?

   Not at all. There are plenty of ways to get the aces to the top of the deck. You could sneak off to the bathroom earlier in the party and set the aces up then. You could make small talk, muttering, "Are all 52 cards in here?" as you run through the deck, slipping each ace to the top as you pretend to "count" them. (That's a very standard magician's move, by the way — setting up the deck before anyone's even aware that you're about to do a trick.)

   Either way, your body language and demeanor should change completely when you're ready to begin performing. Straighten up, clear your throat, look up, start talking. (That's another standard magician's technique: "announcing" that the trick is beginning by taking command of the social situation — even though the dirty work has already been done.)

   "Actually, it's not so hard to find the aces," you could begin (particularly after Aces by Touch). "I bet even you could do it. Want to try? Don't worry, I'll coach you. Here, take the deck — you're going to do this whole trick yourself."

2. **Hand the deck to your volunteer. Instruct him to deal off a bunch of cards into a facedown pile — and to stop whenever he likes.**

   If you read the beginning of this chapter, you already know my feeling about tricks that involve dealing. Fortunately, this trick involves only a *short* amount of dealing — and the climax is worth every bit of it.

Figure 10-5:
Tell your
volunteer
to deal
out four
piles (A).
The climax
is yours to
enjoy (B).

"Just start dealing off cards into a pile here. Not the whole deck — I'd like to be home in time for Letterman. Just a little stack. Stop whenever you feel like it."

If your volunteer deals off 20 cards and is still going, gently remind him: "Remember, you can stop at any time."

3. **Instruct him to pick up the newly dealt packet and deal *it* into four piles, one card at a time (Figure 10-5, photo A).**

"You're finished? Great," you can say after the first dealing is over. "Okay, get rid of the cards you have left.

"Now I'd like you to pick up that pile you dealt onto the table. You're going to deal it off into four piles — here, here, here, and here." Tap the table in four spots to show where (see Figure 10-5, photo A). "One card at a time, one card onto each pile, boom, boom, boom, boom, until you've gotten rid of all the cards."

In other words, he should cycle among the four piles as he deals. After putting the fourth card down to begin Pile D, he puts the fifth one on Pile A, the sixth on Pile B, and so on, until all the cards are dealt.

4. **Make your final speech — and then tell him to turn over the top card of each pile.**

"Excellent! Now, you may not have felt like a professional card shark. But let me tell you, you sure *looked* in command. You did much better than you think!

"Remember: The object of this exercise was for you to locate the four aces, just by instinct. Go ahead and turn over the top card of each pile. Let's see how you did."

And sure enough, there they are: ace, ace, ace, ace (photo B). "Hey, you're good!" you can say. "All right — anyone want to play poker with the two of us?"

The trick works because during the first dealing part, your volunteer unwittingly put those four top-card aces onto the *bottom* of the pile. (That's a side effect of dealing off a pile — you reverse their order.)

So during the four-pile dealing business, the four aces were the *last* cards to be dealt — which means, naturally, that they went on top of the four piles.

The Envelope, Please

Here's another freak-out trick that's pathetically easy — but looks utterly impossible. It's not a pick-a-card trick, either — it's a predict-a-card trick.

The effect: A volunteer shuffles a deck. You hand over a sealed envelope containing a prediction. The volunteer turns over the top card — and it matches the prediction!

The secret: Before you begin the trick, write "3 of Spades" on a piece of paper. Also write the date of a day *last week*. Put this prediction into a standard business envelope — and then seal it shut. Remove the actual 3 of Spades and hold it behind the envelope, face out. (It doesn't have to be the 3 of Spades. Use whatever card inspires you.)

Figure 10-6, photo A shows how you hold the envelope. See how you can't see the card? That's because it's behind the envelope (photo B). Sneaky, eh?

Because the envelope hasn't really been entered into evidence yet, don't make a big deal out of it. Hold it on your hand but away from the action (at your side, for example) until you get to Step 2.

1. **When you're ready to begin the trick, ask the spectator to shuffle the cards.**

    "Before I begin, would you please shuffle these cards? Over and over again. Would you mind? Thanks.

    "You know, I'm a very gifted individual," you can continue as the shuffling goes on. "I have these flashes of the future. Last week I predicted the weather correctly more times than the TV weather guy. I told my best friend that Microsoft stock would go up, and it did. It's really freaky — I'm still experimenting to find just how far my predictive powers go. Let me know when you're finished shuffling."

2. **When the shuffling is over, simply set the envelope on top of the deck, in the process setting the hidden card on top of the cards.**

    That, of course, is the entire trick. It's direct, deceitful, and thoroughly delicious. Under cover of the envelope, you just baldly put a new card onto the top of the deck (photo C) — and not a soul suspects.

Figure 10-6:
You're holding the envelope (A) so that the audience can't see the card hidden behind it (B). When you put the envelope down onto the deck, the card goes along for the ride (C), thus making your prediction (D) come true.

"*This* — " you can say as you set the card and envelope down, right under the spectator's nose, "— is a prediction I made before we ever started. In fact, I wrote down this prediction *last week*. Go ahead — look it over. The envelope is completely sealed."

You're actually *telling* the spectator to focus on the envelope. Oh, the cruelty! The sneakiness! The misdirection!

3. **Ask the spectator to open the envelope and read the prediction.**

The trick is actually long over. But your showmanship keeps the fun alive.

"All right — I'd like you to tear open the envelope and read the prediction I made. Please note that I've never even touched the cards. You've been in charge of this trick from the very first moment."

The volunteer opens the envelope and reads the prediction — out loud, if you're performing for a group. Don't hover. Stand far enough away from the cards that nobody will accuse you later of having manipulated the deck as you were standing there.

"That's *amazing,* isn't it?" you can say after the prediction has been read. "I mean, I wrote that prediction a whole *week* ago — and I was *right!*" Hold your hands in the air as though you're Evita greeting her adoring crowds. "Thank you! Thank you very much!"

Everyone will be staring as though you've just sprouted antlers. "Oh, wait — I forgot. You guys don't know *what* I was predicting. Well, that's easy enough — I was predicting what card would be on top of the deck when you were finished shuffling."

"My *prediction* says the 3 of Spades — it would be a spectacular coincidence if the top card really is the 3 of Spades, wouldn't it? No, not a coincidence — just one of my incredible premonitions. Go ahead. Turn over the top card and have a look."

4. **Tell the volunteer to turn over the top card.**

The volunteer turns over the top card, and you've got yourself a blockbuster (photo D). It's short, sweet, and utterly impossible.

Soul Mates

As a magician, I go through life on an obsessive quest for card tricks that aren't "pick a card" tricks. I much prefer making cards do more impressive stunts — like changing identity, flying around the room, or filling out my tax return.

Truths of Magic, Part 10: The pre-climax recap

In "The Envelope, Please" (see the preceding section), you stop the action (in Step 4) in order to make a speech about the impossibility of what you're about to do. In this step, you recap everything that's happened so far, and you remind the audience that if the outcome is as you've predicted, the trick qualifies as a miracle.

The trick would be much weaker without this pre-climax recap, and magicians worldwide know it. Whenever a trick involves the revelation of something at the end — a prediction that matches, an object that has changed or vanished, and so on — a speech like this makes the impact greater.

Why? Because it reminds and misdirects. The pre-climax recap focuses the audience's thoughts on the impossibility of what you're about to do — and meanwhile, it helps them *forget* any little details that might have started them guessing. Such a speech also summarizes the action so far, clearly lays out the rules of the game, and gets the audience to admit *in advance* that your work will qualify as a miracle — if you pull it off.

Soul Mates, a specialty of Jon Racherbaumer, is one such trick (unusual, that is, not tax-related). It's got a sweet line of patter, a very unusual structure, and a climax nobody's ever seen before. In the lingo of magicians everywhere, this trick *kills*.

The effect: You insert two cards into the deck at positions indicated by an audience member. Although your volunteer is in total control of the deck, the two cards manage to find their mirror-image "soul mates" — same-color, same-number cards.

The secret: The two cards you've chosen correspond to the top and bottom cards of the deck. The rest works itself.

1. **Ask an audience member to shuffle the deck as you talk about soul mates.**

   "Shuffle those, would you?"

   As the shuffling goes on, introduce the trick. "I believe in soul mates," you might begin (whether you actually do or not). "I believe that for every person on earth, there's a perfect mate somewhere else on earth. Not everyone finds that soul mate — after all, yours might be in Liechtenstein or Pakistan. But they're out there. And I can demonstrate how even inanimate objects like cards have soul mate affinity, too."

2. **Scan through the deck. Pull out the "soul mate" cards (the ones that match the top and bottom cards) and put them on the table, face up.**

   By "soul mate" cards, I mean the ones that match the number and color. If the top card on the deck is the 4 of Diamonds, pull out the 4 of Hearts. If it's the Jack of Clubs, pull out the Jack of Spades. And so on. Find the soul mate of the *top* card first, and the *bottom* card second. This way, when you set them face-up onto the table, the bottom card's soul mate is on top (see Figure 10-7, photo A).

   It's safe to pull out these cards out in the open. In fact, you should explain that you're doing so.

   "To show you my little lesson in the love life of cards, let's pick out a couple of lost lovers. Let's use these two."

3. **Hand the deck back to the spectator. Ask him to deal a random number of cards face-down onto the table.**

   "All right. You've shuffled the cards, and I've chosen a couple of lover cards. Now comes the search. Start dealing down any number of cards onto the table here. A few, a lot, whatever. Stop whenever you feel the urge. We're simulating this first card's quest for companionship among the throngs of candidates."

Figure 10-7: Find the cards that match the top and bottom cards (A). Put the lover card face-up on the dealt pile (B). Later, you'll set each lover card with its partner on the table (C) — and prove that its mirror has been found (D).

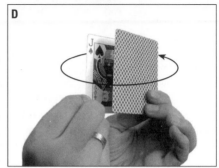

4. **When the dealing stops, put down the first "lover" card *faceup* on the freshly dealt pile. Tell your volunteer to put the rest of the cards on top (photo B).**

   "Excellent," you can say. "I'm going to put the first lonely-heart card right here. Faceup, so we can find it easily later."

   That first "lover" card, you may recall, is the one that matches the *bottom* card of the deck. When the rest of the deck is placed on top of that faceup one, you've just made a sandwich.

5. **Tell your helper to pick up the deck and repeat the dealing business — deal down any number of cards off the top of the deck.**

   "All right. We've got one more lover who's looking for a soul mate, so let's repeat the process. Once again, deal any number of cards onto the table. Stop whenever the spirit moves you."

6. **When the second batch of dealing is over, put the remaining "lover" card faceup onto the freshly dealt stack. Have the volunteer put the rest of the deck facedown on top.**

   "Very good. Once again, I'm going to put a lost-love card faceup here — and if you'd just put the rest of the deck on top — that's great."

7. **Pick up the deck. Fan through it to show your volunteer the two face-up lover cards. Pull out each card along with the card *to its right* and set them on the table.**

As you set each pair of cards down, leave the "lover" card faceup and the card on top of it facedown (photo C).

"Remember, you shuffled the deck. And remember, *you* decided when to stop counting off cards. That's our equivalent of sending each of our single friends out into the dating world. Now let's see how they made out."

8. **Pick up the first pair of cards. Hold them face to face, about an inch apart, and rotate them back and forth, slowly, so that the audience can see that they're mirror images of each other (photo D).**

"As you can see, this 4 of Diamonds has found its true soul mate, the 4 of Hearts. And look here . . ."

9. **Pick up the remaining pair of cards. Again, hold them as though mirroring each other, rotating them to reveal that they match.**

"These soul mates, too, have found each other. A perfect match — against all odds!"

It'd be hard to imagine a trick that's simpler, sweeter, and more mind-blowing.

It'd also be hard to imagine a trick that's more effective at cheering up your perennial single friends.

The "Pick a Number" Spelling Bee

The magic world is teeming with tricks that involve *spelling* a word as you deal cards, one letter per card — and arriving at a previously chosen card on the word's last letter. It's kind of weird, kind of different; audiences eat it up.

Here's such a trick — and it has an unusually powerful effect. In this one, your volunteer only *thinks* of a card instead of actually touching it.

This effect will blow away anyone whose name is spelled with 10 to 15 letters. That requirement rules out people like Ed Bay of Cleveland Heights, OH; for Ed and similarly name-length-challenged spectators, I'll provide an alternate climax.

The effect: A volunteer thinks of a number between one and ten. You show him one card at a time, telling him to memorize the card that comes up at the number he thought of. Amazingly enough, when you count off cards as you spell your volunteer's name, the silently memorized card shows up on the name's final letter!

The secret: The trick works on some mathematical principle that would only bore you. For now, I'll just admit that the whole thing is self-working — and shocking to any audience that's expecting just another card trick.

1. **Ask your volunteer to think of a number between one and ten.**

   "I want to show you a trick that *involves* cards, but isn't really *about* the cards," you can say. "It's actually about *you.* In fact, it can only work if I perform it for you; what we've got here is a designer card trick. Here . . . shuffle these cards, and then think up a number between one and ten. Lock onto that number."

   The shuffling is optional, but shuffling makes almost any card trick seem more amazing.

2. **Instruct him to remove that number of cards from the deck — anywhere — and hide them.**

   "This number you're thinking of is going to be really important in my little demonstration. I'd like you to reinforce that number by taking out that number of cards from the deck. Take them from anywhere — the top, the middle, whatever. Do it behind your back or somewhere else I can't see. Any old cards. Don't let me see how many you've taken, either. Put 'em in your pocket or something."

3. **Take the deck. Show one card at a time from the top of the deck. Tell your volunteer to memorize the card that falls at his number's position. Keep going until you've dealt *one less* than the number of letters in your volunteer's name.**

   There's a lot of patter to learn here, but the instructions are critical. "Okay, this is where it gets interesting," you can say. "Give me the deck — thanks. I'm going to show you the cards, one at a time. When we get to the number you're thinking of, *memorize that card.* So if you're thinking of the number three right now, memorize the third card. Or whatever.

   "But whatever you do, don't tip me off that we've reached your number! Don't blink, don't sweat, don't let your pupils dilate. Just let me keep right on going, and you keep right on remembering your card. Think you can handle this?"

   As promised, you're going to take one card at a time from the top of the deck, hold it up to show your spectator, and then *put the card down* into a little pile on the table (see Figure 10-8, photo A). Believe it or not, this process is the key to the trick — as you show these cards, you're actually reversing their order.

   "All right, here we go. I'm not even going to look at the cards. This trick takes place entirely in your head." (And indeed, don't look at them. Avert your face, as though you're afraid of catching something.)

   "Here we go. One. Two. Three. Four. Five . . ."

Figure 10-8:
Show each card to your volunteer (A). Later, you'll reveal the randomly thought-of card (B).

Now, if your friend is one of the Anointed Ones — someone with 10 to 15 letters in his name — you should know exactly how many letters that is. (To arrive at such a number, you may have to fudge a bit: You can count first and last name, or just the last name, or the company name, or whatever. Or pick a different volunteer. Do what you have to do.)

Keep showing cards to your volunteer until you've reached *one fewer* than the number of letters in his name. If the name is Bill Clinton (11 letters), stop when you say "ten." If it's Saddam Hussein (13 letters), stop when you get to 12.

When you've finished counting, stop and look up at your volunteer. "Okay, I must have gone past your number by now. Have you got a card in mind? Don't forget it. From now on, the card is the important thing."

4. **Put the stack of dealt-off cards (now on the table) back on top of the deck. Give the deck a phony shuffle.**

By *phony shuffle,* I mean shuffle them in such a way that the top batch of cards falls last, undisturbed, as described in "How to Shuffle without Really Accomplishing Anything" at the beginning of this chapter. (This step is optional, but it's a nice psychological touch.)

"All right. Now that you've got a card in mind, the *number* you've got in your head isn't important anymore. Can I have those cards that you took out of the deck before?"

5. **Put the volunteer's cards on top of the deck.**

"Now, this is where things get spooky," you can say. "As I mentioned earlier, this isn't a generic card trick — it's custom-made to be performed for *you.* I'll prove it. Watch: I'll spell your name as we deal off the cards."

6. **Deal off cards as you spell the volunteer's name. Before revealing the final card, ask for the name of the memorized card — and then turn the last card faceup.**

Say each letter as you deal a card off the top of the deck onto the table, all facedown. "M. I. C. K. E. Y. M. O. U. S —"

Now stop. Take the final card and hold it apart from the deck, still face-down (photo B). "All right — loud and clear. What was the name of the card you thought of?" (It's *much* more effective to have the card *named* before you reveal it than to show the card and ask, lamely, "Was that your card?" Do it my way, and the whole audience gets the impact at once — instead of just the volunteer.)

After your volunteer names the card, slowly and dramatically turn over the last-letter card (photo B).

"E!"

All right. So what about when your friend's name is Ed Bay (or, conversely, Sue Kômákûmarynskîschöff)? Those names aren't between 10 and 15 letters long.

In such cases, here's an alternate finale. In Step 3, deal off *ten* cards. Every-thing else in the trick remains the same (except for the patter about "a designer trick," of course) until the grand finale in Step 6.

Instead of spelling your helper's name, give him the deck. Instruct him to announce the name of each card as he turns it over from the top of the deck. But tell him to lie when he comes to his own card — to substitute some other card's name. Explain that after years of practice, you've cultivated a pretty good ear for the tension in a liar's voice. Emphasize that his voice shouldn't waver, get louder, or tense up when lying about the name of his card — just keep dealing cards and go right past it.

Turn your back and let him begin. Of course, you're not actually listening to the names of the cards — instead, you're *counting to 11.* The eleventh card is the one your volunteer has in mind.

After the card-naming has proceeded a card or two beyond 11, stop your volunteer. "Hold on," you should say, as dramatically as possible. "I think you lied a couple cards back. I think you were lying about the King of Spades" (or whatever the card was).

Your volunteer will sheepishly agree — unless, of course, he's lying.

The Shuffling Lesson

This effect, dreamed up by Advisory Pantheon member Chad Long, is mind-boggling. It's got a dual climax, a you-do-as-I-do premise, and a conclusion that leaves your spectator thinking she actually did the magic.

But this trick does require one fleeting bit of manual dexterity. It's not anything that'll require a visit to a chiropractor, but it is something you'll have to practice until you can do it smoothly and reliably. Don't pass over this trick just because there's one sneaky move; some of the best things in life require some effort to attain. (Other examples: juggling ability, frequent-flyer award tickets, and BMWs.)

The effect: You tell your audience a story about how magicians aren't born knowing how to shuffle; they must actually work up to this talent. In fact, you say, magicians work up from very simple shuffles — and you lead a volunteer through several easy ones.

But after a few years, you say, a magician gets good at manipulating cards even when they've seemingly been shuffled. You demonstrate by turning over the top cards of four piles you've made — and they're all kings! That's amazing, but jaws don't really hit the carpet until the spectator turns over *her* four cards — and they're all aces!

The secret: Before you begin the trick, put the four kings at the bottom of the deck; put the four aces at the top. Do this "stacking" of the deck during a moment when nobody's paying attention, or under the premise of removing the Jokers, or as you pretend to make sure all 52 cards are present. As in other tricks, your body language and failure to participate in the current conversation subconsciously lets people know that no trick is going on. Later, when you clear your throat, sit forward, and begin speaking loudly, *then* people tune in and begin paying attention.

1. **Give the deck a phony shuffle or two.**

   The phony shuffle is the one described in "How to Shuffle without Really Accomplishing Anything" at the beginning of this chapter. In this case, shuffle so that the kings fall first, and the aces fall last. (Do it slowly if you're having trouble keeping control.) In other words, don't mess up the order of the top cards or bottom cards as you do your riffle shuffle.

   Don't say, "Kindly note that I am now shuffling the cards." All of this should be casual, comfortable, and automatic, as though you *always* shuffle the cards before beginning a trick.

   What you can say is, "Did you ever notice how often magicians shuffle cards? But you know, magicians aren't born knowing how to shuffle. We have to work at it. We start when we're very young. Here, I'll show you."

2. **Hand the top half of the deck to your spectator.**

   "Here, hold these for a second." You're left with the bottom half in your hands, with the kings on the bottom.

   "See, there's all kinds of ways to mix up a deck cards. Most of them take years of practice."

3. **As you talk, fan the bottom of the deck just enough that you can see the backs of all four bottom cards — and prepare to remove them with your left hand.**

   That's the hard part I warned you about earlier. You can glance down at your hands, but don't stare; be quick about this. Figure 10-9, photo A shows this process from your angle.

   "There's regular cutting, like this . . . "

4. **Pull out the four counted-off cards with your left hand and drop them onto the top of the deck.**

   If you plow right on in to the next step, nobody in a million years will suspect that you've just set up the entire trick. The point was to get your secret four cards on the top of your half of the deck, just as the spectator's aces are on the top of hers.

   "There's also traditional riffle shuffling, like this."

5. **Do a false shuffle with your little packet, keeping the top cards intact.**

   Here's where you do, yet again, the preserve-the-top-cards shuffle described in "How to Shuffle without Really Accomplishing Anything" at the beginning of this chapter.

   So far, your volunteer hasn't done anything but watch. Now it's time to get her into the action.

   "But those are the advanced methods. When magicians are very young, we start out really, really simply. Here, I'll show you what we go through. Hold your deck like this."

   Demonstrate: Hold the deck in your right hand, with the faces of the cards facing your right palm, as shown in photo B.

6. **With your left thumb, slide a card off the right-hand packet and into your left hand. Repeat until you've pulled off five or six cards this way (photo B).**

   "When we're about three years old, we do this kind of baby shuffle. Here, do this along with me. One card at a time. Yeah, that's it. We start out easy. And when we get more advanced, we pull off bigger chunks at a time — right."

Figure 10-9: As you talk, pull over the four bottom cards (A). The first "lesson" involves pulling one card at a time from the stack in your right hand (B), and later bigger chunks from (C). The next involves a "center cut," pulling chunks from the middle (D) and throwing them on top. Finally, you make four piles and deal onto them (E) — in preparation for the grand finale (F).

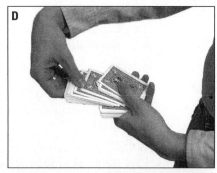

7. **With your left thumb, scrape off thicker chunks of cards (photo C). Finish by dropping the remaining cards from your right hand onto the top of the left-hand deck.**

   In other words, after you've pulled off five or six cards in Step 6, you (and your volunteer) continue with exactly the same movement — but now pull off clumps of cards instead of one at a time.

"And then drop the rest of the deck on top, like that. Right! That's very good. That's actually called an overhand shuffle — now you know. Well, jeez, you're a prodigy! You're ready to advance to the next kind of shuffle — the center cut."

8. **Fan the cards. Pull out the center third (photo D) and drop them on top of the deck. Repeat.**

   Make sure your volunteer does this maneuver along with you.

   "A center cut is when you pull out a bunch of cards from the middle, like this, and drop them on the top. That's it — good! Yeah, they use a center cut in Las Vegas casinos because it disrupts any kind of prearranged order."

9. **Push off a handful of cards and drop them onto the table. Repeat three times, so you wind up with four little piles in a row (and a remaining bunch in your hand).**

   "Man, you're a natural at this stuff! I think you're ready for the *pile mixer*. Take a few cards off the top, like this, and drop them onto the table to make a little pile. That's it. Do it again to make a second pile — right — and a third, and a fourth." The setup should now look like photo E.

10. **Deal the remaining cards on top of the four piles: a card onto pile 1, the next onto pile 2, and so on, until all the cards are gone (photo E). Direct your volunteer to do the same.**

    "Then just deal the rest of the cards onto the four piles, one at a time, until they're all gone, like this. This is called a *distribution shuffle,* also known as a *dealing shuffle.*"

    (***Note:*** Don't use this patter when performing for magicians. These terms aren't real shuffling terminology. But they sure sound good, don't they?)

    "Over the years, though, we magicians get better and better at the various ways to shuffle cards. Eventually, we get so good that we can actually manipulate the cards *as* we do the shuffles. See here? Even with all the mixing up we just did, I managed to wind up with . . ."

11. **Turn over the top cards of your four piles. Then ask the spectator to turn over the top cards of *her* piles.**

    "King, king, king, and king! Of course, I've had years of practice . . . let's see how *you* did. Holy smokes — ace, ace, ace, ace!"

    Let the feeling of utter astonishment register as the scene unfolds (photo F). After all, the cards have been in her hands *the whole time*.

    "Hey," you can say accusingly as you wind up the trick. "Have you been going to shuffling school behind our backs?"

Sleight of Foot

There are restaurant tricks, and there are card tricks — and sometimes, as in this case, there are card tricks to perform *in* a restaurant. Your friends won't soon forget this funny, bizarre, mystifying trick; after all, how often do you ask your friends to remove articles of clothing while out to dinner?

Don't answer that.

This twist on an old idea (see the sidebar "Truths of Magic, Part 11: Whose trick is it, anyway?") comes from Advisory Pantheon member Jamy Ian Swiss, one of the world's greatest card magicians.

The effect: You announce that you've become a pioneer in sleight-of-*foot:* If your volunteer can pick a card with his foot, you'll locate it with yours.

After removing his shoes and socks, a spectator plucks a card from the deck with his toes. After he puts the card back, you nudge the deck with your foot — and somehow manage to cut directly to the chosen card.

The secret: As you point to the deck, indicating that the volunteer should replace the cards, you let a few grains of *salt* (previously dabbed onto your fingertip) fall onto the top card of the deck. The salt grains make the top half of the deck roll away practically on its own.

Before you begin, there's only one step: Get some grains of salt on your index fingertip. Earlier in the evening, for example, salt your food, being sure to get a little excess on your plate. Get the salt to stick to your fingertip either by pressing it firmly into (or wiping firmly across) the loose salt — or, if you're a naturally sticky person, just by tapping your fingertip into it.

1. **Ask your volunteer to shuffle the cards.**

   "Everybody talks about sleight of hand," you can begin. "Sleight-of-hand this, sleight-of-hand that — but come on! There are plenty of other perfectly useful parts of the body!"

   Hand the deck of cards to your volunteer. "Here, shuffle these, will you?"

   As that's taking place, continue. "I mean, why don't magicians ever use sleight-of-*foot?* That seems to be to be just as legitimate. In fact, let's try one like that. I'll tell you what: If you can pick a card using *your* foot, I'll *find* it again with mine. In fact, I'll never even touch the deck with my hands! Fair enough?"

2. **Have the volunteer spread the cards out on the floor, facedown.**

   "Since I can't use my hands, I'm going to have to ask you to spread the cards out on the floor, in sort of an arc. That's good.

"The next part, I'm afraid, is going to take a little bit of pedal dexterity . . . you'll have to take off your shoes and socks."

While this bit of embarrassing disrobing takes place, the stage is yours for jokes and wisecracks. ("This is the part of the trick where you find out who's worn his socks two days in a row," for example.)

3. **Ask your volunteer to pick a card, using her toes alone (Figure 10-10, photo A).**

Only genetically blessed volunteers can successfully pick up a card with one foot; most require two, as shown in photo A. (Alternatively, you could let your volunteer use only one foot — to *push out* a card, which she can then pick up with her hands.)

"All right now: Steady as she goes. Pick a card, any card — but use your toes alone. Yes, I know it's hard. But at least I didn't make you use your feet to *shuffle*."

"Okay, you've got one? Don't let me see it. Show it to everyone but me."

4. **Direct your volunteer to square the deck into a neat stack; lift off the top half of the deck; and put the chosen card onto the bottom half.**

"All right, you've all had a look at the card? Great. Now square up the cards into a nice neat stack — you're allowed to use your hands for this. Excellent. Now lift off about half the deck — good — and put your card right there where you cut."

As you say this, point to the half of the deck that's still on the floor.

5. **Once the card has been put down, point again to the pile on the floor — and in the process, dislodge some salt from your finger onto it.**

You don't actually have to touch the cards on the floor; just let your hand hover directly over it. As you extend your index finger so that you can point down (to indicate where the top half of the deck is to be replaced), it rubs against your thumb, dislodging some of the salt so that it falls directly onto the pile — and, therefore, directly onto the chosen card. Photo B shows this moment.

This is the moment of truth — the part you've practiced at home. You've run through the salt-dislodging business until you know exactly how much salt to dislodge (more than five grains, but less than 50). You've worked on it until you can dislodge the salt smoothly and naturally as you point.

As you point, finish your instructions to the spectator. "And just put the rest of the cards on top. That's it — let's lose that baby deep in the deck where we'll never see it again."

6. **Announce that you'll find the card with *your* foot.**

"Okay, then. Now comes the hard part — this is where I do the sleight-of-foot. Here, let me just take off *my* shoe and sock here."

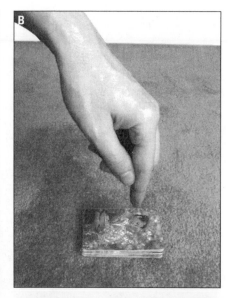

Figure 10-10:
Your volunteer is all thumbs (A). Take this advice with a grain of salt: point to show where the cut cards should be replaced (B). Then, with just the right amount of force (C), kick the deck (D) to make it cut to the chosen card.

Start to undo your shoe, then give up. "Oh, forget it — let's just get this over with. Here we go: the fully clothed Sleight-of-Foot trick."

7. **Nudge the deck with the side of your shoe. Reveal the card you cut to.**

When you knock the deck — very gently — with your shoe, the deck splits apart at that point, thanks to the rolliness of the salt grains, which act like ball bearings (photos C and D).

Truths of Magic, Part 11: Whose trick is it, anyway?

Many magicians think that Sleight of Foot, described in this chapter, has been around "forever," with no discernible date of origin — kind of like knock-knock jokes, the recipe for Italian dressing, or Dick Clark.

In fact, though, it was dreamed up by a magician named Herbert Milton, who first marketed his trick in the 1920's (in a booklet that went for a then-astronomical $25).

Since then, the Sleight-of-Foot idea has been passed on and reprinted in various magic books, such as Hugard and Braue's *Encyclopedia of Card Tricks*.

Although many magicians perform the Sleight-of-Foot trick today, they're not, in fact, all doing the same trick. Advisory Pantheon member Billy McComb doesn't bump the deck with his foot — he uses a golf putter (and he uses sand instead of salt). In other versions of the trick, you get salt onto the card *beneath* the chosen card instead of *on* the chosen card. Jamy Ian Swiss added the hilarious business about asking the volunteer to take off his shoes and socks.

As Jamy points out, this trick is a perfect illustration that magic is an interpretive art: You don't have to be a great inventor to be a great magician, just as most pop singers aren't great composers. What matters is the impression you make, the style you bring to the trick, the personality you bring to it — and not just the trick itself.

As you watch other magicians perform, keep that point in mind: It's not just "How good is this trick?" but "How good is this *magician*?"

This isn't a first-time, every-time operation, by the way. Shiny, slippery cards obediently spill apart at the salted spot; older, dull cards don't. A whisper-soft kick isn't enough force to dislodge the top half of the deck — but kicking too hard will spray the cards across the floor, making it impossible to identify the break you're looking for. Practice — and using the right deck — makes perfect.

"All right, I've made my fancy cut. Let's see how I did. Loud and clear, what was the name of the card you chose with your toes?"

After the card has been named, triumphantly turn over the top card of the bottom pile on the floor, so everyone can see that your shoe actually cut to the correct card.

"Okay — shoes off, everyone! Let's play a game of Toe Poker!"

The Future Deck

This trick involves a great sacrifice on your part — even more than the usual starvation, pain, and callused pinkies that comes from hours of practice. For this trick, you'll have to retire from your household a $1.49 deck of cards and a $1.09 felt-tip pen. Two perfectly good items, trashed forever in the service of your art. I'll wait right here as you mull that over.

You've decided to go ahead? I'm delighted, because this trick — a contribution of Advisory Pantheon member Mike Maxwell — is among the best uses you'll ever find for 52 pieces of cardboard.

The effect: You write a prediction — in permanent marker — on a card, which you stuff into an empty envelope. You invite the spectator to choose any card at all, and you put *it* into the envelope, too.

That's all. When the spectator takes out the two cards in the envelope, sure enough, your handwriting correctly predicts the chosen card.

The secret: In advance, you've written "Ten of Clubs" on *every single card.* When you write your prediction, you do so with a dried-out pen, so that it doesn't leave a mark on the card — and you "write" your prediction on the actual 10 of Clubs. What card the spectator chooses from the facedown deck, therefore, *is* your "prediction" card — not the one in the envelope. The envelope makes it impossible for the audience to realize the cards have been switched.

That doesn't make sense when *I* read it, either. You'll just have to trust me on this and follow along as you read.

Before you begin the trick, uncap your permanent felt-tip marker and set it on a windowsill for a few days. Unless you've found a brand of marker I don't know about, it will dry out to the point where it won't make a mark.

Using a *working* felt-tip pen of the same color, take a deep breath, flex your muscles, and write "Ten of Clubs" across the right edge *every single card* — all except the 10 of Clubs and one other random card. (In this example, let's say the other lucky survivor is the Queen of Diamonds.)

This is the sacrifice part: you'll never again be able to use this deck for any trick except the this one. (Maybe the trick shouldn't be called The Future Deck after all — it's really the No Future Deck.)

Writing anything 50 consecutive times can drive you quietly insane, as anyone who's ever signed the papers for a mortgage can tell you. Listen to the radio or talk on the phone as you work to make your signing more mindless.

When the writing is over, put the unmarked Queen of Diamonds on the bottom of the deck, and the 10 of Clubs somewhere in the middle.

Now survey your handiwork: If you fan the cards from right to left as you look at them, your writing appears on the edge of every card (see Figure 10-11, photo A). But if you fan the cards the way it feels more natural — from left to right, as in photo B — you can't see *any* writing! Now you know why you left that Queen unsigned — to cover the face of the deck.

The fact that you can show all the cards this way will come in very handy. You can shuffle the cards (make sure the bottom card falls first, as described at the beginning of this chapter), fan them left-to-right, and otherwise handle them normally. There are three things you can't ever do, however:

✔ You can't let the spectator handle the cards.

✔ You can't turn any cards end-for-end, so that the writing is now on the left side of some, and the right side of others.

✔ You can't tell a book by its cover.

1. **Shuffle your special deck as you introduce the trick.**

   Remember to shuffle your special deck the special way described at the beginning of this chapter, so that the Queen of Hearts remains on the bottom. And be sure to keep track of which way is up as you shuffle, so that the writing is always on the right side.

   "I met a guy at a magic conference last month who really freaked me out," you might say. "This guy was pushing the boundaries between science and magic tricks. He was experimenting with psychological pressure — trying to affect the behavior of his audience through sheer force of personality."

2. **Fan the deck from left to right, face up, so that your volunteer can see.**

   "I mean, let's say I'm going to do a card trick. This guy said I should be able to *make* you pick the card I want. I should be able to write down the card you're going to pick — before you pick it!"

3. **Close up the deck and uncap your marker.**

   "I'm dying to find out if this guy's theories are right. Will you try it with me? Great! I appreciate your willingness to be mentally controlled."

4. **Holding the deck so that only you can see, find the 10 of Clubs. Pull it out and put it onto the face of the deck.**

   Actually, you can put it anywhere that nobody can see its face — in the palm of your hand, for example — but the deck provides a solid surface for the writing you're about to do.

"To help reinforce my prediction, I'm going to write the name of your future card *on* a card. With permanent ink. This method makes a pretty vivid mental impression on both of us, although you may not *feel* anything. All right, let me just write my little prediction here . . ."

5. **Write "Ten of Clubs" on the edge of your 10 of Clubs (photo C).**

Of course, your marker is all dried up. You don't actually leave a mark; you're faking it. But since you're taking care to keep the card's face hidden, nobody can tell that your pen doesn't work.

"Great!" Cap your marker and put it in your pocket. "I'm going to put my prediction right here in this envelope, where nobody can tamper with it."

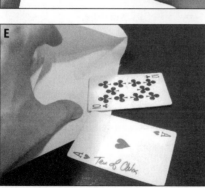

Figure 10-11: Fan the cards the wrong way (A), and you can see the writing on every card. Fan the cards normally (B), though, and the cards look perfectly normal. That makes it easy for you to write nothing (C) on the 10 of Clubs, give the volunteer a free choice (D) — and have your prediction match (E).

6. **Show your envelope empty and then slip the 10 of Clubs into it.**

You can substitute almost any opaque container for the envelope: a box, a hat, a shoe, and so on. The sole qualification is that the container must prevent anyone from noticing the *order* cards get put in; you're going to be putting two cards aside, and you want a plausible reason for them to get mixed up.

For example, it wouldn't work to have your volunteer stick the cards into her own pocket; she'd remember which one went in first.

It wouldn't work to stick the cards into your *own* pocket, either, although for a very different reason — this time, the skeptics in your audience would assume you did some sneaky card-switching in the seclusion of your pocket. It's much better to keep things out in the open, in some third-party container.

7. **Spread the cards out across the table, facedown. Invite your volunteer to push one card, facedown, out of the lineup (photo D).**

"Here's where the psychological influence comes in. There are 51 cards left. I want you to choose one card — don't think too hard about it, just put your finger on one that seems to be calling out to you — and push it forward away from the other cards."

8. **Deliberately and openly, put the chosen, facedown card into the envelope.**

"This one? Very good — it goes into the tamper-proof envelope, too."

All that remains is for you to make a brief speech that summarizes the impossibility of the outcome — and takes people's minds off the possible role of the envelope, hat, box, or shoe.

"That's it — we're done with our little experiment. You can relax your brain now. Remember: I wrote down what card I wanted you to select. You could have chosen any one of these cards."

9. **Scoop up the deck, turn it faceup, and spread the cards in a ribbon across the table — left to right, of course.**

Since you're spreading left to right, of course, the writing on the edges of the cards isn't visible; this tiny bit of psychological manipulation — showing the audience that the deck is normal — is a key strength of this trick.

As always, however, be careful to keep the cards in their original orientation so that the writing will be concealed. In the process of spreading the cards across the table in Step 7, then collecting them and re-spreading them in this step, you don't want to inadvertently rotate the deck so that spreading them *exposes* the writing on all 50 edges!

10. **Ask the volunteer to pour out the contents of the envelope onto the table.**

"Go ahead and dump out that envelope. I'm eager to see how we did!"

As shown in photo E, you've pulled it off: Your prediction, written across the edge of one card, matches the card that has no writing on it. I'm telling you, this one is drop-dead unbelievable.

What the audience doesn't realize, of course, is that the cards that went into the envelope were switched: the one with the writing on it went in *last,* and the 10 of Clubs went in first.

Only one thing could mar the perfection of this trick — and that's if somebody ever catches you doing the trick again. They'll wonder why the pushed-out card always seems to be the 10 of Clubs.

If that concerns you, you could always make up *several* decks, using a different force card each time. Now *that's* sacrifice!

Dream a Card, Any Card

The beauty of this trick, as Advisory Pantheon member Daryl points out, is that you never even *once* touch the cards. (No, I'm not leaving off his last name. He's just Daryl. Like Cher or Madonna, except without the singing.) It's a blockbuster effect that can fry spectators' brains if they think about it too much.

The effect: You mention that you had a dream about a card. A voice in the dream chanted: "value and suit . . . value and suit . . ."

Trying to make sense of the dream, you ask a volunteer to fan the cards facing you, so that you can indicate which card was in your dream. The volunteer removes that card and puts it facedown on the table.

Now the volunteer deals the deck into two piles — and turns over the top card of each. "Value and suit . . . Value and suit . . ." Sure enough, the value of one card and the suit of the other combine to identify the facedown, dreamt-of card!

The secret: You don't actually know the identity of your dream card *until* the spectator is fanning the deck toward you. That's when you sneak a peek at the first two cards, which identify the "dream card." (Step 3 will make all this clear.) Thanks to some clever maneuvering, those two cards wind up on top of the two dealt-out piles.

1. **Ask a volunteer to shuffle the cards.**

   "I had the weirdest dream last night," you might begin. "I had to stand up and give a speech in front of all my friends, and then I realized that I was naked on the stage, and I hadn't prepared anything to say! And then this army of Bill Gates clones started chasing me, but even though I was running and running, I wasn't moving anywhere, and — no, wait a minute. That was my dream the night *before* last.

   "No, last night it was about a card. Yes, that's the kind of things magicians dream about. Cards. This particular card, though, seemed to have a special significance. Here, I'll show you what I mean. Now, I'm *never going to touch the cards.* If I touch the cards during this trick, I'll pay you $10,000."

2. **Ask the volunteer to fan cards toward you.**

   "I'd like to find the card I saw in my dream. But I can't touch the deck to do this — my bank account couldn't take it. So just fan the cards like this. Slide them by me, facing me, so I can see every card." Demonstrate with your empty hands. Figure 10-12, photo A, shows the cards being fanned.

3. **Look at the top two cards of the deck — and find the card that matches their value and suit, respectively.**

   The top two cards are on the *far left,* as shown in photo A. Remember: "Value and suit." That means that you'll notice the *value* of the top card (ace, 2, 3, or whatever) and the *suit* of the card next to it (Clubs, Diamonds, Hearts, or Spades). Combine these two factors to identify your "dream card."

   For example, suppose the top card is the **two** of Hearts and the second card is the King of **Clubs**. Look for the two of Clubs. (And what happens if the top two cards have the *same* value or the *same* suit? Announce that you couldn't find your dream card, and ask the volunteer to cut the deck and start again.)

4. **When you spot your dream card, ask the volunteer to set it facedown on the table.**

   "Stop! Right there. This one here. Take that card out and put it on the table, facedown."

5. **Ask the volunteer to *think* of a number between 1 and 51, and to deal that many cards into a pile on the table.**

   "All right," you say. "You've got 51 cards left. Think of any number from 1 to 51, and then deal down that many cards into a pile on the table, one at a time. Don't tell me the number — just deal off that many cards."

Figure 10-12:
Notice the
value of the
first card
and the suit
of the
second (A).
Later, they'll
identify
the dream
card (B)!

Why do you tell your volunteer in advance that she'll have to deal off that number of cards? Because that way, she'll be less inclined to think of a *high* number, which would force you and the audience to sit there while she deals off most of deck, which is about as entertaining as watching a glacier move.

6. **When she stops dealing, ask her to pick up the dealt-off pile and to deal *it* off into two piles, alternating right and left.**

"Okay, put the rest of the deck aside," you say when she reaches her thought-of number.

"Now, there's one part of the dream I didn't tell you about. All the time I was picturing this one card, a voice kept chanting, 'Value and suit! Value and suit!'" (Use a booming or creepy voice for that part.)

"I didn't know what that meant, but I think I know now. Pick up those cards you just counted off. Deal them into two piles, alternating like this: left, right, left, right. Keep going until all the cards are gone."

As she finishes dealing, notice which of the two piles gets the *last card*. That's going to be your Value pile.

7. **Ask the volunteer to turn over the top card of each pile.**

"I believe that the voice — 'Value and suit!' — was trying to tell me the significance of my chosen card. Here, turn over the top card of this pile." Point to the Value pile — the one that received the last dealt card.

"That's the Value. It identifies the *number* of the dream card. See, it's a two. So the dream card has to be a two of Something. Now turn over the top card of the other pile. That's the suit pile; it tells us the *suit* of my dream card — see, it's Clubs. Two. Clubs. Two of Clubs. So the card in my dream —" and here you point to the face-down card she set aside in step 4 — "has got to be the two of Clubs! Wouldn't that be a miracle?"

8. Ask the volunteer to turn over the facedown Dream card.

"Turn it over and let's see!"

And, of course, it's the 2 of Clubs.

This trick may look long and wordy as you read it on the page. But its impact is *huge*. As this book was going to press, I did the trick for a Harvard-trained doctor. He was absolutely short-circuited by it. "That is a *great* trick," he kept muttering, staring at the cards on the table. "What a *great* trick. And you never even touched the cards . . . I don't understand it!"

(Of course, I'm a Yalie. What did I expect from a Harvard man?)

Chapter 11

The Build-Your-Own-
Card-Trick Kit

• •

In This Chapter

▶ Four ways to say "Pick a card" without meaning it

▶ Seven ways to say "Is this your card?" and know it

▶ Two tales from the trenches of professional card magic

• •

There's an old saying that goes like this: Give a man a fish, and he eats tonight. *Teach* a man to fish, and he eats every night (although without much in the way of Food Groups II, III, or IV).

I often picture you, the blossoming magician, as the main character in that ancient proverb (the person, not the fish). Sure, I could teach you step-by-steps from here until doomsday. But you'd never be able to do any tricks except the ones you got from this book, all written out. Your inner child magician would never grow.

I'd much rather you grasp the *principles* of magic so that when you're in front of a crowd, hooked on the laughter and requests for dates, you won't be limited to a bunch of stale routines. I'd rather give you the tools to make up your own tricks, to improvise, to wing it, to think on your feet.

In that spirit, allow me to offer a chapter that's a menu of components. You can assemble them into your own personalized, designer card miracles.

How This Chapter Works

The most common kind of card trick boils down to two steps:

1. **Somebody picks a card.**

2. **You identify it.**

To pull this off, you, the magician, must either (a) find out the name of the chosen card, or (b) know what it is beforehand. And how could you possibly know the chosen card before it's chosen? Quite easily, if you perform what's known as a *force* — seeming to give the customer a free choice of cards, but actually giving no choice at all.

Just as there are dozens of ways to force a card, so there are dozens of ways to *reveal* a card. Trust me on this: The most common card revelation — "Is this your card?" — is also the lamest, one that brands *AMATEUR* across your forehead in large italic lettering. The revelation is much more impressive when the chosen card leaps out of the deck, floats up out of the deck, or reveals itself in some otherwise mind-numbing manner.

Now you're getting the idea: This chapter contains a choice of several *forces* and several *revelations*. You're invited to mix and match them, creating one new trick after another. You know — pick one from column A, one from column B.

Some magicians, by the way, have made their reputations doing nothing but combining and recombining forces and revelations like the ones in this chapter. For example, they'll repeatedly force the same card, so that every audience member seems to choose the same darned card. That ubiquitous card keeps reappearing, in revelation after revelation. Doing so requires talent, patience, and a longer list of forces and revelations than the ones in this chapter — but at least you know you're in hallowed company.

Forces

This section covers four card forces — clever, easy ways to make a volunteer "choose" a card you already know. It's good to master more than one, just in case you're forced to force more than once for the same audience. The ones described here will serve you well; go force and multiply.

The Cut Anywhere force

Here's one of the simplest and most effective forces on earth. It's the one featured in "Post-It-ive Identification" (see Chapter 4); now that you know it's only one of many card forces, feel free to substitute any other force in this chapter when you do that Chapter 4 trick.

Before you begin the trick, put the card you want to force on top of the deck. As you settle down to do the trick, feel free to give the deck a phony shuffle. (For more on phony shuffles, see Chapter 10.)

1. Ask a volunteer to cut the deck in half (Figure 11-1, photo A).

"What I'd like you to do is to cut the deck in half anywhere."

If you point to a spot on the table next to the deck, your volunteer is less likely to spontaneously *complete* the cut. You want the deck to wind up in two piles.

2. **When that's done, put the *bottom* half on top, crosswise, as shown in photo B. Say something.**

The "say something" part is important. You need to take the spectator's attention — and your hands — off the deck, if even for one second. This, kids, is misdirection.

Say: "You are really good at this, you know that? Next time, *you'll* do the card trick." Or: "You had a free choice there. I had absolutely no mental influence on you — that *you* could feel." Or crack your knuckles and wiggle your fingers, as though you're about to do something impressive.

3. **Lift the top half of the deck, and point to (or tap) the top card of the *bottom* pile. Tell the volunteer to memorize that card.**

"All right — go ahead. Take a peek at the card you cut to. Don't forget its name."

If you study the action so far, you'll realize the brilliance of this fakeout: You've actually just made the poor sap "cut to" what was the top card — the card whose identity you already know!

At this point, your work is done here. Tell the spectator to complete the "cut," putting the top half of the cards back onto the deck, and then to shuffle the cards. Then pick up the deck and proceed to one of the revelations described later in this chapter.

Figure 11-1:
Your volunteer sets aside the top half of the deck (A). (Caution: Most decks don't have the big X.) You put the bottom half on top (B).

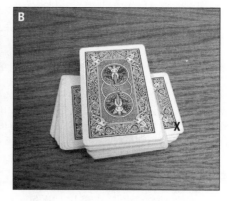

The Under the Hanky force

This force loses points because the action is hidden under a handkerchief or napkin — but gains extra points because it's so far out of the ordinary.

Before the trick begins, put the card you want at the top of the deck.

1. **Hold the deck on your left palm.**

   "In a lot of card tricks, the magician gets too much of an advantage," you can explain. "The magician has every chance in the world to peek at your card, or to peek at the card above it, or whatever. This time, though, not a chance. We're going to blindfold the whole affair, so I can't see any of the action."

2. **Cover your left hand (and the deck) with a napkin, hanky, or opaque scarf, as shown in Figure 11-2, photo A. As you adjust the cloth, however, flip the deck over in your hand.**

   Now the deck is face up, although the cloth conceals this minor detail.

3. **Ask the spectator to lift off half the deck through the cloth.**

   "All right," you can say now. "We're ready. Through the cloth, I'd like you to lift off about half of the deck."

   Your volunteer, of course, now lifts off a stack of faceup cards through the fabric.

4. **Flip over the bottom half of the deck (still in your hand) facedown again. Invite the volunteer to take the top card (photo B).**

   In other words, under cover of the napkin, your left hand should turn its remaining half of the deck back over. The force card is now back on top.

   "Great — now reach under there and take the card you cut to." (In other words, the top card of the packet still in your left hand.)

Figure 11-2: If you had X-ray vision, you'd see something like photos A and B.

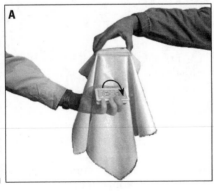
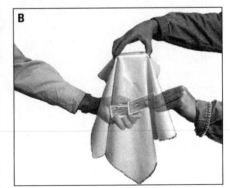

Now that your volunteer has selected a card, you'll have to reverse your double-flipping procedure, so that you wind up with all the cards in your hand, all face down again.

5. **Still under the cloth, flip the packet back faceup. Have your volunteer put his packet back down onto the cards in your hand.**

"You hang onto that card for a minute. Go ahead and put the top half of the deck back down again."

6. **Once the cards are all in your left hand, flip the whole deck face-down one last time, and take away the cloth.**

I realize that a lot of flipping is involved in this force — four in all — but unless somebody with X-ray vision is in the audience, nobody will suspect anything's going on under the cloth.

"Okay — here are the cards. Keep remembering your card, but go ahead and bury it in the deck. Shuffle them so I've got no chance of seeing anything."

You're made in the shade. The volunteer is busy concentrating on a card whose identity you already know. At this point, you can use any of the revelations described in this chapter — but the Feeling by Muscle revelation is particularly apropos, because it lets you re-use the napkin you already have in your hand.

The Bottom-Deal force

Sneaky, sneaky, sneaky! This force is delicious because the very thing that makes it seem extra-fair — your dealing cards from the *bottom* of the deck to prevent fancy deals off the top — is actually how you get away with murder.

Start with the card you want to force on the bottom of the deck. Do a couple of phony shuffles that leave that bottom card in place, as described at the beginning of Chapter 10.

1. **Explain what you're about to do. Ask your volunteer to name a number between one and 52.**

"I did the most amazing card trick the other day," you might begin. "But at the end, this heckler ruined everything — he accused me of doing double dealing. He said any Las Vegas card shark can manipulate the cards he's pulling off the top of the deck.

"I couldn't do trick dealing if I wanted to, but I'll tell you what: I'll deal off the bottom of the deck so I can't get away with anything. Name a number between one and 52. You *can* name a high number if you want, but remember, we're going to be standing here getting older while I deal down that many cards. I'd like to be home in time for *E.R.*"

2. **Hold the deck in your left hand. Using your left fingers, pull back the bottom card half an inch (Figure 11-3, photo A).**

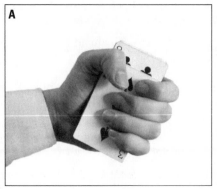

Figure 11-3: The Move, as seen from underneath (A). The Deal (B).

Experiment with your grip on the deck to see what makes this sinister little move easiest for you. If you have short fingers, you may want to shift your left hand around the left side of the deck slightly more than usual.

The deck is mostly suspended by the insides of your thumb and forefinger; your remaining left fingers are left available to glide the bottom card backward. The deck and your hand hide this little slide.

3. **From the bottom of the deck, deal off the number of cards named by your volunteer, one at a time.**

Over and over, your right fingers grab — and pull out — the *next*-to-bottom card. From the top, though, everything looks legit (photo B).

4. **As you reach the volunteer's number, pull the actual bottom card out — and hand it to the volunteer.**

"Here's the card you chose," you can say, turning your face away. "I don't even want to see it. Memorize that card!"

The deed is done. The deck can now be shuffled, given away, or abandoned — your volunteer is convinced he's had a free choice. But you, O Wise One, already knew what it was.

The Countdown force

Here's a force you can do your very first time at the plate. Quick, simple, and foolproof.

Before you start, put the card you want to force at the top of the deck.

Grace under Fire, Part 5

"The Card on the Ceiling" is one of the most famous card tricks in magic. A spectator chooses a card from the deck — and even signs it with a pen. But after it's returned to the deck, the magician whips the deck up into the air so hard that it hits the ceiling. Fifty-one cards shower back down again — but a single card remains stuck to the ceiling. As all can see, it is, of course, the chosen card.

Advisory Pantheon member Harry Lorayne was performing this trick at a resort hotel in the Catskills where he'd been working for years. On one special occasion, though, the manager asked him to do the trick for a special group of guests who were seated in a different room of the building. He was happy to comply.

He went through the trick with his usual polish, almost on automatic pilot. As he had done thousands of times before, he concluded the trick by throwing the cards upward. Too late,

he looked upward to watch the result — and discovered for the first time that this new room had a beamed, vaulted roof. It had no horizontal ceiling to which a card could conceivably stick — only beams and shadows. Harry and his guests watched as the deck disappeared completely into the darkness above the horizontal beams.

Many seconds passed; there was no sign of the deck. But just as Harry was about to apologize, he glanced up again. "And, look!" he exclaimed, pointing.

Thanks to a fluke of aerodynamics, a single card was now floating downward, wafting down alone out of the cavernous darkness of the roof. Sure enough, it was the chosen card; Harry caught it in his hand. The rest of the deck was never seen again.

To this day, Harry doesn't how he did it.

And you know what *that* means, don't you? For added effect, casually give the deck a phony shuffle or two (as described at the beginning of Chapter 10) without actually disturbing that top card.

1. **Ask your volunteer to name a number between 1 and 15. Demonstrate how you'd like her to deal off that number of cards.**

   "Tell you what. Name any number between one and fifteen. Eight? Okay, great. In a moment, I'm going to give you the deck. I'd like you to count down to the *eighth* card, just like this: One, two, three, four, five, six, seven, eight. And I want you to look at, and memorize, that eighth card. Think you can handle that?"

   As you say this, you demonstrate. Deal off eight cards into a little pile on the table.

   Now, in reality, your volunteer is probably smart enough to understand the instruction without seeing you demonstrate first. She's probably feeling vaguely annoyed that you're treating her as though she has the IQ of a walnut.

But your "demonstration" is the key to the whole trick. In dealing down the correct number of cards onto the table, you're *reversing the order* of those eight cards. What was originally the top card (the force card) is now the *eighth* card. Read on.

12. **Put the small pile (now on the table) on top of the deck. Hand the deck to your volunteer. Instruct her to do the dealing business herself.**

"All right, I think you get the idea. Here, go ahead. Deal down to your chosen number, and memorize that eighth card."

Sure enough, when she memorizes the eighth card, it's the one whose identity you already know — the one that was originally on top. Proceed with your favorite revelation.

Revelations

You've just forced a card. You know your volunteer's card, and you know that the volunteer doesn't know that you know. Now what?

Now reveal the card in one of the following delicious ways.

The Geiger Counter

This revelation is the one featured in The Hands-Off, Mixed-Up, Pure Impossibility trick featured in Chapter 10.

This is the revelation where you spread the cards out in a ribbon on the table. Then you run the corner of a single card along the edges of the others, making a neato clicky sound, as though your "detector" is picking up signals. Gradually, you home in on the chosen card.

Flip back to Chapter 10 for photos and more detailed instructions.

The Jumping Out revelation

Talk about befuddling: this card revelation simply short-circuits audience brains. They'll have absolutely no clue how the card leaped out of the deck, all on its own, and flipped over to reveal itself.

1. Get the chosen card on top of the deck.

And how are you supposed to do that? Easy. Depending on how you forced the card, the card may already be on top of the deck. For example, suppose you've just performed the Countdown force (flip back a couple pages). Your volunteer has just looked at, for example, the eighth card. All you have to do is scoop up the pile of cards on the table (with the chosen card on top) and plop them back onto the main deck. Do a false shuffle or two (see the beginning of Chapter 10), keeping the chosen card at the top, and you're home free.

If it's too late for that and the chosen card has already been shuffled into the middle of the deck, no big deal. Simply thumb through the cards until you find it — and then cut the cards in such a way that the chosen card becomes the new top card. (If you feel you must say something during this process, any lame excuse will do: "This only works with complete decks" or "There aren't any Jokers in here, are there?" or "Now I just quickly memorize the order of every card in the deck . . .")

Then, once again, a false shuffle gets you ready for the next step — and the special card is once again on top.

2. Cleanly square up the deck. Hold the deck as shown in Figure 11-4, photo A — with your right fingers holding the ends of the deck. With your left hand, push the top card to the right one inch.

Because your right hand blocks your spectators' view — and because they have no idea what's about to happen — nobody sees this one-card ledge sticking out.

Figure 11-4:
The top card, in cantilevered position (A). After the toss (B).

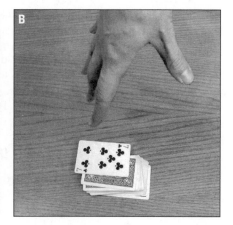

3. **Ask the volunteer to name the card. Hold the deck about two feet over a flat surface. Drop the deck straight down.**

Aerodynamics at work: The airstream catches the overhanging top card and flips it over, face-up, as the deck falls.

Your results may definitely vary on this trick. Depending on your deck, the table surface, and the height of the drop, one of the following may happen:

- The deck lands neatly, with the chosen card still on top of the deck — but face-up, as shown in photo B.

- The deck lands neatly, but the chosen card doesn't turn over — instead, it shoots off to the side somewhere. That's still okay. It's still clearly separated from the pack.

- The deck lands in a mess, maybe even some face-up. Even if this — the worst case — happens, *something* will have happened to your chosen card. It'll be off to one side, either face-up or face-down; just the fact that you can find it amid the mess is impressive enough.

Practice the drop until you can get a consistent result; some magicians prefer to give the deck the tiniest shove downward instead of letting gravity do all the work. Regardless of what happens, the finale is surprising, unusual, and freakish enough to get a rise out of almost any audience.

Feeling by Muscle

If you've got a thespian streak, this psycho-surreal thriller gives you all the opportunity in the world to ham it up. This revelation, an invention of magic consultant Mark Levy, is a natural follow-up to the Under the Hanky force described earlier in this chapter.

1. **Scatter the cards, face-up, all over the floor of the room — cover a huge area.**

The patter is critical to this effect. You must convince your helper that you're not just making this up.

"All right. You've got a card in mind, and I don't know it. But what I do know is that your card is visible somewhere on this floor. As you probably know, lie detectors work by measuring certain involuntary reactions your body makes to mental stress. Your pupils dilate, your mouth gets a little dryer, and your muscles clench. What I want to do is try the same idea here."

2. Hand the volunteer one end of a napkin, handkerchief, or dish towel.

"We're going to use this cloth to make my task even more difficult. I don't want you to squeeze my hand when we walk by your card, or anything."

Each of you should wrap your end of the cloth tightly around your hand, as shown in Figure 11-5.

"We're going to walk among these cards — you have to look down at them. When you see your card, make every effort not to react. Don't tug on the cloth. Don't clear your throat. Don't let your stomach rumble. The idea is for me to feel, through the cloth, any subliminal muscular contractions that your brain triggers when it sees your card. Ready?"

Figure 11-5:
Lead your volunteer as you walk among the cards.

3. Walk slowly among the cards, leading your volunteer. Look for the chosen card. Walk past it, then return to it a couple of times.

"I can't be totally sure, but I think I felt something around this area here. It's gotta be one of these cards — was it this one, maybe?"

4. Finally, drop to your knees and dramatically grab the card.

And, of course, you're right.

Grace under Fire, Part 6

The sidebar "Grace under Fire, Part 5," earlier in this chapter, introduces the classic Card on the Ceiling revelation. In that trick, the magician hurls the deck against the ceiling — and the chosen card sticks.

But Harry Loryane isn't the only one who's had unexpected results with this trick. Advisory Pantheon member John Cornelius was doing the trick for an important guest one day. Everything was going fine: he shuffled the deck, whipped it upward, and watched it hit the ceiling and cascade down again.

As the spectator was quick to point out, however, the card stuck to the ceiling was the *wrong card.*

John was bewildered. How could the trick have gone wrong?

In fact, *two* cards had become stuck to the ceiling (one had adhered to the other). But

now, out of the corner of his eye, John saw the second (bottom) card detach itself and flutter down to the ground behind a couch, unnoticed by his spectator. Inspiration struck.

"Are you sure I had the wrong card?" he asked the volunteer.

"Yes, of course I'm sure," was the response. "My card was the Ace of Clubs."

"Then I'll just have to change the card on the ceiling — by magic!" said John, snapping his fingers. "Look up at your card now!"

And sure enough, the card that remained stuck up there was, indeed, the Ace of Clubs. As far as the spectator was concerned, John had magically changed the identity of a card that was suspended ten feet over his head.

Neither John nor that spectator will ever forget the trick.

The "Name of the Card Is" revelation

This revelation is as clever as can be. But it only works with a single card — the 10 of Hearts — and you *definitely* can't do it twice for the same group.

1. Before you do the trick, write in pencil, on a pad or piece of paper, "THE NAME OF THE CARD IS."

Write each phrase on a separate line, as shown in Figure 11-6, photo A. (If you're performing for a large group, you could also write this on a blackboard.)

Turn the prediction face down (or otherwise conceal it).

2. Force the 10 of Hearts.

Use any of the forces described earlier in this chapter.

3. Ask your volunteer to read the "prediction."

"Now, before we even started," you might say, "I wrote a prediction on this piece of paper. Turn it over and read it, loud and clear."

Figure 11-6:
Your prediction — both before (A) and after your erasing binge (B).

 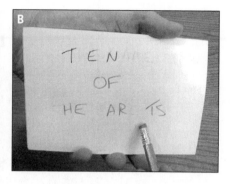

Sit back smugly, arms crossed, pleased as punch. Of course, your powers of prediction seem pretty pathetic. Your volunteer, loudly and clearly, says: "The name of the card is."

Now your attitude changes, big time. "Oh! Jeez, I'm sorry. I forgot to finish it! Here, give me that." Hold the prediction so that nobody can see what you're doing.

4. **Erase letters of your prediction, as shown in photo B — and cross the top of the I in the last word to turn it into a T — so that the "prediction" now says "T E N OF HE AR TS."**

Before you reveal what you've done with the erasing, ask the volunteer to name the chosen card. And then:

"See, it's not that I wasn't finished writing my prediction. I just wasn't finished *erasing* it!"

Turn the prediction around and collect your well-earned applause.

Slap It!

Freaky. That's all anyone can say about this revelation.

Before you start, put the force card on the bottom of the deck. Read "The Jumping Out revelation" earlier in this chapter for suggestions on how to accomplish this.

1. **Ask your volunteer to hold the deck as shown in Figure 11-7, photo A.**

Thumb beneath, fingers on top. "Now, at this point, you're the only one who knows the name of your card. Well, you and Casper, the friendly magician ghost. He'll help me out here . . ."

Figure 11-7:
Have the
spectator
hold the
deck as
shown in
(A). Slap
downward
on your end
(B) — for a
surprising
result.

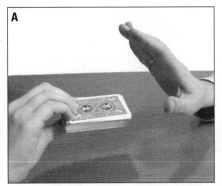

12. **With your fingertips, sharply slap the end of the deck nearest you (If you didn't dislodge all of the cards, keep slapping until you do.)**

    Amazingly, all of the cards fall onto the table except the chosen card, which remains inexplicably clutched in the spectator's hand (photo B)!

The "Above and Beyond" revelation

There are already enough revelations in this chapter to fill a book in the Bible. But I had to mention this favorite, which gets 'em every time.

This trick is what's known as a *sucker trick*. It leads the onlookers to believe they've finally caught you, seen you mess up — only to find out that you had 'em in the palm of your hand.

1. **Explain what's going to happen.**

   "At this point, of course, I have no idea what your card is," you lie, having already forced a card whose identity you know.

   "I'm going to find it again in a very unusual way: I'm going to turn over the cards one at a time. Even though you'll try not to react in any way, I'm going to see if I can tell which card is yours just from the vibes. Don't say anything. Here we go."

2. **One at a time, deal the cards from the top of the deck, putting each one face-up into a ribbon of cards on the table.**

   Stare intently at the cards on the table as you go. Sooner or later, you'll turn over the spectator's card.

3. **Don't stop when you see the chosen card. Deal four or five more cards beyond it, slowing to a stop.**

   Finger the next card, the one currently on the top of the deck in your hand.

4. **Make the bet.**

   "All right, here's the deal. I'll bet you a quarter that the next card I turn over will be your card."

   Of course, deep inside, your volunteer is laughing his head off. He's already *seen* his card — it came up five cards ago! — and so he's sure that the *next* card couldn't possibly be his.

   He's right. But you didn't say that the next card you *deal* would be his. You said that the next card you *turn over* would be his.

5. **Once your spectator has agreed to the bet, reach out to the face-up cards on the table, pull out his card, and turn it face down onto the tabletop.**

   You've just won a quarter, you sneaky snake! Invest it wisely.

The Magic For Dummies Grand Finale

What better way to illustrate how much you've learned from this book than to *use* the book in a trick?

The basic idea is this: A volunteer picks a card, and *this book* reveals it! (Don't think too hard about this one — you'll wind up thinking in circles.)

1. **Force the King of Clubs, using any of the methods described earlier in this chapter.**

   Now comes the juicy part. "All right, I've put the cards down. For the first time, loud and clear: What was the name of your card?"

   After you hear the answer — "the King of Clubs" — continue.

   "I've been learning magic from this book lately," you can say as you casually pick up this book. "The funny thing is, it not only teaches you *how* to do magic tricks . . . "

2. **Open the book to the next page. Hand the book to your volunteer.**

   " . . . it even does them *for* you!"

Part V
Party Time

The 5th Wave   By Rich Tennant

"I really preferred when Stan did simple disappearing coin tricks at parties."

In this part . . .

*I*mpromptu, close-up magic is extremely rewarding — and it's the kind of magic you'll have the most opportunity to *do*. But there's more to life than doing one-on-one tricks up close. Sometimes bigger tricks, tricks that work well for a crowd, are called for — and the next three chapters are devoted to such larger, broader, stand-up tricks.

Chapter 12

Rope

• •

In This Chapter

▶ Cutting rope and restoring it

▶ Making solid gold dissolve through rope

▶ A three-second rope escape

• •

*I*n magic circles, *rope* refers to a very specific item: a soft, white, cotton clothesline. No excuses, now — no nylon cord, twisted-strand brown rope, kite string, or dental floss. Go out to the hardware store and just buy a doggone hank of clothesline.

Thus equipped, you're ready to learn not just Walking through Ropes (see Chapter 5), but also this chapter's three mind-blowers.

The Classic Cut-Rope Restoration

The Cut and Restored [your noun here] is an essential effect in any magician's repertoire. Magicians are *always* cutting up things or breaking them into pieces, including ropes, neckties, and their onstage assistants. (These magicians were probably *very* destructive little children.)

This effect is good enough to perform for almost any size performance: at a table, in the living room, or even onstage.

The effect: You cut a piece of rope in half and promise to restore it to one long piece. Unfortunately for the audience's high expectations, your not-very-impressive solution is to *tie* the two halves together.

Not wishing to disappoint, however, you run your hand along the entire rope — and the two halves are magically rejoined.

The secret: Thanks to a clever twist early on, you never actually cut the rope at its center.

1. **Hold both ends of a piece of rope in your left hand, as shown in Figure 12-1, photo A.**

   The guy in photo A is using a piece of rope about six feet long; anything over four feet is fine.

   "I'm a pretty scientific magician," you might begin. "I like my tricks to be precise. If I want to cut a piece of rope in two, for example, I'd prefer to cut it from the exact center."

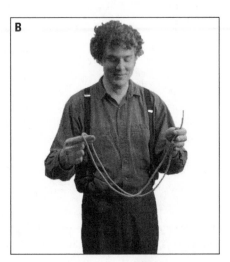

Figure 12-1: Hold up your rope in a U shape (A). As you bring the middle of the rope upward (B), grab the leftmost rope in your hand (C) and pull it up as an impostor for the center of the rope (D). (Photos C and D are what you alone see.)

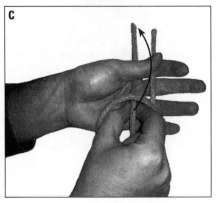

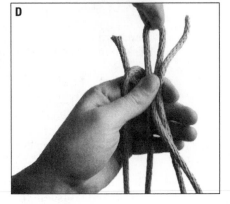

2. **Insert your right thumb and index finger *under* the exact-center loop of dangling rope, as shown in photo B.**

   Your right fingers should be in "I'm gonna pinch you!" position, yet they *don't* pinch the rope. Instead, they slip *under* the bottom loop of rope and lift it up to your left hand.

3. **With your right thumb and index finger, grab the leftmost strand of rope that's hanging from your left thumb (photo C). Pull it upward, forming a loop that you clamp with your left thumb (photo D).**

   Steps 2 and 3 may not feel quite as natural as, say, sneezing or yawning. In fact, they may require numerous rehearsals before the move feels continuous, smooth, and natural. (You want it to *look* like you're simply grabbing the dangling middle of the rope and pulling it up out the top of your left hand.)

   But that's the whole trick. Done properly, it looks utterly normal. After the "center" of the rope is in position (photo D), hand a pair of scissors to a volunteer. (Or if you're onstage and can't be bothered, cut the rope yourself.)

4. **Have a volunteer cut the rope (Figure 12-2, photo A).**

   "There we go," you can continue. "Here's another piece of scientific equipment — a pair of scissors. If you don't mind, I'd like you to snip the rope in half. Right in the center there."

5. **After the cutting, let the rightmost two ends drop from your hand.**

   This startling optical illusion is shown in photo B — you've just cut the rope into two long halves, clear as day. What nobody realizes, of course, is that your left hand now contains a short piece of worthless rope, looped around a still whole, much longer strand.

   "Beautifully done. And precisely, too! Hey look, you've done a magic trick — you've made one rope turn into two!"

6. **Tie the short piece in your hand around the longer piece in a knot.**

   In other words, as you continue to hide the bent middles of the ropes in your hand, tie the two short ends — the ones sticking up out of your left hand — in a single knot (photo C). In real life, of course, you'd require a *double* knot to tie two ropes together. But because your hands block most of the action, and because you're talking and fiddling, nobody will object.

   "Ah, but in this case, I'm afraid, I'm the better magician. Through the use of a simple scientific principle, I can restore the two pieces into one continuous length of rope!"

7. **Triumphantly display the "restored" rope (photo D).**

   "And voilà! Back in one piece!"

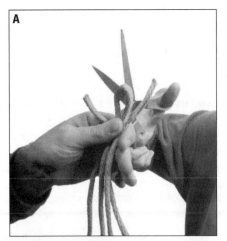

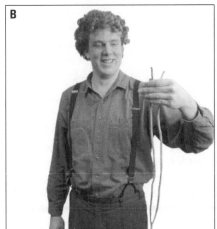

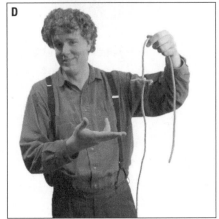

Figure 12-2:
After the rope is cut (A), you seem to have two halves (B). Knot the short piece (C) as a temporary finale (D). Wrap the rope (E) and then display it whole (F).

Unless your entire audience is caffeine deprived, somebody is certain to look disgusted, demand a refund, or lob diseased fruit.

"All right, all right. I admit it. I joined the ropes back together using science instead of magic. But if it's magic you want, it's magic you'll get."

8. **Grab one end of the rope with your left hand. Using your right hand, begin wrapping the rope around your left fist. When your right hand hits the knot, slide it along the rope.**

Even after it grabs the knot, your right hand keeps wrapping — all the way off the far end (photo E).

"Ladies and gentlemen — a scientific marvel . . ."

9. **Unwrap the rope to show it whole (photo F).**

" . . . two rope pieces joined magically into one!"

At this point, you've got a fully restored rope stretched between your hands — and a little knot of incriminating evidence hidden in your right hand. You have several options to get rid of the knot:

- Plan ahead — after Step 8 but before Step 9, reach into your pocket with your right hand. Leave the knot behind as you pull out some magic utensil — a "magic key," a "magic coin," a "magic used Kleenex" — which you then wave over your wrapped-up left hand. Or:

- Do something dramatic with the rope — like whipping it or tossing it gently into the audience — to provide misdirection as you drop the knot onto the floor behind you. Or:

- Don't worry about it; just leave the knot in your hand. Ditch the knot when you reach for the props for your next trick or carry it around with you until you go to bed that night.

Ring off Rope

Here's another trick that involves a borrowed finger ring. Hate to break it to you, but you may actually have to *practice* this one before you perform it. Not everything comes easy.

But the payoff is well worth it: For the rest of your life, you'll have people thinking you're some kind of genius.

The effect: You thread a ring onto a rope. While somebody holds both ends of the rope, you manage to make the ring dissolve and reconstitute *off* the rope.

The secret: It's all in the handling; the ring is actually off the rope much sooner than anyone suspects.

As with just about every rope-centric magic trick (see the beginning of this chapter), you need a piece of clothesline for this, in this case about 15 inches long.

1. **Borrow somebody's ring. Thread the ring onto the rope. Display the setup in your left hand, as shown in Figure 12-3, photo A.**

   "I'd like to show you a simple demonstration of escapology. That's *escape*-ology, the study of escapes, not to be confused with *eschatology*, the study of the end of the world, or *ichthyology*, the study of fishes."

   (Note to the phonetically impaired: Those useful patter words are pronounced "ess-kit-TAH-luh-jee" and "ick-thee-AH-luh-jee.")

   Here comes the part that you should practice in front of a mirror or video camera endlessly before you ever venture into public. It should *look* like you're just turning your left fist over, palm down, *as* you wrap the lower part of the rope (emerging from your left pinky) around your fist (underneath, away from you, and finally back over the top).

   As you'll see, much more is going on: You're actually going to secretly remove the ring from the rope during the act of turning your left fist over.

2. **Close your left hand. Begin turning it palm down. As it approaches the upright position, thumb on top, grab the lower rope with your right hand.**

   This particular tenth-of-a-second arrangement is frozen in time in photo B. The ostensible reason of your grabbing the lower rope is so that you can wrap it around your left hand *away* from you. For a split second, though, your fists are together, which presents a perfect opportunity for that ring to slip down the rope and into your right hand.

3. **Without stopping the motion of your hands, loosen your grip on the ring so that it slides into your right hand (photo C).**

   Photo C shows the same instant as photo B — but this time, from your viewpoint.

   Imagine that both hands form a cocoon: tight at the top and bottom, wide in the middle. That is, keep your right *upper* (and left *lower*) fingers open enough so that the ring will slide unencumbered — but keep your *pinky* closed hard on the rope to prevent the ring from siding completely off the rope and clattering to the floor.

   So far, only another tenth of a second has elapsed.

4. **Finish turning your left hand knuckles down. Wrap the right hand's rope end away from you, over the top of your left hand, and over to a spectator's hand (photo D). As you hand the end to her, slip the ring off that end of the rope and keep it in your right hand.**

   "Could you hold onto this end for me, please?"

   (In case I didn't mention it, keep your right hand *closed* so that nobody knows the ring is inside.)

Figure 12-3:
The only honest part of this trick is the beginning (A). From the audience's point of view (B), you're just grabbing one end of the rope. But, as seen from your side (C), the ring slides down the rope into the lower hand. You wrap the rope around your left fist — and finally you hand the rope to someone to hold (D). Then hand the other end to someone, say some magic words, and mystically remove the ring (E).

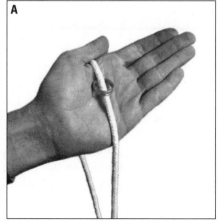

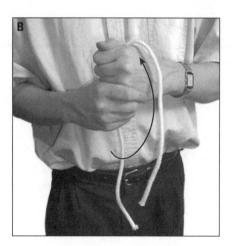

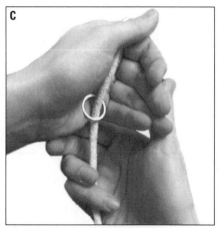

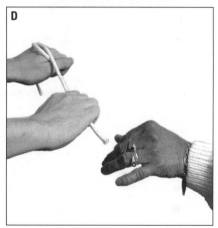

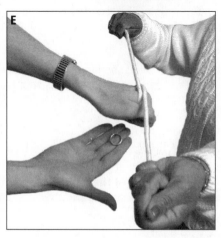

I'm perfectly aware that at first, you'll feel incredibly self-conscious performing this move. You won't believe that everybody won't immediately know what you're doing. However, three things conspire in your favor. First, you've practiced until you can do this business smoothly and without even looking; second, nobody even knows what you're up to yet.

And third, you don't look at your hands when you do it! Remember the basic rule of misdirection: The audience looks where you look. And in this case, you're looking at *the spectator's hand* as you ask her to hold onto the end for you.

5. **With the ring still in your right hand, grab the other end of the rope — the one coming from the thumb side of your left fist — and hand it to another spectator, wrapping it over the top of your left hand.**

"And if you could just hold that end . . ." (If you only have one audience member, she can hold both ends of the rope, one in each hand, at this point.)

"As you can see, both the ring and I are thoroughly tied up at the moment. But here's where the escapology comes in. Remember, that's the study of escapes. So here . . ."

6. **Place your right hand directly under the left. Rub gently. Open your right hand to show that the ring has dissolved off the rope (photo E).**

"Study *this!*"

Grace under Fire, Part 7

A few years ago, Advisory Pantheon member Mike Bent had an audition in New York for a TV show. Since his plan was to drive down from Boston with a friend, do the audition, and fly back, he packed light — all he brought with him was a small suitcase containing his magic props.

Mike's audition went well; afterward, he took a cab to the airport. He got there just in time to make his flight. He quickly bought his ticket and headed to the gate. (Under normal circumstances, he'd check his suitcase, but there wasn't time on this occasion.) And so, at the security checkpoint, he placed his prop case on the X-ray machine's conveyor belt, momentarily forgetting what was inside.

Just after the case emerged from the scanner, Mike noticed that the conveyor belt stopped moving. The security guard was studying the contents with some interest. And no wonder: Mike's props included a fake knife, a human skull, a baby doll, props with electronics inside (wires, batteries taped together, and so on) — and, to top it off, a prop blank pistol. (Mike isn't what you'd call a dull magician.)

The guard asked, "What is all this stuff?"

"I'm a magician," Mike replied.

"Oh, okay," said the guard. He let Mike through without another word.

Escape from the K-Mart Tie

This book doesn't offer you much in the way of escape tricks, even though they made Houdini one of history's most famous magicians. That's because handcuffs, straitjackets, and padlocks aren't everyday objects found around the house. (Well, at least not around *my* house.)

But here's a miniature escape that's plenty powerful, if only because it takes place right under your friend's noses, while they're holding you in place with an ordinary rope and a necktie.

The effect: You're handcuffed (or just tied by the wrists). A piece of rope is thrown over the chain between cuffs — yet in a matter of seconds, you're free of the rope.

The secret: Read on. The three-step rope-removal twist is too complicated to pithily summarize here.

1. **Let an audience member put the "cuffs" on you.**

   If you really do have handcuffs, use 'em. But in the absence of handcuffs — which is almost always — substitute a scarf, necktie, or even another piece of rope. A tie is probably the best alternative to real cuffs — it's easier to tie than a scarf, yet easy to distinguish from the long rope you'll be using.

   "You've probably all heard of Houdini, the master of escapes," you can begin. "This guy could wriggle out of anything — straitjackets, handcuffs, underwater trunks, swim trunks — anything. But Houdini didn't just appear one day, you know. He started with simpler escapes and worked up to the big ones. When he was only four years old, he probably began by performing escapes like the one I'm about to show you."

   Hold up the necktie. "I'm supposed to use handcuffs for this trick, but I couldn't find any where I usually shop — K-Mart. They did, however, have this attractive necktie. I figured it's just as good. Would you be so kind as to tie my wrists with this? We'll *simulate* handcuffs. That's it. Now tie the other end around my other wrist. Make sure I can't slip out. That's excellent."

2. **Ask the volunteer to throw a rope around the center portion of the necktie and then to hold both ends of the rope firmly.**

   This rope, by the way, can be as long as you like — but no shorter than about ten feet. You need enough slack that you can turn your back on your volunteer — who's holding the ends — without violating his personal space.

"On my table there, you see that I've got a long piece of rope. Would you mind picking it up and throwing it over the tie between my wrists? That's good — and now hold both ends. Tight. At this point, I'm help- less. I'm a dog on a leash. I belong to you." Squint your eyes accusingly. "You're *enjoying* this, aren't you?"

After you're tied, by the way, contribute to the impression of helpless- ness by letting your wrists dangle. Don't use your hands for anything — let them hang, impotent. That's why you ask your *volunteer* to handle the rope. Yes, you're perfectly capable of picking it up yourself — but this way, you create the subliminal impression of a magician who's been incapacitated by a Father's Day gift.

The setup should now resemble Figure 12-4, photo A.

"The challenge, then, is for me to escape. After all, if there's one thing a magician hates more than being imprisoned, it's being imprisoned by a piece of polyester. I'm going to turn my back and do my thing — whatever you do, don't let go of the ends of that rope."

Optional dramatic element: After you get good at the following steps and can do all of them smoothly and quickly, heighten the tension — like thousands of magicians before you — by billing your escape as a race against *time*. At this point, you'd ask another volunteer (or the same one) to watch the sweep second hand of a watch. The challenge: If you can't escape within five seconds (or ten, or whatever can't-lose interval you've worked out in rehearsal), you'll pay the volunteer $20, leave the party immediately, mow his lawn, or whatever.

3. **Turn your back (photo B). With your left hand, pick up the piece of rope that's draped over the "chain" (the piece of tie that connects your wrists). Push this loop underneath your right handcuff.**

   Please notice, as shown in photo C, that the *lower* piece of rope be- comes the *top* of the loop you wedge under the tie against your wrist. You wind up giving a single twist toward you as you move the rope to your right wrist.

   Difficult as this is to grasp as you read, in practice, it's really not a big deal. With your left hand, just grab the rope that loops around your "chain" and rotate that loop clockwise as you bring it to your right wrist; it's now the top side of the loop you shove underneath.

4. **Pull the rope loop through the right "cuff." When it's big enough, throw it over your right hand (photos D and E).**

   Although your right hand doesn't technically have to be palm up, as shown in photos D and E, turning it seems to feel better. Note that the rope loop goes *down* over your hand (photo E).

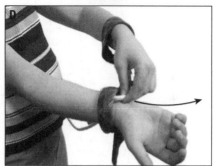

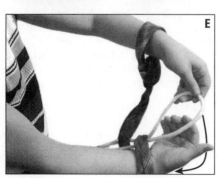

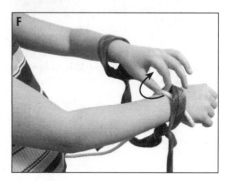

Figure 12-4:
You're all tied up (A). Turn your back (B). Grab the rope, twist it inward (C), and shove it under your right "cuff" (D). Pull it through and over your hand (E). Then pluck the top-of-wrist, near-side-of-cuff piece of rope (F) and throw it over the top of your hand (G). You're free!

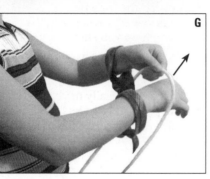

5. Let go with your left hand. Grab the piece of rope that's now lying on top of your right wrist, on the near side of the "handcuff" (photo F). Throw it over your right hand and away from you (photo G).

If the gods are with you, you should now be completely free of the rope. Make the most of your sudden freedom — in one dramatic move, pivot to face the volunteer, throw your hands up in the air, and fling the rope away from you.

Because about only three seconds have elapsed since you first turned away, this sudden centrifugal gesture looks deeply impressive. Especially if you yell something triumphant as you spin around, something along the lines of:

- "Yessss!"

- "Freebird!"

- "I'm comin' home, mama!"

- "Hasta la vista, baybeeee!" (Works best with an Austrian accent.)

- "Time!" (To be said only if you are, in fact, being timed. I know it doesn't make much sense, but it's just a great thing to yell.)

You've done what you set out to do — you've released yourself from the rope. Which leaves you, of course, standing there still knotted up in your necktie, which you must now ask your volunteer to untie for you.

This is a bit humiliating, of course, but hey — you're a *novice* magician, remember? If your ego won't rest until you can free yourself of the handcuffs as well, see *Magic For Convicts*.

Chapter 13

I Knew That!

In This Chapter

▶ Picking out cards from a deck by touch

▶ Reading your spouse's (or friend's) mind

▶ Doing magic over the radio

▶ "Forcing" your audience to select an object of your choosing

▶ Reading people's minds using books

▶ Knowing your friends' preferences for vegetables

▶ Reading minds over the phone

*Y*ou're about to enter a special zone in the magic world, a realm of mind reading and prediction tricks known as *mentalism*.

But be warned: When you do this kind of trick, you're instantly saddled with a moral dilemma. These tricks make it look like you know what other people are thinking. The dilemma: Do you pretend that you really can read minds? Or do you make clear that these are for entertainment purposes only — great tricks, sure, but nothing supernatural?

Among pro magicians, this debate rages endlessly. Some magicians relish making audiences wonder if ESP really exists — making spectators admit the possibility that you really *can* sense what they're thinking. Other magicians, realists all the way, recoil in disgust at such a presentation style. Pretending to *really* have ESP, this second group feels, is lying, cheating, and taking advantage of your spectators' trust — even more than other kinds of magic do.

As a hobbyist magician, you probably won't lose much sleep over the mind-reading debate. If you're philosophical, however, decide which magical camp you're in — and adjust your performance accordingly.

The Three-Card "Pick by Touch" Test

Here's a great trick for getting your feet wet in the exciting new field of paranormal events. It isn't mind reading, *exactly,* but it definitely falls into the category of Sixth-Sense Stunts that Scare the Psychologically Susceptible.

The effect: You scatter a deck of cards face down on the table. You challenge a spectator to hold his hand over the cards. You tell him to let it fall on one he *thinks* could be, say, the 2 of Hearts. You set his selection aside.

You ask another spectator to see if she can find the Jack of Diamonds in the same way; then you announce that *you'll* find the 10 of Spades. When the three set-aside cards are revealed, you've made your point: all three of you were successful in choosing cards by touch alone.

The secret: The trick relies on a classic magic concept called the *one-ahead principle.* There's a good reason you don't turn over each card as it's selected — because they're off by one, as you see in a moment.

1. **Invite a spectator to shuffle the deck.**

   "Have you ever read up on card sharks? You know, these guys who go around making thousands of dollars in poker games? Everybody knows that they're cheating — but nobody can ever figure out how. Actually, I think that at least some of them use *card sensing.* Have you ever done any experiments in card sensing? Here, shuffle these."

2. **As you take back the deck, glimpse and memorize the bottom card. Scatter the deck all over the table — but keep track of where the bottom card winds up.**

   Doing all that isn't as hard as it sounds. For example, your opening speech gives you plenty of time to peek at the bottom card.

   Then put the deck on the table. Start your messing-up process by spreading the deck from right to left as though it were a particularly large pat of nonfat dairy spread. As a result, the bottom card is easily accessible to you. Now, as shown in Figure 13-1, slide your hands all over the table as you mix the cards — but keep one finger (your right thumb or pinky, for example) permanently pressed against what was originally the bottom card.

   After enough swirling around on the table, leave the card somewhere near the edge of the mess. Don't forget where you left it; you'll need to find it again later.

3. **Instruct your volunteer to touch the card he guesses is the [name the bottom card here].**

Figure 13-1:
As you slide the cards all around the table keep a finger on the bottom card, as shown. (Note: When *you* do the trick, no circle will appear around your pinky.)

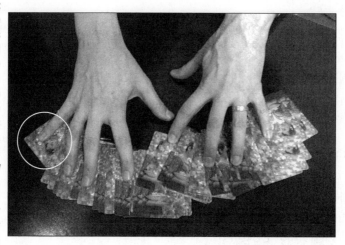

"In card sensing, you choose cards by feel, kind of like playing your hunches at the horse-race track. Here, try it. Hold your hand over the deck. Just move it around. Try to guess which card is, I don't know, the 10 of Hearts." (Of course, here's where you name whatever the bottom card was.)

"Just let your instinct take over. When you think you've got it, touch the card with your finger."

4. **Set aside the selected card — but look at it first, as though to see how he did.**

"This one? Let's see . . ." Pick up the card he touched, memorize it (peek at it without letting anyone else see), and set it carefully aside, well apart from the other cards. You'll name this card in the *next* "test" — that's why it's called a one-ahead trick.

For this example, let's say that he touched the Jack of Hearts.

"Good — you did better than you probably think. See, most people have never even *tried* card sensing, so they don't appreciate how often it really works. All right, let's try another test."

If several people are present, choose a different volunteer for the second round. "This time, I'd like *you* to try to find the — well, the Jack of Hearts," you tell her. "Hover until you get an impression, and then touch what you believe could be the Jack of Hearts."

5. **Set the second card aside — but once again, peek and memorize it first.**

   "Let me see . . ." (And here, once again, you look at the card, memorize it, and set it aside. Let's say it's the 10 of Spades.) "Another good guess."

   Set the second card on top of the first.

   "Hey, let me try one. I may not be as good at it as you are, but I've been working on it. Let's see if I can find the 10 of Spades."

6. **Pretend to get "vibes" from the mixed-up cards — and finally select the edge-of-pile card that was originally the bottom card.**

   Peek at this one, too, just for consistency.

   "Hey, all right!" you might say approvingly.

7. **Slip your card underneath the first two chosen cards as you pick up all three.**

   "Okay, let's see how we did. Remember, the cards we tried to find were the 10 of Hearts, Jack of Hearts, and 10 of Spades. If you stop to think about it, the odds of our having been right all three times is pretty astronomical — we're talking one out of 50, three times in a row. But that's where the sixth sense prevails over logic. Because look at this."

8. **Reveal the three cards, in order.**

   "There they are: 10 of Hearts, Jack of Hearts, and 10 of Spades. So the moral of the story is — never play poker with a good card-senser!"

The Triple-Prediction Spouse-Clincher

If you're familiar with the *one-ahead* principle described in the previous trick, you're ready for a slightly more difficult version of the same concept. Your body language, acting, and verbal skills will be put to the test in this one.

The "Triple-Prediction" part of the title is easy to understand. Why are the words "Spouse-Clincher" part of the name? Because I did this trick on a first date with a beautiful woman — and she wound up marrying me.

Your mileage may vary.

The effect: You make three predictions about impossibly obscure aspects of your volunteer. You're correct all three times.

The secret: You make your predictions on a "one-ahead" basis. You don't make the second prediction until you already know the answer to the first, and so on.

As with the Three-Card "Pick by Touch" Test, however, you must know *one* of the answers before you start. If you know in advance that you'll be performing this trick for someone specific, do a little research. Ask your victim's friends, relatives, or bosses for some obscure factoid you couldn't otherwise know. (In my wife's case, I sneakily found out from a former classmate the name of her med-school dorm building. Talk about obscure!)

Of course, sometimes such research isn't practical. If you're performing the trick for strangers or for people you can't find dirt on beforehand, I'll provide a backup plan in the following instructions.

1. **Tear up a sheet of paper into six strips. Keep one set of three for yourself and give the other set to your subject.**

   "Here we are. Three slips for you, three slips for me." Set three of the strips into one little pile for your subject, and three near you.

   "Now, I don't know you very well," you might begin. (Or as appropriate: "Now, I've never met you before" or "Now, we've only been married for 30 years.")

   "I know your name, and that you're a nice person, and that you've obviously got at least a little bit of patience for watching magic tricks.

   "But some things about a person are harder to pick up. Sherlock Holmes was a special case. He'd notice a speck of toothpaste on your pinky fingernail — and he'd extrapolate from that clue everything you'd done in the last 24 hours. I'm not *that* good, but I've gotten pretty good at picking up subtle signs along those same lines.

   "I'll tell you what. Let's do a test. Right now I'd like you to clear your mind." And then, after one-third of one second: "Well, *that* didn't take long. Okay, now I'd like you to focus on something — I don't know, something from your youth that I couldn't possibly know. I've got it: Think about your best friend when you were a little kid. What was your best friend's first name? Focus on that first name. Say it over and over in your head. I'm going to take one of my slips and write down an impression."

2. **Take a slip of paper from your set of three. So that nobody can see, write 35. Cross it out and write 37 next to it (see Figure 13-2, photo A).**

   I realize that the odds of the friend's name being *37* are fairly slim, unless your volunteer grew up in prison. But that's not the point. You're now writing your answer to the *third* question, which is several minutes away. You're using the one-ahead principle, you trickster, you.

   By the way, writing 35 and 37 is the backup plan I mentioned earlier. If you were able to find out a piece of obscure trivia about your subject beforehand, write *that* on the first slip instead.

Figure 13-2:
Your first
prediction
actually
gives
you two
chances
(A). As you
go, have
your
volunteer
clamp your
guesses
in one
hand and
her own
answers in
the other
(B). If all
goes well,
you're right
all three
times (C).

3. **Fold your first prediction. Ask your subject to hold it in her right hand — and to now reveal the childhood friend's name.**

"All right, I've made my guess," you can say as you fold the slip. "Here: Clamp my guess in your hand with your thumb until the end of the trick — that's it. Now my prediction is safely locked away. The truth can be told: What was the name you've been thinking of?"

4. **So that everyone can see, write down the friend's name on one of the *subject's* slips of paper. Fold it and ask her to hold it in her left hand.**

"Xerxes? Wow, I can see why you were able to remember his name after all these years. I'm going to write that name down on one of *your* slips of paper — there we go — Xerxes. Okay, now if you'd just clamp *this* slip of paper in your *other* hand. That hand's going to be *your* pile."

Your volunteer's dual hand-clamps should look like photo B.

Now you're in a great position: You know the kid's name. Unfortunately, your original prediction was wrong — but you'll fix that. You're about to go another round with your subject — another mind-reading test.

But you don't want your volunteer thinking about the fact that she just gave you the answer before the trick was completely over. Using your body language and face, establish the fact that Round 1 is over — it was a complete trick in itself. Straighten up, shift position, scoot your chair, whatever, but make it seem like you're now beginning fresh.

"All right, let's try something a little different now. Something harder. Once again, I want you to think of something and focus on it nonstop. But this time, I want you to think of a place. A city, a park, a building — anything with some emotional resonance for you. A place you can picture. A place where something important happened. Let me know when you've got that place's name in your head."

5. **Take a second slip from "your" pile. Write *Xerxes*. Fold it *and* ask your friend to hold it.**

In other words, write whatever name was given to you in Round 1. Once again, don't let anyone see your prediction. Fold the slip when you're finished writing. Ask your volunteer to clamp it, once again, under her right thumb.

"All right, I've made a guess here. Once again, if you'd just clamp that together with my first prediction — excellent."

Her right hand has now been established as your Prediction Pile.

"All right, I've written my guess. You can tell us now: What's the name of the place you were thinking of?"

6. **Write the place name on one of "her" slips.**

Write so that everyone can see it. "Prague? Ah, Prague! I've never been to Prague, although I love dealing with Czechs. Especially when they're made out payable to me."

Or whatever. "Like that? Okay, great. Let's add this one to your pile, here in this hand." Fold the slip and add it to her "answers" hand.

Now you're ready for Round 3. Once again, psychologically cleanse your palate: Shift in your chair, crack your knuckles, make a break with the previous round.

If, as mentioned earlier, you've clandestinely learned a morsel of deep, dark dirt about your subject, ask her to concentrate on that tidbit now. ("Now I'd like you to think back to the time you were in college. What was your English professor's name?" or whatever.)

If not, and you're using the Plan B (and you wrote numbers on your first prediction), read on.

"All right, I'm ready to make one more attempt. Let's do something easier this time; sometimes I do better with numbers than with touchy-feely names and places. How 'bout — okay, I know. Think of any number between 1 and 50. Make both digits odd, and make the digits different from each other. Lock that number in your head."

That wording is critical. If you're going to memorize any line of patter in the book, memorize that one. "Make both digits odd" forces her to think of a two-digit number (without your having to say so).

It so happens that there *aren't* very many two-digit, both-odd numbers between one and 50. There's 13, 15, 17, 19, 31, 35, 37, and 39 — but in 100 performances, 99 people will choose 35 or 37. I'm not exactly sure what that tells us about human nature, but what do you care? You've got what's almost a sure thing.

That's why, way back in Step 2, you wrote "35," crossed it out, and wrote "37." Now you're covered either way. Basically, you're cheating. (Get over it — that's what magicians *do*.)

7. **Pick up the final slip of paper from "your" pile. Concentrate for a moment. Write the place name on it. Fold it and put it into your volunteer's "guesses" hand. Ask for the actual number and write it on the final slip of paper.**

"Got it. At least I hope so. All right, loud and clear — what was the number you thought of? 37? All right, I'll write that on your final slip, like this. Go ahead and clamp that final slip in your left hand with the other answers."

Your volunteer winds up holding three slips in each hand, as shown in photo B.

8. **Take your pile from her right hand, open your *bottom* slip, and compare answers.**

"All right — three rounds, three guesses. I was going purely from vibes here. My spelling may have been wrong, I may have been way off — but let's see how I did. Here, let me have my stack of guesses."

Now, because you've been "one ahead," your answer to Round 3 is actually at the bottom of the slips of paper your subject has been holding for you. For that reason, you must unfold the bottom slip to correspond with her opening her *top* slip.

Doing so undetected isn't such a big deal. It's your friend, Mr. Misdirection, to the rescue. *Look* at, and even nod toward, the three slips still in your volunteer's hand. (Don't look at her face. Look at her *pile*.)

Say, "Okay, unfold that top slip and put it down on the table." During the tenth of a second when she's looking down at her hands, simply grab the bottom slip from *your* pile. Bring it toward the table just as your subject brings hers there. Add, "And I'll open my prediction at the same time."

Look — just because I've dwelled on this issue for three whole paragraphs, don't get nervous. You know what? *Your audience won't care.* Your subject, frankly, is much more interested in how *she's* doing than in what you're doing. You've given her a task, and she's seized by performance anxiety — especially if other people are watching. Even if you didn't use that clever instant of misdirection to grab your bottom slip, it's likely that nobody would notice, or care, which slip you're unfolding from your pile. Everyone's too eager to see you fail.

"You chose the number 37. And I correctly predicted you'd say — yes, 37!"

If you were right, quell the riot and proceed — you've got two surprises to go. (And if you'd secretly found out some piece of life-history trivia beforehand, same thing — you're batting 1,000. Proceed with the other slip-openings.)

If you were wrong — that is, if you've got some nonconformist socio-path subject who didn't pick 35 or 37 — don't sweat it. After all, you *were* attempting the impossible.

"Oh, darn — I'm oh for three so far. Let's see how I did on the significant-place test." And go right on.

If your subject chose 35 but not 37, no biggie. Unfold your slip and show that your first instinct (the crossed-out number) had, indeed, been 35. "Well, you can see that that was my first guess," you can say. "It's like on the SAT — they always say that you should leave your first guess. I get half a point for that — let's see how I did on the next test."

9. Unfold your next two slips along with your helper (photo C).

"Okay. The next test would have been — well, that was the place name, right? You said — oh, right, Prague. And I said — yes! I said Prague!"

You'll greatly enhance the effect if *you* look surprised and delighted, too.

"Finally, we have your childhood friend's name. You said your friend's name was Xerxes, and I — well, I did pretty well on that one, too. I did predict you'd say Xerxes."

Smile and accept whatever gifts are showered upon you.

"Can you imagine how good I'd be on *The Newlywed Game*?"

The Math/Geography/Animal/Color Test

In the middle of a recent radio interview, the host asked me: "Why don't you do a trick for our listeners right now?"

I stared at him as though he'd just grown a third eye. Do a trick on the *radio?* Where nobody can see me? Was he nuts? My career flashed before my eyes.

But then I remembered this ancient and freaky little mind-reading test, which once had its 15 minutes of fame on TV's *Regis & Kathie Lee* and in *Esquire* magazine. Since it's completely verbal, you *can* do it over the radio — and, for that matter, over the telephone, via e-mail, while driving the car, and so on.

The effect: You ask a volunteer to think of a number; do some math with it, all in his head; convert the resulting number to a letter; think of a country that begins with that letter; think of an animal that begins with the country's second letter; and focus on the color of the animal.

You make a guess about the color — and get it right.

The secret: The math at the beginning ensures that the volunteer winds up with the same number — 4 — every time you do the trick. From there, the spectator really doesn't have any choice, thanks to the clever way the questions are structured.

There's only one tricky part to this stunt, and that's remembering what to say. Because this is a purely verbal, very unusual trick, I'll list the patter *as* the steps.

1. **"Think of a number between one and ten. Don't tell me what it is. Got it?"**

   In fact, this is the only free choice your volunteer will have.

2. **"Okay. In your head, multiply it by nine. All right?"**

   At this point, you're still in the dark.

3. **"If the answer is two digits, add the two numbers together."**

   Now you're home. No matter what number was chosen in Step 1, your volunteer now arrives at the number 9. If you follow Steps 2 and 3 using *any* number between 1 and 10, you get 9.

4. **"Subtract 5 from the answer."**

   You know that your volunteer gets 4 as the result, but she doesn't know that you know.

5. **"Now, find the letter of the alphabet that corresponds to that number. So if your number is 1, pick A; if it's 2, pick B; and so on."**

   The number 4 corresponds to the letter D. All is going according to your master plan.

6. **"You've got the letter in mind? Great. Now we move on from math into geography: I want you to think of a country that begins with the letter you're thinking of."**

Here's where the manipulation gets really sinister: although you seem to be offering a free choice, there *are* only four countries that begin with D: Denmark, the Dominican Republic, Djibouti, and Dominica. Hard as it may be to believe, in 15 years of performing this trick, I've never yet met a volunteer who chose Djibouti or Dominica.

Trust me on this: Your volunteer is now thinking about Denmark.

(About one time in 100, somebody will think of the Dominican Republic. In that case, the trick derails. No big deal; change the subject or do a different trick, using the line "Is that really a country? I thought it was just an island republic" as your transitional excuse.)

7. **"You're now thinking of a country, right? Okay, great: Now take the second letter of the country's name. Got it? On to biology: I'd like you to pick an animal that begins with that letter."**

Here again, you've psychologically stacked the deck against your hapless volunteer: there are only two reasonably common animals that begin with E: the elephant and the emu. Guess which one almost everyone picks?

8. **"Finally, I'd like you to focus on the *color* of this animal. Picture it. Don't think about anything else. I'm going to see if I can pick up the image of this color — by brain waves alone."**

Elephants are generally considered gray, by the way.

9. **"I'm getting the impression that it's — gray!"**

You won't believe how good the rush of power, control, and triumph feels when your dumbfounded volunteer admits that you're right — a handy sensation to keep in mind during your next radio interview.

Divide & Conquer

In this puzzling little prediction trick, all you'll have to do is play a little game.

The effect: You assemble a bunch of different objects on the table — cards, different CDs from your collection, matchbooks that don't match, a stack of business cards from your last trade show, or whatever. You and a volunteer take turns eliminating objects until only one is left on the table — whereupon you slowly and deliberately take off your shoe to reveal a prediction. Needless to say, you correctly predicted which item would be left.

The secret: The rules of this little elimination game make your success a sure thing. Your unsuspecting victim actually has no choice — you *force* the outcome so that it matches your prediction.

Before you begin, then, write a prediction on a slip of paper. It can simply name the object: "Yanni Live in New Haven CD," for example. If you're using something that's openable (matchbooks, CD cases) or turn-overable (coasters, business cards), you could write on the *bottom* of one of them: "I knew we'd wind up with this one!"

Hide your prediction in your shoe or in a sealed envelope (see the following sidebar, "Truths of Magic, Part 12: Distance yourself from the prediction"), and begin.

1. **Arrange the objects on the table. Explain the rules.**

   You need a fairly large group of objects for this one — between 9 and 20, for example. They can't be identical, either; you can't use nine quarters. (It wouldn't be much of a trick if your prediction said: "I knew we'd wind up with the quarter!")

   "When I was a kid," you can explain, "I used to fight with my brother over everything. I always accused my mom of giving him the bigger bowl of ice cream, the better piece of the cake, the less wormy piece of fruit. So finally mom got smart — she instituted the principle of Divide and Choose.

   "It works like this: My brother gets to cut the two pieces of pie, but *I* choose which piece I want. That way, he's got an incentive to cut the slices exactly evenly. Or I pick out which two apples we'll have, but *he* gets to choose which one he wants. So obviously, I'm not going to pick out an apple that's like an ant farm, because I might get stuck with it.

   "I'd like to show you a trick that works along the same lines. I've got a bunch of CDs here" (or whatever you've got). "It's a game of elimination. We take turns. I choose two, and *you* get to pick which one gets taken away. Then you choose two, and *I* get to take one away. We just keep going until there's only one left. Get it? Here, let's try."

   You'll "win" this game no matter who begins — if you remember this:

   If you have an odd number of objects, you must begin the game. If there's an even number, your *buddy* goes first.

   If you have any trouble remembering this rule, just keep saying this quietly to yourself: "I'm odd. I'm odd. I'm odd."

2. **When it's your turn, touch two objects that *aren't* your predicted one. When it's her turn, take away the one that's *not* your predicted one.**

   Suppose there's an odd number of cards on the table. You, of course, begin.

   "All right, I'll start. I choose these two. Now you can take away whichever one you want." She should take it completely away from the other objects.

"Great. Now it's your turn. You choose any two, and *I'll* take one away."
If one of the objects she touches is The Predicted One (see Figure 13-3,
photo A), take the *other* one off the table. If neither of her two touched
objects are The Predicted One, take away whichever you want.

"My turn again? Okay, I choose these two. Take one of them away."

And so on. If you think this through or program it as a 3-D vector-graph
computer simulation, you'll soon realize that you can't lose. The
predicted object is within your control. After several rounds, there'll be
only two objects left on the table — and it's your choice to remove one.

Remove the one that's not the prediction object.

"All right, we've got one object left on the table," you can say. "Now, the
funny thing about my rivalry with my brother was that even with the
new, super-fair rules, I still always got the best of him. Somehow I
always managed to know which one he'd choose."

3. **Reveal the prediction (photo B).**

"See, before we even started playing the game, I made a prediction. I
wrote it down on a little slip of paper which, to avoid tampering by
marauding bands of hecklers, I've stashed inside my *sock,* inside an
envelope. Let me take off my shoe here — really, this is nothing personal — and look! Here's my envelope . . . the remaining CD is *Sounds of
Aboriginal Australia,* and I correctly predicted we'd have — yes, *Sounds
of Aboriginal Australia!*"

(Or "the 4 of Spades!" Or "The pack of Juicy Fruit!" Or whatever.)

Figure 13-3:
Always
eliminate
the one
that's *not*
your
prediction
object (A).
When
there's only
one left,
reveal your
prediction (B).

Don't be swayed by the simplicity of this trick's description. In practice, it's absolutely unsolvable — a real mind-bender.

The Book Test

You gotta know a Book Test. You practically can't even *apply* to be a card-carrying magician without knowing a Book Test. Don't leave home without one.

A Book Test is a classic mind-reading act. A volunteer picks a word from a book and concentrates on it. You, the magician, announce the chosen word. There've been as many different methods to pull this off as there have been Madonna hairstyles — but this method, an invention of magic consultant Mark Levy, is unusual, baffling, and clever.

Truths of Magic, Part 12: Distance yourself from the prediction

In Divide & Conquer, I wrote that you should pull the prediction out of some difficult-to-access location — such as your shoe. There's a good reason for storing your prediction in an awkward, distant, or sealed-up location: Believe it or not, if the prediction were any easier to get to, you'd be accused of making the prediction *after* you knew what to write.

For example, suppose you play the Divide & Conquer game and wind up with the Electric Light Orchestra CD on the table. If you then reach into your pants pocket to pull out the prediction, some wiseacre in the crowd — I kid you not — will yell out, "You wrote down 'Electric Light Orchestra' in your *pocket!*"

We won't, for the moment, preoccupy ourselves with why people with such farfetched theories are allowed to roam the streets (let alone vote). Suffice it to say that such ridiculous claims greatly weaken the climax of your trick, even if they're patently absurd.

Why not avoid the problem entirely? Remove all doubt. Whenever you do a prediction trick, store the prediction someplace that's completely inaccessible — and yet, preferably, in full view during the entire performance. In a restaurant, put the prediction under the centerpiece of the *next table* (if, that is, the table is unoccupied). A sealed envelope almost anywhere works well (such as under the tablecloth or under your volunteer's seat cushion). You could write the prediction on a sticky note and put it underneath the table. Inside your shoe or sock is always good (albeit hygienically questionable).

But you get the point: Don't wreck your own masterful performance by leaving the door open to moronic theories from the crowd.

The effect: A volunteer arrives at a number by adding together the page numbers from two newspaper pages. He chooses a book from a pile, turns to the page that corresponds to the total, and concentrates on the first word on the page — or even the *image* of the action in the first paragraph — and you're able to read his mind.

The secret: You've already memorized the first word or paragraph on the page. And how did you know what page to consult? Easy — you've ripped off the corners of *paired* newspaper pages, such that the total is always the same. Read on.

Before you begin, locate a newspaper that fits the bill. A tabloid-shaped newspaper (*National Enquirer, New York Post,* and so on) is ideal. If all you can find is a full-size newspaper (*The New York Times, The Boston Globe, San Francisco Chronicle),* you'll have to make do with one *section* of the paper. But do your best to find a tabloid one — using only a section of a paper greatly diminishes the mystery, thanks to the reduced number of pages.

Here's how to decide if your paper is acceptable:

- ✔ Is the page number of the back page divisible by four? If so, then your paper (or section) is what we want — printed like a book, with four pages printed on each double-width sheet. (The left-hand newspaper in Figure 13-4, drawing A shows this pleasant scenario.) Skip the next three paragraphs.

- ✔ Is the page number of the last page even but *not* divisible by four (such as 62)? In that case, something funny is going on inside the paper. There's probably a single loose sheet inside that hasn't been folded in half like all the other pages. (The right hand newspaper in Figure 13-4, drawing A shows this problem.) In this case, read on.

- ✔ If there is a single loose sheet inside, is it at dead center? If so, you're still in luck. Throw away that center sheet and you're ready to begin.

- ✔ Unfortunately, some sneaky papers (such as the *The New York Times*) sometimes put a loose single page into a section *off-center,* which throws off the mathematical principle behind this trick. Go back to the newsstand and pick up a more magically suitable publication.

All right — you've got your paper. Add up the page numbers of *both sides* of *one giant sheet.* For example, if you were using the left hand newspaper in drawing A, you'd add up page numbers 1, 2, 7, and 8 — all four page numbers that appear on a single sheet of folded newsprint. The total is 18. (The key to the trick, of course, is that the total is 18 regardless of which sheet of newsprint you choose.)

If you were using the right hand newspaper in drawing A, you'd add up 1, 2, 9, and 10, for a total of 22.

Figure 13-4:
The
newspaper
at left is
ideal (A).
The second
paper is
okay if you
toss the
loose sheet.
Pick up
two page
corners at a
time (B).

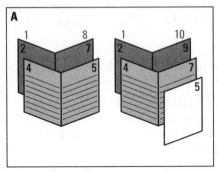

Collect three books. If they're from your personal library, fine. If you're performing at someone else's house, take them from his library. Choose one — say it's *Moby Dick* — and turn to the page that matches your total. Memorize the first whole word on the page. If you can find a book whose first paragraph depicts some interesting action, better yet; you'll be able to end the trick by drawing a picture instead of simply announcing a word, which is even creepier.

In the instructions for this trick, I'll show you how to manipulate the proceedings so that a volunteer "chooses" the book whose word or image you've just memorized. As you get comfortable doing the trick, however, consider memorizing the first word or image on the specified page of *all three* books. That way, you can eliminate the "Magician's Choice" shenanigans described in Step 5 — and just plow ahead with a spectacular revelation regardless of which book was chosen.

Put the books at a place between you and your audience, such as on an end table. You're ready to go.

1. **Introduce your literature.**

   "Funny thing about the publishing industry," you might begin. "Every day, we chop down miles of rain forest to feed our society's hunger for reading material. But look at the contrast between the results! On one hand, we've got newspaper — cheap, fast, and disposable. Nobody here would consider me a vandalistic thug if I started tearing up a newspaper."

2. Open the newspaper to the center. Tear off the corners — the ones where the page numbers are printed — of each side.

Set down the torn-off corners in two piles — one from each "wing" of the newspaper section.

"But if I were to start ripping up the pages of these *books* —" Pick one up, open it, and get into tearing position, but stop. "Well, you'd throw me out of the joint."

Ask for a volunteer and greet him. "I'll tell you what. What I've done here is to tear off all the page numbers from the newspaper. I'm going to go through my piles of page corners — just tell me to stop whenever you feel like it. No pressure . . . just whenever the urge strikes you."

3. Begin picking up two page-number corners at a time — one from each pile in each hand. Until you're told to stop, let them flutter to the floor.

Photo B makes this clear: Each time, you pick up the top page corner from both piles simultaneously. Throw them away, pick up the *next* corner from each pile, and repeat — until you're told to stop.

4. When you're stopped, give whichever two page corners are in your hands to your volunteer. Ask him to add all four page numbers together.

"Right here? These two? We can keep going if you want — no? All right, here you are. These are yours to keep as a souvenir, by the way. But before you go get these page corners bronzed, add up the page numbers. I think, actually, you've got *four* page numbers there, on the fronts and backs. Add them *all* up, all four. Let me know when you've arrived at a total."

Offer him a calculator or pad to do the addition. The last thing you want is a volunteer with no math skills to ruin a great trick.

5. Let the volunteer "select" a book, using "the Magician's Choice."

Ah, the Magician's Choice! This little con has been serving magicians well since the first camel salesman unloaded his laziest, most flea-bitten animal on an unsuspecting rich guy.

Although they may not call it the Magician's Choice, you'll see the same technique used by companies, parents, and Congress: offering what seems to be a free choice — but manipulating the game so that you choose the one the *magician* wants. (It's akin to a card force — see Chapter 11 — but the Magician's Choice scam refers to a *specific* sequence of steps.)

"I've picked out a few fine works of fiction from our host's bookshelves," you can say. Point to the three books you'd laid out beforehand. "Would you hand me any two of those?"

In the next ten seconds, the action may take any of several paths. If the volunteer hands you the two books that aren't *Moby Dick,* you're in like Flynn. "Excellent. Grab that remaining book and don't let me near it." Skip down to Step 6.

If, on the other hand, one of the two books you're handed *is* your target book, your little game continues without skipping a beat. Hold out the two books he just handed you. "Thanks very much. Okay — here — take either one of these two books . . . "

If your volunteer now takes *Moby Dick,* finish your sentence like this: " . . . and hold it so I can't see the pages." Toss the book left in your hands aside, as though you intended to discard it all along.

But if your volunteer takes the *other* book out of your hands, leaving *you* with *Moby Dick,* finish the sentence like this: " . . . so I'm left with one very special choice. Hey, look at this — you've chosen the world's greatest fish story. *Moby Dick.*"

As you can see, the Magician's Choice involves a series of forks in the road. The idea is to think on your feet, to pretend that the whole thing is going according to some standard plan.

(Although I'm glad you just learned about the Magician's Choice, remember that this trick works even better if you don't use it — which is the case if you pre-memorize the key word or scene in all *three* books.)

6. **Ask the volunteer to open the chosen book to the chosen page number.**

   "What I'd like you to do with this book is open it to a certain page — the page whose number you arrived at when you added the newspaper numbers together. When you get to that page, focus in on the first complete word on that page. In your head, repeat that word."

   Of course, if you're interested in the Book Test — Paranormal Edition, say instead, "When you get to that page, take a moment to read the first paragraph. Try to picture what's going on in the story. Imagine the scene."

7. **Take a pad and magic marker. Hold it so that the audience can't see it — and record your "mental impression."**

   "The idea here is for me to detect what you're thinking about," you can continue. "Try to blot everything else out of your head except that one word" (or: "except that scene in the story").

Write the word on your pad — or draw a simple picture of the scene. (The drawing-a-picture business works especially well if the scene involves a monomaniacal sea captain attacking a giant albino whale.)

8. **Ask your volunteer to announce the thought-of word (or read the paragraph).**

"All right, I've made my guess," you can say. Put down the marker. Clutch the pad to your chest so that nobody can see its face.

"Loud and clear: What was the word you were thinking of?" (Or: "Loud and clear: Please read to us the paragraph you arrived at.")

Smile broadly. Look relieved. "You know, I'm actually getting pretty good at this. I got exactly that impression, thanks to your superior powers of concentration. Look at this!"

Show the audience your pad for the first time. It's a shocker!

The Great Vegetable Prediction

Few magic tricks involve vegetables. A shame, I say — maybe we'd grow up stronger and healthier if more of our popular entertainment incorporated fine produce and legumes.

This one, though — a favorite of Advisory Pantheon member Johnny Thompson — scores highly on the Food Group I Relevance Test. Try it at your next picnic!

The effect: You place a sealed box onto the table next to you. You take vegetable-name suggestions from the audience, writing each onto a slip of paper and dropping it into a paper bag. Once you've had enough suggestions, an audience member chooses a slip from the bag; incredibly, when the sealed box is opened, it contains the very vegetable whose name was on the chosen slip!

The secret: You write the same thing on every slip going into the bag. Even a vegetable could predict the outcome.

Before you begin, place a fairly common vegetable into your little box. Actually, you can use fruits instead of vegetables — believe it or not, the trick will work just as well. (For that matter, you could use a sealed bag to contain the fruit instead of a box. And you could use a bowl for the slips of paper instead of a paper bag. Express yourself!)

For this example, let's say you've chosen a banana. I know it's not a vegetable, but it's all I had in the fridge at picture-taking time. (Don't choose something offbeat like kumquat or radicchio — when you take suggestions from the audience, nobody will propose what's actually in the box, and you'll look extremely foolish.) Close up the box so that nobody can see the contents.

Equip yourself with a piece of paper torn into strips, a magic marker, and a bowl or bag into which you can stuff the suggestions. You're ready.

1. **Ask for vegetable (or fruit) names from the audience.**

   "Ladies and gentlemen, I'm going to need your assistance for this little miracle. I need you to provide me with the names of some fruits. Can anybody think of one?"

2. **When an audience member shouts out a name, write *banana* (the name of your predetermined fruit) on a slip of paper. Fold it and stuff it into the bag.**

   "Apple? All right, very nice — apple it is. Into the fruit bowl goes 'apple.' How about another one?"

3. **Continue taking fruit names. Each time, write *banana* on a slip of paper, fold it, and drop it into the bag.**

You'll help your cause if you make subtle comments about the written forms of these vegetable/fruit names: "Broccoli — let's see, is that two Cs and one L?" Or: "Lettuce. Jeez, I've never realized how much that word looks like it should be 'la-TOOCE.'"

In other words, in every respect, act as though you're actually writing down the audience's suggestions. Make a party out of it:

- "Oh, *good* one! What're you, a farmer?"

- (When someone suggests, say, jícama): "Ah, I see we have the chef from Le Cirque here tonight."

- "Is it just me, or does all this make you just crave a big juicy Big Mac?"

Another sneaky fakeout: If somebody names something that could be considered confusingly spelled — say, kumquat or fennel — write its actual name down (instead of *banana*). Make such a mess of crossouts and re-writing the name that you wind up throwing the slip away (preferably in such a way that the audience can see it) and starting fresh on a new slip of paper. And on *this* one, of course, you write *banana*.

When you've filled out enough slips of paper — and after somebody's actually suggested "banana" — cap your pen.

"All right, that should be fine," you can say. "We've got enough fruits in there for a salad."

4. **Invite an audience member to select a slip from the bag (Figure 13-5, photo A).**

Figure 13-5:
A volunteer
picks fruit
(A). You
bear
fruit (B).

"Pick a fruit, any fruit," you might say. "Now, so everyone can hear it: What fruit did you pick?"

It should come as no surprise to you that the chosen slip says *banana*.

5. **Present the box or bag that contains the fruit or vegetable.**

"Now, when most magicians do tricks that involve telling the future, they make *written* predictions of the outcome. But not me. I *shop* for my predictions. Inside this box, in fact, is my prediction — in the form of a piece of fruit. Obviously, I had no idea which fruit you'd choose — but open the box and show everybody how I did."

The spectator displays your accurate prediction (photo B) — one large banana, comin' up.

"Ever since I mastered this trick, I don't bother making grocery lists anymore. I just read my own mind!"

The Telephone Trick I: Call This Number

As with the Book Test, the Telephone Trick is another classic. Performed competently, this trick can short-circuit some of the smartest minds in your social circle — and give you an overnight reputation as a really good magician.

The effect: Though there are as many variations on this trick as there are "Seinfeld" reruns, the premise is always the same: You do a card trick at a party. But unlike in the other 104,345 card tricks on earth, *you* don't reveal the chosen card's name. This time, you pick up the telephone and call someone else who reveals the card's name over the phone. (Reason enough to invest in a speakerphone right there.)

The freakishness of this miracle is that the person you're calling isn't even in the same building. How could he possibly have known what card was being chosen in a party miles away?

I'll give you two different versions of this trick. Choose one and become an expert at it.

Any version of the Telephone Trick requires the assistance of a friend who's willing to sit at home and play the part of the distant assistant. Discuss the project with this friend of yours. Decide which version of the trick you prefer — and practice together.

And then go out and blow minds.

The secret: The strength of this first version of the Telephone Trick, proposed by Advisory Pantheon member Jeff Sheridan, is that you, the magician, do almost nothing. You never handle the cards — indeed, you can do the trick *without* cards, asking someone simply to think of a card — and you never handle the telephone. An audience member picks the card, dials the phone, and speaks to the mystery assistant. These points won't be lost on your jaw-dropped audience.

The secret hinges on a code — a name code. You tell the volunteer whom to ask for when she calls. And in the process of asking for the appropriate person, *she* unwittingly reveals to him the name of the selected card.

If you were a professional magician, I'd suggest that you memorize a person's name for each of the 52 cards in the deck. (Your assistant doesn't have to memorize anything — at his end, he can have a six-foot wall poster of the code's translation, for all you care.)

But because you've probably got a life outside of magic, here's a simpler idea: the *first name* of the person your volunteer asks for (when making the phone call) indicates the suit. Let the *last letter* of the first name reveal the card's suit.

Sarah or Jonah	*Hearts*
Eric or Brooke	*Clubs*
Ingrid or Ed	*Diamonds*
Tess or James	*Spades*

(Yeah, yeah, I know, it'd be simpler to use the *first* letter of the first name. But that'd also be easier to figure out. After you've provided the name to ask for, the Mensa nerds in your audience may quietly test their theory that the card's name was somehow embedded in the assistant's name. *This* will throw them off the track.)

As for the number of the card — that's easy, too. Make up a last name whose first letter corresponds to the card number, like this:

Ace	**A**nderson
2	**B**uford
3	**C**renshaw
4	**D**onaldson
5	**E**ngland
6	**F**rench
7	**G**ray
8	**H**arris
9	**I**reland
10	**J**ohnston
Jack (11)	**K**ravitz
Queen (12)	**L**ang
King (13)	**M**oore

Using this system, then, how would you name your assistant if the chosen card were, say, the 4 of **H**earts? You'd ask for Ric**h D**enison. The Ace of **S**pades? How 'bout: Alexi**s A**rthur. The Queen of **D**iamonds? Davi**d L**ee.

Prepare a tiny cheat-sheet of this code system if it will make you feel more relaxed. Paste it into a little pocket-sized phone book. During the trick, you can glance at the code while you pretend to look up your assistant's phone number.

But in time, you won't need the code. As you talk about the magic of long-distance telepathy, you'll have plenty of time to count in your head ("A, B, C, D, E . . .") to find the letter that corresponds to the card's number — and even *make up* a last name that begins with that letter.

I realize that this is a lot to contemplate. But if you've grasped all of it on the first reading, then (a) you're ready to begin, and (b) *you* must be a Mensa nerd.

Explain the code to your friend, arrange for him to be home during the party, practice many times, and then head out.

1. Have a deck of cards shuffled as you introduce the trick.

"I'd like you to shuffle these cards very well. See, I've got a particular bias about card tricks. I don't see why the magician should ever have to handle the cards at all. If there's real magic in the world, I shouldn't ever have to touch the cards. In fact, if there's real magic in the world, we shouldn't even have to *use* cards! Here, give me that."

2. Take away the deck of cards.

"You know what cards are in that deck as well as I do! What's the point of saying 'Pick a card'? Just *name* a card. Say it out loud. Make one up. You've got a totally free choice."

If *that* doesn't get your audience's attention, take up streaking.

3. As you get the telephone ready, calculate (or look up) your name code.

"Now, at this moment, everyone in this room knows that you thought of the 8 of Clubs. But in principle, nobody *outside* this room knows your card. That's where telepathy comes in.

"Did you ever have one of those experiences where you and someone close to you started saying exactly the same thing at the same time? I've got this one friend like that. Jack. We've been best friends since we were babies. One time in high school, I got this cold, dark, sickened feeling one afternoon. Turns out later he'd been in a car accident.

"Over time, we began to realize that these weren't just coincidences. We had somehow advanced our sense of each other to the point where we could communicate mentally. Just small stuff, you understand. Not whole sentences. And not when one of us was trying to keep private — just when one of us was broadcasting.

"So let's try something wild. We all know your card, but my friend Jack doesn't know it. He does know, however, that I planned to test our little telepathic link tonight. He agreed to be on call for this little experiment."

4. Give your friend's phone number to a volunteer. Ask her to call the number — on speakerphone, if possible — and ask for him by name.

"Here's the number where he's going to be tonight. Give them a call. Ask for Jack Hamilton. When he comes on, don't give him any help. Just ask him what your card is. I'm just going to sit here in the corner and broadcast — mentally. I won't say a word."

The volunteer calls your buddy's number and asks for Jack Hamilton. Your friend replies, "This is Jack" (or "speaking" or whatever) — and gets busy translating "Jack Hamilton" into a card name (in this case, the 8 of Clubs). (If the spectator just asks for "Jack," your friend should ask, "Which Jack?")

After he's figured out the name of the chosen card, he should say: "I'm getting the impression of — of a black card. A Club. I believe that it's the 8 of Clubs."

I'm telling you, they'll talk about this trick for *weeks*.

The Telephone Trick II: Call the Phantom

Every version of the Telephone Trick has its strengths. The beauty of the Call This Number method is that you never touch the cards, and you never talk to the person on the other end of the line.

The strength of *this* method is that you don't have to learn any kind of code, and there's no chance that your volunteer can screw up (in dialing or asking for the name). In this version, you do the dialing — but all you do is ask for the Phantom; when she comes on the speakerphone (or when you hand the phone to your volunteer), she immediately announces the chosen card.

Furthermore, you don't necessarily have to plan ahead with this method. After you and your friend have done the trick a few times, you'll both know: When a call begins, "Is the Phantom there?," that's the cue to get to work. You can do the trick whenever you happen to call (and she's at home).

The effect: Once again, a card is chosen (or just thought of). You place a call to someone called The Phantom, who promptly names the card.

The secret: As soon as your friend knows it's you and why you're calling, she starts naming card suits. You interrupt her at the appropriate moment, thus signaling her — and you repeat the process with the number of the card.

   1. **Ask a volunteer to choose a card.**

      You can use the astonishing "We're not even going to use an actual deck" method, if you like (see Steps 1 and 2 of the previous trick).

      "Now, you've seen my first attempts at magic tricks tonight," you might continue (if, in fact, you've *done* any other tricks tonight).

      "But it's incredible what the really great magicians can do. Like I know this one woman. She calls herself the Phantom. She's really unbeliev-able. She'll actually read your mind over the phone! She lets people like us just call her up and have her tell us what we're thinking. It's kind of like the Psychic Friends Network, except she's always right and she never asks for your Visa number. You wanna try? C'mon, let's try it!"

2. Dial your friend. Ask for the Phantom.

"Hello — is the Phantom there please?"

As you've rehearsed beforehand, your accomplice at the other end of the line immediately recognizes that cue. It means it's *you,* calling to do this trick.

As soon as she hears that line, she begins saying slowly into the phone (which only you can hear): "Clubs. Hearts. Diamonds. Spades."

All you have to do is *interrupt her* at the key moment. Say, "Sure, I'll hold."

Now your friend knows the card's suit. She immediately begins saying, "Ace. Two. Three. Four. Five . . ." and so on. Once again, you signal the card by interrupting her. This time, say: "Hi — is this the Phantom?"

That's it! She now knows the card's name.

Put her on speakerphone (act as though the idea of doing so just occurred to you). If you don't have a speakerphone, hand the telephone to your volunteer. Whisper to the volunteer: "Ask her what your card is!"

When he does so, he'll be floored to hear the Phantom's voice — reading his mind. Scary.

Chapter 14

Group Hysteria

In This Chapter

▶ Parlor magic

▶ Group magic

▶ Stand-up magic

▶ Big magic

Most of the tricks in the preceding chapters fall into the category known as *close-up* magic — tableside, under-their-noses, up-close tricks. But not all tricks are appropriate for close-up performance. For example, you'd never do the Flaming Guillotine of Death over dessert and coffee. Not only would the cabinet be ungainly, but you'd almost certainly be asked to leave the restaurant.

No, those jumbo illusions, the ones you often see on TV specials, the kind that require massive custom-built trunks and cabinets, belong under the heading *stage magic.* (There aren't any of those tricks in this book. I figured the odds of your having an acrylic trunk and stagehands lying around your house are pretty slim.)

In between, however, is a happy-medium category known as *parlor magic* — tricks sized appropriately for a living room or backyard. In parlor magic, your audience is generally seated in front of you, and you're generally standing up. (There's plenty of crossover between magic categories, by the way — mindreading tricks can often be done close-up, onstage, *or* as parlor tricks, for example. Still, the terms *close-up, parlor,* and *stage* are useful in describing not only a scale of magic performance, but also a certain *magician's* preferred performance arena.)

Parlor magic is the domain of this chapter: tricks that are big enough to be enjoyed by a roomful of people — and, for that matter, *designed* to be performed for a roomful of people because they're rich with audience participation, humor, and fun.

The Torn and Restored Toilet Paper

Sure, sure, we all know that magicians can tear up and restore dollar bills, neckties, and newspapers. Old hat, man. Not even worth e-mailing home about. But go to a party and tear up some Charmin, and you better *believe* they'll be talking about you the next morning. That's exactly what you'll do in this offbeat gem, a favorite of Advisory Pantheon member Chris Broughton.

The effect: You hand a square of toilet paper to each guest at the party. You bid them to shred the tissue into a million fluffy little scraps; you do the same. You show them how to rub the shredded TP on the elbow to mash it back into one piece — but alas for their budding magic careers, only your toilet tissue is restored. Everyone else is left with nothing but a pathetic wad of bathroom tissue — and a newfound respect for your abilities.

The secret: While you're in the bathroom fetching a roll of toilet paper, you wad up a duplicate square and wedge it behind your ear. Foolproof misdirection and clever handling do the rest.

1. **Return from the bathroom carrying a roll of toilet paper.**

   If you ask me, the opportunity to parade into the center of a party trailing a garland of ScotTissue — and yet winding up, four minutes later, looking like you have magical powers — is worth the price of this book right there.

   Anyway, as mentioned above, don't emerge from that bathroom until you've squeezed a wadded-up square of toilet paper behind your right ear. Don't be nervous about it — nobody will notice. Frankly, once you hand out a square of TP for each guest, they'll be much too interested in their own progress to worry about you.

2. **Distribute a square of toilet paper to each guest (Figure 14-1, photo A).**

   Either hand out individual squares — or just hand the roll around, with instructions to tear off one square per person. (Take a square yourself, too.)

   "Would you like to participate? Would you like to participate?" That's all you need to say as you distribute the toilet paper. Trust me: You'll have their full attention.

3. **Lead your friends through the process of shredding the square of toilet paper.**

   "What we're going to do here," you could say, "is conduct a small experiment in particle physics. But first, of course, we're going to need some particles. So what we'll do — here, everybody do this with me — is tear the square of toilet paper in half, just like this."

Figure 14-1:
Enter the party zone with a square of toilet paper behind your ear (A, shown from behind). Shred the paper (B). As you rub against your elbow, steal the previously hidden piece from your ear (C, shot from behind). Swap bundles (D) — and then drop the shredded wad down your collar (E). Finally, unveil your restored masterpiece (F).

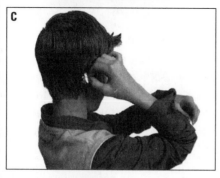

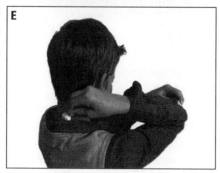

Rip your square right down the center. Then put the two strips together and tear *them* in half, so that you now have four bite-sized pieces. Continue ripping the square into ever smaller shreds.

"Good," you can say as you do this (see photo B). "Now rip it into quarters, like this. Okay, and now into eighths. Care to try for sixteenths?"

4. Roll your shreds into a tight little wad.

"Now roll this mess into a compact little pellet between your hands, like this. Looking good. Now here's where the science comes in . . ."

5. **With your left hand, press the pellet against your right elbow — and begin rubbing.**

"We've compressed the pieces quite a bit, but we can help the process along by applying some further compression. If you start rubbing it against your elbow, like this — that's it, good — the pulpy molecules of the shredded tissue start to adhere. Hey, this stuff really *is* squeezably soft! Rub it in tight little circles, like this."

6. **As you peer at your own elbow, grab the previously hidden TP wad from behind your right ear (with your right hand), as shown in photo C.**

The beauty of the elbow-rubbing business is that your audience is now distracted in two different ways: First, they're preoccupied with their own rubbing. Second, if anyone does look over at you, they'll look at the action on your elbow, just as you are.

7. **Bring your hands together, as though to further compress your wad (photo D). Mash the two wads together, handling them as one.**

Here's a perfect line of patter to explain this hands-together action: "If you feel the shreds starting to fall apart, take a moment to re-compress it, if you want" — and pretend you're using both hands to further mash down your pellet.

Don't be skeptical about getting away with this exchange. It's completely hidden by your hands — and, as before, your spectators will be concerned with their own little "science projects."

Nothing to see here, folks, your actions seem to say. *Nobody here but us fingers.*

8. **In the process of further squishing your wads, exchange your right-hand wad with your left-hand wad.**

The best way to pull off this swindle is simply to rotate the doubled wad as you handle it, so that the shredded bundle is now on the right.

Okay — you've done it. You've now got the shredded pieces hidden in your right hand, and a whole, unshredded wad in your left.

9. **Resume the rubbing action against your right elbow (with your left hand). Meanwhile, drop the pellet in your right hand down the back of your shirt (photo E).**

You may remember this convenient and undetectable method of ditching small objects from Chapter 3's "The Vanishing Quarter, Showoff Edition." As in that trick, your right hand is naturally at your collar, thanks to its elbow-out position.

"Now, do you feel anything happening?" you should say. Take command of the room — be a squadron leader here. Start getting excited. "You may begin to feel the paper sort of changing texture. Maybe tingling a little. Okay, slow it down, now — slow it down — all right, I think we can take a look and see what we've accomplished."

10. **Pull your wad away from your elbow. Slowly and carefully unfold it to its full non-shredded size (photo F).**

"And if all's gone well, you should see that the wonders of particle physics have pretty much joined the ripped edges together. You should wind up with a fully restored square of toilet paper, ready to use."

You may want to handle the tissue with your fingers splayed out, fully open, so that everybody can see you've got nothing concealed in them.

Everyone around you is now unraveling a pulpy mess of shriveled Charmin scraps, most *definitely* not restored into a whole piece. Pretend to be stumped.

"Huh! Well, that's odd — it worked for me. Maybe you guys didn't rub long enough. Tell you what — you can keep those shreds of tissue with my compliments. Take 'em home and when you have a moment, rub them some more. You never know, you know?"

You Can't Do as I Do

For years, magicians, comedians, and other public speakers have amused and intrigued audiences with a cute little gag that goes like this:

"Before I begin my talk, I think it'd be nice if we all got to know one another. At the count of three, I'd like each of you to turn around and shake hands with the person sitting directly behind you. Just to be friendly. Here we go: One, two, three!"

Sounds good on paper — but of course, when each audience member actually turn around, there's nobody to shake hands with — because *everybody else* has turned around, too! The result is an entire auditorium of laughter, as people catch on.

It's a clever gag, but it's old as Moses' toes and twice as corny. Here, courtesy of Advisory Pantheon member Aye Jaye, is a fresher way to loosen up a crowd — and this time, they'll be completely stumped by your quadruple-jointedness.

The effect: You ask your audience to warm up by clasping their hands in front of them — with arms twisted. All they have to do now is untwist their arms, which you easily demonstrate. But much to their bewilderment, everyone in your audience remains twisted.

The secret: In the process of helping somebody attain the correct positioning, you momentarily unclasp your hands. Read on, and be grateful for the invention of photography.

1. Invite the onlookers to try a warm-up with you.

"I realize you'd like to get on with the magic show" (or dinner, or reunion, or group therapy, or whatever people have gathered for). "But it's always good to go into this kind of thing warmed up. C'mon, sit up straight — let's get loosened up. Do as I do."

2. Stick your arms stiffly in front of you, palms facing outward.

"Start by sticking your arms out like this. Palms outward, like you're prying open some elevator doors. Thumbs down. Good, that's it."

Figure 14-2:
Clasp your hands, wrists crossed (A, and then B). Help out one of your spectators (C) — but when you re-clasp your hands, your right hand rotates clockwise instead of counterclockwise (D). Only you can straighten your arms at this point (E) — definitely not your audience (F).

3. Clasp your hands (see Figure 14-2, photos A and B).

"Now cross your wrists like this, and clasp your hands together. Good!"

If you were to bend your elbows at this point, they'd point outward, more or less.

4. Pretend to notice that somebody's not clasping quite right. Unclasp your right hand in order to "correct" her positioning.

"Nice and tight," you say as you "help out" the spectator by gripping her clasped-hand assembly with your right hand (photo C).

Of course, this is only a fake-out. The real reason you took your right hand away from the left for a moment is so that, when you re-clasp your hands, you do so in a *different way*.

Therefore, this moment of helping to adjust another spectator's positioning shouldn't be a big deal. It's all over in two seconds, and it should feel like it's not really part of the ritual. Put the whole episode in parentheses — then pretend to go right back to your original position.

5. As you bring your right hand back to clasping position, rotate your wrist *clockwise* so far that your thumb is once again pointing downward (photo D). Re-clasp.

It doesn't matter whether your right arm goes under your left (as in the photo) or over. Either way, this position is unbelievably awkward and may even be slightly painful. That's okay; you're suffering for your art.

Truths of Magic, Part 13: Humans make terrible witnesses

One hour after performing "You Can't Do as I Do," you could ask each spectator, one by one, to describe exactly what you did. "Well, let's see," they'll say. "The magician stood there, arms out, hands clasped like this, and told us to do the same thing. But the magician was able to untwist 'em, and we couldn't."

All of which is correct — but incomplete. People won't remember the *critical moment* — when you took your hands apart for a minute to correct somebody else's positioning! Your body language made sure they'd forget it; you acted as though you were going "off the record" for a moment.

That's a perfect illustration that you, the magician, have a terrific advantage in your effort to create magic in your spectators' minds: as a species, human beings have lousy memories. When onlookers try to re-create in their heads exactly what the steps of a particular trick were, they inevitably edit out what they thought at the time was irrelevant static.

Selective memory, in other words, is a magician's best friend. Just hope those same onlookers aren't asked to serve as witnesses in a trial!

If you've done this properly, if you were to bend your elbows *now* (don't actually do it when performing), both elbows would bend to the left. You've just re-clasped your hands in a completely different arrangement, although not a soul will know it.

So there you stand in quiet agony, your hands in a totally different configuration.

"Now, to complete this warm-up, all you have to do is — straighten out. Like this!"

6. Untwist your hands. Remain clasped. Smile.

If you clasped correctly in Step 5, you'll find that untwisting your arms is easy — they'll practically untwist themselves, leaving you standing there with two perfectly straight, parallel arms (photo E), grinning like Garfield the Cat.

Everybody else, however, will be unable to untwist (photo F). They'll sit there, contorted into peculiar-looking knots, absolutely bamboozled. Let them writhe for a minute.

"Well, I guess it helps if you have an extra elbow in each arm, like I do!"

The Strength Test

In the late 1800's, a teenager named LuLu Hearst, calling herself the Georgia Wonder, traveled across America with a most unusual act: She performed incredible feats of strength. In one demonstration after another, she'd outlift and outmuscle all comers, male or female. She became a celebrity, raking in $1,000 per week and even being accused of having caused an 1884 earthquake.

Scientists from the Naval Institute to the Smithsonian tested her — and concluded that she was the real thing. Little did the humiliated musclemen, scientists, and musclemen scientists know that she was actually using the principles of magic and psychology to fool the crowds.

Here's exactly such a phony demonstration of strength. There's really no secret to it — except for Isaac Newton's little secrets concerning physics. You probably won't get visited by the Naval Institute, but that's okay; they'd probably muddy up your carpet anyway.

The effect: You stand with your arms straight against a wall. You challenge everybody else at the party to try to squash you against the wall. Yet no matter how many people line up behind you, pushing with all their might, you manage to remain with your arms straight (see Figure 14-3).

The secret: There's no secret. Because of a loophole in the laws of physics, you'll only feel the force of *one person* pushing on your back. If your living room were big enough, you could have 10,000 people lined up behind *that* person, all pushing in a giant chain — but all that force dissipates by the time it reaches you.

1. **Find a very sturdy wall.**

   And I mean sturdy — you'd be surprised at the number of walls these days that seem to have been constructed from leftover cereal boxes. A concrete or plaster wall is good; one made from that wallboard stuff may not be up to the task.

   "Hey, c'mere, everyone," you can begin, as you flex and stretch and roll up your sleeves. "The way they drive us at work" (or school, or whatever) — "it's like we're the slaves who had to build the pyramids or row the Viking ships. But working so hard does have one nice benefit — it sure builds muscles! You might not think it to look at me, but I've gotten very strong lately. In fact, I'll make you a little bet: I'll bet you that I'm stronger than all of you put together. Look, I'll prove it."

2. **Stand in front of the wall. Plant your hands against the wall: arms straight, palms flat, fingers up.**

   You might want to plant one leg in front of you, too, to help counter the pressure.

   "Okay, I'm ready. Everybody line up behind me. Jake — put your hands on my back and get ready to push. Susan, you stand behind Jake. And so on. We're going to build one giant train of muscle fiber."

Figure 14-3: It doesn't matter how many people are pushing. You're stronger!

When you name the person who's going to stand immediately behind you, choose wisely — remember, all you really have to do is withstand the pushing of *one person*. That doesn't mean you have to choose some little weakling wimp — after all, you're the one with an entire house to push against — but don't choose Mr. T, either.

"Here's the challenge: When I say go, you all try to push me flat against the wall. Believe it or not, I'm stronger than all of you put together!"

(If somebody reminds you that this is a *bet,* and wants to know what they get if they succeed, stare sardonically at them and say, "You get to see me pressed against the wall!")

3. Let 'em push (see Figure 14-3).

"On three: ready? One, two, three!"

Amazingly enough, regardless of how many people are pushing, they won't be able to budge you! The law of inertia, Chapter XI, Article 7, says that no person can transmit more force than he can create himself.

Give it about 20 seconds, or as long as you feel ready to withstand the pushing, and then yell, "Okay, stop! Everybody stop!"

Dust off your hands, mop your brow, and beam generously. "I'd be happy to lift you all with one hand, too — but I've got to be strong for work tomorrow."

Grace under Fire, Part 8

Sometimes a good magician cuts his trick short — and winds up with a much better miracle than the regularly scheduled ending.

Advisory Pantheon member Looy Simonoff, for example, was getting ready to perform a card trick. He borrowed a deck of cards and asked a volunteer to shuffle it thoroughly. "Then I'd like you to deal down 12 cards and shuffle *them,*" he told the spectator. "Finally, choose any four cards out of the stack of 12. Put them face-down on the table here."

The volunteer did as he was told. "Now turn those four cards face up," Looy continued, ready to launch into the body of his trick.

To his absolute astonishment, however, the four cards the volunteer turned over — by sheerest, one-in-a-million coincidence — were the four Aces!

Looy was too smart — and too stunned — to continue with the trick he had planned. He just looked around the roomful of jaw-dropped faces and said — "Thank you!"

The Phantom Photo

As you advance to parlor-magicianship, you acquire certain perks: the option to perform standing up, for example, and the right to use a table. That's lucky, since this surprising audience-pleaser, a creation of Advisory Pantheon member George Schindler, requires both a standing magician and a table.

The effect: You take apart an empty picture frame, displaying each piece of it separately — the cardboard back, the piece of glass, and the frame itself. It all looks perfectly normal (if a little on the cheap side). You reassemble the empty frame and cover it with a handkerchief.

Now you offer a spectator a choice of five movie-star photos. Bizarrely enough, when you remove the cloth from the picture frame, it's no longer empty — it's got the chosen movie star's photo in it!

The secret: As you're showing the pieces of the frame, you show the back panel first — and set it onto your table, face-down onto double-sided tape attached to one star's photo. That's how the photo gets into the frame.

And how do you know which star's photo will be chosen? Easy: You use the Magician's Choice technique — you force the issue.

You'll have to assemble a few components for this one:

- A picture frame that can, in fact, be taken apart into three pieces — frame, glass, and easel back.

- Double-sided tape.

- A cloth napkin, handkerchief, or dishrag.

- Photos of five celebrities. (Hint: You can make your own job much easier in the upcoming steps if you include, say, one Harrison Ford- or Tom Cruise-level movie star among four, er, slightly less box-office-dynamite ones.) The photos should be big enough to fill most of the frame, although not big enough to fill it completely. You'll probably want to rubber-cement the five originals to cardboard so they'll be easier to handle.

  And where, you might ask, are you supposed to get these photos? Fly to Hollywood and wait with a camera outside the fanciest restaurants? Nah — two words: *People* magazine.

By the way: the celebrity photos make this a handy, good-looking, and entertaining trick, filled with the opportunity for jokes about flopped movies and derailed careers. But the beauty of this trick is that it's so flexible. You could substitute almost anything for the movie-star photos, depending on the occasion. If you're performing for teenagers, use five rock stars. If you're performing for people who don't get out much, use five playing cards (enlarged on a photocopying machine). If you're performing at your corporate picnic, use five stock certificates or corporate logos. If you're performing at a PAQ convention (Parents of American Quintuplets), use five birth certificates. You get the idea.

✔ A duplicate photo of the most popular celebrity.

Put the duplicate photo face-down on your table, and put pieces of double-sided tape on the back corners. Later in the trick, you'll place the easel back of the frame directly on top of this tape — thereby installing that photo into the frame when you reassemble it.

This face-down, tape-stuck photo is on your table during the beginning of the trick; your audience shouldn't be able to see it. For that reason, this is not a trick you can perform at dinner or up close. You can easily hide the face-down photo however, if:

✔ The audience's eyes are below your table height, so that they can't see the table surface. That delightful condition is true if, for example, you're up on a stage or platform — or if you're performing for kids who are seated on the floor.

✔ You have a box of props on your table. In that event, you can position the face-down photo behind the box, blocking the photo from the crowd.

✔ You've got a whole bunch of paraphernalia on your table, such that one more piece of face-down paper won't be particularly noticeable. Besides, nobody knows what you're going to attempt, so there's nothing particularly suspicious about a piece of paper on your table.

You've checked your props; you've practiced diligently; you've memorized the names of your movie stars. It's showtime.

1. **Show your picture frame.**

   "I was reading about the future of photography," you might begin. "They say that in the future, all of our pictures will be digital, and they'll be displayed on TV screens on the walls of our houses." (A mention that Microsoft chairman Bill Gates *already* has this system in his house is optional.)

   "But I've been fooling around with something even better. This is the equipment right here. Cost me $150,000 for the prototype. You probably can't even see the electronics — it basically looks just like a cheap picture frame."

2. **Take the frame apart.**

   You're about to show each of its three components individually, front and back (see Figure 14-4, photo A). Start with the back. "It comes with a cardboard back . . ."

3. **After showing the back panel, lay it face-down on top of the pre-taped photo on your tabletop (photo B).**

   Ta-daa! You've just sneakily attached the duplicate photo — let's say it's Tom Cruise — to the cardboard back.

   If you can set the back panel down so that the picture is more or less upright and centered, great — but don't make a big deal of it. A little crookedness is a small price to pay for keeping the action moving along; as far as your audience is concerned, all you've done is set the back panel down so that you can go on to display the next piece of the frame.

4. **Show the sheet of glass, and finally the empty frame.**

   " . . . a piece of solid, see-through glass" (and set *that* down on the table), "and the frame itself."

   Put the frame down. Wink conspiratorially at the audience. "The electronics are all hidden in the glass," you can tell them.

5. **Put the frame back together facing you (photo C).**

   Start by putting the glass back into the frame. Then pick up the face-down back panel, which now has Tom Cruise's picture taped to its face. The key move: As you pick it up and put it back into the frame, keep its back to the audience!

   Doing so isn't suspicious — the little clasps that hold the cardboard back in place are visible only from the back. The audience will simply assume that you've got the frame facing the wrong way in order to show what you're doing as you fasten the frame together.

   "Normally, this new digital photo system requires a certified installation technician to visit your house. Putting the thing together is an extremely technical and difficult process, as you can see; fortunately, I've had extensive training," you can say as you put the frame back together. "There we go."

   At this point, you've got a reassembled frame sitting on your table with its back to the audience — and Tom smiling at you through the glass front.

   "Here, let me install the dust cover to protect the delicate electronics." Pick up your napkin or handkerchief and show it on both sides.

6. **Cover the frame with the handkerchief and turn it to face the audience.**

   At last, Tom Cruise's face is toward the audience — but he's covered up.

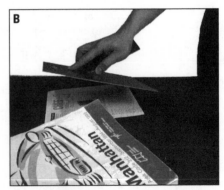

Figure 14-4: Show each piece of the frame individually (A) — but set down the cardboard back onto your pre-taped Tom Cruise photo (B). When you reassemble the frame, have its back to your audience, as shown here from behind you (C). Perform the Magician's Choice (D) — and finally, unveil the picture in the frame (E).

7. **Show your five movie-star photos. Use the Magician's Choice to force Tom Cruise upon a volunteer (photo D).**

If you've read Chapter 13, you already know about the Magician's Choice. It's an age-old swindle in which you offer several objects to a volunteer. By a process of elimination — a game that *you* control — you force the volunteer to choose a particular one.

The key to the Magician's Choice is to march right along, confidently and suavely, never letting on that you're actually making up the rules as you go along. Rehearse it enough times in private that you can fake out the volunteer every time, without stumbling; once you've mastered it, the Magician's Choice routine will serve you well in many future tricks.

I'll be the first to admit that a five-item Magician's Choice looks ridiculously complex on paper. The following discussion isn't beach reading, not by a long shot. But in practice, it's actually amazingly simple: you just keep Tom Cruise in the game until he's the only one left.

Here's how it works. Start by showing your five photos. (Put Tom Cruise at position 2 or 4 — for some reason, people choose those photos more often than the ones at the ends.)

"I'll admit it: I'm the first person in line to buy *People* magazine's 'Most Beautiful People in the Universe' article every year," you can say. "Every year, I run for the newsstand and grab that issue to find out the answer to one key question: Am I in it?

"But once again, I didn't make it this year; seems like you have to be a major movie star to be even considered for the contest. Anyway, here were some of the winners: five of Hollywood's best and brightest. Here, take two of 'em off my hands, will you?"

The wording in the Magician's Choice scam is important. Don't ever use the word "choose" — doing so will imply that the "chosen" pictures will be the ones kept in the game. The two that the volunteer takes may wind up being ones that you *eliminate*.

When the volunteer takes two pictures, the road forks. Your next step depends on whether Tom Cruise was one of the two *taken-away* pictures or one of the three *left in your hand*.

If Tom was taken: Immediately toss the three photos remaining in your hand onto your table. They're out of the game. Congratulations — you've just narrowed the choice from five photos down to two. (If you've surrounded Tom with somewhat less heart-throbby stars, odds are pretty good that Tom will be among the two first chosen.)

"Okay — and now I need you to give me back one of those two."

Once again, you're about to play a mind game. If your volunteer hands Tom Cruise back to you, hold the photo up to admire it. "Tom Cruise — you like Tom Cruise, eh? You must not have seen *Cocktail*. Well, whatever — Tom Cruise it is!"

But if the volunteer hands the *other* picture back to you, discard it immediately (by tossing it onto your table). Tom Cruise is left in her hands. Point to Tom's picture. "So we're left with Tom Cruise, eh? Okay, great — Tom Cruise it is!"

You're done. The audience is convinced that it just saw a volunteer choose Tom Cruise. Either way, thank your volunteer and invite her to take her seat again. Skip to Step 8.

If Tom was left in your hand: "All right, you can set those down for a moment," you tell your volunteer (in reference to the two photos she took from you). You've got three photos left in your hand. One of them is the Cruise-man.

"Now take two of these remaining ones." Once again, you'll have to think fast.

If your volunteer takes the two photos that *aren't* Tom Cruise, then you're done; he's left alone in your hands. "Which leaves us with that mega-blockbuster-heartthrob, Tom Cruise. All right, Tom Cruise it is!" Invite the volunteer to take her seat again; skip to Step 8.

But if, on this second round, your volunteer *takes* Tom and another photo, you've got to play a third round. Immediately throw away the photo left in your hand, point to the two in your volunteer's hand, and say: "Great — of those two, which one shall I take?"

See how that wording works either way? It could mean "take away," and it could mean "choose as our selection." Sleaze city!

Anyway, if you're now handed Tom, hold him aloft triumphantly. Or if you're handed the *other* picture, point to Tom, who's finally alone in your volunteer's hand. Either way, finish with your neat verbal wrapup: "Tom Cruise, eh? All right, Tom Cruise it is!"

The flow chart in Figure 14-5 illustrates all the possible outcomes of this five-way Magician's Choice. If the diagram helps you follow the preceding discussion, great. If it does nothing but make you think I'm some kind of computer nerd gone berserk, then ignore it. Instead, just focus on the *logic* of the Magician's choice: no matter what happens, keep Tom Cruise in the game. Play the game by these two rules:

- Whenever you're left holding pictures that don't include Tom, throw away your pictures (by tossing them onto your table).

- Whenever you volunteer is holding a pair of pictures, ask for one of them back.

Either way, you'll eventually wind up with Tom Cruise as the only remaining picture.

8. Give the final buildup to the climactic unveiling.

"All right," you continue. "Out of all the pretty faces in the world, you chose Tom Cruise. Now the cool thing about my super-high-tech, extremely expensive digital frame system is that you don't control it by pushing buttons or flipping switches. You control it *mentally*. Its sensors pick up brainwaves and convert them into digital imagery."

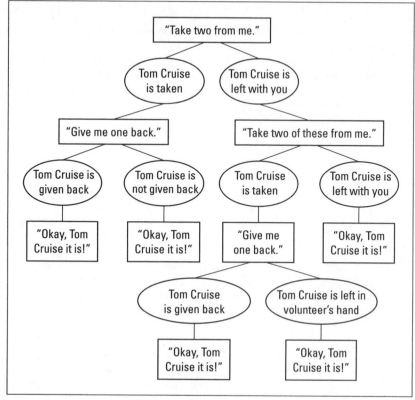

Figure 14-5:
The
Magician's
Choice
involves
quick
thinking —
but these
are the only
possible
outcomes.

Stop for a moment. Pretend to notice that not a single person in your audience is buying your spiel.

"What — you don't believe me? C'mon — I'm a magician. Would I lie to you? No, really, it's true! I can prove it! Check this out: We're a whole crowd thinking of nothing but Tom Cruise. And if I've installed the batteries the right way, we should see that in the frame is . . ."

9. **Remove the handkerchief to reveal what's in the picture frame (photo E).**

". . . Tom Cruise!"

What's especially attractive about this trick is that it has a *double* surprise ending. Not only is the picture frame suddenly filled at the end of the trick, but it's filled with the correct photo!

The Late-Night Party Murder Mystery

At its heart, this last trick in the book is a simple mind-reading effect — a great one, to be sure, but simple. But the trappings — the feeling you create, the story you tell of a grisly murder, the psychological mastery you'll display, and the fact that you're pitting yourself against the crowd — elevate it to the level of an unforgettable and chilling mystery.

You don't need much in the way of props for this one — beyond a roomful of people and at least one friend.

The effect: You tear out a paper cutout of a hapless victim. You place him, along with a murder instrument (such as a pencil) on the floor in the middle of the room. You leave the room; while you're gone, one of the spectators is to get up, stab the paper doll through its heart, and sit down once again.

At that point, the group is to call you back into the room. You move slowly among them, looking deeply into each person's eyes, challenging the group not to tip you off through nervous breathing or increased perspiration. Just as the group is getting seriously spooked out, you leap in front of one person and make your accusation of virtual murder. Naturally, you're correct.

The secret: You know which person is the murderer because somebody *signals* you — your confederate (which is magic-ese for "secret assistant"). You can read more about confederates in Chapter 7 (see Three-Object Monte, Freakout Edition); for now, it's enough to note that confederates should be used extremely sparingly in your repertoire. Reserve them for tricks — like this one — that have maximum impact.

In this trick, your silent helper tips off the murderer's identity by sitting in exactly the same *position* as the culprit. (You've explained the trick to this discreet friend before performing.) You know instantly when you re-enter the room who your target is . . . the rest is acting.

1. **Tear or cut a human figure out of a piece of paper as you introduce the setup.**

You'll make a more attractive paper doll if you fold your sheet of paper in half — and then tear out, from this doubled-up page, *one side* of a person's body. When you unfold the torn-out half-body, you'll have a nice, symmetrical silhouette of your victim.

Set up the trick as you do your tearing. "Did you guys ever play Clue when you were a kid?" you might ask.

"It was a pretty cool murder-mystery game where you'd have to guess which character committed the murder. Well, when I was little, I played a variation of that game. It was called *No* Clue."

2. Introduce Mr. Snee — and the instrument of his doom.

"This is Mr. Snee — a little-known investment banker. Except for Bill Gates, Mr. Snee is the richest man in the world — well, on paper."

As the crowd chuckles appreciatively at your little pun, pick up the pencil.

"What Mr. Snee doesn't realize, though, is that tomorrow morning, he's going to wake up dead. He'll find this evil-looking, razor-sharp dagger plunged into his heart.

"Here's how you play No Clue. I'm going to leave the room. While I'm gone, one of you will quietly volunteer to be the murderer. Get up, pick up the murder weapon, and stab the poor guy right through the heart."

As a sweet little sinister touch, draw a heart shape on Mr. Snee in the appropriate place, for the benefit of any audience member whose knowledge of anatomy is a little fuzzy. Set the paper doll and pencil down in the middle of the room (on a coffee table, perhaps, or on the floor).

"Once you've done the evil deed, sit right back down. At that point, the whole group should scream bloody murder. That's to summon me, the No Clue detective, back into the room — to see if I can figure out who the murderer was. All right — ready? I'm outta here."

3. Leave the room.

And I mean *really* leave the room. You don't want some smart aleck ruining the trick for you by claiming you were secretly peeking. If you can go into an adjoining bathroom, closet, or basement and close the door, great. If you can go outside where you and your turned back are visible through the window, that's good, too. On subsequent repetitions of the trick — yes, this is one of the rare tricks you can perform two or three times — you may even have to take an audience member with you as a witness to verify that you're not somehow watching the murder take place.

Once you've left the room, and somebody has stabbed the paper doll, you'll be summoned. Some crowds actually scream the words, "Bloody murder!" Some just politely call your name. It depends entirely on the group, their mood, and how many family members are asleep upstairs.

4. Burst into the room — in Detective Mode.

"Oh, no!" you can exclaim in mock horror as you pretend to stumble across the corpse. "Oh, dear Lord, not Mr. Snee!"

Pick up the paper doll and remove the pencil. Inspect both. *Sniff* the pencil. Hold the hole in the paper cutout right up to your eye.

"Somebody has murdered an innocent man — the second richest man on earth, true, but innocent nonetheless! This evil deed must not go unpunished — and I, the brilliant detective Dr. Davidini" — or whatever your name is, plus "-ini" tacked onto the end — "intend to find out who's responsible!

"Whichever one of you did this — you probably think you're off the hook. You think there's no evidence. Ah, but that's where you're wrong. Your own body will betray you. As I look into each of your eyes, I will know the murderer in the same way a lie detector knows a liar — by faster breathing. By perspiration. By the pulse in the neck. And most of all, by your eyes — you cannot control the dilation of your eyes when you feel guilt!"

By now, of course, you already know who the murderer is. How? Because you took one sneaky glance at your confederate — who's sitting in the *same position* as the guilty party. Arms, hands, legs, general posture — all should match.

Don't be rigid about this system. Suppose the murderer is sitting on the floor, but your confederate is on a chair — your confederate should not get off the chair. If the murderer has a drink and your confederate doesn't, no big deal. Your confederate should *approximate* the same positioning. You'll still get the idea; no two people have the same posture in any grouping. (If the murderer changes position, by the way, your confederate can discreetly shift, too.)

Look at Figure 14-6. Your secret friend is the guy with glasses in the middle of the couch. Can you figure out whose position he's matching? Of course you can — even though the murderer isn't on the couch and has a glass in her hand.

5. Put down the paper and pencil. Begin walking around the room. Stare for several long seconds into each person's eyes.

Ham it up. Stand in front of each person long enough to make the audience think that, just maybe, you really can see their pupils dilate.

Perform this kind of silent interrogation of everyone in the room. Staring into one of your friend's eyes may feel a little awkward, but remember — it's all in the name of art. Staring into the eyes of your confederate, which you must do as part of the universal interrogation, is even more awkward. But do it anyway. It's required for this potent trick — and besides, this is where you get to find out which of your friends has been secretly wearing tinted contacts for the last three years.

6. After inspecting everyone's eyes, stand boldly in front of the wrong person.

Make your final speech standing in front of some random person, so everybody gets thinks that you're about to blow your own trick in a huge and dramatic way.

Figure 14-6:
Your confederate is the guy with the glasses. Can you spot the murderer?

"Now, we know the that murderer is somewhere in this room. We know that nobody has said anything — and yet the human body is a funny thing. The brain sends out signals whether we will it to or not — and there's not a thing you can do about it. Especially when it comes to guilt . . . guilt about *murder.* And that's how I figured out that the murderer . . . is . . ."

7. Whirl on your heel and point directly at the real murderer.

". . . *you!* Mua-ha-ha-ha-haaaaaa!"

Laugh evilly and triumphantly, and then interrupt yourself. Ask meekly: "Am I right?"

And, of course, you are.

There aren't many tricks that can be repeated without giving away the secret, but this is one of them. You can do the whole murder mystery two or three times, provided the audience *wants* to see it more than once. Repeating the trick is especially useful if some wise guy thinks he knows how you're doing it — "You peeked" and "You guessed" are perennial favorites — because you can prove him wrong simply by doing it again.

Don't expect to see the fireworks of excitement and delight in your audience's faces after this incredible trick. Dull befuddlement is more like it.

But deep down inside, everyone's profoundly impressed. You can see it in their eyes.

Part VI
The Part of Tens

The 5th Wave   By Rich Tennant

WHERE **NOT** TO PERFORM MAGIC TRICKS

IRS

"...and magically, the $50 dollar bill has disappeared into thin air as if it never actually existed. Its exact location known only by me, The Amazing Brad—Hider of All 'Things Valuable'."

In this part . . .

*W*hy a series of top-ten lists? Because they're concise, they're informative, and they make the outline look more complete.

Here they are, for your continued magical education: ten ground rules of magic, ten moments in history that changed the art of magic forever, ten famous dead magicians worth knowing about, and ten things to say when you mess up.

Finally — as a send-off — I'll offer you ten ways to pursue this hobby. I can think of no better blessing than to wish you a rich and rewarding journey deeper into one of the world's greatest performing arts.

Chapter 15
Ten Basics of Good Magic

• •

*T*hroughout the chapters of this book, I've drawn your attention to some of the *technical* rules of magic. But to set your mental stage for this new hobby of yours, let the following general guidelines be your magician's compass.

Don't Reveal the Secret — Ever

Even if you've never learned a magic trick, you've probably heard this one: Never tell how you did it.

Sounds easy. But wait until your *spouse* or your *date* or your *father* or your *boss* or your *kid* looks you straight in the eye, pinning you to the wall, begging, "Oh, come on. Just tell me. I won't tell anyone — look, how's it gonna hurt you? Just tell me, all right? What's the big deal? Come *on!*"

Don't do it.

See, at the moment you complete a trick, you've created a temporary psychological personality warp: In a very subtle way, you've done something they can't do. For one split second, you've established your superiority without offending anyone. Not only that, you've cracked open, in your audience's mind, just the faintest possibility that what you did was real magic. You've created a reasonable doubt.

But if you tell how you did the trick, you burst your own aura of masterfulness. Now people know that you're not really magic *and* you're a sap. In fact, now *they* feel superior for having suckered you into revealing your methods.

Worse — much worse — is that revealing a trick erases that delicious doubt you've created in your audience's mind. You've crushed their microscopic, budding belief that the impossible *might* sometimes be possible. Believe it or not, finding out how a great trick was done doesn't make your audience feel good. It makes them feel *terrible.* It leaves a sour taste in the mouth. Not only were they tricked, but their subconscious hopes — that maybe they've seen a tiny miracle — are dashed.

A few years ago, I was teaching a beginning magic course in New York City. One of my students ignored this advice. After the magic class, he went home and showed his little girl one of the tricks. "How'd you do it, Daddy?" she begged him afterward. This was no ordinary five-year-old, mind you; she was blonde *and* curly. She had huge, blue, beseeching eyes. "C'mon, Daddy, just tell!"

So he caved. He told her how he did the trick. She burst into tears and ran from the room.

Very few grown-ups burst into tears when you expose a trick. But deep inside, they'll feel the same sense of letdown.

Don't Repeat a Trick

In general, don't do a trick twice at the same sitting, no matter how much the audience begs you. Because you no longer have the element of surprise in your favor, repeating a trick just gives your audience a better chance to figure out how you did your illusion. And as you know, that's not a good thing. Instead, either leave, change the subject, or launch into your next trick.

A very few tricks, on the other hand, are *supposed* to be repeated; in this book, I've pointed them out. Such tricks tend to be less dazzling than others, but because they're so solidly un-figure-outable, the mystery builds the more times you repeat the trick.

Know When to Start

When you're learning to be a magician and trying out tricks, it's okay to be an annoying magic nerd, bugging your spouse or mom or office mate to watch some new trick you've just learned.

But in public, be cool. Do tricks when nothing else is going on — *if* somebody expresses interest. Do tricks after ordering in a restaurant, but before the food has arrived. Do tricks when the party conversation lags. Do tricks waiting for the check, waiting for cabs, waiting in line.

And, of course, do tricks when you're asked.

Know When to Stop

Knowing when to stop doing magic is equally important as knowing when to start. You can't lose by stopping too soon. If you do only one trick and stop, you're a sure winner. You leave them wanting more, wanting to see you again, wanting to be around you, and this is a positive thing. If you do *three* great tricks and there's nothing else going on, you're still okay. In fact, now you've established yourself not just as Someone Who Knows a Trick, but as a real magician, too.

If you do 45 minutes of tricks, however, and the applause after each one is getting noticeably sparser, you've gone on too long. You've become an annoying magic nerd.

Build Up Your Audience

If you ask me, there's nothing more pathetic than a magician who makes fun of his audience. For goodness' sake, they're humoring *you,* taking time out to support your stage-strutting habit; it's hardly fair to repay them by making fun of their looks or performance. (If insulting your audience would never even cross your mind, great; you obviously haven't seen some of the magicians I've seen.)

On the other hand, it *is* great to build *up* your audience, especially the volunteers who assist you with a trick. In this book, in fact, you can read about tricks where you claim that your helper, not you, did the trick. You lose no status by praising your volunteer in this way — and, in fact, you make everybody impressed with what a generous and secure human being you are.

I've got a favorite quote from Jeff McBride, a famous illusionist (and a contributor to this book): "A good magician doesn't say, 'I'm a magician and you're not.' A good magician says, 'I'm a magician — and *you are, too!*'"

Suit the Tricks to the Crowd

Magic isn't a one-size-fits-all proposition. Being a good magician means being versatile enough to adapt to different situations and different people. For example:

- ✔ Preschoolers already believe in magic — and they don't tell time or count money. So mind-reading, money, card, and other intellectual, non-colorful, non-funny tricks shoot right over their heads. (Tricks that involve scissors, matches, and the insertion of writing implements up your nose are also worth reconsidering for these audiences.)

- ✔ Be careful with card tricks when performing for people from other countries — the words for "Clubs, Hearts, Diamonds, and Spades" are different in every language. Nobody will know what you're talking about when you name the cards (even if they speak English).

- ✔ Performing outdoors? If there's likely to be any wind at all, forget all your match, card, and scrap-of-paper mentalist tricks — unless your idea of suave showmanship is chasing your props across somebody's back yard.

Keep the scale of your performance in mind, too. Your close-up tricks will bomb if you're supposed to stand up at the front of an auditorium to perform. And watch out for *angles;* if you find yourself surrounded by the audience, abandon tricks whose secret methods might be glimpsed by people behind you.

One Great Trick Is Worth Ten Not-Ready Ones

I'll be up-front with you: If I'm lucky, you'll be doing *five tricks* from this book a year from now.

That's just the way it is with magic books, tapes, and classes; no matter how many hundreds of tricks are described, only a handful match your style, your work habitat, the stuff you carry around with you, your tolerance for practice, your fondness for talk, and so on. I'm lucky to add *one* trick to my permanent repertoire from a particular book; I'm hoping this book has a higher average for you because (a) the tricks are all geared for first-timers, and (b) I've already thrown out the duds.

But you know what? Knowing only five or six tricks is *great.* If you do them well, and polish them, and you freak people out every time you do them, that's perfect. You will be considered a real magician, very talented, the life of the party.

It's a thousand times worse to do a whole bunch of tricks not very well. Nobody is served by a trick the audience can figure out. They're not entertained or mystified, and you look like a doofus.

Learn a *few* tricks and make them rock-solid!

Keep at It

It's an unfortunate fact of magic life: You will have magic bad-hair days. Spectators will occasionally spot your secrets and loudly let you know. Partygoers will leave your circle of admirers to go freshen their drinks — and not return. You'll dramatically whip a card out of the deck — the wrong card. Failure is part of learning. No matter how great your skill, circumstance will lob you the occasional curve ball.

The best way to deal with these set-backs is to laugh at yourself, recite an endearing, self-deprecating line (see Chapter 18), and go on to the next trick (if you still have an audience). Later, you can do an autopsy on your dead trick: How did you contribute to its demise? Did you practice it enough? Did you misjudge the kind of audience it would be good for?

But press on — you sure won't get better by quitting. Instead, react to your flubs the way all the great magicians have: practice and perform.

Act the Part

Jean Eugene Robert-Houdin, the venerable French conjuror, once said that a magician is "an actor playing the part of a magician." That 150-year-old advice can still be of incalculable value as you perform the tricks in this book.

In other words, if you perform the tricks in this book as goofs, throw-aways, or fluffy puzzles, your audience will take them that way. They'll undervalue what you're doing.

The people watching you perform don't know how your tricks are done. Okay, most of them don't think that you actually have magic powers, but they're giving you license to convince them that you do. Just as they go to movies and want Robert DeNiro to convince them that he's a psychopath, they want you to convince them that their quarter really vanished, the dinner roll really floated, and you can really find cards merely by spelling out their names.

So value the opportunity they're giving you to delight them. In the privacy of your own bedroom, run through the trick *without* applying the secret method, and understand what the trick would look like if it worked by real magic. Know what you'll say and how you'll act as you show each effect to your audience. Cultivate a sense of occasion. Act the part of a magician.

Make It Yours

Without a doubt, you should learn all you can about magic by watching others perform. Be inspired by them; borrow panache from them; learn showmanship and pacing from them.

But you won't do yourself any favors by copying them directly. Your performance should reflect *your* personality, style, and environment. You'll never get away with performing silently — accompanied only by a music CD — when you're performing after-dinner tricks at the table. A tuxedo won't gain you anything but laughter if you're a teenager on the bus to school.

When you do a trick in a style that doesn't fit you, the audience just thinks you're weird. "Why is this joker acting like such a phony?" they wonder.

On the other hand, if you make your magic fit your lifestyle and personality, you'll be unstoppable. Doug Henning expresses his personality in a "Gee whiz, even *I'm* amazed!" way. David Blaine got his own TV special just by doing little close-up effects to passersby on the street (okay, also at parties where TV producers hang out). Others, like David Copperfield, express themselves in a confident "the magic happens through me, and I'm in control" way. There are a million variations on how to act, and they're all correct — as long as your style is a natural expression of your personality and it honors the trick you're performing.

Chapter 16

Ten Classic Moments in Magic History

• •

Magic isn't the oldest profession, but it's probably the oldest hobby. If they looked hard enough, scientists could probably find cave drawings of early Neanderthals making woolly mammoth bones float against their hands.

Yet magic is different in every era and every place. At one time or another, magicians were considered religious figures, representatives of the devil, or elegant guys in tuxedos. This chapter offers a glimpse into some of the most famous moments in the history of magic, days that changed magic, directly or indirectly, forever.

Robert-Houdin Prevents War with a Trick

Many people consider the French magician Jean Eugene Robert-Houdin (1805-1871) the father of modern conjuring. Before Robert-Houdin came along, magicians dressed in robes and made quasi-religious incantations over clunky-looking props. Robert-Houdin changed all that. Dressed in the evening clothes of the time, performing with natural-looking props and using plausible-sounding scientific explanations as patter, Robert-Houdin levitated his son, grew oranges on a tree in seconds, and constructed an *automaton* — a mechanical, moving statue — that could beat the world's most celebrated chess players. (Ever hear of Houdini? He gave himself that stage name as a tribute to his idol, Robert-Houdin.)

In 1856, the French government asked Robert-Houdin for help in squelching unrest in its Algerian territory. Not because of the magician's physical strength or military savvy, but because of his supreme magic skill.

It seemed that the Marabouts, a group of Algerian holy men who, by the way, frequently performed magic tricks, were stirring up the country against their French occupiers. The French government asked Robert-Houdin to travel to Algiers. His assignment: to demonstrate to the Algerian people that French magic was greater than the homegrown variety.

At a demonstration of his powers, Robert-Houdin performed his Light and Heavy Trunk illusion: He invited a girl onstage and asked her to lift a small trunk; she did so easily. He then asked the strongest Algerian man to come up and do the same.

But after Robert-Houdin made a few mystic passes, the powerful Algerian couldn't budge the trunk an inch. He tried so hard, the story goes, that he let out a scream and eventually hobbled off the stage with a herniated disk. For Robert-Houdin's patriotic efforts, the French government awarded him a medal. (No report on whether or not insurance covered the Algerian's back problem.)。

Herrmann Pulls a Coin from a Roll

Even if you've never seen his photograph, you can imagine what Alexander Herrmann (1843-1896) looked like. With slicked-back black hair, goatee, and sharp handlebar mustache, Herrmann was the classic portrait of a dark-souled magician (or the devil). While he was noted for many dramatic illusions, including his own version of the dangerous bullet-catching trick, he also enjoyed whimsical close-up effects as well.

Once, while waiting in a bakery, Herrmann made a spectator's coin vanish, picked up a freshly baked roll from the counter, broke it open, and revealed the same coin nestled inside. The baker, blown away, became frantic with the notion that perhaps there might be more money hidden elsewhere in his baked goods. He began wildly ripping open his freshly baked inventory in pursuit of more free money.

(See The $100 LifeSaver trick in Chapter 6 if you're interested in starting just such a riot yourself.)

Malini Produces a Block of Ice

Max Malini (1873-1942) was a bold and boastful performer, idolized by today's magicians as a man who could astonish without using prepared props. In one of his best-known effects, Malini borrowed a gentleman's hat and set it over a heads-up coin. After a series of unsuccessful attempts to make the coin flip over by itself, the wizard would whip away the hat to reveal a substantial block of dripping ice — so big that it barely fit under the hat.

Making objects appear from under a hat, in fact, has a proud tradition among magicians. Some of these items-from-nowhere have included vegetables, fruits, bricks, birds, snakes, insects, and — in the hands of Advisory Pantheon member Dan Sylvester — an *anvil.*

Houdini Becomes Dangerous

Harry Houdini (1874-1926), the most famous name in magic even decades after his death, was not always well-known. For a time, before he changed his name from Erich Weiss, Houdini performed small-scale effects — mostly card tricks, plus the occasional escape — on the low-paying stages of the country's "dime museums."

One day, broke and depressed, Houdini didn't even have enough money to pay for a necessary train ticket. Inspired by necessity, Houdini had a quick brainstorm. He handcuffed himself to the railroad tracks, in hopes that the conductor would stop, take pity on him, and let him ride for free. That's not quite what happened — instead, another passenger on the stopped train paid for the magician's ticket out of pure impatience.

But besides the free ride, Houdini got something else from the trip — something far more valuable. He realized at that moment that danger sells. Shortly thereafter, he began incorporating similar elements of life-and-death drama into his escape routine. By moving his escapes from the dusty confines of the dime-museum stage to outdoor locales with dangerous conditions, Houdini made an international name for himself. From that point on, Houdini's tricks were on a substantially more dramatic scale — escaping from a straitjacket while hanging 30 stories above the street, for example, and freeing himself from a sealed trunk dumped into sub-zero water.

Blackstone Saves His Audience

More than one youngster (and adult) dreamed of a career in magic after seeing a performance by Harry Blackstone (1885-1965) (whose real name was Harry Broughton). During his show, the famous Blackstone performed such impossible feats as making a lightbulb float out into the audience and making a handkerchief dance across the stage.

While performing at one Saturday matinee, Blackstone and his crew were interrupted by a fire marshal, who asked them to evacuate the packed theater; the drugstore next door had caught fire. Several containers of volatile chemicals were burning out of control. An explosion was possible, and there was a risk that poisonous gases could fill the theater.

Blackstone realized that a panicked stampede could result in injuries to the large number of children in his audience. Thinking quickly, he appeared on stage and couched his evacuation instructions in the form of a trick. He announced that he wanted to perform the greatest effect they'd ever seen, but it was so big, they'd have to witness it outside of the theater. Blackstone and his crew lined up the audience in orderly fashion, and ushered them out the back to safety.

Richiardi Jr. Bisects His Daughter

Aldo Richiardi (1923-1985) thrilled audiences with the energetic, yet graceful, style he brought to his stage illusions. At the end of his show, which featured all forms of magic, Richardi Jr. (as he was known on stage) ended the night's effort with his controversial version of Sawing a Woman in Half.

For this trick, Richiardi, Jr., wearing a white lab coat, directed his assistants to wheel out a stainless-steel overhead buzz saw. He had his own daughter lie down on the saw table. The sound system blared a funeral dirge. The smell of hospital chloroform filled the air.

After Richiardi Jr.'s daughter was secured in the apparatus, the spinning saw blade descended upon her, whipping flesh and spraying blood all over the stage. Richiardi then stopped the saw — and invited the audience onstage to file past his daughter!

For 40 minutes, the audience walked past the girl's body as an exhausted-looking Richiardi Jr. bowed his head and wiped his hands. When all were reseated, the magician's assistants helped the girl uneasily to her feet — still alive and in one piece.

The Great Tomsoni Capitalizes on His Mistakes

Johnny Thompson (b. 1934, also known as "The Great Tomsoni") is one of the funniest and most entertaining magicians working today. But he wasn't always an expert in comedy magic. Early in his career, he made his doves appear and his silk handkerchiefs vanish, exactly like many performers before him.

But one night, Thompson was trying out a new act — one that required several rapid costume changes. As he hurled himself onstage after a change, he realized, to his horror, that he had left his fly open. As the audience began to notice, they roared with laughter. *Hmmmm,* thought Thompson.

At a show a few weeks later, he flawlessly produced a dove from inside the folds of a silk handkerchief — but it pooped a white streak down Thompson's suit (the bird, not the handkerchief). The audience howled. Not only did Thompson not mind — he figured out a way to make the dove relieve itself on his jacket at *every* performance.

Later, just before an important performance in California, Thompson's assistant bowed out. With no time to train a new helper, Thompson enlisted the service of his actress wife, Pam. She had to wear the *old* assistant's dress and shoes, both of which were several sizes too small. During the performance, then, Pam wobbled out in tight shoes and bodice-ripping gown, literally forcing her into the role of dizzy blond. And when Pam one day forgot to take the chewing gum out of her mouth . . . one of the funniest acts in magic was born.

Today, thanks to his ability to take advantage of his early mistakes, Johnny has become a comedy icon to magic's top talent — Lance Burton, Penn & Teller, and Jamy Ian Swiss, among others. He's influential far beyond his riotously laughing audiences.

Doug Henning Comes to Broadway

On May 28, 1974, Canadian Doug Henning (b. 1947) brought magic, with a jolt, into the pop-culture mainstream with a Broadway show that (like Robert-Houdin before him) modernized the look and style of magic. Forsaking the tuxedos of 100 years of magicians before him, Henning bounded about the stage in a sequined leotard, shoulder-length hair bouncing. *The Magic Show* combined rock ballads (by *Godspell* composer and *Pocahontas* lyricist Stephen Schwartz), dance numbers, and a fleshed-out story line (good magician vs. bad magician) to keep patrons coming back for four years.

Among the illusions Henning performed in the show were a version of Houdini's Metamorphosis (in which the magician and his assistant exchange places instantly while one is locked in a trunk) and The Zig-Zag Lady (in which the assistant's body, in a thin cabinet, is pushed into several disjointed sections).

Copperfield Changes the Scale of Magic

In 1977, a 20-year-old David Copperfield (b. 1957, as David Kotkin) starred in the first of his annual splashy TV specials. Since then, he's gone on to become magic's biggest name, second only to Houdini as the most widely recognized person in the art.

Many factors have played a part in Copperfield's success — including his skill, inventiveness, looks, stage sense, dancing ability, and team-building. But Copperfield's trademark, the feature that took the public by storm, is huge illusions. He made a Lear jet vanish; floated himself over the Grand Canyon; walked through The Great Wall of China; and made the Statue of Liberty disappear. Ask a Copperfield spectator for a classic moment drawn from one of the magician's performances, and you'll undoubtedly hear an enthusiastic description of one of these Godzilla-sized show-closers.

You See Your First Magic Trick

As "classic" as the previous nine moments were, none of them could ever have the power of that moment, years back, when you saw your first magic trick. You wouldn't be reading this book if someone, somewhere, hadn't piqued your interest when you were very young.

Looy Simonoff remembers seeing his father vanish a card barehanded. Billy McComb recalls a sideshow fakir who vanished a ring, and then reproduced it in a set of sealed boxes. Steve Fearson can still picture his uncle magically changing a stack of nickels into dimes. Harry Lorayne describes a camp counselor who used a reversed card to locate a selected card.

What's your first magic memory? Chances are that your first trick was shown to you not by a pro, but by a family member, babysitter, waiter, friend, or just some other "regular" person who wanted to delight you.

And now it's your turn. Which tricks in this book will you practice to perfection — and who will see their very first magic tricks in *your* hands?

Chapter 17

Ten Dead Magicians Worth Knowing

• •

*T*his chapter started out as "The Top Magicians of All Time" — but unless this book were expanded into a handsome 26-volume set, some of the greats would have to be eliminated.

Furthermore, magic is like opera or sports: there are as many opinions about this art as there are practitioners. Just publishing a list of the ten greatest *living* magicians would be an exercise in futility (and a sure way to get myself letter-bombed).

Here, then, are ten of the most famous *dead* magicians — men who changed the art forever. They may not be the *top* ten — no two magic experts would ever agree on such a list — but they're among the most important. Because the tricks, techniques, and principles of showmanship these magicians introduced affect nearly everyone performing today, they're worth getting to know.

John Henry Anderson (1814-1874)

Ask the average person to draw a magician, and you'll get a little cartoon of a guy in a tux pulling a rabbit out of a hat.

The funny thing is, not many people have actually ever *seen* a magician do the hare-from-headgear trick. But the audiences of John Henry Anderson, who was known alternately as "The Wonder of the World," "The Napoleon of Necromancy," and "The Great Wizard of the North," saw exactly that: a bunny pulled from a top hat.

Anderson, who made and lost fortunes at conjuring, was also an early advocate of splashy self-promotion, announcing his appearances with tall, colorful posters and lavish parades. And pulling a rabbit out of a hat was by no means Anderson's most glorious effect. Among other things, he produced his son from inside a giant book, communicated with the late President

Lincoln through spirit rapping, and, in an effect called The Inexhaustible Bottle, poured various different drinks — called for by audience members — all from a single bottle.

Harry Kellar (1849-1922)

Before becoming an illusionist of extravagant stage shows, Kellar (born Heinrich Keller) worked as a magician's assistant, first to the exotically named (but actually British) "Fakir of Ava;" then to John Henry Anderson, Jr.; and, most importantly, to The Davenport Brothers.

The Davenports were a charismatic duo who became famous performing an early *spirit cabinet* act. In this trick, they were tied to chairs inside a large cabinet. (Picture a dressing room at The Gap, and you'll have it.) Once inside, with the curtains drawn, spirits manifested themselves by playing trumpets and drums inside the box, ringing bells, and tossing objects around. Sometimes a gentleman from the audience was invited to enter the cabinet — only to burst forth a moment later, screaming, his hair disheveled and his coat turned inside out. The Davenports claimed that their act was a genuine display of ghosts.

After serving his apprenticeship with the Davenports, Kellar split off and developed his own stage show. His act included all forms of magical illusions, from levitation to the tried-and-true spirit cabinet. But instead of claiming that he could produce genuine ectoplasmic buddies, Kellar presented the cabinet as the illusion it was — a great stage trick, but not true spirit communication.

Kellar built quite a reputation with this act, and he influenced decades of future magicians with his style of high-entertainment magic. During one performance, he asked spectator John L. Sullivan, the heavyweight champion of the world, to join him inside the cabinet. Sullivan got the usual rough treatment inside the cabinet — and wound up, at the end of the trick, tossed onto his butt inside the cabinet.

Servais Le Roy (1865-1953)

Le Roy (born Jean Henri Servais Le Roy) was the mastermind behind a much-loved turn-of-the-century magic act called Le Roy, Talma, & Bosco. The act featured deft sleight-of-hand and riotous comedy. But what magicians recall best were Le Roy's inventive, sophisticated illusions, many of which are still performed today.

Previous magicians had made women seem to float in the air. But Le Roy's twist was to whip the draping cloth off the woman as she levitated — only to reveal that she had vanished! In another Le Roy creation, the magician drapes three large silk handkerchiefs in front of an empty box — whereupon the silks begin dancing wildly around the stage. At the trick's conclusion, assistants pop out from beneath each spooky foulard.

Although Le Roy created these illusions during the same time Henry Ford was still knocking out the kinks of his first "horseless carriage," they still stun today's slick, savvy, sophisticated crowds.

Howard Thurston (1869-1936)

On the night before his entrance exam at the University of Philadelphia, young ministry student Howard Thurston was floored by the spectacular performance of the most famous magician of the time, Herrmann the Great.

Thurston was still thinking about the show as he bought his train ticket to Philadelphia. But when Thurston examined the ticket, he discovered that the clerk had accidentally made it good for passage to the wrong city — to Syracuse, in fact. Before returning it, however, the youngster saw Herrmann the Great boarding the Syracuse-bound train!

On a whim, Thurston decided to keep the ticket and follow Herrmann aboard the train, jettisoning his ministry plans. (Thurston never did muster the courage to speak with Herrmann that day. But just being near the famous wizard was enough to give him the magic bug.)

Thurston later went on to purchase Harry Kellar's show. After incorporating some of his own illusions, Thurston became the leading stage wizard of his day. If you're old enough to have seen him perform, you may remember him making a man magically turn upside-down in a box far too small to permit such movement; vanishing a singing woman and her piano in mid-air — on mid-note; and making a girl disappear, only to reappear in a trunk that had been suspended over the audience's heads the entire night.

Horace Goldin (1873-1939)

Today, it's not uncommon to see a dynamic young magician run through his routine at breakneck speed, producing a bright orange scarf in one hand and a squawking macaw in the other — only to vanish them both on the way to 30 other mini-climaxes. The father of such high-speed pacing in magic was Horace Goldin (born Hyman Goldstein), also known as "The Whirlwind Wizard."

Necessity was the mother of Goldin's breathless style — he had a thick Polish accent and a pronounced stammer. Those impediments meant that Goldin couldn't accompany his tricks with the usual spiel of patter. Instead, Goldin stuffed 45 tricks into a 17-minute show: appearances, vanishes, transformations, and whimsy. His best known effect was the now classic "Sawing a Woman in Half" illusion (which he may even have invented, depending on whom you ask).

Joseph Dunninger (1892-1975)

Dunninger, a brilliant and flamboyant mentalist, was the first magician to use radio and television to his distinct advantage.

For years, mentalists had performed such various high-visibility stunts as reading local politicians' minds or driving blindfolded through city streets. Dunninger took these publicity stunts to a grand scale.

Using the new, national mediums of radio and TV as a forum to showcase his feats, Dunninger gave his electric performances to America at large. He read the minds of celebrities: Babe Ruth, Jack Benny, Pope Pius XII, Thomas Edison, and Franklin Delano Roosevelt. Dunninger also chose unique venues for his demonstrations: He once divined the name and address of an envelope chosen at random by the postmaster general in his own post office. Another time, he read the thoughts of Brooklynites who were parachuting off a Coney Island amusement-park tower.

Cardini (1899-1973)

Calling himself Cardini, Richard Valentine Pitchord's performance became the gold standard for stage magicians everywhere.

His act was unforgettable. Wearing a monocle and tuxedo, Cardini tottered out onto the stage, acting the part of a bewitched — and drunken — British gentleman. While trying to remove his elegant white gloves, fans of cards appeared at his fingertips — again and again and again. No matter how many times he dropped these materialized decks to the stage floor, more kept appearance at his fingertips, apparently against his will. Hundreds of playing cards littered the stage, as the poor "drunk" Cardini tried vainly to undo his gloves.

And cards were not the only things troubling him. Cigars appeared, cigarettes vanished, billiard balls changed color, lapel flowers spun, silks untied themselves — all with astonishing grace and without a word from Cardini.

Slydini (1901-1991)

Like many close-up performers, Tony Slydini (born Quintino Marucci) never became a household name. The reason was simple: He performed most of his beautiful magic at a table surrounded by a close group of spectators — rather than the enormous auditoriums played by the grand illusionists. But to the magic world, Slydini was an influential giant, inspiring dozens of other performers to pursue his ideal of elegant close-up magic requiring almost no props at all.

Few magicians were performing in Argentina, where Slydini grew up. As a result, the creative youngster was forced to dream up his own moves, subtleties, and routines. Using only a few coins, some sheets of paper, a pack of cards, cigarettes, and a purse frame with no bag, Slydini created some of the most elegant, original magic of his day.

Ed Marlo (1913-1992)

Edward Malkowski was a profoundly influential force in the crazy field of card magic. As Ed Marlo, he wrote over 60 books on every conceivable aspect of cards, contributing over 2,000 tricks and subtleties to the art form.

To say that Marlo was obsessive about cards is an understatement. For example, one night, two magicians and their wives took Marlo and his wife to dinner to celebrate his birthday. During the drive to the hotel restaurant, one of the magicians told Marlo about having seen a new card trick. Marlo whipped out a deck and began figuring out a way to perform the trick he'd just heard described. While in this frenzied state, he shut out the world. By the time they arrived at the parking garage, Marlo's cards were all over the back seat.

The driving magician handed his keys to the valet, and the group piled out of the car. Shortly after entering the hotel, however, one of the magicians suddenly stopped and asked: "Hey — where's Ed?"

The group ran back to the garage to find the valet who had parked the car. "Excuse me — did you see the older gentlemen who came with us?" The valet nodded. "You mean the guy with the cards? Yeah — he's upstairs in the car. I left him in the back seat playing with his cards!"

The magicians ran up two parking tiers and found the car. There was Ed Marlo, hunched over the cards. They opened the door and cried, "What are you doing, Ed?!"

"Working on the twentieth method," was all he said.

Dai Vernon (1894-1992)

Canadian David Frederick Winfield Vernon — Dai for short — was known to the magic world as "The Professor." Vernon's genius was in knowing how to separate the wheat from the chaff. Like Marlo, Vernon meditated on every aspect of every trick, searching for the best possible method. He was known to deliberate for weeks on how to properly put a deck on the table or turn a single card face up onto the deck.

Although he didn't write books, his input shaped the writing of numerous classic magic books, including the classic sleight-of-hand book *Expert Card Technique*, *The Dai Vernon Book of Magic*, and *The Inner Secrets of Card Magic* series. During his long and illustrious life, Dai Vernon probably influenced more magicians to become dedicated students than anyone this century.

Blackstone's donuts

Dai Vernon, a master storyteller, once told of a breakfast he had with another famous magician, Harry Blackstone (Sr.), and several other magicians. On the way into the restaurant, Blackstone spotted an uneaten plain donut at a table just vacated. He put the donut in his pocket as the magicians sat down.

Blackstone ordered a chocolate-covered donut and a plain donut. But after the waitress delivered the food, he switched the chocolate-covered donut on his plate for the plain one he'd swiped. He called the waitress back. "Sorry," he said, "but didn't I order one chocolate-covered donut? It seems I have two *plain* donuts!"

The waitress looked at his plate, puzzled. She apologized, took Blackstone's plate, and soon returned two different donuts. After she left again, Blackstone switched the chocolate-covered donut in his pocket for the plain one on the plate. He called the waitress back. "I know I've already troubled you too much, but I just wanted *one* chocolate-covered and I seem to have two!"

The waitress was beginning to doubt her sanity. She began looking around, trying to figure out what happened. While her head was turned away for a moment, Blackstone swapped the donuts one more time, winding up with just what he had ordered. "Never mind," he told the waitress. "Everything is okay now!"

Chapter 18

Ten Things to Say When Things Go Wrong

● ●

*1*n a perfect world, this chapter wouldn't exist. The noble view, the pure approach, the idealistic thing to say is: You should *never* screw up. You should practice a trick until you're incapable of making a mistake.

Unfortunately, life isn't like that. Circumstance and bad luck rear their ugly heads. Magic has bad hair days. There will be shows when the balloon won't pop, the tape won't stick, and the volunteer won't cooperate.

When a trick goes wrong, graceful performers don't stomp offstage and take up stamp collecting. Instead, they shrug it off with humor, recover if they can — and if they can't, they plunge on into the next trick.

By showing what a witty and quick-thinking performer you are, your audience will more than forgive you for whatever trick you messed up. For your face-saving pleasure: here are ten things to say when you mess up a trick.

- ✔ I forgot to compensate for the rotational effect of the Earth.
- ✔ Hmm. It worked in the magic store!
- ✔ It's all part of the show, folks — the part that hasn't been rehearsed.
- ✔ That's the first time that ever happened again.
- ✔ Did — did I show you the [Pencil up the Nose] trick? *(Name whatever trick you last did successfully.)*
- ✔ It doesn't look as bad from my side.
- ✔ It's moments like these when I feel like taking that new tranquilizer — Damitol.
- ✔ The real magician will be here shortly.
- ✔ I *knew* I should've had decaf.
- ✔ Wait — come back!

Those ten should be all you need for the next few years' worth of performances. But just for entertainment value, here's another ten:

- ✔ For God's sake, Jim — I'm a doctor, not a magician!

- ✔ I'm curious to see how I get out of this myself!

- ✔ Just relax — this trick has a natural build.

- ✔ *(Shouting back over your shoulder)* Start the car!

- ✔ Wow, it's so quiet in here, you could hear a career drop.

- ✔ I've actually got a very consistent track record — that trick has *never* worked.

- ✔ You know, there's only one thing this trick is missing — talent.

- ✔ When I get that trick right, it won't be a trick. It'll be a miracle!

- ✔ That's what we magicians call *misdirection.* I pretended to mess up the trick — but while I had your attention, my assistants sneaked by with an elephant into the other room for a trick I'm doing later. If you don't believe me, go check.

- ✔ Hey, what do you expect? I got this trick out of *Magic For Dummies!*

Chapter 19

Ten Ways to Get More into Magic

● ●

*A*fter you've seen what magic can do for your reputation, style, and social desirability, you will, like thousands of magicians before you, begin to seek out more magic. Here are ten important ways to increase your magic quotient — both to become a better performer and also to appreciate good magic when performed by others.

Watch Other Magicians

You'd be shocked to discover just how little professional, *live* magic the average person has seen (other than the occasional uncle who pulls quarters out of ears). You can quickly increase your sophistication as a magician by seizing every opportunity to see pros perform — at restaurants, night clubs, performance spaces, theaters, outdoor areas, corporate events, trade shows, or wherever else you may find them.

These working magicians will inspire you with their professionalism and entertainment know-how. Many's the novice magician who dismissed some trick as too simple or unconvincing — and who later saw it become, in the hands of another magician, the highlight of the evening.

For example, if you're ever in California (Los Angeles, to be exact), do whatever it takes to visit the Magic Castle. It's the most prestigious performance space for magic in the world — a private club where all the greats of magic, and near-greats, come to perform. Located in an old Victorian mansion, you enter the club by whispering "Open Sesame" into the face of a carved owl. When the door opens, you get ushered past "Invisible Irma," a player piano manned — or rather, not manned — by a ghost. She plays requested tunes, sips a glass of milk (as you watch its level go down), and even answers questions (via the titles of the musical snippets she plays). From there, you can enter various rooms devoted to different types of magic. The wrinkle: To get in the door, you must be invited by a member. (What better incentive to practice, support magic, and network like crazy?)

Magic museums

Because magic has such a grand and glorious history, magic museums have been cropping up — and are worth a visit if you're in town. For example, the Houdini Historical Center (Appleton, Wisconsin, 920-733-8445, *www.foxvalleyhistory.org*) houses the largest collection of Houdini memorabilia for public viewing. You can see all manner of Houdini-owned straightjackets, handcuffs, and milk-can escapes, plus videos of his performances. You can even hear the only existing recording of his voice. The Center also makes a resource library available for serious students.

The American Museum of Magic is in Marshall, Michigan (616-781-7666). Founded by avid magic collectors Bob and Elaine Lund, this museum is open by appointment only. It's the home to over 12,000 books, 40,000 negatives, 500 antique magic sets, and original magic equipment from Houdini's and Blackstone's shows.

Finally, there's The Magic and Movie Hall of Fame in the American capital of magic — Las Vegas, Nevada (702-737-1343). This 20,000-square-foot museum houses memorabilia collections that pertain to magic, ventriloquism, automata (mechanical dummies), and movies — a collection worth $4.5 million. Many of the pieces on display were donated by celebrities, including Shari Lewis and Siegfried & Roy.

Read

For centuries, books and magazines have been the chief method of passing down magic knowledge from one generation to the next. As a matter of fact, if you ever overhear a conversation among professional magicians, you'll be astounded at how well-read they seem to be. They quote not only books but individual *issues* of classic magic magazines:

Magician #1: "Yes, Annemann wrote about that Dunninger-blindfold-thing way back in *The Jinx,* issue #94, I think."

Magician #2: "You're right, but the method I'm thinking of was a Sam Dalal thing, which he wrote up for *Swami.* Paul Harris took it, substituted playing cards for the blindfold, and published it, with Mike, in *Astonishment #4.*" (Professional magicians are also fanatical about tracing the lineage of their tricks, bending over backward to credit the inventor of each new twist.)

The effects in this book are mostly "self-working" — which *doesn't* mean they work themselves. Instead, that term describes tricks so simple that you can concentrate on your *presentation.* For more tricks in this vein, hit the bookstore or library for books written by Mark Wilson, John Scarne, Karl Fulves, Walter Gibson, George Schindler, Bob Longe, and Freidhoffer. And read all the Penn & Teller books; their tricks require more chutzpah than most, but the lessons you'll get in showmanship and entertainment are invaluable.

You won't find the more specialized books — about the manipulation of cards, coins, thimbles, rubber bands, and so on, for example — at bookstores or libraries. For those, you have to order from a catalog or visit a magic shop (read on).

Go to Magic Shops

Fifty years ago, magic shops were secretive places where you could only see "the good stuff" if the shop owner knew you personally. Today, you can walk in off the street and ask to see nearly any trick demonstrated for you — a great way to learn what's state of the art and which tricks are within your abilities.

Develop a relationship with your local magic shop. The staff can point out the most effective tricks, books, and videos to further your magic career. On Saturdays, furthermore, many magic shops become unofficial hangouts for local magicians. Check the phone book for the nearest shop, but be on the lookout for other shops when you travel. (Another great source of magic-shop information: magic magazines, which print ads from many prominent shops. More on magazines in a moment.)

While you're at the shop, make sure to pick up a copy of the shop's catalog — or as Advisory Pantheon member Richard Robinson calls it, a "dream book." The fires of many a magic career have been stoked by the wild and wonderful promises offered in these catalogs. Sure, they oversell and mislead. They offer each trick as a rousing "crowd pleaser" in which the secret gimmick is "indetectable," enabling you to carry out the effect with "no false moves" and always letting you end "clean."

But exactly as in magic itself, the delight you'll experience reading about self-tying silks, color-changing cards, and silver bowls that pour never-ending fountains of water will more than outweigh a little friendly deception.

Watch TV Magic Specials

Armed with yellow highlighter and the week's television listings, you'll discover something amazing: Magic is hotter than ever. Practically every month brings another magic special, especially during the "sweeps week" periods (when the TV networks trot out their most attractive material to win the highest possible ratings). Magic magazines are also good sources of information about upcoming televised shows.

Let's hope that by the time you read this, those Fox exposé shows, in which a sarcastic "masked magician" exposes one stage illusion after another for no other purpose than to boost ratings, are a thing of the past. These specials focus on the *method* behind a trick — to the exclusion of the much more important ingredients: presentation, style, and personality.

Join a Magic Association

Chief among the magic associations are The International Brotherhood of Magicians (I.B.M.), and the Society of American Magicians (S.A.M.). Don't be intimidated by these organizations' austere names. Rather, think of them as what they are: organized groups trying to further the cause of magic by offering information and meeting places for local and visiting magicians to ply their craft. Each association has local chapters in most major cities; each accepts amateurs; and each has its own magazine brimming with industry news, tricks, and interviews. (See Appendix A for contact information.)

Each of these two prominent organizations offers a special class of membership (and events) for young magicians (under 18).

Read Magic Magazines

If you're sitting in a restaurant and everything on the table looks like a trick prop to you ("The salt shaker has a recessed bottom! I wonder. . . ."), then you're hooked — you've got the magic bug.

In that case, consider subscribing to one of the great magic magazines. Two of the best are *Genii: The International Conjuror's Magazine* and *The Magic Magazine: The Independent Magazine for Conjurors*. (Contact info is in Appendix A.)

At first, you'll probably understand only every tenth word; as in any industry, these trade magazines use jargon and assume that you know the basics of live magic performance. (This book should help you along quite a bit in that regard.)

But as you become more impassioned about magic, you'll start recognizing terms, classic sleight-of-hand moves, and magicians' names. Soon you'll be hovering around your mailbox at the first of the month, waiting to grab your next issue the moment it arrives.

Surf the Web

Today, most major magicians have their own Web sites. These pages tell you where to catch a future performance; sell professionally-constructed tricks; and, occasionally, teach you a simple effect or two. Try these for starters:

General magic

- **All Magic Guide** (*www.uelectric.com/allmagicguide.html*): Richard Robinson's stunning, lavishly illustrated online magic show teaches a new trick each week, features news of magic everywhere, and offers copious links to other online magic resources. Use this as a starting point; all of the following Web sites can be reached by clicking links at the All Magic Guide.

Magic history

- **Magical Past-Times: On-Line Journal of Magic History** (*www.uelectric.com/pastimes*)
- **Doug Henning's World of Magic** (*vellocet.insync.net/~tracy/ doughenning*)

Magic dealers

- **The All Magic Dealers Guide** (*www.uelectric.com/allmagicdealers/*)
- **Hank Lee's Magic Factory** (*allmagic.com/magicfactory/*)
- **Stevens Magic Emporium** (*allmagic.com/stevensmagic/*)
- **Magic Express** (*allmagic.com/magicexpress/*)
- **L & L Publishing** (*allmagic.com/llpub/*)
- **Owen Magic Supreme** (*www.owenmagic.com/index/cell2.htm*)
- **Magic Auction** (*www.magicauction.com/*)
- **Meir Yedid Magic** (*www.mymagic.com/*)

Individual magicians

(For the Web pages of this book's Advisory Pantheon members, see the front of this book.)

- ✔ **The Magic of David Copperfield** (*www.dcopperfield.com/*)
- ✔ **Siegfried and Roy: Masters Of The Impossible** (*www.sarmoti.com/*)
- ✔ **Lance Burton: Master Magician** (*www.lanceburton.com/*)
- ✔ **David Blaine: Magic Man** (*members.aol.com/sperrycito/blaine.html*)
- ✔ **Rudy Coby Launching Pad** (*www.bobself.com/rudycoby/index.html*)
- ✔ **Jeff McBride** (*www.mcbridemagic.com/*)
- ✔ **John Houdi** (*www.houdi.se/*)
- ✔ **Rebekah Yen** (*www.magicyen.com/*)
- ✔ **The Conjuror: David Ben** (*www.theconjuror.com/index.html*)
- ✔ **Paula Paul** (*members.aol.com/paullepaul/index.html*)
- ✔ **Richard Robinson** (*allmagic.com/robinson/*)
- ✔ **Illusions By Zigmont** (*www.zigmont.com/*)

Current events

- ✔ **Magic Show** (*allmagic.com/*)
- ✔ **MagicTimes: A Monthly Magic Magazine With Daily Updates** (*www.magictimes.com/*)
- ✔ **MAGIC - The Independent Magazine For Magicians** (*www.magicmagazine.com/*)
- ✔ **The Magic Menu** (*allmagic.com/magicmenu/*)

Watch Magic Tapes

As recently as 20 years ago, the only way to catch the performance of a good magician was to attend a live performance. Now, virtually every magician worth his deck of cards has produced a video of outrageously high-quality magic. Not just footage of performances, but tapes that actually show you how these tricks are done.

Critics say that such tapes are making good effects too accessible to the masses. Magic students, they feel, are missing the benefit of doing the research themselves and learning along the way.

Well, okay; then here's a modest proposal: Buy the tapes, yes (and thereby support the magicians who create them) — but don't make them your exclusive source of new material. Ask your magic store for recommendations; you can't go wrong with the videos created by this book's Advisory Pantheon members (see the Acknowledgments).

Take a Course

These days, you can attend magic classes in a number of different places:

- ✓ **Adult-education centers.** The Learning Annex, which operates in several major cities, is one example (*www.learningannex.com,* if you're on the Web; otherwise, hit the phone book).

- ✓ **Local colleges.** For example, Advisory Pantheon member Looy Siminoff has taught at the University of Las Vegas since the 1970s.

- ✓ **Magic associations,** such as those listed earlier in this chapter.

- ✓ **Magic camps.** Tannen's Magic Shop has run a Long Island-based magic boot camp for the past quarter of a century. Kids from 12 to 18 live, sleep, eat, drink, and love magic. For one August week, they attend seminars on every branch of magic imaginable (stage illusions, close-up, dove work, and so on) — taught by some of magic's most gifted teachers. (Past faculty members have included Harry Blackstone, Jr. and Doug Henning.) For information, call Tannen's at 212-929-4500, or write to Louis Tannen, Inc., 24 W. 25th St., 2nd floor, NY, NY 10010, or e-mail *spinamagic@aol.com.*

  Equally fun and instructive is Dave Goodsell's West Coast Wizard's Magic Camp, now in its seventh year. Here, children 9 to 17 learn magic from such learned Pantheon Advisors as Billy McComb and Daryl. Campers also see nightly professional magic shows, after which is a question-and-answer session with the performer. Dave Goodsell (who also runs an astronomy and physical sciences camp called Astro Camp) ends the days' instruction with a fascinating look at the stars through telescopes. (Info: Dave Goodsell, P.O. Box 338 26855, Saunders Meadow Dr., Idyllwild, CA 92549. Or e-mail *super13@aol.com.*)

- ✓ **Conventions.** Most conventions last only a few days, but attendees talk about them for months afterward. Visiting professionals offer some of the most worthwhile magic instruction at these conventions. A prominent magician, like Advisory Pantheon member Gregory Wilson, may be teaching knuckle-bending coin sleights in one room, while down the hall, a world-class children's performer is demonstrating how to twist a balloon into a giraffe. While these conventions aren't cheap ($300 to $400 for a few days), the chance to get this top-flight instruction, peruse the dozens of magic-dealer booths, and gain the inspiration of seeing professional shows every night certainly help reduce the pain of paying.

Some of the biggest and best conventions are run by The International Brotherhood of Magicians (I.B.M.), The Society of American Magicians (S.A.M.), Tannen's, and Hank Lee's Magic Factory. Dozens of other quality get-togethers take place in most major cities. Check the magic shops, magazines, and association newsletters for more information on a convention near you.

You may also be able to find a working magician who's willing to teach you privately. Instruction from a professional can often spell the difference between making magic a permanent part of your life or letting it drop by the wayside, along with your juggling balls and sketch pad.

Perform

All of the preceding nine magic resources combined aren't worth the single most instructive action you can take: *doing magic*. Do tricks as often, and as well, as you can without becoming annoying. Sweetly ask your significant other to serve as a guinea pig for a new trick you're working on. Look for lulls in conversation. Wait for that moment at the restaurant after ordering, but before the food has arrived. Use good taste, polished tricks, and lots of charm.

In the process, you'll learn — I guarantee it — the equivalent of a four-year course in psychology and sociology. You'll learn intricacies of the human mind — that it can't, for example, focus on two things at once. You'll learn surprising insights about people you thought you knew well — that the soft-spoken woman in Accounting, for example, goes *ballistic* when she can't figure out how a trick was done. And above all, you'll learn things about yourself: that thanks to magic, you're becoming more comfortable in the spotlight, a better conversationalist, and more natural in almost any social situation.

Maybe that's why magic remains an irresistible hobby, a breathtaking art, an underground science — after 2,000 years.

Part VII
Appendixes

"And next is Rob Filmore, who's promised me he's worked out the kinks in that disappearing wasp's nest trick he performed for us last week."

In this part . . .

The following Appendixes are for your reference pleasure: A list of places to see, buy, and read about magic; a glossary of magic terms; and a Trickography that traces the lineage of the tricks in this book.

Appendix A

Magic Stores, Publishers, Societies, and Magazines

• •

*I*f you've got the magic buzz, here's how to contact the companies that can lead you deeper into magicianhood.

Magic Shops

These shops carry a variety of magic props, books, and videos. Some make their own products; others take a department-store approach, importing items from around the world. Ask for a catalog! (The shops listed here are some of the best known, but there are dozens of others. Support the one near you!)

A-1 MultiMedia Magic Supplies
800-876-8437
916-852-7777
916-852-7785 (fax)
www.A1MultiMedia.com (Web)
3337 Sunrise Blvd., #8
Rancho Cordova, CA 95742

Abbott Magic Company
616-432-3235
124 South Saint Joseph St.
Colon, MI 49040

Al's Magic Shop
202-789-2800
202-347-8682 (fax)
1012 Vermont Ave. N.W.
Washington, DC 20005

Chazpro Family Fun Shop
800-730-0032
541-345-0032
P.O. Box 41415
Eugene, OR 97404

Davenport's
7 Charing Cross/The Strand/Underground
Concourse
London, England WC2 4HZ

Daytona Magic shop
800-34-Magic
904-252-9037 (fax)
136 South Beach St.
Daytona Beach, FL 32114

Hank Lee's Magic Factory
800-874-7400
781-395-2034 (fax)
MagicFact@aol.com (e-mail)
www.hanklee.com (Web)
127 South St.
Boston, MA 02111

Hollywood Magic, Inc.
213-464-5610
213-464-0162 (fax)
6614 Hollywood Blvd.
Hollywood, CA 90028

Kennedy Enterprises
949-262-1164
949-262-1165 (fax)
johnkennedy@earthlink.net (e-mail)
8 Winchester
Irvine, CA 92620

Lance Burton's Magic Shop
702-730-7518
Monte Carlo Hotel
3770 Las Vegas Blvd. South
Las Vegas, NV 89119

Louis Tannen Inc.
800-72-MAGIC
212-929-4565 (fax)
spinamagic@aol.com (e-mail)
www.tannenmagic.com (Web)
24 West 25th St., 2nd Floor
New York, NY 10010

Magic, Inc.
773-334-2855
773-334-7605 (fax)
magicinc@uss.net (e-mail)
5082 North Lincoln Ave.
Chicago, IL 60625

Mecca Magic
973-429-7597
49 Dodd St.
Bloomfield, NJ 07003

Meir Yedid
201-703-1171
201-703-8872 (fax)
meir@mymagic.com (e-mail)
www.mymagic.com (Web)
P.O. Box 2566
Fair Lawn, NJ 07410

Robinson Wizard's Magic Shop
www.allmagic.com (Web)

Steven's Magic Emporium
316-683-9582
316-68-Magic (fax)
sme@southwind.net (e-mail)
2520 East Douglas
Wichita, KS 67214

Twin Cities Magic and Costume Co.
612-227-7888
241 West Seventh St.
St Paul, MN 55102

Book and Video Sources

These companies publish or sell books and videos for magicians. These materials are usually sold either through magic stores or directly to customers.

H & R Magic Books
713-454-7219
3702 Cyril Drive
Humble, TX 77396-4032

Hermetic Press
206-768-1688 (fax)
hermeticpress@worldnet.att.net (e-mail)
1500 S.W. Trenton St.
Seattle, WA 98106-2468

L & L Publishing
800-626-6572
LLPUB@aol.com (e-mail)
P.O. Box 100
Tahoma, CA 96142

Richard Kaufman and Co.
202-237-0497 (phone and fax)
www.kaufmanandcompany.com (Web)
4200 Wisconsin Avenue, NW, Suite 106-292
Washington, DC 20016

Organizations

If you're serious about magic, join one or several of the following organizations. Each publishes a magazine, which you'll get as part of your membership package. Both the I.B.M. and the S.A.M., listed below, have special programs and memberships for magicians under 18.

Academy of Magical Arts, Inc.
213-851-3313
7001 Franklin Ave.
Hollywood, CA 90028

International Brotherhood of Magicians
314-845-9200
www.magician.org (Web)
11137C South Towne Square
St. Louis, MO 63123-7819

The Magic Circle
63-79 Seymour Street
Marble Arch, London W2
England

The Society of American Magicians
314-846-5659
*www.uelectric.com/sam/
events.html(Web)*
P.O. Box 510260
St. Louis, MO 63151

Magic Magazines

These two magazines keep you up to date on what's happening in the world of magic.

Magic
The Independent Magazine for Magicians
702-798-4893
702-798-0220 (fax)
magicmag3@aol.com (e-mail)
7380 S. Eastern Ave., Suite 124-179
Las Vegas, NV 89123

Genii
The International Conjurors' Magazine
213-935-2848
213-933-4820 (fax)
TheGenii@aol.com (e-mail)
geniimagazine.com (Web)
P.O. Box 36068
Los Angeles, CA 90036

Appendix B
Magic Words: A Glossary

Y ou won't find a lot of jargon in *Magic For Dummies*. You will, however, hear a lot of jargon at magic conventions, in instructional magic videos, and when using high-wattage microwave transceivers to eavesdrop on magicians' cell-phone conversations.

Now you'll know what they're talking about. This collection of magic-industry terminology includes magic techniques, magic slang, and even the names of some ubiquitous or particularly famous magic *tricks*. (I can practically hear you asking: "If they're so famous, why aren't they in the book?" And you can practically hear me answering: "Because most of them involve buying specially rigged props, and I couldn't fit the props between the book's pages.")

abracadabra — A very tired cliché magic word used to trigger the moment of magic. You could probably think of something funnier and more entertaining without even trying.

Ambitious Card — A much performed, much loved card trick in which the spectator's selection is repeatedly buried in the deck — and repeatedly winds up on top. Virtually all top card performers can stun onlookers with variations on this trick.

Ball in Tube — A close-up effect, particularly popular among beginners, in which a steel ball mysteriously drops through a brass tube that looks far too narrow to accommodate it.

beat — To admit you've been fooled by a trick. "He beat me with his version of Card to Pocket."

Blindfold Drive — A classic publicity stunt, normally performed by mentalists who profess to "see" psychically. The performer is blindfolded, yet manages to drive a car for blocks without hitting anybody or anything. (The drive often ends at the theater where the performer is appearing.) Caution: Driving blindfolded can get you two points on your license in many states.

blitz — To overload another person's brain with excessive stimuli and information. After a particularly long session of performing and showing off between brother magicians, one will frequently say of the other, "He blitzed me with a hundred things, and I don't remember anything!"

Bullet Catch — A famous stage effect, in which a marked bullet is loaded into a gun and fired at the magician, who staggers, drops to his knees, and reveals the marked bullet caught between his teeth. Today, the effect is still performed by such headliners as Penn & Teller and The Pendragons. But accidents while performing this trick have claimed the lives of 12 magicians.

burn — To watch a trick intensely, with an unblinking stare, immobile head, and general resistance to conventional misdirection. A spectator who's burning you clearly isn't there to be entertained.

busted — When you're caught in the act of performing a "sleight," "move," or subtlety. You're busted, for instance, when a spectator yells, "You dropped the coin into your pocket when you showed us the pencil behind your ear!"

busy — Obvious, strained, or frenetic hand or finger movement that's supposed to be hidden. For example, a magician offering helpful criticism to a fellow magician might say, "It looks a little busy under your right hand when you're doing the 'side steal.'"

card fan — To hold the deck in a circular spread, so all the spectators can see all the cards' faces. Although no conventional magic happens during this flourish, the magician's handling of the fan indicates to the audience that they're watching someone skilled.

Card on the Ceiling — A famous trick in which the magician throws the deck against the ceiling — and the spectator's signed card gets stuck there. Many magic shops, as well as many bars and restaurants, leave these cards stuck to the ceiling as a conversation piece. Michael Ammar, one of this book's Advisory Pantheon members, does a variation of this trick where a torn-off *corner* of the spectator's card sticks to the ceiling.

Card to Wallet — A popular close-up trick, in which the spectator's card winds up in the magician's wallet — in the zippered compartment.

Chop Cup — A classic close-up trick in which several balls repeatedly vanish and reappear from a silver cup. (Invented by a magician whose stage name was Chop Chop.)

clean — The blissful state when a magician's hands and props can be examined because they're not rigged in any way. Example: You're "clean" at the end of the Ring off Rope trick (see Chapter 12), because no extra rings or knots are involved. The audience can inspect the props from now until doomsday without learning how you did the trick.

Coins Across — A well-known trick in which coins invisibly jump from one hand to the other — either one at a time or all at once.

Coins through the Table — There are endless variations of this close-up trick, but in the basic effect, four coins pass through "a soft spot" in the table top, one at a time. The magician "catches" each as it penetrates the table. As with many classic tricks, this trick is available in both easy-to-do and finger-breaking versions.

confederate — A secret assistant pretending to be an audience member. The confederate may, for example, subtly feed the magician information. Confederates should be used infrequently, and rarely as the primary "spectator" in an audience-participation trick (their assistance will be too obvious). See The Late-Night Party Murder

Mystery (see Chapter 14) and Three-Object Monte, Freakout Edition (see Chapter 7) for subtle, effective uses of confederates.

control — To move a card into a specific position in the deck — without the audience's catching on. "Control the chosen card to the bottom of the deck," you'll often read in the particularly unhelpful instructions for a new trick you've just bought.

cop — To remove something secretly from the performing space (usually a card). Magician instructing a fellow magician: "Cop the gaffed card from the deck, so you can end clean." (Translation: "Secretly remove the doctored playing card, so you can hand out the deck for inspection at the end of the trick.")

cull — To prearrange the cards at the top or bottom of the deck, either openly or secretly. Culling is often done under the ruse of checking the completeness of the deck, removing the jokers, or "finding" requisite cards.

Cups and Balls — Many believe this to be the oldest trick in magic. Three balls penetrate, then congregate beneath three cups. Even if you think you know how this one's done, a good magician can still amaze you with one of the 2,000 variations he probably knows.

Cut and Restored Rope — Thick volumes have been written about this famous effect, in which the pieces of a cut rope become whole again. This book has a great version (see Chapter 12).

ditch — Getting rid of an item that the magician has secretly removed from the performing space. To end the spoon bending trick in Chapter 7, for instance, you ditch the concealed nickel as you toss the spoon onto the table.

dive — A sudden, or inconsistent, movement that signals that a secret sleight is occurring. "He dives whenever he laps a coin!"

double lift — A basic sleight in which the magician appears to take a card off the top of the deck — but, in fact, two cards are lifted off. If you want to become proficient at card magic, this maneuver is essential. (The real pros can even do *triple* and *quadruple* lifts, although such sleights are very difficult to make look natural.)

effect — Trick. Many magicians avoid the word *trick,* preferring the more sophisticated-sounding term *effect.* They feel, perhaps, that *trick* somehow connotes more deception and less real magic. *Effect* is a euphemism, along the lines of Customer Service Specialist (instead of "clerk") or ground sirloin (instead of "hamburger").

Egg Bag — A store-bought trick, full of humor potential, in which a wooden egg repeatedly vanishes and reappears inside a small, cloth bag.

false shuffle — To simulate shuffling the deck without actually altering the position of certain cards. Some false shuffles are designed to keep all 52 cards in their original locations. Other false shuffles, such as the one described at the beginning of Chapter 10, keep only some cards — such as the top or bottom one — in their original locations.

faro shuffle — An advanced shuffling technique, allowing the magician to control card movement with mathematical precision.

fast company — Very knowledgeable, experienced magicians or gamblers whose expertise, cunning, and perceptiveness are difficult to defeat. They are rarely fooled; their confidence, composure, and impenetrability are unnerving to average magicians.

finger break — A sleight that enables the magician to hold his place in the deck, using his finger as a marker.

flash — To expose something accidentally that's supposed to be hidden. A magician practicing a new trick might ask a fellow magician: "Did I flash?"

Flash Paper — Thin, chemically treated paper, available from magic stores or magic catalogs, that — when touched by a lit match or cigarette — incinerates in a flash, instantly, safely, and completely, leaving no ash or scraps behind.

flash-and-filigree — A showy performing style marked by fast, delicate, and highly skilled movements. Members of this school love flourishes and manipulative embellishments. They tend to flaunt their skill with stony demeanors or faint smirks. They hold a deck as though it were about to bloom.

flourish — A demonstration of manipulative skill, normally using cards, coins, cigarettes, billiard balls, or other small items. One example of a flourish is the coin roll, in which the magician uses only one hand to "walk" a half dollar over the back of his knuckles.

force — A standard procedure in which an audience member is offered what seems to be a fair choice (usually of cards) — but, in fact, the magician has predetermined the outcome. See Chapter 11 for several easy card forces.

French Drop — A sleight usually used to vanish a coin held at the fingertips. Magicians today rarely use the French Drop because of its unnatural appearance.

fried — An extreme form of *beat.* "That trick really fried me!"

gimmick — A piece of equipment, unseen by the spectator, that helps the magician accomplish the effect. For example, in Chapter 9's Three-Matchbox Shell Game, the matchbox rubber-banded to your wrist is the gimmick. (You may also hear the adjective form, used to describe a prop that's been specially rigged: "You probably have a gimmicked pretzel.")

glide — A relatively simple card sleight that lets the magician switch the deck's bottom card for the card behind it. The Bottom-Deal force in Chapter 11 relies on a glide.

glom — To steal a card from the deck. "Just glom it out!"

go south — To get rid of a hidden object, usually in the palm. Frequently used when discussing an unobservant spectator: "In front of *that* guy, I could have gone south with an elephant!"

grabber — A spectator who can't suppress the desire to touch, grab, or aggressively examine any magic props within reach.

Hindu shuffle — A type of shuffling in which the magician pulls off cards, singularly or in blocks, from the top deck in an elegant, continuous motion.

hook-up — A slight, barely perceptible misstep or snag in the performance of a sleight. The magician always feels this snag, even if it whizzes undetected past lay people. "I keep hooking-up on the dice switch."

impromptu — Without advanced preparation, using the materials at hand. Most of the tricks in this book can be done impromptu because they involve ordinary, unprepared objects.

Invisible Deck — A trick, available in all magic stores, in which the spectator reverses a card in an "invisible deck," only to discover that the magician reversed the identical card in a real deck — before the trick began!

key card — A specific card in the deck that the magician keeps track of to help locate the *spectator's* card. Most key cards sit on the top, or bottom, of the deck. (Chapter 10's You Do as I Do involves a key card.)

kill — An action that blocks or conceals something from the audience. Suppose you have two face-up cards on top of the deck. You want to deal the top one to the table without revealing the one below it. Therefore, as you deal the top one, your left hand turns palm-down to *kill* the face-up card on top of the deck.

lap — To secretly drop something into your lap (when seated at a table) — or to retrieve an object already there. (See Chapter 7's The Classic Salt Shaker Penetration.) Never lap anything that has an open flame.

layman — A non-magician. "This doesn't play well for magicians, but laymen eat it up."

leak — To show something that's *palmed* in the hand (usually a card) by accidentally opening the fingers. When the fingers slightly separate, the whiteness of the card's face or the color of its back "leaks" through the gap between these fingers.

Linking Rings — A classic, famous, and ancient trick in which solid metal rings link and unlink before the spectators' eyes.

load — Something the magician slips into a hat (for example) before pulling it out as though it's appearing magically. In Give That Purse a Hand (see Chapter 5), the rubber hand and its contents are a load.

mechanics grip — The standard way of holding a deck: Cards lie in the face-up palm, thumb curled around one side, other four fingers curled around the opposite side.

mentalist — A magician who specializes in mind-reading or mind-control "demonstrations." Mentalists normally weave their patter around themes involving clairvoyance, prediction, hypnotism, mind reading, and psychic phenomena.

miscall — To mislead the audience by deliberately misreading written material (or names of cards). In The Great Vegetable Prediction (see Chapter 13), you *miscall* the information you're writing on the slips of paper.

misdirection — Audience distraction. Misdirection is an essential magic skill — probably *the* most important one. By directing the audience's attention, you create opportunities to do tricky maneuvers where the audience *isn't* looking. In Chapter 2's Pencil-and-Quarter Double Vanish, revealing the pencil behind your ear is misdirection for the important part of the trick: pocketing the quarter.

Miser's Dream — A classic trick in which the magician plucks countless coins out of the air and drops them into an increasingly full bucket. Several members of this book's Advisory Pantheon, including Torkova and Dan Sylvester, regularly perform world-class versions of this trick.

move — Another name for a sleight. An experienced magician teaching a newcomer: "Don't draw attention to your hands as you do the move."

packet trick — A card trick involving a small group of cards. Packet tricks often involve cards that are gimmicked — that is, specially printed or manufactured — so that you can perform startling effects with an ease of handling not possible with a conventional deck. Multiple packet tricks during a single performance, however, are a direct tip-off to the audience that something's fishy. Some of the most famous packet tricks are The Wild Card and The McDonald's's $100 Aces.

palm — If you know any magic terminology, you better know this one, which is both a noun and a verb. It's a tricky move in which a card, coin, or other object is concealed in your hand — for example, by pinching it between opposite sides of your cupped hand. There are many forms of palming: finger palms, thumb palms, back palms, and so on. As long as you keep your hand cupped and its back to the audience, nobody will see what's inside; and as long as you keep the hand looking relaxed, nobody will suspect that you're carrying something inside.

patter — What a magician says while performing. For some fast, sleight-driven tricks, patter can be kept to a minimum — the magician's actions speak eloquently. For premise-driven tricks, entertaining patter can be crucial to the trick's effectiveness (as in Chapter 4's Sheep and Thieves).

peddle — To maneuver the top card of the deck to the bottom while the deck is being cut. "He peddled the top card!"

penetration — A type of trick in which one solid object apparently goes through another. Chapter 6's Straw through the Jaw is a penetration effect.

play — To work as rehearsed (and to be enthusiastically accepted by the audience). Professionals often recommend tricks or presentations by saying, "This definitely plays."

production — To pull an object out of thin air. In The Unforgettable "Cloudy" Toilet Paper (see Chapter 6), you *produce* a fountain of water from a wad of toilet paper.

restoration — To bring an object back to its preperformance, pre-damaged condition.

retention vanish — A sleight in which you pretend to transfer something from one hand to the other, so that the receiver hand can then seem to make the object disappear. (Chapter 3's The Vanishing Quarter, Show-Off Edition contains a good example.)

retrograde analysis — When magicians "retro" a trick that fooled them, they think backward through the trick until they've worked out what they believe to be the method.

riffle — To flip the corners of a deck of cards with (for example) your thumb, making a satisfying *fffffwwwwwt* sound and looking good at the same time.

riffle shuffle — The most common way to shuffle a deck of cards: The two halves of the deck are butted against each other, interlaced by riffling, and finally mixed by pushing the two halves together.

Rising Card — A classic card trick in which the spectator's card seems to move, all by itself, upward out of the middle of the pack.

routine — A series of tricks performed in a logical sequence, such as the two sugar-packet tricks described in Chapter 8.

roxing — Unethically photocopying magic books, manuscripts, notes, letters, and other copyrighted material — especially if the material is rare, limited, and expensive. Like computer hackers, roxers want "information to be free."

sleight — See *sleight-of-hand.*

sleight-of-hand — The secret manipulation of props (usually by the fingers) to generate a miraculous effect. When magicians speak, they drop the last two words: "He did a version of the trick involving sleights."

sponge balls — A standard set of magic props: vividly colored, easily compressible, foam-rubber balls. They're easier to manipulate than many other small objects. Using sleights, you can make the balls appear, disappear, penetrate, and multiply.

Spooky — A classic, self-contained, store-bought trick in which a spirit, "trapped" under a handkerchief, makes the material rise and fall as you pin it down to the tabletop. Tony Spina, owner of Tannen's Magic Store, says that this is the bestselling trick in the history of his shop. (Sold under various other names, including Glorpy the Ghost.)

square up — To align a deck of cards into a neat block, often by rapping the deck's edge against the table.

stacked deck — Also known as a "set-up" or "prearranged" deck. A deck whose cards the magician has prearranged, unbeknownst to the audience.

stage illusion — A trick that's big enough to be performed in a large auditorium. Examples of famous stage illusions: The Levitation; Sawing a Woman in Half; The Water Torture; Vanishing an Elephant.

strolling magic — A stand-up magic performance, done for a small group of spectators. Magicians who specialize in strolling are hired for work at, say, a private party. They go from one cluster of people to the next, performing tricks that don't need much advance preparation. (There's little room to set up props when you're in a crowd.)

Substitution Trunk — Also known as The Metamorphosis. A famous, beautiful stage illusion in which a magician, standing on top of a sealed steamer trunk, magically and instantaneously switches places with his assistant, who's been locked inside of the trunk. Houdini invented this trick; modern performers have taken it to an art form.

sucker effect — A trick in which you let the audience believe that they understand how a trick is done — only to have their "understanding" dashed. Use sucker effects sparingly; they can make an audience feel foolish and angry.

Svengali deck — A gimmicked deck. Every other card has been manufactured to a slightly shorter-than-standard length. The short cards are all duplicates of the same card, so that the magician can easily perform a force or "magically" change the entire deck into the same card.

talk — To inadvertently expose hidden objects through a tell-tale sound. If, for instance, you throw a coin against one concealed in your palm, the coins will clink — or *talk*.

thumb tip — A plastic, flesh-colored gimmick that fits over the magician's thumb for the purposes of concealing very small objects, liquid, and so on.

tip — To divulge the secret of a trick, especially one known to only a few.

transformation — A broad category of trick in which one object changes into another.

transposition — To magically switch places. The Substitution Trunk is a transposition trick.

Triumph — A famous card trick in which face-up and face-down cards are shuffled together, only to sort themselves out by the end of the trick. In most versions, the spectator's selected card mysteriously turns face-up by itself to end the trick.

vanish — To make an object disappear. "He vanished my wallet!"

vidiots — Magicians who rely solely on video-tape instruction to learn and understand magic — often prime players in the business of making illegal copies to trade with other vidiots.

wired — Prearranged (used to describe a deck of cards). A card cheat might confess: "I was wired going in."

You Do as I Do — A standard trick theme, in which the magician and the spectator hold the same materials and perform the same actions. (Chapter 10 contains a great You Do as I Do trick.) Sometimes, the magician uses this theme to show that he and the spectator have come to the same miraculous end (such as blindly selecting the same card). Other times, he uses it to reveal a magical outcome, which the spectator fails to duplicate (see You Can't Do as I Do in Chapter 14).

Appendix C

Trickography

W hen you really get down to it, all the magic tricks in the world boil down to only a handful of basic effects. Something disappears or vanishes, dissolves through a solid object, is broken and restored, changes places with something else, or floats in the air — or you read a mind. That's pretty much it.

As a result, there's a lot of overlap in the world of magic, both in effects and the methods used to achieve them. Furthermore, as noted in the Introduction, you can't copyright an idea; there's no law to stop one magician from merrily incorporating another magician's trick into his act without permission.

Still, that happens surprisingly infrequently. Because a trick is the magician's livelihood and stock in trade, professional magicians are unusually scrupulous in asking permission to teach, publish, or perform another's new trick. (And for their part, the inventors generally grant such permissions generously.) Pro magicians are also remarkably thorough in crediting the inventors and refiners of each new effect and method.

Many of the tricks in this book are "public domain" — they're so old, and their origins are so obscured, that no one can claim credit for inventing them. A second category of tricks in this book were contributed by the Advisory Pantheon members who invented them; you'll find such contributions credited in the introductions of the tricks in question.

Tricks in a third category were suggested by Advisory Pantheon members, but may have longer histories that deserve mention. Here's the *Magic For Dummies* Trickography — our best effort to credit the magicians who, through the decades, have designed and adapted the traceable tricks in the book.

Chapter 1

Off the Wall was originally published by Looy Simonoff in a book by Paul Harris. Looy called this trick The False Count because it mimics Count Dracula's wall-climbing technique. When Looy performs his trick, by the way, he uses a slightly different technique: He bends the leg he's putting all his weight on. That way, when he straightens up and "falls" out of the doorframe, he appears to fall upward, rather than across the wall.

Chapter 2

The Tale of the Tightrope Walker was dreamed up by stage illusionist Harry Kellar (see Chapter 17).

Although the idea of ditching a pencil behind your ear is an old one; the idea behind Chapter 2's The Pencil-and-Quarter Double Vanish was originated by Harry Crawford. It appeared in the seventh volume of *The Tarbell Course on Magic,* an indispensable series of books that has fed the minds of many an amateur and professional magician. This is one of the first tricks Advisory Pantheon member Tony Spina teaches novices because it so powerfully illustrates a key magic principle: misdirection.

Chapter 3

Sheep and Thieves is a brilliant standard suggested by Johnny Thompson. It's also known as The Sheep, the Thieves, and the Shephard.

Many magicians know of The 7-Penny Reflex Test as Lynn's Pennies, named for its inventor, Terry Lynn. The trick has appeared in books by Arthur Buckley and J.B. Bobo, as well as in Bruce Elliott's *Best in Magic* (as a trick by Harry Baker called Pennytration).

Jack Yates came up with the method behind Don't Show Me the Money. Harry Lorayne dressed up the idea as an act of mindreading, and he published it in *The Magic Book.*

Chapter 4

The rubber-band trick called Cheapskate Houdini was invented by Stanley Collins. This venerable old trick has appeared in many books, including *The Tarbell Course on Magic.*

Mike Bent invented Chapter 4's Post-It-ive Identification. He originally sold it through mail-order and magic shops, before contributing it to this book.

The Photocopied Card was invented by Advisory Pantheon memeber Michael Ammar while working with Gary Plants on Michael's video, *Easy to Master Card Miracles, Volume 3.*

Chapter 5

The basic moves in the Scarf Decapitation are based on Tenkai's Rope through Neck trick.

Meir Yedid originally published Give That Purse a Hand under the title Handy Load in his lecture notes, *Off the Wall.*

Chapter 6

The Missing Spray-Paint Marble and The Ninja Key Catch were both invented and contributed by Advisory Pantheon member Chad Long. Chad first published these in — where else? — his lecture notes.

Mike Caveney's witty Straw-Wrapper Restoration is a twist on a famous old-standby magic principle.

A note about lecture notes

You won't go far in the magic community without hearing about "lecture notes." They're pamphlets that go into greater detail about certain tricks that are described during magicians' lectures to other magicians.

Lecturing to other magicians is a common source of revenue for today's magicians. During a lecture, a magician will demonstrate her own original tricks, methods, and handlings to the assembled group. These lectures, which are usually held in reception halls and last from one to three hours, give local magicians a chance to hob-nob, learn new stuff, ask questions of a source they respect, and eat lousy hotel food. You can find the lecture schedules of visiting magicians in the various magic magazines, on the Web, and at magic shops.

Be forewarned, however: The lecture participants are usually extremely knowledgeable about magic; the talk at these get-togethers is often fast and slangy.

Bob Farmer came up with The Creepy Little Baby Hand after reading about a totally different Paul Harris trick that also used a doll hand. Bob himself has several different ways to reveal that doll hand; for use in *Magic For Dummies*, he recommended a version that's based on a handling by Gary Ouellet and Gilles Couture. Gary, who is both magician and TV producer, originally wrote about this version in *Genii* magazine. (This book's magic consultant, Mark Levy, first saw the trick while dining with magician Aye Jaye at an elegant French restaurant in Manhattan. When the waiter brought a plate of oysters, Aye reached his cupped hands down into the plate, yelled "What did you bring me?" and pulled out the wriggling doll hand, much to the delight and/or horror of the other restaurant patrons.)

The idea of pulling money out of a roll of LifeSavers isn't new. But Bill Herz's $100 Lifesaver Trick introduces the wonderful handling of this memorable version.

The Unforgettable "Cloudy" Toilet Paper was originally featured in the act of an award-winning stage magician — Jeff McBride. He used this trick as the opening of a series of tricks — a routine — all tied around the idea of producing water from nowhere. (In addition to the toilet-paper concept, he has also used the basic balloon idea to produce water from a crumpled newspaper, a bunched-up silk handkerchief, and so on.) Jeff originally published this trick in his lecture notes.

Chapter 7

The origins of The Bendy Spoon, Part One are cloudy. While the spoon-bending technique is as old as the hills, the addition of the nickel has been ascribed to both Slydini (in *Gen* magazine) and Derek Vernon (in Bruce Elliott's book *The Best in Magic*).

The Three-Mug Monte is credited to Bob Hummer, although many people associate it with British stage mentalist Al Koran.

Chapter 8

A Sugar Substitute is a creation of Advisory Pantheon member Gregory Wilson. He based the handling on J.C. Wagner's Charisma Change move, which first appeared in J.C.'s own book *Seven Secrets*.

The Evaporating Sugar is another Gregory Wilson special. He added his own handling to an invention of Brad Stine, which originally appeared in volume one of Paul Harris' *Art of Astonishment*.

Beans through the Orifices features some refinements by Advisory Pantheon member Tom Mullica. The original trick is generally credited to Scottish magician John Ramsey, who called it The Four Bean Trick or Ramsey's Four Bean Trick.

Magician Joe Given is credited with the ingenious idea of linking pretzels as seen in The Linking Pretzels. The version in this book features Advisory Pantheon member Christopher Broughton's handling of the effect.

Bouncing the Roll was an old standard made famous by the revered Jay Marshall.

The origins of The Floating Dinner Roll are unclear. But the trick has been performed by such famed magicians as Jay Marshall and Karrell Fox. George Schindler published his handling — the one that appears in this book — in his book *Magic with Everyday Objects*.

Chapter 9

Nobody can pinpoint the originator of Weighing the Matchbooks. But this book's presentation, recommended by Advisory Pantheon member Jim Sisti, was devised 50 years ago by "Hen" Fetsch.

Intermission

The tale of a young semi-pro magician was based on interviews with Torkova, Steve Fearson, Jim Sisti, Paul Harris, Mike Bent, Chad Long, and Gregory Wilson.

Chapter 10

The card trick called The Hands-Off, Mixed-Up, Pure Impossibilty is based on the Honolulu Shuffle or Waikiki Shuffle, made famous by Eddie Fields.

Dealing to the Aces is a very old, very standard trick dealing procedure. It appeared in Hugard and Braue's *The Royal Road to Card Magic*.

The Envelope, Please dates back to the late 1800s. It's the work of "Professor Hoffman," who published the legendary book *Greater Magic*.

Soulmates is an Annemann-Fulves trick recommended by Jon Racherbaumer. While the names Ted Annemann and Karl Fulves are linked by this trick, they weren't even contemporaries. Annemann, mentalist and publisher of *The Jinx* magazine, died in the mid-1940s. Fulves is a modern writer who's written magic books both for novices and "inner circle" magicians. Fulves built upon the effect of the older Annemann — and their names are forever linked. (This trick's origins show what's great about magic: the way modern magicians both show respect for the work of their predecessors and improve upon it.)

The "Pick a Number" Spelling Bee (Chapter 10) is based on an effect by the influential cardician Bill Simon.

Chapter 10's The Shuffling Lesson was devised and contributed by Chad Long, as originally published in Paul Harris' *Art of Astonishment, Volume 3*.

The idea of using your foot to reveal a card (Sleight of Foot) was developed by Herbert Milton in the 1920s. Jamy Ian Swiss contributed his handling of the idea.

Dream a Card, Any Card, devised and donated by Daryl, is based on the old dealing principle mentioned earlier in the Trickography entry "Dealing to the Aces." Other magicians, including Glenn Gravatt, have come up with similar tricks. But Daryl made the trick memorable by keeping the deck in the spectator's hands and adding the dream theme.

The Future Deck was performed by Mike Maxwell on his outstanding *Mike Maxwell on Self-Working Card Tricks, Volume 2* video. The original trick is credited to Jack Voshburgh, and it appears in the book *Scarne on Card Tricks*.

Chapter 11

The Cut Anywhere Force is attributed to magic dealer Max Holden.

The Under the Hanky Force is attributed to Jean Hugard.

The Bottom-Deal Force is based on a force by J. N. Hofzinser.

The Geiger Counter revelation was devised and contributed by John Cornelius, based on an idea by Jerry Andrus.

The Name of the Card Is is credited to Norman Ashworth, who published the revelation in the book *Annemann's Practical Mental Effects.*

The Above and Beyond Revelation is an old gem, suggested to us by John Cornelius. It appeared in *The Tarbell Course on Magic,* among many other places.

Chapter 12

The Ring Off Rope is based on an invention of Japanese magician Nemoto.

Chapter 13

The concept behind mixing up cards on a table, while tracking one of them with your pinky, as in The Three-Card Pick by Touch Test, came from Chicago magician Matt Schulien, back in the 1940s.

In The Triple-Prediction Spouse-Clincher, my "backup plan" (thinking of a two-digit number that always turns out to be 35 or 37) is an old scam, ingeniously refined by Harry Lorayne.

Divide & Conquer is based on an excellent idea by Roy Baker called the Pateo Principle.

Mark Levy invented and contributed The Book Test, which he based on Alan Shaxon's handling of the newspaper-number force. Alan, the chairman of Britian's prestigious "Magic Circle" and four-time performer at Buckingham Palace, wrote about his handling in his lecture notes.

The Great Vegetable Prediction is Johnny Thompson's twist on an old favorite.

Advisory Pantheon member Jeff Sheridan remembers The Telephone Trick 1 as one of the first tricks he ever performed. (It's an old standard.)

Chapter 14

You Can't Do What I Do is an old effect, brilliantly performed and contributed by Aye Jaye.

Advisory Pantheon member George Schindler invented The Phantom Photo, which he used to sell through mail-order catalogs and in magic shops.

Chapters 16 and 17

The historical information relied on these excellent books:

- *Conjuring* by James Randi. St. Martin's Press: New York. 1992
- *Illustrated History of Magic* by Milbourne and Maurine Christopher. Heinemann: Portsmouth, NH. 1973, 1996
- *Paul Daniels and the Story of Magic* by John Fisher. Jonathan Cape: London. 1987
- *The Encyclopedia of Magic and Magicians* by T.A. Waters. Facts on File: New York. 1988
- *The Art of Magic* by Douglas and Kari Hunt. Atheneum: New York. 1967
- *Magic: A Pictorial History of Conjurers in the Theater* by David Price. Cornwall Books: Cranbury, NJ. 1985

Additional information was provided by Johnny Thompson, George Johnstone, Richard Robinson, Billy McComb, Mike Caveney, Terry Seabrooke, and Torkova.

Chapter 18

The list of funny things to say were written in a creative fit by Gregory Wilson; it was supplemented by clever lines from George Schindler. (Greg also contributed most of the hilarious lines on this book's Cheat Sheet.)

Appendixes

The information in the three appendixes was provided by Erika Larsen and Jim Krenz of *Genii* magazine, Jon Racherbaumer, Daryl, Billy McComb, Looy Simonoff, Rich Marotta, Dick Zimmerman, Ron Bauer, Milt Kort, and Lee Asher — and was written up by Mark Levy.

Index

• *Numbers & Symbols* •

$100 LifeSaver trick, 113–116, 348
7-Penny Reflex Test trick, 57–61, 346

• *A* •

Above and Beyond revelation,
    236–237, 351
abracadabra, defined, 339
Aces by Touch trick, 193–195
adult-education centers, magic
    classes, 331
Advisory Pantheon
  Michael Ammar, 2, 82, 347
  Mike Bent, 78, 250, 346, 349
  Christopher Broughton, 150, 168,
    282, 349
  Eugene Burger, 86
  Lance Burton, 1, 193, 330
  Mike Caveney, 106, 347, 352
  John Cornelius, 234, 350–351
  Daryl, 219, 331, 350, 352
  Bob Farmer (Roberto Farini), 109, 348
  Dan Harlan, 173
  Paul Harris, 326, 345, 348, 350
  Bill Herz, 113, 115, 348
  Jade, 165
  Kevin James, 105
  Aye Jaye, 285, 348, 351
  Mark Levy, 232, 268, 348, 351–352
  Chad Long, 99, 102, 104, 162, 207, 347,
    349–350
  Harry Lorayne, 61, 229, 234, 316,
    346, 351
  Jay Marshall, 349
  Rich Marotta, 352
  Mike Maxwell, 215, 350

  Jeff McBride, 116, 307, 330, 348
  Billy McComb, 214, 316, 331, 352
  Tom Mullica, 152, 349
  Jon Racherbaumer, 201, 350, 352
  Richard Robinson, 10, 327,
    329–330, 352
  George Schindler, 159, 291, 326, 349,
    352
  Jeff Sheridan, 276, 351
  Looy Simonoff, 25, 290, 316, 345, 352
  Jim Sisti, 134, 171, 349
  Tony Spina, 38, 346
  Jamy Ian Swiss, 211, 214, 350
  Dan Sylvester, 116, 312
  Johnny Thompson, 2, 49, 273, 314–315,
    346, 351–352
  Torkova, 110, 349, 352
  Gregory Wilson, 64, 138, 143, 146, 331,
    348–349, 352
  Meir Yedid, 94–95, 329, 347
Ambitious Card, defined, 339
American Museum of Magic, 326
American Science and Surplus,
    magnets, 100
Ammar, Michael, 2, 82, 347
Anderson, John Henry, 317–318
Andrus, Jerry, 350
Annemann-Fulves trick. *See* Soul Mates
    trick, 350
Anti-Gravity Pencil trick, 10–13
Antigravity Ring trick, 76–78
anti-gravity tricks
  Antigravity Ring, 76–78
  pencil, 10–13
Asher, Lee, 352
Ashes through Someone Else's Palm
    trick, 165–167

Ashworth, Norman, 351
Astonishing Straw-Wrapper Restoration
    trick, 106–109, 347
audience
  building up, 307
  suiting tricks to the crowd, 307–308
automaton, described, 311

• B •

Baker, Harry, 346
Baker, Roy, 351
Ball In Tube, defined, 339
balloon tricks, Cloudy Toilet
    Paper, 116–120
Bauer, Ron, 352
Bay, Ed 203, 206
Beans through the Orifices
    trick, 152–156, 349
beat, defined, 339
Bendy Spoon I trick, 123–126, 348
Bendy Spoon II: The Return
    trick, 126–128, 348
Bent, Mike, 78, 250, 346, 349
Big Money Rises trick, 54–56
Blackstone, Harry, saves his audience's
    lives, 313
Blaine, David, 1, 310
Blindfold Drive, defined, 339
blitz, defined, 339
Bobo, J.B., 346
Book Test trick, 268–273, 351
Bottom-Deal force, card tricks, 227–228
Bouncing the Roll trick, 157–158, 349
Braue, Hugard, 349
Broughton, Christopher, 150, 168,
    282, 349
Broughton, Harry. *See* Harry Blackstone
Bubblous Glasses trick, 116
Buckley, Arthur, 346
build-your-own-card-trick kit
  Bottom-Deal force, 227–228
  Countdown force, 228–230

Cut Anywhere force, 224–225
Feeling by Muscle revelation, 232–234
Geiger Counter revelation, 230
guidelines, 223–224
Jumping Out revelation, 230–232
Magic For Dummies Grand Finale
    revelation, 237
Name of the Card Is revelation, 234–235
revelation types, 230–237
Slap It! revelation, 235–236
Under the Hanky force, 226–227
Bullet Catch, defined, 339
Burger, Eugene, 86
burn, defined, 339
Burton, Lance, 1, 193, 330
busted, defined, 339
busy, defined, 339

• C •

camcorders
  as learning aide, 5
  versus practicing in front of a mirror, 5
card fan, defined, 340
Card on the Ceiling trick, 229, 340
card sensing, Three-Card "Pick by
    Touch" Test Trick, 256–258
card shuffling, 185–186
Card to Wallet, defined, 340
card tricks
  Aces by Touch, 193–195
  build-your-own guidelines, 223–240
  Card on the Ceiling, 229
  Dealing to the Aces, 195–198
  Dream a Card, Any Card, 219–222
  Envelope, Please, 198–200
  false shuffle, 83
  force types, 224–230
  forcing a card, 81, 83
  Future Deck, 215–219
  Hands-Off, Mixed-Up, Pure
    Impossibility, 190–193
  phony shuffle, 205

Photocopied Card, 82–84. 347
Pick a Number Spelling Bee, 203–206
Post-It-ive Identification, 78–82
revelation types, 230–237
riffle shuffle, 186
shuffling cards, 185–186
Shuffling Lesson, 207–210
Sleight of Foot, 211–214
Soul Mates, 200–203
Three-Card "Pick by Touch"
    Test, 256–258, 351
Two-Card "Sleight of Hand", 29–32
You Do As I Do, 187–189
Cardini (Richard Valentine
    Pitchord), 320
Catch the Money Reflex Test trick, 60
Caveney, Mike, 106, 347, 352
Cheapskate Houdini: Triple Rubber
    Band Escape trick, 70–76
Chop Cup, defined, 340
Classic Cut-Rope Restoration
    trick, 243–247
Classic Saltshaker Penetration
    trick, 129–132
clean, defined, 340
close-up magic, described, 281
Cloudy Toilet Paper trick, 116–120, 348
Coins Across, defined, 340
Coins through the Table, defined, 340
colleges, magic classes, 331
Collins, Stanley, 346
condiment tricks
  Classic Saltshaker Penetration
    trick, 129–132
  Evaporating Sugar, 146–149
  Sugar Substitute, 143–146
confederate, defined, 340
control, defined, 340
cop, defined, 340
Copperfield, David, 1, 76, 310, 315–316
Cornelius, John, 234, 350–351
Countdown force, card tricks, 228–230

Couture, Gilles, 348
Crawford, Harry, 346
Creepy Little Baby Hand
    trick, 109–113, 348
critical moment, truths of magic, 287
cull, defined, 340
Cups and Balls, defined, 340
Cut and Restored Rope, defined, 340
Cut Anywhere force, card
    tricks, 224–225, 350
cutlery tricks
  Bendy Spoon I, 123–126
  Bendy Spoon II: The Return, 126–128
  Forks a Lot, 132–134
Cut-Rope Restoration trick, 243–247

• D •

Daryl, 219, 331, 350, 352
Davenport Brothers 318
Dealing to the Aces, 195–198, 349
Disappearing Anything trick, 13–15
ditch, defined, 340
dive, defined, 340
Divide & Conquer trick, 265–268, 351
doll arm tricks, Creepy Little Baby Hand
    trick, 109–113
Don't Show Me the Money
    trick, 61–63, 346
double lift, defined, 340
Dream a Card, Any Card trick,
    219–222, 350
Dunninger, Joseph, 320

• E •

effect, defined, 341
Egg Bag, defined, 341
Elliot, Bruce, *Best in Magic*, 346
Envelope, Please trick, 198–200, 349
Escape from the K-Mart Tie
    trick, 251–254

escape tricks
    Cheapskate Houdini: Triple Rubber
        Band Escape, 70–76
    The Escape from the K-Mart, 251–254
    Triple Rubber Band Escape, 70–76
ESP (extra sensory perception),
        mentalism tricks, 255–280
Evaporating Sugar trick, 146–149, 348
eye contact, aiming versus staring, 14

• F •

fake rubber hand tricks, Give That
        Purse a Hand, 94–98
false shuffle, defined, 341
Farmer, Bob, (Roberto Farini), 109, 348
faro shuffle, defined, 341
fast company, defined, 341
Fearson, Steve, 316
Feeling by Muscle revelation, 232–234
Fetsch, Hen, 349
Fields, Eddie, 349
finger break, defined, 341
Fingertip Munch trick, 18–19
Flash Paper, defined, 341
flash, defined, 341
flash-and-filigree, defined, 341
Floating Dinner Roll trick, 158–161, 349
flourish, defined, 341
food tricks
    Beans through the Orifices, 152–156
    Bouncing the Roll, 157–158
    Floating Dinner Roll, 158–161
    Linking Pretzels, 149–152
force, defined, 341
forces
    Bottom-Deal, 227–228
    Countdown, 228–230
    Cut Anywhere, 224–225
    Magician's Choice, 291–297
    Under the Hanky, 226–227

forcing a card, described, 81, 83
Forks a Lot trick, 132–134
Four Bean trick, 349
Fox, Karrell, 349
French Drop, defined, 341
fried, defined, 341
Future Deck trick, 215–219

• G •

Geiger Counter revelation, 230
Geller, Uri, 126–128, 348
Genii: The International Conjuror's
        Magazine, idea source, 328
Georgia Wonder (LuLu Hearst), 288
gimmick, defined, 341
Give Me a Ring Sometime — and a
        String trick, 85–88
Give That Purse a Hand trick, 94–98, 347
Givens, Joe, 349
glide, defined, 341
glom, defined, 341
go south, defined, 341
Goldin, Horace, 319–320
Goodsell, Dave, West Coast Wizard's
        Magic Camp, 331
grabber, defined, 341
grace under fire
    Mike Bent, 250
    John Cornelius, 234
    Chad Long, 162
    Harry Lorayne, 229
    One-Legged Leg Vanish trick, 16
    Looy Simonoff, 290
    Torkova, 110
Gravatt, Glenn, 350
Great Tomsoni See Johnny Thompson
Great Vegetable Prediction
        trick, 273–275
The Great Wizard of the North. See John
        Henry Anderson

guidelines
  act the part, 309
  audience build up, 307
  importance of practice, 308
  keep at it, 309
  know when to start, 306
  know when to stop, 307
  make it yours, 310
  never repeat a trick, 306
  never reveal the secret, 305–306
  suiting tricks to the crowd, 307–308

• *H* •

Hands-Off, Mixed-Up, Pure Impossibility
    trick, 190–193, 349
Harlan, Dan, 173–176
Harris, Paul, 326, 345, 348–350
Heads or Tails: The Shadow Knows
    trick, 64–65
Hearst, LuLu (Georgia Wonder), 288
Henning, Doug, 310, 315, 329
Herrmann, Alexander, 312
Herz, Bill, 113, 115, 348
Hindu shuffle, defined, 341
history of magic
  Blackstone saves his audience, 313
  Blackstone's donuts, 322
  Cardini (Richard Valentine
      Pitchord), 320
  Copperfield changes the scale of
      magic, 315–316
  Dai Vernon (David Frederick Winfield
      Vernon), 322
  Doug Henning comes to Broadway, 315
  Dunninger, Joseph, 320
  Ed Marlo (Edward Malkowski), 321
  Great Tomsoni capitalizes on his
      mistakes, 314–315
  Harry Kellar, 318
  Herrmann pulls a coin from a roll, 312
  Horace Goldin, 319–320
  Houdini becomes dangerous, 313
  Howard Thurston, 319
  Jean Henri Servais Le Roy, 318–319
  John Henry Anderson, 317–318
  Malini produces a block of ice, 312
  Richiardi Jr bisects his daughter, 314
  Robert-Houdin prevents war with a
      trick, 311–312
  seeing your first trick, 316
  Tony Slydini (Quintino Marucci), 321
Hoffman, Professor, 198–200, 349
Hofzinser, J. N, 350
Holden, Max, 350
Honolulu Shuffle. *See* Hands-Off, Mixed-
    Up, Pure Impossibility trick, 349
hookup, defined, 342
Houdini Historical Center, 326
Houdini, Harry, as a dangerous man, 313
Hugard, Jean, 350
Hummer, Bob, 348

• *I* •

I.B.M. (International Brotherhood of
    Magicians), 328, 332
idea sources
  individual magicians, 330
  magazines, 337
  magic associations, 328
  magic classes, 331–332
  magic publications, 326–328
  magic shops, 327, 335–336
  magic video tapes, 330–331
  museums, 326
  organizations, 337
  TV magic specials, 327–328
  watching other magicians, 325
  Web sites, 329–330
impromptu, defined, 342
instant gratification tricks
  Pencil-and-Quarter Double Vanish
      trick, 37–41, 346

(continued)

instant gratification tricks *(continued)*
  Tale of the Tightrope Walker,
      33–37, 346
  Two-Card "Sleight of Hand" trick, 29–33
Invisible Deck, defined, 342

• J •

Jade, 165
James, Kevin, 105
jargon, 339–344
Jaye, Aye, 285, 348, 351
Johnstone, George, 352

• K •

Kellar, Harry (Heinrich), 318, 346
key card, defined, 342
key tricks, Ninja Key Catch, 102–104
kill, defined, 342
Kort, Milt, 352
Kotkin, David *See* David Copperfield
Koran, Al, 348
Krenz, Jim, 352

• L •

lap, defined, 342
Larsen, Erika, 352
Late-Night Party Murder Mystery
    trick, 298–302
layman, defined, 342
Le Roy, Jean Henri Servais, 318–319
leak, defined, 342
learning process,
  camcorders as learning aide, 5
lecture notes, importance of, 347
Levy, Mark, 232, 268, 348, 351–352
lining pretzels idea, Joe Givens, 349
Linking Pretzels trick, 149–152, 349
Linking Rings, defined, 342
load, defined, 95, 342

local colleges, magic classes, 331
Long, Chad, 99, 102, 104, 162, 207, 347,
    349–350
Lorayne, Harry, 61, 229, 234, 316,
    348, 351
Lund, Bob/Elaine, American Museum
    of Magic, 326
Lynn, Terry, 346
Lynn's Pennies, 7-Penny Reflex Test
    trick, 346

• M •

magazines, 337
magic
  level presented in this book, 1–2
  modern day uses, 1
The Magic and Movie Hall of Fame, 326
magic camps, 331
Magic Castle, magical experience, 325
magic dealers, Web sites, 329
Magic For Dummies Grand Finale
    revelation, 237–239
*The Magic Magazine: The Independent
    Magazine for Conjurors*, 328
magic museums, 326
magic publications, idea sources,
    326, 328
magic shops, idea source, 327, 335–336
Magician's Choice force, 291–297
Making an Ash of Yourself trick, 163–165
Malini, Max, produces a block of ice, 312
Malkowski, Edward. *See* Ed Marlo
manual dexterity, versus
    showmanship, 2
Marlo, Ed (Edward Malkowski), 321
Marshall, Jay, 2, 349
Marotta, Rich, 352
Marucci, Quintino. *See* Slydini, Tony
match tricks
  Making an Ash of Yourself, 163–165
  Static-Electricity Test trick, 173–176

Three-Matchbox Shell Game
    trick, 168–171
Weighing the Matchbooks, 171–173
Math/Geography/Animal/Color Test
    trick, 263–265
Maxwell, Mike, 215, ,350
McBride, Jeff, 116, 307, 330, 348
McComb, Billy, 214, 316, 331, 352
mechanics grip, defined, 342
mentalism
    Book Test, 268–273
    described, 255
    Divide & Conquer trick, 265–268
    Great Vegetable Prediction
        trick, 273–275
    Math/Geography/Animal/Color Test
        trick, 263–265
    one-ahead principle, 256
    Telephone Trick I: Call This Number,
        275–279
    Telephone Trick II: Call the Phantom,
        279–280
    Three-Card "Pick by Touch"
        Test, 256–258
    Triple-Prediction Spouse-Clincher
        trick, 258–263
mentalist, defined, 342
Milton, Herbert, 214, 350
mirrors
    practicing in front of, 5
    versus camcorders for trick
        practicing, 5
miscall, defined, 342
misdirection
    7-Penny Reflex Test trick, 57–61
    Astonishing Straw-Wrapper
        Restoration, 109
    Bendy Spoon trick, 126
    Big Money Rises trick, 56
    Classic Saltshaker Penetration
        trick, 131

Cut Anywhere farce, 225
defined, 5, 13, 342
Disappearing Anything trick, 13–15
Envelope, Please trick, 199
Missing Spray-Paint Marble trick, 102
Pencil-and-Quarter Double Vanish
    trick, 37–41
Shuffling Lesson trick, 208
Torn and Restored Toilet Paper, 284
Unforgettable "Cloudy" Toilet Paper
    trick, 120
Weighing the Matchbooks trick, 172
Miser's Dream trick, Torkova, 110, 342
Missing Spray-Paint Marble
    trick, 99–102, 347
mistakes, what to say when things go
    wrong, 323–324
money tricks
    7-Penny Reflex Test, 57–61
    Big Money Rises, 54–56
    Catch the Money Reflex Test, 60
    Don't Show Me the Money, 61–63
    Heads or Tails: The Shadow Knows
        trick, 64–65
    Pencil-and-Quarter Double Vanish
        trick, 39–41
    Pencil-Breaking Cash trick, 46–49
    Sheep and Thieves, 49–51, 346
    Vanishing Quarter, Show-Off
        Edition, 52–54
move, defined, 342
Mullica, Tom, 152–156, 349
museums
    American Museum of Magic, 326
    Houdini Historical Center, 326
    idea source, 326
    magic, 326
    Magic and Movie Hall of Fame,
        The, 326

• N •

Name of the Card Is revelation, 234–235, 351
The Napoleon of Necromancy. *See* John Henry Anderson
Nemoto, 351
Ninja Key Catch trick, 102–104, 347

• O •

Off the Wall tricks, 24–26
office supply tricks
    Antigravity Ring, 76–78
    Pencil up the Nose, 67–70
    Post-It-ive Identification, 78–82
    Triple Rubber Band Escape, 70–76
one-ahead principle, mentalism tricks, 256–258
One-Legged Leg Vanish trick, 15–17
organizations, 337
Oriental Trading Company, fake rubber hands, 95
Ouellet, Gary, 348

• P •

packet trick, defined, 342–343
palm, defined, 343
parlor magic
    described, 281
    Late-Night Party Murder Mystery trick, 298–302
    Phantom Photo trick, 291–297, 352
    Strength Test trick, 288–290
    Torn and Restored Toilet Paper trick, 282–285
    You Can't Do as I Do trick, 285–288
Pateo Principle, Roy baker, 351

patter
    $100 LifeSaver trick, 114–116
    7-Penny Reflex Test trick, 57–61
    Above and Beyond revelation, 236–237
    Aces by Touch trick, 194–195
    Anti-Gravity Pencil trick, 11
    Antigravity Ring trick, 76–78
    Ashes through Someone Else's Palm trick, 166–167
    Beans through the Orifices, 153–156
    Bendy Spoon I trick, 124–126
    Bendy Spoon II: The Return trick, 127–128
    Big Money Rises trick, 55–56
    Book Test trick, 270–273
    Bottom-Deal force, 227–228
    Bouncing the Roll trick, 157–158
    Classic Cut-Rope Restoration trick, 244–247
    Classic Saltshaker Penetration, 129–132
    Cloudy Toilet Paper trick, 117–120
    Countdown force, 229–230
    Creepy Little Baby Hand trick, 111–113
    Cut Anywhere force, 224–225
    Dealing to the Aces, 196–197
    defined, 10, 343
    Disappearing Anything trick, 14
    Divide & Conquer trick, 266–267
    Don't Show Me the Money trick, 61–63
    Dream a Card, Any Card trick, 220–222
    Envelope, Please, 198–200
    Escape from the K-Mart Tie trick, 251–254
    Evaporating Sugar trick, 147–149
    Feeling by Muscle revelation, 232–234
    Fingertip Munch trick, 18
    Floating Dinner Roll trick, 159–161
    Future Deck trick, 216–219
    Give Me a Ring Sometime - and a String, 86–88

Give That Purse a Hand trick, 96–98

Great Vegetable Prediction trick, 274–275

Hands-Off, Mixed-Up, Pure Impossibility trick, 191–193

Heads or Tails: The Shadow Knows trick, 64

Jumping Out revelation, 231

Late-Night Party Murder Mystery trick, 298–302

Linking Pretzels, 150–152

Magic For Dummies Grand Finale revelation, 237–239

Making an Ash of Yourself trick, 164–165

Math/Geography/Animal/color Test trick, 263–265

Missing Spray-Paint Marble trick, 100–102

Name of the Card Is revelation, 234–235

One-Legged Leg Vanish trick, 15

Pencil up the Nose trick, 68–70

Pencil-and-Quarter Double Vanish trick, 39–41

Pencil-Breaking Cash trick, 46–49

Phantom Photo trick, 292–297

Photocopied Card trick, 82–84

Pick a Number Spelling Bee trick, 204–206

Post-It-ive Identification trick, 80–82

Ring off Rope trick, 248–250

Scarf Decapitation, 94

Sheep and Thieves trick, 49–51

Shuffling Lesson trick, 207–210

Slap It! revelation, 235–236

Sleight of Foot trick, 211–214

Soul Mates trick, 201–203

Static-Electricity Test trick, 174–176

Straw-Wrapper Restoration trick, 107–109

Strength Test trick, 289–290

Stretchiest Arm in the World trick, 23–24

Stretchiest Finger in the World trick, 21–22

Stretchiest Thumb in the World trick, 19–20

Sugar Substitute trick, 144–146

Tale of the Tightrope Walker, 35–37

Telephone Trick I: Call This Number, 278–279

Telephone Trick II: Call the Phantom, 279–280

the card you chose reference, 84

Three-Card "Pick by Touch" Test Trick, 256–258

Three-Matchbox Shell Game, 169–171

Three-Mug Monte trick, 135–137

Three-Object Monte, Freakout Edition trick, 138–141

Torn and Restored Toilet Paper, 283–285

Triple Rubber Band Escape, 70–76

Triple-Prediction Spouse-Clincher trick, 259–263

Two-Card "Sleight of Hand" trick, 30–32

Under the Hanky force, 226–227

Vanishing Quarter, Show-Off Edition trick, 52–54

Walking through Ropes trick, 88–92

Weighing the Matchbooks trick, 172–173

what to say when things go wrong, 323–324

You Can't Do as I Do trick, 286–288

You Do As I Do trick, 187–189

peddle, defined, 343

pencil tricks
  Anti-Gravity Pencil, 10–13
  Pencil up the Nose, 67–70
  Pencil-and-Quarter Double Vanish trick, 37–41, 346

Pencil-Breaking Cash trick, 46–49
penetration, defined, 343
performance, make it yours, 310
Phantom Photo trick, 291–297, 352
phony shuffle, described, 205
Photocopied Card trick, 82–84, 347
Pick a Number Spelling Bee
    trick, 203–206, 350
Plants, Gary, magic video with Michael
    Ammar, 347
play, defined, 343
postal mail
    Dave Goodsell's West Coast Wizard's
        Magic Camp, 331
    Tannen's Magic Shop, 331
Post-It-ive Identification trick, 78–82, 346
production, defined, 343
props
    ashes, 165–167
    balloons, 116–120
    beans, 152–156
    cards, 28–33, 185–240
    coffee cups, 134–137
    coins, 123–126, 129–134
    dinner rolls, 157–161
    doll arm, 109–113
    fake glasses, 116
    fake rubber hands, 94–98
    forks, 132–134
    keys, 102–104
    LifeSavers, 113–116
    loads, 95
    magnets, 100–102
    matchbooks, 171–173
    matchboxes, 168–171
    matches, 163–176
    money, 37–66
    office supplies, 67–84
    Oriental Trading Company, 95
    pencils, 37–41
    Post-it Pop-Up Note Dispenser
        refills, 78–82

pretzels, 149–152
purses, 94–98
rings, 76–78, 85–88
ropes (white braided cotton), 88–92,
    243–254
saltshakers, 129–132
scarves, 92–94
spoons, 123–128
spray paint cans, 99–102
straw wrappers, 106–109
straws, 104–106
string, 85–88
sugar packet, 143–149
sugar substitute packet, 143–146
toilet paper, 116–120
white cotton string, 34
publications
    Art of Astonishment, Paul Harris,
        348, 350
    The Art of Magic, Douglas and Kari
        Hunt, 352
    Best in Magic, Bruce Elliot, 346, 348
    Conjuring, James Randi, 352
    The Dai Vernon Book of Magic, Dai
        Vernon, 322
    Encyclopedia of Card Tricks, Hugard
        and Braue, 214
    *The Encyclopedia of Magic and
        Magicians*, T. A. Waters, 352
    Expert Card Technique, Dai Vernon, 322
    Genii magazine, 328, 348
    Greater Magic, 349
    Illustrated History of Magic, Milbourne
        and Maurine Christopher, 352
    The Inner Secrets of Card Magic, Dai
        Vernon, 322
    The Magic Book, 346
    Magic with Everyday Objects, George
        Schindler, 349
    *Magic: A Pictorial History of Conjurers
        in the Theater*, David Price, 352
    Off the Wall, 347

Opera For Dummies, 6
Paul Daniels and the Story of Magic,
John Fisher, 352
reading about magic tricks, 326–327
The Royal Road to Card Magic, 349
Scarne on Card Tricks, 350
Seven Secrets, J. C. Wagner, 348
The Tarbell Course on Magic, Harry
Crawford, 346
purse tricks, Give That Purse a
Hand, 94–98

• R •

Racherbaumer, Jon, 201, 350, 352
Ramsey, John, 349
Ramsey's Four Bean trick, 349
reading, idea source, 327
restoration, defined, 343
retention vanish, defined, 343
retrograde analysis, defined, 343
revelations
Above and Beyond, 236–237, 351
Feeling by Muscle, 232–234
Geiger Counter, 230
Jumping Out, 230–232
Magic For Dummies Grand
Finale, 237–239
Name of the Card Is, 234–235, 351
Slap It!, 235–236
Richiardi, Aldo (Richiardi Jr.), bisects
his daughter, 314
riffle, defined, 343
riffle shuffle
defined, 186, 343
faking, 185–186
right-handed presentations, conventions
used in book, 2
Ring off Rope trick, 247–250, 351
ring tricks
Antigravity Ring, 76–78
Give Me a Ring Sometime — and a
String, 85–88

Rising Card, defined, 343
Robert-Houdin, Jean Eugene, 309,
311–312
Robinson, Richard, 10, 327, 329–330, 352
rope tricks
Classic Cut-Rope Restoration, 243–247
Escape from the K-Mart Tie, 251–254
Ring off Rope, 247–250
Walking through Ropes, 88–92
routine, defined, 343
roxing, defined, 343
rubber band tricks
Antigravity Ring, 76–78
Triple Rubber Band Escape, 70–76
rubber bands, how to shoot off your
finger, 76

• S •

SAM (Society of American Magicians),
328, 332
Scarf Decapitation trick, 92–94, 347
scarf tricks, Scarf Decapitation, 92–94,
347
Schindler, George, 159, 291, 326, 349, 352
Schulien, Matt, 351
Seabrooke, Terry, 352
secrets, never reveal, 305–306
self-mutilation tricks
Beans through the Orifices, 152–156
Pencil up the Nose, 67–70
Straw through the Jaw, 104–106
Shaxon, Alan, 351
Sheep and Thieves trick, 49–51, 346
shell game tricks
Three-Matchbox Shell Game, 168–171
Three-Mug Monte, 135–137
Three-Object Monte, Freakout
Edition, 137–141
Sheridan, Jeff, 276, 351
showmanship
acting the part, 309
aiming versus staring eye contact, 14

(continued)

showmanship *(continued)*
  developing, 9
  importance of patter, 10
  learning techniques from other
    magicians, 325
  looking above audience's heads, 14
  nobody questions the procedure, 13
  versus manual dexterity, 2
  what to say when things go
    wrong, 323–324
shuffling cards, 185–186
Shuffling Lesson trick, 207–210, 350
Simon, Bill, 350
Simonoff, Looy, 25, 290, 316, 345, 352
Sisti, Jim, 134, 171, 349
Slap It! revelation, 235–236
Sleight of Foot trick, 211–214
sleight, defined, 343
sleight-of-hand, defined, 343
Slydini, Tony (Quintino Marucci),
    321, 348
Social Climbing trick, 25–26, 345–346
Soul Mates trick, 200–203, 350
Spina, Tony, 38, 346
spirit cabinet trick, 318
sponge balls, defined, 343
Spooky, defined, 343
square-up, defined, 344
stacked-deck, defined, 344
stage illusion, defined, 344
stage magic, described, 281
Static-Electricity Test trick, 173–176
Stine, Brad, 146, 348
Straw through the Jaw trick, 104–106
straw tricks, Straw through the Jaw
    trick, 104–106
straw wrapper tricks, Straw-Wrapper
    Restoration trick, 106–109
Strength Test trick, 288–290
Stretchiest Arm in the World trick, 22–24
Stretchiest Finger in the World
    trick, 21–22

string tricks
  Give Me a Ring Sometime — and a
    String trick, 85–88
  Tale of the Tightrope Walker,
    33–37, 346
strolling magic, defined, 344
Substitution Trunk, defined, 344
sucker effect, defined, 344
sucker trick, Above and Beyond
    revelation, 236–237
Sugar Substitute trick, 143–146, 348
Svengali deck, defined, 344
Swiss, Jamy Ian, 211, 214
Sylvester, Dan, 116, 312

• T •

talk, defined, 344
Tannen's Magic Shop, magic camp, 331
telephone numbers
  American Science and Surplus, 95
  Oriental Trading Company, 95
  Tannen's Magic Shop, 331
Telephone Trick I: Call This
    Number, 275–279
Telephone Trick II: Call the
    Phantom, 279–280
Tenkai's Rope through the Neck
    trick, 347
Thompson, Johnny (The Great
    Tomsoni), 2, 49, 273, 314–315, 346,
    351–352
Thompson, Pam, 315
Three-Card "Pick by Touch"
    Test, 256–258, 351
Three-Matchbox Shell Game
    trick, 168–171
Three-Mug Monte trick, 134–137
Three-Object Monte, Freakout Edition
    trick, 137–141
thumb tip, defined, 344
Thurston, Howard, 319

tip, defined, 344

toilet paper tricks, Cloudy Toilet Paper, 116–120

Torkova, 110, 349, 352

Torn and Restored Toilet Paper, 283–285

transformation, defined, 344

transposition, defined, 344

tricks

$100 LifeSaver, 113–116, 348

7-Penny Reflex Test, 57–61, 346

Aces by Touch, 193–195

Anti-Gravity Pencil, 10–13

Antigravity Ring, 76–78

Ashes through Someone Else's Palm, 165–167

Astonishing Straw-Wrapper Restoration, 106–109, 347

Beans through the Orifices, 152–156, 349

Bendy Spoon I, 123–126, 348

Bendy Spoon II: The Return trick, 126–128, 348

Big Money Rises, 54–56

Book Test, 268–273, 351

Bottom-Deal force, 227–228

Bouncing the Roll, 157–158, 349

Bubblous Glasses, 116

Catch the Money Reflex Test, 60

Cheapskate Houdini: Triple Rubber Band Escape, 70–76

Classic Cut-Rope Restoration, 243–247

Classic Saltshaker Penetration, 129–132

Cloudy Toilet Paper, 116–120, 348

Creepy Little Baby Hand, 109–113, 348

Cut Anywhere force, 224–225, 350

Dealing to the Aces, 195–198, 349

Disappearing Anything, 13–15

Divide & Conquer trick, 265–268

Don't Show Me the Money, 61–63, 346

Dream a Card, Any Card, 219–222, 350

Envelope, Please, 198–200, 349

Escape from the K-Mart Tie, 251–254

Evaporating Sugar, 146–149, 348

Fighting Off An Assailant, 26–27

Fingertip Munch, 18–19

Floating Dinner Roll, 158–161, 349

Forks a Lot, 132–134

Four Bean, 349

Future Deck, 215–219, 350

Give Me a Ring Sometime — and a String, 85–88

Give That Purse a Hand, 94–98, 347

Great Vegetable Prediction, 273–275

Hands-Off, Mixed-Up, Pure Impossibility, 190–193, 349

Heads or Tails: The Shadow Knows, 64–65

importance of practice, 308

Late-Night Party Murder Mystery, 298–302

learning process, 5

learning techniques from other magicians, 325

level presented in this book, 1–2

Linking Pretzels, 149–152, 349

magicians credit, 2

Making an Ash of Yourself, 163–165

Math/Geography/Animal/Color Test, 263–265

Miser's Dream, 110

Missing Spray-Paint Marble, 99–102, 347

never repeat, 306

never reveal the secret, 305–306

Ninja Key Catch, 102–104, 347

Off the Wall, 24–27, 345–346

One-Legged Leg Vanish, 15–17

Pencil up the Nose trick, 67–70

Pencil-and-Quarter Double Vanish, 37–41

Pencil-Breaking Cash, 46–49

Phantom Photo, 291–297, 352

Photocopied Card, 82–84, 347

(continued)

tricks *(continued)*
    Pick a Number Spelling Bee,
        203–206, 350
    Post-It-ive Identification, 78–82, 346
    presentation (showmanship) versus
        manual dexterity, 2
    reading about, 326–327
    right-handed conventions, 2
    Ring off Rope, 247–250
    Scarf Decapitation, 92–94
    Sheep and Thieves trick, 49–51
    Shuffling Lesson, 207–210, 350
    Sleight of Foot, 211–214
    Social Climbing, 25–26, 345–346
    Soul Mates, 200–203, 349
    spirit cabinet, 318
    Static-Electricity Test, 173–176
    Straw through the Jaw, 104–106
    Strength Test, 288–290
    Stretchiest Finger in the
        World, 21–22
    Stretchiest Thumb in the
        World, 19–21
    Sugar Substitute, 143–146, 348
    suiting to the crowd, 307–308
    Telephone Trick I: Call This
        Number, 275–279, 351
    Telephone Trick II: Call the
        Phantom, 279–280
    Tenkai's Rope through the Neck, 347
    Three-Card "Pick by Touch"
        Test, 256–258, 351
    Three-Matchbox Shell Game, 168–171
    Three-Mug Monte, 134–137, 348
    Three-Object Monte, Freakout
        Edition, 137–141
    Torn and Restored Toilet
        Paper, 282–285
    Triple Rubber Band Escape, 70–76
    Triple-Prediction Spouse-Clincher,
        258–263, 351
Two-Card "Sleight of Hand", 29–33
Under the Hanky force, 226–227
Vanishing Quarter, Show-Off
    Edition, 52–54
Walking through Ropes, 88–92
Weighing the Matchbooks, 171–173,
    349
what to say when things go wrong,
    323–324
You Can't Do as I Do, 285–288, 351
You Do As I Do, 187–189
Triple Rubber Band Escape trick, 70–76
Triple-Prediction Spouse-Clincher
    trick, 258–263, 351
Triumph, defined, 344
troubleshooting
    Chad Long, 162
    Harry Lorayne, 229
    John Cornelius, 234
    Looy Simonoff, 290
    Mike Bent, 250
    One-Legged Leg Vanish trick, 16
    Torkova, 110
truths of magic
    anticipate the dumb guesses, 38
    Bent, Mike, grace under fire, 250
    chosen card, 84
    confederates (secret helpers), 138
    Cornelius, John, grace under fire, 234
    cutting cards doesn't accomplish
        much, 190
    distance yourself from the
        prediction, 268
    don't pre-announce the trick unless
        you're lying, 134
    element of surprise, 54
    give 'em something to believe in, 34
    humans make terrible witnesses, 287
    Long Chad, grace under fire, 162
    Lorayne, Harry, grace under fire, 229
    Simonoff, Looy, grace under fire, 290

nobody questions the procedure, 13
One-Legged Leg Vanish, grace under fire, 16
pre-climax recap, 200
third times the charm, 48
Torkova, grace under fire, 110
whose trick is it anyway, 214
TV magic specials, idea source, 327–328

• *U* •

Under the Hanky force, card tricks, 226–227

• *V* •

vanish, defined, 344
Vanishing Quarter, Show-Off Edition trick, 52–54
vendors
  American Science and Surplus, 95
  Oriental Trading Company, 95
Vernon, Dai (David Frederic Winfield Vernon), 2, 322
video cameras, as learning aide, 5
video tapes, magic, 330–331, 350–451
vidiots, defined, 344
Voshburgh, Jack, 350

• *W* •

Wagner, J. C., *Seven Secrets*, 348
Waikiki Shuffle. *See* Honolulu Shuffle
Walking through Ropes trick, 88–92
Web sites
  All Magic Dealers Guide, 329
  All Magic Guide, 329
  The Conjuror: David Ben, 330
  current events, 330
  David Blane: Magic Man, 330
  Doug Henning's World of Magic, 329

Hank Lee's Magic Factory, 329
Houdini Historical Center, 326
Illusions By Zigmont, 330
individual magicians, 330
Jeff McBride, 330
John Houdi, 330
L & L Publishing, 329
Lance Burton: Master Magician, 330
MAGIC - The Independent Magazine for Magicians, 330
magic dealers, 329
The Magic Menu, 330
Magic of David Copperfield, 330
Magic Show, 330
Magic Times: A Monthly Magic Magazine with Daily Updates, 330
Magical Past-Times: On-Line Journal of Magic History, 329
Meir Yedid Magic, 329
Owen Magic Supreme, 329
Paula Paul, 330
Rebekah Yen, 330
Richard Robinson, 330
Rudy Coby Launching Pad, 330
Siegfried and Roy: Masters of the Impossible, 330
Stevens Magic Emporium, 329
Weighing the Matchbooks trick, 171–173, 349
Weiss, Erich. *See* Harry Houdini
West Coast Wizard's Magic Camp, Dave Goodsell, 331
The Whirlwind Wizard *See* Horace Goldin
Wilson, Gregory, 64, 138, 143, 146, 331, 348–349, 352
wired, defined, 344
The Wonder of the World. *See* John Henry Anderson

• Y •

Yates, Jack, 346
Yedid, Meir, 94–95, 329, 347
You Can't Do as I Do trick, 187–190,
    285–288, 344, 351

• Z •

Zimmerman, Dick, 352

Notes

Notes

Notes

 FOR DUMMIES®

The easy way to get more done and have more fun

PERSONAL FINANCE

0-7645-5231-7

0-7645-2431-3

0-7645-5331-3

Also available:

Estate Planning For Dummies
(0-7645-5501-4)

401(k)s For Dummies
(0-7645-5468-9)

Frugal Living For Dummies
(0-7645-5403-4)

Microsoft Money "X" For
Dummies
(0-7645-1689-2)

Mutual Funds For Dummies
(0-7645-5329-1)

Personal Bankruptcy For
Dummies
(0-7645-5498-0)

Quicken "X" For Dummies
(0-7645-1666-3)

Stock Investing For Dummies
(0-7645-5411-5)

Taxes For Dummies 2003
(0-7645-5475-1)

BUSINESS & CAREERS

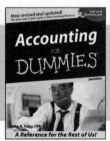
0-7645-5314-3

0-7645-5307-0

0-7645-5471-9

Also available:

Business Plans Kit For
Dummies
(0-7645-5365-8)

Consulting For Dummies
(0-7645-5034-9)

Cool Careers For Dummies
(0-7645-5345-3)

Human Resources Kit For
Dummies
(0-7645-5131-0)

Managing For Dummies
(1-5688-4858-7)

QuickBooks All-in-One Desk
Reference For Dummies
(0-7645-1963-8)

Selling For Dummies
(0-7645-5363-1)

Small Business Kit For
Dummies
(0-7645-5093-4)

Starting an eBay Business For
Dummies
(0-7645-1547-0)

HEALTH, SPORTS & FITNESS

0-7645-5167-1

0-7645-5146-9

0-7645-5154-X

Also available:

Controlling Cholesterol For
Dummies
(0-7645-5440-9)

Dieting For Dummies
(0-7645-5126-4)

High Blood Pressure For
Dummies
(0-7645-5424-7)

Martial Arts For Dummies
(0-7645-5358-5)

Menopause For Dummies
(0-7645-5458-1)

Nutrition For Dummies
(0-7645-5180-9)

Power Yoga For Dummies
(0-7645-5342-9)

Thyroid For Dummies
(0-7645-5385-2)

Weight Training For Dummies
(0-7645-5168-X)

Yoga For Dummies
(0-7645-5117-5)

Available wherever books are sold.
Go to www.dummies.com or call 1-877-762-2974 to order direct.

 WILEY

FOR DUMMIES®

A world of resources to help you grow

HOME, GARDEN & HOBBIES

0-7645-5295-3

0-7645-5130-2

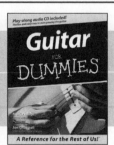

0-7645-5106-X

Also available:

Auto Repair For Dummies
(0-7645-5089-6)

Chess For Dummies
(0-7645-5003-9)

Home Maintenance For
Dummies
(0-7645-5215-5)

Organizing For Dummies
(0-7645-5300-3)

Piano For Dummies
(0-7645-5105-1)

Poker For Dummies
(0-7645-5232-5)

Quilting For Dummies
(0-7645-5118-3)

Rock Guitar For Dummies
(0-7645-5356-9)

Roses For Dummies
(0-7645-5202-3)

Sewing For Dummies
(0-7645-5137-X)

FOOD & WINE

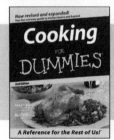

0-7645-5250-3

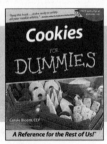

0-7645-5390-9

0-7645-5114-0

Also available:

Bartending For Dummies
(0-7645-5051-9)

Chinese Cooking For
Dummies
(0-7645-5247-3)

Christmas Cooking For
Dummies
(0-7645-5407-7)

Diabetes Cookbook For
Dummies
(0-7645-5230-9)

Grilling For Dummies
(0-7645-5076-4)

Low-Fat Cooking For
Dummies
(0-7645-5035-7)

Slow Cookers For Dummies
(0-7645-5240-6)

TRAVEL

0-7645-5453-0

0-7645-5438-7

0-7645-5448-4

Also available:

America's National Parks For
Dummies
(0-7645-6204-5)

Caribbean For Dummies
(0-7645-5445-X)

Cruise Vacations For
Dummies 2003
(0-7645-5459-X)

Europe For Dummies
(0-7645-5456-5)

Ireland For Dummies
(0-7645-6199-5)

France For Dummies
(0-7645-6292-4)

London For Dummies
(0-7645-5416-6)

Mexico's Beach Resorts For
Dummies
(0-7645-6262-2)

Paris For Dummies
(0-7645-5494-8)

RV Vacations For Dummies
(0-7645-5443-3)

Walt Disney World & Orlando
For Dummies
(0-7645-5444-1)

Available wherever books are sold. Go to www.dummies.com or call 1-877-762-2974 to order direct.

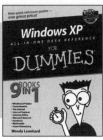

FOR DUMMIES®

Helping you expand your horizons and realize your potential

INTERNET

The Internet For Dummies
0-7645-0894-6

The Internet All-in-One Desk Reference For Dummies
0-7645-1659-0

eBay For Dummies
0-7645-1642-6

Also available:

America Online 7.0 For Dummies
(0-7645-1624-8)

Genealogy Online For Dummies
(0-7645-0807-5)

The Internet All-in-One Desk Reference For Dummies
(0-7645-1659-0)

Internet Explorer 6 For Dummies
(0-7645-1344-3)

The Internet For Dummies Quick Reference
(0-7645-1645-0)

Internet Privacy For Dummies
(0-7645-0846-6)

Researching Online For Dummies
(0-7645-0546-7)

Starting an Online Business For Dummies
(0-7645-1655-8)

DIGITAL MEDIA

Digital Photography For Dummies
0-7645-1664-7

Photoshop Elements 2 For Dummies
0-7645-1675-2

Digital Video For Dummies
0-7645-0806-7

Also available:

CD and DVD Recording For Dummies
(0-7645-1627-2)

Digital Photography All-in-One Desk Reference For Dummies
(0-7645-1800-3)

Digital Photography For Dummies Quick Reference
(0-7645-0750-8)

Home Recording for Musicians For Dummies
(0-7645-1634-5)

MP3 For Dummies
(0-7645-0858-X)

Paint Shop Pro "X" For Dummies
(0-7645-2440-2)

Photo Retouching & Restoration For Dummies
(0-7645-1662-0)

Scanners For Dummies
(0-7645-0783-4)

GRAPHICS

PowerPoint 2002 For Dummies
0-7645-0817-2

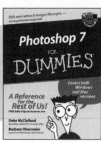

Photoshop 7 For Dummies
0-7645-1651-5

Macromedia Flash MX For Dummies
0-7645-0895-4

Also available:

Adobe Acrobat 5 PDF For Dummies
(0-7645-1652-3)

Fireworks 4 For Dummies
(0-7645-0804-0)

Illustrator 10 For Dummies
(0-7645-3636-2)

QuarkXPress 5 For Dummies
(0-7645-0643-9)

Visio 2000 For Dummies
(0-7645-0635-8)

Available wherever books are sold. Go to www.dummies.com or call 1-877-762-2974 to order direct.